Katrin Susanne Mühlfeld

Strategic Shifts between Business Types

Dear Ursula, dear Philip,

many thanks to both of you: for the
encouragement when I first started thinking
about doing the PhD, and for the (always
much too short) perfect recreation at
Pegasus Cottage and its "subsidiaries"
on the beach & in the garden — in the summer
of 1998 it also proved to be the ideal
setting for preparing the presentation that earned
me the PhD offer in the first place!

Love, Katrin

GABLER EDITION WISSENSCHAFT

Business-to-Business-Marketing

Das Business-to-Business-Marketing ist ein noch relativ junger For-
schungszweig, der in Wissenschaft und Praxis ständig an Bedeutung
gewinnt. Die Schriftenreihe möchte dieser Entwicklung Rechnung tra-
gen und ein Forum für wissenschaftliche Beiträge aus dem Business-
to-Business-Bereich schaffen. In der Reihe sollen aktuelle For-
schungsergebnisse präsentiert und zur Diskussion gestellt werden.

Katrin Susanne Mühlfeld

Strategic Shifts between Business Types

A transaction cost theory-based approach supported by dyad simulation

With a foreword by Prof. Dr. Klaus Backhaus

Deutscher Universitäts-Verlag

Bibliografische Information Der Deutschen Bibliothek
Die Deutsche Bibliothek verzeichnet diese Publikation in der Deutschen
Nationalbibliografie; detaillierte bibliografische Daten sind im Internet über
<http://dnb.ddb.de> abrufbar.

Dissertation Universität Münster, 2003

D 6 (2002)

1. Auflage Juli 2004

Alle Rechte vorbehalten
© Deutscher Universitäts-Verlag/GWV Fachverlage GmbH, Wiesbaden 2004

Lektorat: Brigitte Siegel / Sabine Schöller

Der Deutsche Universitäts-Verlag ist ein Unternehmen von
Springer Science+Business Media.
www.duv.de

Umschlaggestaltung: Regine Zimmer, Dipl.-Designerin, Frankfurt/Main
Druck und Buchbinder: Rosch-Buch, Scheßlitz
Gedruckt auf säurefreiem und chlorfrei gebleichtem Papier
Printed in Germany

ISBN 3-8244-7989-3

Foreword

The range of products and services that are traded on business-to-business markets is very broad. It encompasses such heterogeneous goods as standardized software, machine tools, and power stations. Against this background of heterogeneity, the development of undifferentiated „one-for-all" marketing programmes is neither promising from the practitioner's perspective, nor consistent with an application-oriented approach in marketing science. Yet, at the same time, the pitfalls of overemphasizing the particularities of individual transactions, which lead to a lack of generalizability, are to be avoided. As a response to this dilemma, various conceptions for systematizing transactions on business-to-business markets have been developed in the past years. Common to all of these concepts, which are rather varied in terms of their methodology, are the objectives of identifying meaningful types of transaction processes (usually referred to as transaction or business types) and of deriving corresponding recommendations to guide marketing practice. Common to all of them is, however, also a deficit: The approaches presented to date take into account only the heterogeneity that prevails at a certain point in time. They do not capture the potential change of market offerings over time, that is, the heterogeneity that arises from shifts between the different types in the course of time. The existent approaches are, hence, static in the sense that they treat the criteria that are used for categorization as given. They do not interpret them as variables that are susceptible to the transaction parties' design. In the light of the multitude of examples of shifts between business types that can be observed in the marketplace – in the automotive industry, the chemical industry or the IT sector – a broadening of perspective in order to account for this dynamic aspect was overdue. The present study addresses this research deficit in that it represents a first-time systematic exploration of the motivations and prerequisites of such fundamental strategy changes that take the form of shifts between business types.

The recent literature on business-to-business marketing discusses the identification of business types increasingly from a neo-microeconomic perspective. Transaction cost economics, in particular, have been found to provide suitable theoretical foundations for analyzing the differences between various selling and purchasing processes and for deriving recommendations that are useful to marketing practice. The present analysis follows this tradition: First, in view of her research objective, the author modifies a particular selected typological approach that is rooted in transaction cost economics. This approach originally identifies three distinct business types: product business, project business and relational business. The distinction bases on the criterion of which particular specificity is associated with a transaction either in technological or contractual terms. In modifying this approach, the author introduces an explicit differentiation between the seller and the buyer perspective that allows for a systematic analysis of balanced and imbalanced transaction relations. These relations and differences between them are later identified as decisive impacts on the seller's motivation for initiating a shift between business types, and also on its prospects of success. Drawing on transaction cost economics and market process theories, the author develops an analytical framework that places the specificity involved in a transaction or transaction series, respectively, at the center of the analysis. Specificity is interpreted as a core decision variable with regard to the shift issue. Furthermore, the author examines the influence of varying initial business types constellations that differ primarily with respect to the parties' power over each other. She also analyzes potential sources of impulses that might trigger shift considerations on the part of the seller. The second part of the analysis takes as its point of departure the assumption that a seller firm is contemplating a particular shift direction based on such qualitative considerations. The author then proceeds to examine conditions of efficient assertability of the envisaged shift direction. She develops a formal model, which is illustrated by means of a case study from the chemical industry. A simulative solution to the model sheds light on, for example, the impact of varying amounts of R&D investment and on the effects of different developments of the competitive environment on the shift decision.

The present study constitutes an important contribution to the theoretically-grounded research on business-to-business marketing. At the same time, it represents a pioneering piece of work that creates a systematic reference framework for further research on strategic shifts between business types. It also offers impulses for application-oriented research in economics and provides valuable references for marketing practice.

I hope that this publication will see the broad dissemination and considerable recognition that it deserves, both in the scientific community as well as in business practice.

Klaus Backhaus
Professor of Marketing

Preface

"It is, perhaps, worth stressing that economic problems arise always and only in consequence of change." (F. A. Hayek 1945)

Fundamental changes of market offerings represent an empirically observable phenomenon in the market place. From the viewpoint of the concerned companies, such a change constitutes a considerable challenge. A challenge arises also from the perspective of marketing science: typological approaches to business-to-business marketing that have proven to be as meaningful from an empirical viewpoint and as valuable from a theoretical perspective have so far restricted themselves to static analysis in the sense that they have focused on the analysis of marketing for or within particular (business) types. Shifts *between* these types have not been at the centre of such analysis.

This thesis provides a dynamics-oriented perspective and analyzes motivations of and influences on shifts between business types. It was written while I was working as an assistant teacher at the Institute of Business-to-Business Marketing (IAS) and was accepted as a PhD thesis by the Faculty of Commerce at the Westfälische Wilhelms-Universität Münster in February 2003. To my supervisor, Dr. Klaus Backhaus, Professor of Marketing, I am indebted not only for encouraging me to address this important and challenging research issue. His constructive support throughout all phases of my PhD project and the generous provision of academic freedom have allowed me to work on and complete this PhD project in its present form. Beyond these experiences immediately related to my PhD project, working at the IAS provided me with the much appreciated opportunity to learn from him in many other respects. Among these was the insight that an institution's (work) spirit is inextricably associated with and dependent on the person of the institution's head or chairperson, in this case Dr. Klaus Backhaus. Therefore, my special thanks go to him for creating the exceptionally pleasant and stimulating environment that I enjoyed working in so much for the past years. Also, I am deeply indebted to Dr. Theresia Theurl, Professor of Economics, for the kind willingness to render the second opinion on this thesis.

Furthermore, I am much obliged to Dr. Thomas Lueb (BASF Coatings AG) who provided me with important exemplifying insights into the reality of strategic shifts between business types, ensuring that the theoretical considerations are well complemented by illustrations from business practice.

I am also indebted to many other people for their contributions in terms of time, knowledge and encouragement that helped me in completing this project. First of all, I would like to thank my colleagues at the IAS: for always being prepared for discussion, for taking over many of my duties and responsibilities as assistant teacher during the most pressing times of writing up the thesis, and last but not least for their contributions to the kind of friendly and stimulating atmosphere that made working at the IAS and with them such a valuable and enjoyable experience as it was. In particular, I would like to thank Dipl.-Kfm. Gregory Theile for his inexhaustible willingness to discuss my latest scientific ideas, as well as for his encouragement and helpful critical comments during all phases of my PhD project. I am also grateful to Dipl.-Vw. Jens Hardenacke and Dipl.-Kfm. Holger Werthschulte for their valuable comments on an earlier version of this thesis. Special thanks go to my former „office colleague", who later became my „PhD colleague", Dr. Lars Brzoska, for being an always present and reliable „motivational anchor". I am indebted to PD Dr. Detlef Aufderheide for numerous helpful discussions and for his comments on an earlier version of this thesis. With his profound expertise in economics he proved to be a just as important „scientific anchor".

I am also highly indebted to Dipl.-Kffr. Angela Broer and Dipl.-Kffr. Valerie Feldmann: not only could I share my scientific ideas with them and received many valuable comments on my work. Perhaps even more importantly, they did an excellent job at motivating me during the unavoidable dry spells of the project, and also provided distraction from the seriousness of science whenever it was needed.

Finally, I would like to thank my parents, Hans-Horst and Sabiene Mühlfeld, who supported me so generously during all stages of my education, and my boyfriend Sven Florian Kerstan: they unreservedly kept me grounded at all times and supported me in so manifold ways. To them, I dedicate this work.

Katrin Mühlfeld

Table of contents

List of figures and tables

Figures

Tables

XVI

List of abbreviations

ABB	Asea Brown Boveri
AG	Aktiengesellschaft
Anon.	Anonymous
Approx.	Approximately
AV	Added value
BK	Betreiberkonzept ("BOT" = build-(own)-operate-transfer")
BT^B	Business type of buyer
BT^S	Business type of seller
Bspw.	beispielsweise ("for example")
c.p.	ceteris paribus
CAC	Comparative advantage over competition
CAD	Computer Aided Design
CIB	Computer Integrated Business
CIM	Computer Integrated Manufacturing
Co.	Corporation
DBW	Die Betriebswirtschaft (journal)
DIN	Deutsche Industrie-Norm (German Industry Norm)
E_	Example_
ed.	Edition
Ed(s).	Editor(s)
e.g.	exemplum gratum
Esp.	Especially
et al.	et alii
etc.	et cetera
F	Following
Ff	forth following
Fig.	Figure
Fn	Footnote
GE	Geldeinheiten ("monetary units")
i.d.R.	in der Regel ("usually")
i.e.	id est
IFF	International Flavors & Fragrances, Inc.

Kg	Kilogramm/ kilogram
KWU	Kraftwerk Union AG (German powerstation manufacturer)
LAN	Local area network
NIE	New Institutional Economics
OEM	Original Equipment Manufacturer
p.	Page
PC	Personal Computer
PDB	Product business
PDB^B	Buyer product business
PDB^S	Seller product business
PJB	Project business
PJB^B	Buyer project business
PJB^S	Seller project business
pp.	Pages
PPS	Produktionsplanung und -steuerung
R&D	Research & Development
RB	Relational business
RB^B	Buyer relational business
RB^S	Seller relational business
Repr.	Reprint
SET	SET
SL	Systemlieferantenschaft ("cooperative system supply")
Tab.	Table
TCA	Transaction cost analysis
U.S.	United States of America
VC $^{(B)}$	Value created from the buyer's view
VC $^{(S)}$	Value created from the seller's view
Vs	Versus
Vol.	Volume
WiSt	Wirtschaftswissenschaftliches Studium (journal)
ZfB	Zeitschrift für Betriebswirtschaft (journal)
Zfbf	Zeitschrift für betriebswirtschaftliche Forschung (journal)
ZFP	Zeitschrift für Forschung und Praxis (journal)

1 Strategic shifts between business types as essential elements of the market process

1.1 Recognizing and seizing opportunities for shifts between business types as a touch-stone of firm strategy

When firms fundamentally change the strategic orientation of their market offerings, success and failure are immediate neighbors.

> Continental changes its supply strategy.[...] Continental Automotive Systems partially abandons plans to become a systems supplier. Expectations of high profits from developing into a systems supplier have fallen through for most companies. [...] Many companies that have changed from producers of components to systems suppliers now realize that they come off worse with that strategy. [...] Not only Conti, but also Bosch and Siemens Automotive draw their largest profits from selling basic components such as sparkplugs, radiator tubes or tires.[1]

> „Owing to intensive market surveys, we have realized that more and more customers perceive modularly pre-planned conceptions for power stations as advantageous", explains Ingo D. Paul, head of product management steam power stations at KWU. This is linked up with the fact that in the course of the liberalization of many electricity sectors, more and more Independent Power Producers (IPP) push into the market." [...] Siemens and the ABB Kraftwerke AG (Mannheim) were the first to respond to these trends and develop according concepts for modular power stations „off-the-shelf". [...] First experiences [...] have shown that the goals which are aspired to – the reduction of costs and construction times – can indeed be attained in this way.[2]

Long-term oriented, strategic decisions in terms of a *basic redesign of the firms' offering* as illustrated by the examples usually carry along high hopes of substantially improving a firm's

---

[1] Translated from *Reinking* (2002). The quotation represents a currently not uncommon view on the automotive supply industry. The described experiences suggest that at least a considerable number of suppliers have not been able to profit from closer cooperation with their Original Equipment Manufacturer (OEM) customers targeted at the production of more specific, large modules (see for associated recommendations e.g. *Layer, G. B.* (1992)). See for detailed analysis of the issue e.g. *Freiling, J.* (1995), whose analysis, though, also points in the cooperative direction; in this context also *Männel, B.* (1996).

[2] Translated from *Jopp, K.* (1998), p. 25. Already in the 1980's Siemens KWU began to develop and market a new concept for selling power stations which was called "KWU-convoy-concept". Simplification of the process for obtaining approval by relevant authorities, and thereby reducing construction times and costs were primary goals attached to the concept. Standardization and general approval of whole modules was the key to the strategy. There is good reason to infer that along came a decrease in seller dependence owing to the inceased substitutability of customers with respect to the modules.

(long-term) financial situation.[3] Often enough, though, their realization does not meet the expectations but brings about the exact opposite, whether due to miscarried implementation or erroneous choice of the new strategy. Nevertheless, persistent refusal to consider change is not an option, either: in a world that consists of a ceaseless sequence of transient states, adaptation to varying conditions poses a constant challenge. Maladaptation ultimately causes lastingly unaltered marketing strategies to run into problems. *Hayek* (1945) has captured this fundamental condition in the well known and frequently quoted statement that "...economic problems arise always and only in consequence of change."[4] Such change has many faces. Globalization, entry of new competitors, dynamic developments of customer needs, alterations in the legal frame to name just a few examples: environmental change and perpetual interaction between economic actors which call for adaptive action can take an infinite variety and number of realizations.[5] Resistance to this challenge can have detrimental effects when competitive offers gain ground and a firm's customer and profit basis is eroded as a result. However, a crucial precondition for adaptation is information on relevant changes.

In view of a constant flood of information, aggravated during the last decades through the emergence of new information and communication technology[6], the task of deciding on appropriate reactions to impulses from environmental and market dynamics seems difficult enough. Yet, the claim of marketing reaches even beyond: scholars such as *Dickson* (1996) have argued that "... marketing is the art and science of creating change (disequilibrium) in markets in such a way that the change benefits the firm..."[7], thereby highlighting not only the close link between marketing and (strategic) change, but also its proactive dimension. Whether or not one agrees with this particular definition, its essence is reflected in many other definitions of marketing. Most of them carry, at least implicitly, some notion of heading for "new horizons" of customer satisfaction and, hopefully, resulting company success through

---

[3]   The term "strategic" refers here to long-term oriented decisions that considerably affect intra-firm resource allocation. For a more detailed exposition see chapter 2.2 and 3.3.2.

[4]   *Hayek, F.* (1945), p. 523.

[5]   See e.g. *Porter, M. E.* (1991), p. 98; *Drucker, P. F.* (2002). On the difference between spontaneous, decentralized adaptation as described by *Hayek, F.* (1945) and intentional adaptation as described by *Barnard, C. I.* (1938) see extensively *Williamson, O. E.* (1991b).

[6]   See e.g. *Shapiro, C./Varian, H. R.* (1999), p. 1ff; *Kotler, P.* (2003), pp. 2, 33 ff.

[7]   *Dickson, P. R.* (1996), p. 102.

2

implemented exchange.[8] In the words of *Sudharshan* (1995), this idea reads as: "marketing strategy creates pathways to a desirable future. Marketing management is travel through these pathways to achieve the desirable future."[9] It is widely held that the vehicle for traveling these roads is the (comparative) competitive advantage.[10] The firms' constant quest for finding and, if possible, sustaining such competitive advantage, bears considerable resemblance with the continuous search for improvement and innovation that Austrian economics ascribe to entrepreneurial actors, and which fills in the part of the engine of the market process.[11] Summing up, strict resistance to the dynamic challenge of market processes is likely to lead to a dead-end in the long run. Empirical evidence shows that firms respond to this insight by implementing strategically-motivated changes to their market offerings at times.[12]

By no means does such behavior *guarantee* any success. However, if one suspects that it is not pure luck that distinguishes successful from unsuccessful redesign endeavors, there is some value to a *systematic* investigation into the conditions that are conducive to a positive outcome. Hence, reaching beyond the case particularities of the changes undertaken by the example companies, two key issues about the strategic design and redesign of offerings in industrial goods marketing are paradigmatically highlighted.

First, *fundamentally* distinct ways of conducting transactions exist: beyond the obvious divergence in terms of product (technology), transactions can be presumed to differ in a

---

[8] Some definitions of marketing center explicitly around the notion of exchange and its promotion (see e.g. *Dwyer, R. F./Schurr, P. H./Oh, S.* (1987), p. 11; *Hunt, S. D./Lambe, C. J.* (2000), p. 29, in reference to *Kotler, P.* (1972); *Bagozzi, R. P.* (1975); *Hunt, S. D.* (1976); see also *Kotler, P.* (2003), p. 9). The underlying idea is that (voluntary) exchange is per definition value creating (see for such assessment e.g. *Foss, N. J.* (2003).

[9] *Sudharshan, D.* (1995), p. 1.

[10] See e.g. *Day, G. S.* (1999), p. 128ff; *Varadarajan, P. R./Jayachandran, S.* (1999), p. 120; from a strategic management perspective e.g. *Porter, M. E.* (1985); *Teece, D. J./Pisano, G./Shuen, A.* (1997). It constitutes itself in an offering which is perceived as superior compared to the relevant competitive offerings by the buyer, and is at the same time more profitable for the seller. In view of its relativity, the construct has also been referred to as "comparative advantage over competition" (CAC) (see e.g. *Backhaus, K.* (2003), pp. 7f, 35ff, who defines marketing as the management of CACs; related: e.g. *Plinke, W.* (2000), p. 77ff.

[11] Seminal contributions to this topic include *Schumpeter, J. A.* (1926); *Schumpeter, J. A.* (1928); *Schumpeter, J. A.* (1942); *Kirzner, I. M.* (1973); *Kirzner, I. M.* (1979); recently, e.g. *Fu-Lai Yu, T.* (2001).

[12] See e.g. *Hamel, G./Prahalad, C. K.* (1994), p. 136; *Leker, J.* (2001); *Burmann, C.* (2001), *Burmann, C.* (2002a). Note that the latter two authors, though, base their investigations on a broader conception of strategic change.

number of other basic respects such as e.g. the kind of contract applied[13], or the degree of dependence experienced by the seller and the buyer[14]. In recognition of such fundamental differences between transactions, marketing science has developed a large number of concepts for more or less systematically categorizing different kinds of transactions.[15] A basic idea inherent to most of these categorizations is the aim of simultaneously achieving maximum internal homogeneity and external heterogeneity of the identified groups. Apart from this similarity, the approaches developed so far in the literature differ substantially, with respect to the applied criteria, their theoretical and/or empirical foundations, the recommendations which may or may not be derived from them, or the specific area of marketing (industrial or consumer goods) which they focus on. Regardless of prevailing variations in the terms that have been coined for referring to such categories, the notion of "business types" is adopted here for general reference to such categorizations of transaction situations.[16]

Starting with such categorization of transaction processes, a **second**, crucial issue emerges which has not yet been subject to similarly extensive, systematic treatment: empirical observation suggests that fundamentally different ways of trading *functionally identical* products exist and, first, that they are employed by different companies in a market at the same time, and, second, that, over the course of time, individual companies may shift from one way of transacting to another in selling functionally identical products, that is, firms make changes in the way they transact which – from the seller's viewpoint – imply strategic redesigns of their offerings.[17] This analysis focuses in particular on the second issue. The central questions are then what motivates companies to shift from one way of transacting, that

---

[13] See related e.g. *Macneil, I. R.* (1974); *Macneil, I. R.* (1978); *Williamson, O. E.* (1985); *Backhaus, K./Aufderheide, D./Späth, G.-M.* (1994).

[14] See related e.g. *Emerson, R. M.* (1962); *Blau, P. M.* (1964); *Williamson, O. E.* (1985); *Heide, J. B./John, G.* (1988); *Backhaus, K./Aufderheide, D./Späth, G.-M.* (1994).

[15] Already in 1980, *Enis, B. M./Roering, K. J.* (1980), p. 186, concluded that "...the search for a conceptually logical and managerial useful classification of products is a continuing theme in the marketing literature." A few, non-representative examples include *Mathur, S. S.* (1984); *Kaas, K. P.* (1992); *Kaas, K. P.* (1995b); *Weiber, R./Adler, J.* (1995); *Plinke, W.* (1997); *Bensaou, M.* (1999); *Cannon, J. P./Perreault, W. D. J.* (1999); *Backhaus, K.* (2003) (see chapter 2.1.1.3 for a more detailed and systematic overview).

[16] Later, the term will be narrowed down to apply to the groups resulting from a particular categorization, a transaction cost-based typology developed primarily by *Backhaus, K./Aufderheide, D./Späth, G.-M.* (1994); *Backhaus, K.* (1998) and related publications.

4

is, from one business type, to another at a certain time, and under what conditions is this change likely to be successful?[18] In a nutshell: why was Siemens successful where Continental failed? Such puzzlers are at the heart of this research. A key factor to their answer might lie in adopting a dynamic perspective on structuring the observable variety of transaction processes. The criteria for categorization are no longer viewed as data, but as variables which are susceptible to deliberate design by the transaction partners and, in particular, the seller.[19] The focus on the seller's active role in molding the shift results from the inherent normative orientation of this research which is adopted in accord with many contributions in the strategic management tradition[20]: the explicit aim is to gain insights that provide some guidance for management practice in deciding which "knobs to turn".

Recapitulating, in view of a continually evolving environment and dynamic market processes, firms face several challenges associated with the search for sustainable competitive advantages and with the related task of shaping their market offering in terms of a particular business type. First, they need to recognize general opportunities for strategic shifts between business types. Second, they must draw the "right" inferences regarding the direction of a shift.[21] Finally, the firm needs to examine whether the specifically envisaged shift really improves its situation compared to a continued pursuit of the previous business type. This concerns the question of whether the particular firm is in the position to seize the opportunity. Taken together, these issues represent an important touch-stone of a firm's (marketing) strategy.

---

[17] Although related issues (e.g. building competitive advantages in rapidly evolving environments) have extensively been discussed by researchers adopting a dynamic capabilities approach (see e.g. by *Teece, D. J./Pisano, G./Shuen, A.* (1997)), such analysis building on transaction types is largely lacking.

[18] The number of contributions to the investigation of various aspects of strategic change in general is impressive (see e.g. *Gilbert, X./Strebel, P. J.* (1987); *Ginsberg, A.* (1988); *Boeker, W.* (1989); *Hamel, G./Prahalad, C. K.* (1989); *Huff, J. O./Huff, A. S./Thomas, H.* (1992); *D'Aveni, R. A.* (1994); *Chakravarthy, B.* (1997); more recently *Burmann, C.* (2001); *Burmann, C.* (2002a); *Leker, J.* (2001)). Yet, it has been largely detached from research on structuring transaction processes. Noteworthy exceptions include e.g. *Mathur, S. S.* (1984); *Mathur, S. S./Kenyon, A.* (1997). By no means results from these first, tentative treatments a systematic and exhaustive investigation to this topic.

[19] See in a more general governance context *Heide, J. B.* (1994), p. 82.

[20] See e.g. *Saloner, G.* (1991), p. 131; *Ambrosini, V./Jenkins, M.* (2002). With respect to marketing's normative orientation see e.g. *Robin, D. P.* (1979), p. 3; *Varadarajan, P. R./Jayachandran, S.* (1999), p. 133; *Donnan, M. P./Comer, J. M.* (2001), p. 256.

[21] Given that the outlined conditions are fulfilled, a further requirement is a succesful shift implementation. This is, however, a distinct problem in its own the analysis of which is beyond the scope of this work.

5

Although the basic answer to these key questions is a clear "*it depends*", a well founded, systematic approach to structuring business transactions should allow at least for figuring out, "*...what* the solution depends *on*...".[22]

1.2   Research purpose and organization of the analysis

"There is nothing so practical as a good theory."[23]

In view of the foregoing discussion, the central **objective** of this research is the proposition of a framework for the analysis of seller-initiated shifts between business types that is solidly grounded in economic theory and allows for deriving answers to such questions as: what circumstances (should) trigger shift considerations and which are the underlying motivations? Under what conditions are they likely to be successful from the seller's perspective, that is, assertable on efficient terms in consideration of the buyer's interests?

In approaching the outlined research purpose, the analysis is organized as shown in *Fig. 1*. Following the introductory remarks in this **first chapter**, the **second chapter** is dedicated to an outline of the static foundations of this analysis. Building on a general substantiation of the usefulness of applying a systematic and, in particular, a typological structure to the variety of transactions that can be found in business reality, various approaches to this structuring task are presented. Since it has been the domain of industrial marketing that has recently been characterized by a particularly intensive discussion about various ways of systematically structuring transactional variety, the analysis focuses on this subarea of marketing.[24]

---

[22] *Shapiro, C./Varian, H. R.* (1999), p. x, who advance exactly such a line of argument.

[23] *Lewin, K.* (1945), p. 129.

[24] For comprehensive overviews see e.g. *Kleinaltenkamp, M.* (1994); *Backhaus, K.* (2003), p. 300ff; *Kleinaltenkamp, M./Jacob, F.* (2002).

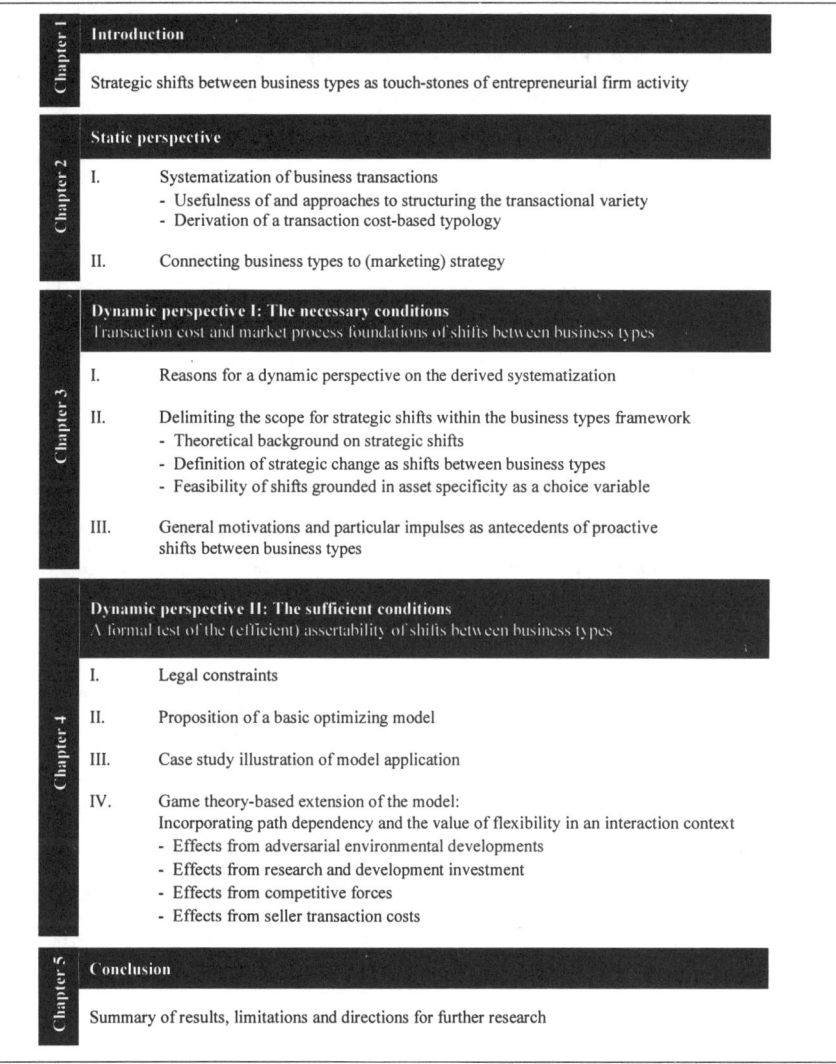

Chapter 1

Introduction

Strategic shifts between business types as touch-stones of entrepreneurial firm activity

Chapter 2

Static perspective

I. Systematization of business transactions
    - Usefulness of and approaches to structuring the transactional variety
    - Derivation of a transaction cost-based typology

II. Connecting business types to (marketing) strategy

Chapter 3

Dynamic perspective I: The necessary conditions
Transaction cost and market process foundations of shifts between business types

I.   Reasons for a dynamic perspective on the derived systematization

II. Delimiting the scope for strategic shifts within the business types framework
     - Theoretical background on strategic shifts
     - Definition of strategic change as shifts between business types
     - Feasibility of shifts grounded in asset specificity as a choice variable

III. General motivations and particular impulses as antecedents of proactive shifts between business types

Chapter 4

Dynamic perspective II: The sufficient conditions
A formal test of the (efficient) assertability of shifts between business types

I.   Legal constraints

II. Proposition of a basic optimizing model

III. Case study illustration of model application

IV. Game theory-based extension of the model:
     Incorporating path dependency and the value of flexibility in an interaction context
     - Effects from adversarial environmental developments
     - Effects from research and development investment
     - Effects from competitive forces
     - Effects from seller transaction costs

Chapter 5

Conclusion

Summary of results, limitations and directions for further research

Fig. 1: Organization of the analyis

Industrial marketing is understood as marketing that is targeted at organizational buyers who acquire the products and services for the purpose of further production (intermediate goods and services). Hence, their demand for the exchanged objects is derived from subsequent

7

market stages.[25] Based on the presentation of various approaches, a market sides balancing typological concept that builds on New Institutional Economics (NIE), or, more specifically, transaction cost theory, is held as most appropriate with respect to the research purpose.

After a brief sketch of the relevant foundations of transaction cost theory, existing transaction cost-based systematizations of business transactions are described. From these approaches which are very similar at their core, the concept developed by *Backhaus* and colleagues is chosen as the basis for the following shift analysis. It centers mainly around asset specificity as the discriminating criterion and is regarded as the most coherent and, with respect to the integration of dynamics, furthest developed concept.[26] Nevertheless, some modifications are proposed in order to facilitate the shift analysis. In particular, the notion of "business types constellation" is introduced: building on a more explicit distinction between the buyer and the seller positions in terms of transaction-specific investment, the business types (product, project and relational business) as outlined by *Backhaus* and colleagues are reinterpreted and assigned to each transaction partner individually. A combination of a particular seller business type and a particular buyer business type is referred to as constellation. As a result, the formal clarity of the subsequent analysis is enhanced, and more conducive conditions for uncovering distinct shift motivations are created. Next, the constitutive elements of a business types constellation are identified. The considerations are guided by an idea that has received only little explicit attention in the literature so far, yet bears important consequences for the analysis of shifts between business types: it is the proposition that asset specificity may stem from technological properties of a transaction (object), but also from the transaction's contractual dimension. Following a brief outline of type-specific marketing problems, the business types concept is connected to the issue of (industrial marketing) strategy with the result that the pursuit of a particular business types constellation is viewed as a strategy.

---

[25] See for related, fundamental definitions of industrial marketing e.g. *Engelhardt, W. H./Günter, B.* (1981), p. 24; *Anderson, J. C./Narus, J. A.* (1999), p. 4; *Backhaus, K.* (2003), p. 8; *Hutt, M. D./Speh, T. W.* (2004), p. 4f.

[26] See the seminal contributions by *Backhaus, K./Aufderheide, D./Späth, G.-M.* (1994); *Backhaus, K.* (2003); *Backhaus, K./Plinke, W./Rese, M.* (2004). Asset specificity describes a condition where investments are tailored idiosyncratically to a particular transaction partner with the consequence that a large difference prevails between their value in this original use and in the best alternative use (see e.g. *Williamson, O. E.* (1985), p. 52ff). See chapters 2.1.2.3.3 and 3.2.3 for in-depth characterization.

Proceeding from this presentation of the static foundations, the **third chapter** begins with a sketch of arguments from business practice and economic theory that suggest the need for a dynamic view on the business types framework in which the structuring criteria are variables instead of given data. Against this background, fundamental considerations on necessary conditions for a shift to occur are advanced and presented in a purely qualitative manner. First, a definition of the research object, shifts between business types constellations, is derived. Building on this characterization, the general feasibility of such shifts is established based on the idea of asset specificity as a choice variable.[27] The discussion of individual influencing factors prepares the ground for the subsequent identification of shift motivations. Arising from the position that value creation, claim and protection are the central objectives guiding the individual firm in this framework, the impact of different initial constellations and of various kinds of impulses on the potential desirability of certain shifts is explored on a general level. In investigating these issues, insights from transaction cost theory are combined with arguments from Austrian economics in order to better capture the subjective and dynamic dimension of the market process within which proactive shifts between constellations take place.

Based on these fundamental qualitative considerations, the individual firm needs to (quantitatively) assess its capacity to have the buyer accept the newly envisaged constellation at terms that are efficient and profit-enhancing from the seller's perspective ("assertability"). This is the topic of the **fourth chapter**. After a brief discussion of the problems that legal constraints may impose restrictions on particular constellations or shifts, a formal economic model is developed which comprises two distinct steps. First, drawing on three related transaction cost theory-based models, an optimizing perspective is adopted, and the resulting model is illustrated by means of application to a case study.[28] Second, the model is extended to capture the interactive dimension of the transaction. Based on the principal ideas of the optimizing approach, a very simple game theoretic model of the dyadic relationship between a seller and a buyer is proposed which incorporates issues of path dependency and valuing flexibility. It is linked to two basic goals: the first objective is to provide a theoretically-

---

[27] Explicit consideration of this idea can be traced back to *Riordan, M. H./Williamson, O. E.* (1985). It has later been taken up e.g. by *Aufderheide, D.* (1993); *Sanchez, R.* (2000); *Aufderheide, D.* (2000).

[28] Note that the despite the use of the term optimization, no notion of equilibrium is embodied (see for a similar assessment on his approach *Porter, M. E.* (1991), p. 98).

guided heuristic framework for thinking about some important aspects of shifts between business types constellations. The second goal is to derive some instructive insights into various impacts (e.g. adversarial environmental developments throughout the game) on the efficient assertability of the shift which is aimed at. The results are obtained by means of a computer simulation. Finally, some findings from the model are presented.

To conclude, the **fifth chapter** summarizes the principal findings of the analysis, discusses some limitations and hints at directions for future research.

2 Strategic decisions for business-type specific marketing in industrial goods markets

2.1 Static perspective: structuring business transactions

2.1.1 Foundations of systematic approaches to industrial marketing

2.1.1.1 On the usefulness of systematizing business transactions

In considering the benefits from a structured approach to industrial marketing, the starting point is given by business reality: industrial marketing practice covers an immense and highly heterogeneous variety of transactional processes in marketing industrial goods, ranging from marketing standard screws to computer integrated manufacturing systems or nuclear power stations.[29] If marketing science (or, as *Kotler* (1972) puts it, marketing management science) aims at reaching beyond pure description in order to develop recommendations for business practice as it has been demanded by many scholars, it is faced with a dilemma[30]: the heterogeneous variety of transaction situations in business practice renders any attempt to develop a marketing program which is universally applicable regardless of particularities of the transaction situation pointless. On the other hand, normative statements that solely refer to one specific situation or marketing problem will hardly deserve the label "science".[31] Hence, there is a need for a systematic approach which combines some abstraction from parti-cularities in order to go beyond considerations of individual cases, with a more differentiated view on marketing problems than can be achieved by a general "one-for-all" marketing

---

[29] See also regarding the following argument *Backhaus, K./Aufderheide, D./Späth, G.-M.* (1994), p. 14; *Kleinaltenkamp, M.* (1994), p. 78; *Backhaus, K.* (2003), p. 299.

[30] See *Miracle, G. E.* (1965), p. 18; *Schwartz, G.* (1965), p. 19; *Lilien, G. L.* (1979), p. 191; *Backhaus, K.* (2003), p. 299; *Varadarajan, P. R./Jayachandran, S.* (1999), p. 133; *Donnan, M. P./Comer, J. M.* (2001), p. 256; *Ambrosini, V./Jenkins, M.* (2002), p. 264, on the need to develop recommendations for marketing practice. A recent investigation with 241 German and US-Amercian marketing researchers by *Franke, N.* (2002) has revealed that for more than 60% of the respondents, the normative design-oriented purpose of marketing science is at least as important as mere knowledge gains (p. 55f). *Kotler, P.* (1972), p. 52, distinguishes between "marketing" as a descriptive science and "marketing management" as a normative science. In this context, no such differentiation is made. Both terms are synonymously used following the normative orientation. The notion of a "normative" marketing science is understood in this paper in terms of a practical-normative orientation as opposed to a declarative-normative perspective (see *Bamberg, G./Coenenberg, A. G.* (2002), p. 11f.).

[31] See e.g. more generally on this position *Lamnek, S.* (1995), p. 16.

programme.[32] Grouping transactions according to some criteria which are decisive for the way buyers and sellers come to agree on the exchange and carry it out seems a promising way to handle this. This procedure is referred to as "structuring" in the following, regardless of the concrete method and attributes of the grouping (content of criteria, number of groups, etc.). In industrial marketing, a particularly popular approach to structuring is the typological approach.[33]

2.1.1.2 Methodological aspects: emphasizing the role of typological theories in structuring

"... typologies have proved to be a popular approach for thinking about organizational structures and strategies."[34] Their particular usefulness for structuring complex economic and organizational phenomena in a rather parsimonious manner has been widely recognized, both from a theoretical perspective and in practical applications in various fields of research.[35] However, there is considerable debate about the definition of the term "typology", particularly in comparison to other methods of structuring and grouping such as "classification schemes" or "taxonomies".[36] Moreover, a large variety of different conceptions of typology construction

---

[32] See e.g. *Meyer, M./Kern, E./Diehl, H.-J.* (1998), p. 118. Essentially, the approach encompasses both traditional purposes of business management as a science as outlined, for instance, by *Kosiol, E.* (1964), p. 745ff: a theoretically-oriented purpose concerned primarily with explicating is distinguished from a pragmatically-oriented purpose which is predominantly directed towards developing recommendations.

[33] See e.g. *Kaas, K. P.* (1992); *Plinke, W.* (1997); *Meyer, M./Kern, E./Diehl, H.-J.* (1998); *Backhaus, K.* (2003). Early contributions to the use of typologies with a more general focus on business administration include *Leitherer, E.* (1965); *Riebel, P.* (1965).

[34] *Doty, D. H./Glick, W. H.* (1994), p. 230

[35] See *Bacharach, S. B.* (1989); *Rich* (1992); *Doty, D. H./Glick, W. H.* (1994) for theoretical discussions. Drawing on subsequent argumentations, complexity in that context can roughly be understood in terms of a large number of varied elements that are related in ways which make it difficult to separate (1) them and (2) the links between them. Detailed overview of characterizations and measures of complexity are provided by *Holm, H. J.* (1993) or *Edmonds, B.* (1999), p. 2 appendix VI, who summarizingly defines complexity as "...that property of models which makes it difficult to formulate its overall behaviour in a given language or representation, even when given almost complete information about its components and their inter-relations." Early examples of structuring concepts labelled as typologies can be found, for instance, in *Woodward, J.* (1965); *Perrow, C.* (1967); *Kotler, P.* (1972); *Etzioni, A.* (1975); *Mintzberg, H. T.* (1979); *Porter, M. E.* (1980); *Mintzberg, H. T.* (1983).

[36] The following remarks provide an illustration for these difficulties: *Doty, D. H./Glick, W. H.* (1994) in their definition of "classification schemes" essentially follow *Rich* (1992), p. 758, who regards them as "a means for ordering and comparing organizations and clustering them into categorical types." *Doty, D. H./Glick, W. H.* (1994) regard both "classification schemes" and "taxonomies" as elements of "classification systems" which in turn are regarded as decision rules for categorizing "...phenomena into mutually exclusive and

have been proposed. As a consequence, the ability of typologies to go beyond purely descriptive categorizations is a controversial issue.[37] Less unequivocal seems to be that those concepts for structuring complex phenomena that are grounded and woven into a solid underlying theory are more likely to fully exploit their explanatory potential.[38] *Doty/Glick* (1994) have recently argumented that, contrary to frequent criticism, typologies may possess exactly this potential. They define typologies rather restrictively as "...conceptually derived interrelated sets of ideal types"[39]. By that, they focus on a certain kind of typological concept, namely the ideal-types-concept which is predominantly concerned with the consequences of departures from a proposed normative ideal.[40] This kind of typological approach has been identified by *Hempel* (1965) as belonging to the domain of theoretical systems. He contrasts it with more descriptive, essentially empirically-based typological approaches, namely the classificatory-types- and the extreme-types-concept.[41] While in the former case, types are construed as classes, extreme types are referred to by *Hempel* (1965) as purely comparative ordering types which represent an intermediate stage on the way from descriptive, classificatory concept formation to thoroughly theoretical conceptualization.

Doty/Glick (1994) argue that such ideal-type-typologies are complex theoretical concepts when they are fully developed and specified. Their complexity is seen as caused by the incorporation of multiple levels of theory. In order to qualify as such a typological theory, *Doty/Glick* (1994) propose that a typology has to fulfill three central requirements: first,

---

exhaustive sets with a series of discrete decision rules" (p. 232; this definition also draws on *McKelvey, B.* (1982) p. 40). *McKelvey, B.* (1982) identifies "taxonomies" as theories of classification, with "classifications" aiming at the "actual construction of a classification scheme and the identification and assignment of organizational forms to formally designated classes" (p. 13). He considers "typologies" as "...simple one-or two-dimensional schemes based on an a-priori theorizing" and hence as a subgroup of special classifications that group "...objects together on the basis of a small, selected number of attributes of particular interest".

[37] See *Emerson, R. M.* (1962); *Mechanic, D.* (1963); *Blalock, H. M. J.* (1969); *Scott, W. R.* (1981); *McKelvey, B.* (1982); *Bacharach, S. B.* (1989); *Doty, D. H./Glick, W. H.* (1994).

[38] See *Bloom, B. S./Engelhart, M. D./Furst, E. J., et al.* (1956), p. 17; *Bacharach, S. B.* (1989), p. 497f; *Doty, D. H./Glick, W. H.* (1994) p. 230 ff. The term "structuring" will be used in the following in a very basic sense and as synonymous with the terms "grouping" and "classifying". It is used in *Hempel's* tradition who, very fundamentally, defines a classification as dividing "... a given set or class of objects into subclasses" (*Hempel, C.* (1965), p. 137).

[39] *Doty, D. H./Glick, W. H.* (1994), p. 232.

[40] See *Campbell-Hunt, C.* (2000), p. 142.

[41] See *Hempel, C.* (1965), p. 156ff.

13

identification of relevant constructs, second, specification of the relationships among these constructs, and third, falsifiability of these relationships.[42]

First, the proposed ideal types represent a reduction of the real world's complex variety in that they should "provide an abstract model, so that deviation from the extreme or ideal type can be noted and explained."[43] Thus, they are viewed as *complex* constructs that consist of multiple *one-dimensional* constructs and bring them together in a holistic representation. Defined as such, some important aspects have to be noted with regard to the ideal types: they represent rather "artificial", pure constructions than actual and observable realizations of the analyzed phenomena. In fact, real designs will only imperfectly correspond to the ideal types. Since their nature is complex, they usually have to be captured using multiple dimensions. Each ideal type is characterized by specific levels of underlying one-dimensional "first order" constructs. Depending on the concrete research question, these could include factors such as age or size of an organization or environmental uncertainty.[44] Second, in order to figure as a typological theory as characterized by *Doty/Glick* (1994) the concept must also include hypotheses regarding the relationships among these constructs.[45] It focuses on the internal consistency of characteristics within an ideal type and develops an explanation for a resulting effect on the dependent variable of the typology. The (implicit or explicit) surmise in some organizational typologies is that real organizations that are more similar to any of the proposed ideal types will also be characterized by a higher level in the dependent attribute.[46]

---

[42] See *Doty, D. H./Glick, W. H.* (1994), p. 233. Also see *Blalock, H. M. J.* (1969), p. 8, and *Bacharach, S. B.* (1989) who advocates falsifiability and utility as criteria (p. 500ff). Fundamental discussions of criteria for evaluation of theories are *Popper, K. R.* (1959); *Hempel, C.* (1965); for an outline of a position which takes a more skeptical approach towards the thought pattern of falsification with respect to the development of theories in economics see the seminal contributions by *Lakatos*, for instance *Lakatos, I.* (1971).

[43] *Blalock, H. M. J.* (1969), p. 32. *Miles, R. E./Snow, C. C.* (1978) identification of organizations as prospectors, analyzers, and defenders constitutes an example for typological ideal types (that in the particular case are argued to be maximally effective).

[44] See *Doty, D. H./Glick, W. H.* (1994), p. 233f. The authors additionally claim a third point, namely that ideal types are not categories themselves, because empirical example of the phenomena may be more or less similar to an ideal type. This argument, however, is essentially implied by the first aspect and, therefore, redundant.

[45] See *Blalock, H. M. J.* (1969), p. 2, 30; *Dubin, R.* (1969), p. 87ff; *Whetten, D. A.* (1989), p. 491ff; *Doty, D. H./Glick, W. H.* (1994), p. 234.

[46] See *Doty, D. H./Glick, W. H.* (1994), p. 234. The dependent variable is selected in relation to the specific context. Examples for dependent variables are effectiveness *Miles, R. E./Snow, C. C.* (1978) or competitive advantage *Porter, M. E.* (1980).

Third, the concept must be susceptible to tests of falsifiability. Its predictions must be testable and be open to disconfirmation.[47] Such a typology would ideally consist of two different theoretical levels: the first element is a grand theory that explains the particular level of the dependent variable in a real example as a result of its similarity or dissimilarity with regard to an ideal type. The second element is a middle-range theory which consists of causal arguments substantiating the interaction of first order constructs within each ideal type.[48]

Now, what insights could possibly be gained from a typology in the described sense when developed for the field of industrial marketing? The main point is that, if referring to typological theories as outlined by *Doty/Glick* (1994), structuring business transactions should not only allow for description and explanation of differences between the groups and their common characteristics, but should also offer the advantage of an explicit normative orientation, that is, a theoretically-guided derivation of recommendations addressed to practitioners in strategic marketing management. Hence, taking into account the benefits that can generally be expected from structuring, a rich tradition of systematic approaches has evolved in the industrial marketing literature. Myriads of groupings for various objects of reference and based on different methods of structuring have been proposed.

2.1.1.3   Overview of different streams of structuring industrial marketing transactions

Textbooks dealing with the particularities of marketing industrial goods[49] (or intermediate goods) have been published as early as 1934/1935.[50] They may be regarded as marking the beginning of the emergence of industrial marketing as a distinct subject matter within the field of marketing.[51] The idea of developing an industrial marketing approach that is structured

---

[47]   See *Lave, C. A./March, J. G.* (1975), p. 60f; *Popper, K. R.* (1959), p. 78ff; *Doty, D. H./Glick, W. H.* (1994), p. 234.

[48]   See *Doty, D. H./Glick, W. H.* (1994), p. 234f.

[49]   Unless it is explicitly stated, the use of the term "industrial goods markets" in this paper implies provision of products as well as services if they fulfill the criteria of being traded to organizational buyers who purchase the products for the purpose of further production (see e.g. *Engelhardt, W. H./Günter, B.* (1981), p. 24). Their demand is, hence, derived from subsequent market stages. The inclusion of products and services is in line with a focus on the total value delivered to a customer and the resulting holistic perception and assessment (see *Anderson, J. C./Narus, J. A.* (1999), p. 4ff).

[50]   See *Frederick, J. H.* (1934); *Elder, R. F.* (1935).

[51]   See *Backhaus, K.* (1998), p. 2; *Reid, D. A./Plank, R. E.* (2000), p. 10.

15

according to some attributes of the transaction essentially dates back to the 1960's.[52] The core idea is that transactions can be classified according to some basic characteristics which are decisive for the way in which buyer and seller view the transaction. Among the first and, with regard to structuring transactions on industrial markets, most influential of such approaches were commodity school concepts.[53] These concepts focus on the objects of transaction, that is the physical characteristics of the goods and related customer buying habits in order to establish different categories of products.[54] Early applications on industrial marketing include:

- *Miracle* (1965) who uses nine different product characteristics for the identification of five different classes of products (including both consumer and industrial goods),

- *Marrian* (1968) who develops a two-level-classification that distinguishes on the first level four classes according to usage (equipment, materials, supplies and services) and subsequently develops up to six sub-categories for each class with regard to the degree of essentiality, or

- *Rowe/Alexander* (1968) who consider the degree of standardization and the intended application (established or newly developed) as discriminating criteria.[55]

---

[52] See *Backhaus, K.* (2003), p. 303f. The emergence of industrial marketing as a separate stream could be regarded as the result of superordinate structuring, based on the criterion "institutional", on the level of general marketing (see e.g. *Baumgarth, C.* (1998b), p. 15). The roots of the latter can be traced back to the beginning of the 20th century and nearly as long, a tendency to form categories requiring different marketing programs can be observed (see *Bartels, R.* (1965)). The main economics-based schools were the commodity school, the functional school and regional school as noninteractive approaches, and the institutional school, the functionalist school and the managerial school as interactive approaches (for an overview see *Bartels, R.* (1962); *Sheth, J. N./Gardner, D. M./Garrett, D. E.* (1988); *Kleinaltenkamp, M./Jacob, F.* (2002), p. 149 f.

[53] See e.g. *Backhaus, K.* (1992), p. 777, and the literature referred to there on their significance. An overview of the various schools in marketing (e.g. commodity, functional, regional, institutional, functionalist and managerial for the economic perspective and buyer behavior, activist, organizational dynamics, systems, social exchange and macro for the noneconomic perspective), each inhibiting its own structuring approach, is provided by *Sheth, J. N./Gardner, D. M./Garrett, D. E.* (1988), p. 19ff. For alternative systematization ("classical schools" are institutional, commodity, functional; "modern" paradigms are grounded in behavioral science, decision theory, systems theory, or modern microeconomic theory) see e.g. *Meffert, H.* (2000), p. 19ff.

[54] See *Sheth, J. N./Gardner, D. M./Garrett, D. E.* (1988) (p. 23, 36ff). *Copeland, M. T.* (1923); *Rhoades, E. L.* (1927); *Aspinwall, L.* (1958) are thought of as founders of the commodity school. Less systematic but conceptually related classifications can, for instance, be found with *Frederick, J. H.* (1934), p. 1ff.

[55] See *Miracle, G. E.* (1965); *Marrian, J.* (1968); *Rowe, D./Alexander, I.* (1968). Marquard provides a critical overview of 11 typological approaches most of which concentrate on industrial goods, as well as an empirical investigation into usefulness and feasibility of commodity approaches in industrial goods marketing.

16

Approaches in the tradition of these early commodity concepts still play an important role in the recent industrial marketing literature: on the one hand, some authors still advocate them as such, although in most cases, they do not derive a complete marketing conception from such structuring.[56] Right from the start, this deficiency, together with an underdeveloped focus on the characteristics of the buyer-seller-relation, rules these basic approaches out as potential foundations for this research. Yet, on the other hand, commodity concepts have provided the foundations for further developments, particularly into some recent and advanced structuring approaches which are typically also used by the respective authors as basis for deriving marketing programs.

To date, a great variety of approaches for structuring industrial marketing has been developed. In principle, they can be systematized according to the method which is used to derive the structure.[57] In principle, three main streams can be distinguished.

- First, and closest related to the original commodity approaches, there are **morphological approaches** that derive categories of goods in a formal deductive way. Taking as a starting point the complete spectrum of goods, they follow a top-down procedure based on some criteria in order to establish a hierarchy of goods. The result is usually a descriptive classification. Examples include *Pfeiffer/Bischof* (1974) who develop a comprehensive goods categorization, or, with respect to industrial marketing, *Hutt/Speh* (2004) who distinguish entering goods, foundation goods and facilitating goods and several subcategories for each. *Homburg/Garbe* (1996) have developed a morphological systematization of industrial services.[58]

- The second stream is formed by approaches that derive their structure in an **empirically-inductive** manner. Catalogues of attributes are established for certain objects, e.g. exchanged goods or business relationships, based on empirical studies. Different levels of these attributes are then assigned to the individual objects. A recent example has been

---

[56] See, for instance, *Brierty, E. G./Eckles, R. W./Reeder, R. R.* (1998), p. 54ff; *Hutt, M. D./Speh, T. W.* (2004), p. 19ff; *Jarrat, D./Fayed, R.* (2001), p. 64.

[57] This systematization has been developed by *Backhaus, K.* (2003), p. 299ff. For alternative systematizations see e.g. *Kleinaltenkamp, M.* (1994), p. 79ff.

[58] See *Pfeiffer, W./Bischof, P.* (1974), p. 919f; *Homburg, C./Garbe, B.* (1996); *Hutt, M. D./Speh, T. W.* (2004), p. 19ff.

proposed by *Bensaou* (1999), who develops a framework for choosing different types of relationships contingent on specific product and market conditions.[59] A very sophisticated approach has been advanced by *Cannon/Perreault* (1999), who combine reasoning from various theoretical streams on relationships with empirical research. Finally, they arrive at an empirically-based classification of eight different clusters of business relationships. The clusters are characterized by four dimensions (importance of supply, complexity of supply, availability of alternatives, supply market dynamism).[60] Recently, *Baumgarth* (2001) has developed a typology specifically targeted at branding in business-to-business markets. He distinguishes four types according to (1) the degree of individualization (low= standardized vs. high = customized) and (2) the vertical reach of markets processes (single-stage vs. multiple-stage). Despite lacking explicit reference to empirical data, the approach can be categorized as empirically inductive in nature. Its basis is formed by existing (empirical) concepts from the literature in combination with the author´s own observations from business practice.[61]

- Third, there are approaches that follow a **theoretically-deductive** path. Building on some theoretical framework, a systematic structure of transaction processes of exchanged goods is derived. In terms of theory applied, modern microeconomic theory and, in particular, New Institutional Economics (NIE) have recently gained significant recognition as potentially promising foundations. This development is mainly due to the substantially less restrictive assumptions regarding the level of information and the degree of rationality adopted by these approaches compared to neoclassical microeconomics. Examples of concepts drawing on NIE include *Backhaus* et al. (1994), *Kaas* (1992, 1995), *Weiber/Adler* (1995), *Kleinaltenkamp* (1997), *Plinke* (1997), and *Kleinaltenkamp/Jacob* (2002).[62] In many of these concepts, the identification of different types of transactions on industrial

---

[59] See *Bensaou, M.* (1999). Some practice-oriented classifications are developed without empirical basis from argumentative inferences drawn from business practice e.g., *Hutt, M. D./Speh, T. W.* (2004) p. 19ff.

[60] See *Cannon, J. P./Perreault, W. D. J.* (1999). The eight clusters are: basic buying and selling, bare bones, contractual transaction, custom supply, cooperative systems, collaborative, mutually adaptive, and customer is king.

[61] See *Baumgarth, C.* (2001), p. 276 ff.

[62] See *Kaas, K. P.* (1992); *Kaas, K. P.* (1995b); *Backhaus, K./Aufderheide, D./Späth, G.-M.* (1994); *Weiber, R./Adler, J.* (1995); *Kleinaltenkamp, M.* (1997); *Plinke, W.* (1997); *Kleinaltenkamp, M./Jacob, F.* (2002). Related literature includes for instance *Schade, C./Schott, E.* (1993b).

markets, in particular the distinction of transaction and relationship marketing, plays a prominent role.

- Finally, a number of approaches has been developed that cannot be unambiguously placed in one category but draw on a broader methodological basis. *Mathur's* (1984) four-fields-matrix of offerings that is built on the distinction of software vs. hardware and differentiated vs. undifferentiated marketing, respectively, represents an early example which has subsequently been elaborated on by *Mathur/Kenyon* (1997).[63] The structure does not rely on a particular theoretical background, nor is it derived on the basis of empirical evidence. Emphasis on the claim that basically every product could be marketed in each of the four cells is, however, not in line with the usual morphological approach either. The classification schemes by *Coviello et al.* (1997) or *Day* (2000) are other examples.[64] Both are rooted in relationship marketing. *Coviello et al.* (1997), for instance, base their structure on a literature review of relationship marketing and arrive at four different, but not mutually exclusive categories: transactional marketing and relational marketing, with the latter including database, interaction, and network marketing. Approaches that are rooted in relationship management deserve a special note because they share a common element of analysis with many concepts based on NIE: they also tend to draw, implicitly or explicitly, on *Macneil's* (1974, 1978) work on modern contract law.[65] Thereby, they focus on the continuum between the two extremes of simple, discrete market transaction, conducted at an arm's-length, and complex relational exchange, often in the form of longer-term, collaborative strategic partnerships.[66] Some authors like *Gundlach/Murphy* (1993) follow

---

[63] See *Mathur, S. S.* (1984), p. 103; *Mathur, S. S./Kenyon, A.* (1997), p. 106ff; other examples include e.g. *Cannon, J. P./Perreault, W. D. J.* (1999); *Jarrat, D./Fayed, R.* (2001), p. 64.

[64] See *Coviello, N. E./Brodie, R. J./Munro, H. J.* (1997); *Day, G. S.* (2000).

[65] See *Macneil, I. R.* (1974); *Macneil, I. R.* (1978). On an assessment of *Macneil's* influence on relationship marketing see e.g. *Hunt, S. D./Lambe, C. J.* (2000), p. 29.

[66] Despite variations in the terminology used by the authors, the approaches correpond to a remarkable degree regarding essential characterisctics. See *Jackson, B. B.* (1985); *Dwyer, R. F./Schurr, P. H./Oh, S.* (1987); *Morgan, R. M./Hunt, S. D.* (1994); *Day, G. S.* (2000); *Freytag, P. V./Clarke, A. H.* (2001), p. 474ff; Recently, there have also been attempts to identify and outline intermediate types, e.g. *Day, G. S.* (2000); *Lambe, J. C./Spekman, R. E./Hunt, S. D.* (2000).

19

Macneil (1974, 1978) more closely in explicitly distinguishing three forms of exchange (transactional, contractual, relational).[67]

An assessment on which of these many approaches might best be suited for structuring industrial marketing is a complex task and, arguably, to some degree prone to subjective influence. Building on the reasoning in the previous chapter, it seems promising to base the analysis on a systematization of industrial marketing which might satisfy the criteria for a typological approach according to *Doty/Glick* (1994). Out of the three outlined streams, it is likely that the theoretically-deductive approaches possesses a, if not the, strongest potential in this area.[68] Yet, the question as to what theory would be most suitable remains unanswered. Essentially, this issue concerns a choice between an economic and a noneconomic theoretic orientation with the latter including concepts from fields such as psychology, sociology and behavioral research.[69] These noneconomic theories are integral elements of the so-called neo-behaviorist perspective and have unfolded their greatest impact in consumer marketing.[70] The understanding of marketing has profited from research in this tradition in mainly two ways.[71] First, the neo-behaviorist paradigm has provided the theoretical foundations for the investigation of intervening variables and processes (e.g. emotions, perception, decision making and learning processes) that precede actual (and directly observable) behavior.[72] Second, methodological progress regarding multivariate analysis methods has been spurred by such research in the neo-behaviorist tradition. On the other hand significant weaknesses of this perspective have been identified. Essentially, they are rooted in the lack of a coherent, yet parsimonious theoretical framework. This deficiency has been held responsible for the difficulties associated with bringing together findings on various issues in the field.

---

[67] See *Gundlach, G. T./Murphy, P. E.* (1993), p. 36.

[68] A more detailed evaluation will be provided in chapter 2.1.2.1 for that approach which is ultimately selected from this stream.

[69] See *Bartels, R.* (1988), pp. 157ff, 185ff; *Sheth, J. N./Gardner, D. M./Garrett, D. E.* (1988), p. 22; *Meffert, H.* (2000), p. 22ff; *Franke, N.* (2002), p. 190f.

[70] See *Kaas, K. P.* (2000), p. 63, also on the weaknesses of the perspective. A recent, extensive treatment of the behavioral science perspective on consumer marketing is e.g. *Blackwell, R. D./Miniard, P. W./Engel, J. F.* (2001).

[71] See for more detailed argumentation *Kaas, K. P.* (2000).

[72] See also *Müller-Hagedorn, L.* (1983) for such assessment.

20

It is exactly this latter issue that constitutes a major strength of the economic perspective. This view offers a stringent theoretical basis that, in addition, has been subject to sophisticated mathematical formalization in many subfields (e.g. neoclassical microeconomics). Hence, although constrained to a narrower perspective by the assumptions of the particular school, economics-based approaches to marketing facilitate a very focused and precise analysis within their specific boundaries.[73] Furthermore, they allow for relating "...back to the origins of marketing as a subdiscipline of economics, providing a distinct identity for marketing by associating it with a distinct domain of human behavior."[74] Also, the economic perspective exhibits greater tendency towards normative analysis than non-economic perspectives such as, for instance, psychology. Therefore, those areas of marketing research which are concerned with normative issues may find greater congruence with their objectives when applying economic instead of noneconomic theory. Finally, among the different areas of interest in marketing, industrial marketing can be expected to profit to a particularly high degree from economics-based analysis, because industrial markets are often argued to be characterized, on average, by a higher degree of rationality in buying, thereby coming closer to the relevant assumptions.[75] However, strong assumptions regarding rationality and availability of information, a high degree of abstraction in its models and related problems of operationalization and empirical testing have usually been regarded as main weaknesses of the economic perspective. Yet, some of these weaknesses have been overcome by recent developments in microeconomic theory, particularly in terms of the NIE with its focus on *limits* to rationality and consequences of information *deficiencies*.[76] Perhaps at least partially

---

[73] This may, in some contexts, considerably enhance chances to uncover the decisive determinants in the otherwise complex network of influences and interrelations (see *Weiber, R./Adler, J.* (2002) , p. 79).

[74] *Sheth, J. N./Gardner, D. M./Garrett, D. E.* (1988), p. 22.

[75] See *Industrial Marketing Committee Review Board* (1954), p. 153. This view is illustrated by the argument that "industrial goods are required for the highly complex processes of producing profit. [...] The industrial buyer [...] is largely concerned with them as elements in a profit-producing system" (*Rose, D.* (1968), p. 124). See also *Dodge, H. R.* (1970), p. 29ff; *Williamson, O. E.* (1985), p. 396f; *Baumgarth, C.* (2001), p. 277.

[76] See *Kaas, K. P.* (2000), p. 60ff; *Franke, N.* (2002), p. 215ff.

due to these developments, the economic perspective on marketing has gained considerable and increasing support during the past 20 years.[77]

As is evident from this brief outline, the choice between the two is highly dependent on the concrete research question. Taking into account that this research focuses on industrial marketing issues from a management-oriented, normative point of view, a concept based on economic reasoning might provide a particularly well-suited basis for deriving generalized recommendations for business practice. With respect to the concrete choice of a theoretical basis for this work, a steadily growing body of industrial marketing literature drawing on NIE with its various, related concepts points in the neoinstitutional direction.[78] Whether and why this framework might be suitable and which particular concept within this stream might be appropriate in view of this work´s research topic calls for more detailed evaluation.

2.1.2   Derivation of a market sides-balancing typology on the basis of New Institutional Economics reasoning

2.1.2.1   A basic outline of the foundations of New Institutional Economics as relevant to the marketing perspective

Neoclassical microeconomic reasoning, in essence, assumes frictionless functioning of economic exchange processes on markets between perfectly informed, rational utility-maximizing individual players on the supply-side as well as on the demand-side. In the paradigm of perfect competition, a faceless seller and a faceless buyer, each insignificant in relation to the market and each drawn from a large pool of actors, meet for an instance in order to exchange goods at the equilibrium market price which summarizes all relevant information.[79] No cost for using the market mechanism is incurred by the actors, i.e. there are no costs for conducting a transaction. In this world, there is no real need for the organization

---

[77]   See Sheth, J. N./Gardner, D. M./Garrett, D. E. (1988) p. 22; Kaas, K. P. (1992); Kaas, K. P. (1995a), p. 4ff; Backhaus, K. (2003), p. 300ff; Homburg, C. (2000), p. 355; Kleinaltenkamp, M./Jacob, F. (2002), p. 150ff; Backhaus, K./Plinke, W./Rese, M. (2004).

[78]   See, for instance, Jackson, B. B. (1985); Heide, J. B./John, G. (1988); Anderson, E./Weitz, B. (1992); Rangan, V. K./Corey, E. R./Cespedes, F. (1993); Homburg, C. (1995).

[79]   This condition which implies that the transacting individuals know all relevant facts about past, present and future conditions is associated with the term "perfect information". See Stiglitz, J. E. (1989); Milgrom, P./Roberts, J. (1992), p. 27; Richter, R./Furubotn, E. G. (1999), p. 11.

of economic activity in (for instance) firms, nor is there any scope for marketing activity promoting market exchange.[80] Real business life without firms is, however, hard to imagine and marketing plays a prominent role in most of them. A different approach to economic reasoning is, thus, needed that conceptually accounts for these empirical facts in order to gain insight into the reasons for their existence and organization.[81]

With the development of the NIE, an alternative framework has emerged that allows marketing scholars to relate back to the origins of the field without being restricted by the tight assumptional constraints of neoclassical microeconomic theory. NIE explicitly acknowledges the existence of information deficiencies, which are also crucial to marketing, and emphasizes their significance for economic transactions: their conduct itself is not costless.[82] NIE is centered around the existence, development, and (efficient) design of institutions that emerge in response to incomplete and asymmetrically dispersed information and resulting uncertainties – conditions that figure as assumptions to the analysis.[83] The term institution is interpreted in a broad sense. In essence, it covers all regulations and organizational provisions that aim at influencing the behavior of actors in order to achieve a higher degree of attainment regarding a certain goal.[84] This interpretation comprises both formal constraints (like for instance laws or formal contracts) and informal constraints (like for example customs, traditions, or codes of conduct).[85] In the NIE perspective, institutions

---

[80] For a brief review of neoclassical economics in comparison to NIE and TCA see, for instance, *Furubotn, E. G./Richter, R.* (1998), pp. 1f, 8ff; *Erlei, M./Leschke, M./Sauerland, D.* (1999), p. 44ff; *Richter, R./Furubotn, E. G.* (1999), p. 9ff; *Rickard, S.* (2002), p. 18ff.

[81] In as far as neoclassical economics recognized that in practice firms existed this was seen as a passing stage. The empirical phenomena were not integral parts of the theoretical concept.

[82] This has been expressed as the "costs of running the economic system..." by *Arrow, K.* (1969), p. 48.

[83] This implies a positive element (systematic analysis of effects) as well as a normative element (efficient design) of the theory.

[84] The understanding of the term "institution" has mainly been shaped, for instance, by *North* who defines institutions as "...the humanly devised constraints that structure political, economic, and social interactions" *North, D. C.* (1991), p. 97, and characterizes them as consisting "... of a set of constraints on behavior in the form of rules and regulations; and finally, a set of moral, ethical, behavioural norms which define the contours and that constrain the way in which the rules and regulation are specified and enforcement is carried out." *North, D. C.* (1984), p. 8. The latter argument emphasizes that institutions have to be binding, i.e. must imply mechanisms for sanctions, in order to serve their purpose of channeling behavior in a desired direction.

[85] See *North, D. C.* (1991), p. 97.

are viewed as endogenous elements: they represent incentive structures or restrictions, respectively, that are created and can be altered by the human actors.[86]

Since information is not freely available, it is a scarce good and obtaining information is costly in the world of NIE. Therefore, complete elimination of information deficiencies is either impossible or not worthwhile against the background of a rational cost-benefit-analysis from the viewpoint of the individual actor.[87] In this setting, the transaction between interacting players is examined: due to the assumed information deficiencies, market prices do not (necessarily) convey perfect information. As a result, not all transactions are market transactions, but some are conducted via other institutions, for instance firms.[88] This gives rise to the emergence of a large variety of different kinds of contracts between transacting parties, the examination of which becomes the predominant issue in economics.[89] Associated is a transformation of perspective from the traditional focus on *unilateral actions* of individual economic actors to their *interaction*.[90] The underlying conditions for these processes are then examined on several levels. Broadly speaking, NIE incorporates two related areas of research: the first perspective originates with *Coase* and focuses on the institutional environment, i.e. the rules of the game.[91] The second stream concerns the institutions of governance, i.e. the play of the game, and traces its origins to *Coase* and *Williamson*.[92]

---

[86] See, for instance, *Buchanan, J. M.* (1990), p. 2f, who contrasts the view held by orthodox economics that choices are made within constraints with the choice among constraints as analyzed by constitutional economics..

[87] Rationality in this context implies that at least actors intend to maximize their individual benefit under the given restrictions. *Williamson, O. E.* (1985), p. 45. This idea also illustrates that the classical tool of marginal analysis is still of some importance in NIE (see *Williamson, O. E.* (1985),p. 41).

[88] The market itself is considered as an institution, the use of which is not costless.

[89] See *Buchanan, J. M.* (1975), p. 229. *Williamson* actually sees the "contractual man" in the center of analysis of complex systems through the lens of NIE. Referring to *Rawls*, he contrasts it with the economic man, the working man and the political man (see *Rawls, J.* (1983), p. 13; *Williamson, O. E.* (1985), p. 43).

[90] See *Backhaus, K./Aufderheide, D./Späth, G.-M.* (1994), p. 23.

[91] See *Coase, R. H.* (1960).

[92] See *Coase, R. H.* (1937); *Williamson, O. E.* (1975); *Williamson, O. E.* (1985). For a recent review see *Williamson, O. E.* (1998), p. 24f. For considerations on the impact of changes in the institutional environment on institutions of governance see e.g. *Williamson, O. E.* (1991a). The term "New Institutional Economics" has first been used by *Williamson* and serves as a distinction from earlier theoretical discussions of institutions not only with regard to content but also regarding terminology. Despite their recognition of the importance of institutions for society, these earlier contributions were more dispersed and were lacking a coherent theoretical basis. See, for instance, *Menger, C.* (1871 (repr.: 1990)); *Menger, C.*

NIE is no unified theory but consists of various concepts that are related to each other, partially interdependently, and sometimes even overlap in their argumentations. However, they differ in their assumptions, particularly regarding the level of information or knowledge that characterizes the actors and regarding the coordination costs associated with transactions. These assumptions vary with the particular perspective taken on the institutional arrangements that evolve in response to information deficiencies. By that, the various concepts within NIE focus on a variety of problems associated with institutions. The main schools of thought within NIE are property rights theory and agency theory which emphasize incentive alignment, and transaction cost theory which examines the economies of transaction costs.[93]

Property rights theory examines the effects of rights of ownership and of changes in these rights with regard to the behavior of economic actors and to the allocation of scarce resources.[94] The right of ownership of an asset consists of three elements: first, the right to use the asset, second, the right to appropriate returns from the asset and, third, the right to change its form and/or substance.[95] Hence, property rights theory is concerned with the efficient

---

(1883); *Veblen, T. B.* (1899 (repr.: 1998)); *Schmoller, G.* (1900 (repr.: 1989)); *Veblen, T. B.* (1904 (repr.: 1975)); *Commons, J. R.* (1934 (repr.: 1961)).

[93]   There is no universally accepted, unambiguous systematization of the different concepts within NIE. The above distinction is based on *Williamson, O. E.* (1985), p. 24ff. All three streams of research are argued to belong to the efficiency branch of contract theory in economics. In addition, several other concepts have been developed that relate to NIE. They often focus, however, on other parts of social science such as law (economic analysis of law), politics (public choice theory and constitutional economics) and history (new economic history). Another theoretical concept associated with NIE is information economics. Seminal work includes for instance *Hayek, F.* (1945); *Stigler, G. J.* (1961); *Nelson, P.* (1970); *Darby, M. R./Karni, E.* (1973); *Stiglitz, J. E.* (1975); *Stigler, J. G./Rothshild, M.* (1976); *Spremann, K.* (1990). Despite the common focus on information and information deficiencies, a clear outline of the relationship between the two has not yet been established in the literature. Three broad interpretations have been advanced: first, information economics is regarded as its own subject matter distinct from NIE (see *Hopf, M.* (1983)). A second view considers it to be rather one stream within NIE (see *Kaas, K. P.* (1995a), p. 3f; *Kaas, K. P.* (2000), p. 63; *Kleinaltenkamp, M./Jacob, F.* (2002), p. 152). Finally, some authors hold the view of information ecocomics as a generic term for all theoretical concepts dealing with the distribution of information (see *Spremann, K.* (1990)).

[94]   See *Williamson, O. E.* (1985), p. 27; *Barzel, Y.* (1997), p. 2ff; *Furubotn, E. G./Richter, R.* (1998), p. 69ff; *Richter, R./Furubotn, E. G.* (1999), p. 35.

[95]   See *Furubotn, E. G./Pejovich, S.* (1974), p. 4; *Williamson, O. E.* (1985), p. 27.

alignment of incentive structures as represented by the patterns of rights of ownership, assuming the possibility of ex ante conclusion of contingent contracts.[96]

Agency theory also deals with the efficient design of incentive structures, though on the level of individual transactions between a principal and an agent. The latter is assigned a task by the principal and receives a reward in response to execution. The emphasis is on (contracting) problems arising from the separation of ownership and control in the presence of information asymmetries.[97] Either implicitly or explicitly, feasibility of contingent contracts is assumed.[98] Three classes of problems are distinguished depending on, first, whether the agent's behavioral attribute that is critical to the outcome which accrues to the principal is exogenously given or whether it can be impacted on by the agent (*ex ante* perspective). The second criterion relates to the issue of whether the attribute becomes at least *ex post* known to the principal. *Hidden characteristics* prevail when the critical behavioral attributes are exogenously given and are susceptible to ex post assessment by the principal. *Hidden intention* relates to situations with ex post observability of a behavior that was subject to the agent's influence. *Hidden action*, finally, also covers cases where the agent chooses a certain behavior and where this chosen behavioral realization (e.g. level of effort) cannot be observed by the principal.[99]

Transaction cost economics originates from ideas first expressed by *Coase* (1937) and has been developed into a distinct theoretical framework mainly by *Williamson* (1971, 1975, 1985).[100] Despite recognizing the significance of property rights and *ex ante* incentive

---

[96] See *Williamson, O. E.* (1990), p. 62. Contingent contracts refer to complete contingent claims contracts that specify the terms of supply and reward for all present and all possible future conditions. They represent the economic counterpart to the legal term of complete presentation. (*Williamson, O. E.* (1985), pp. 69f, 333).

[97] Agency theory has mainly been established by *Alchian* and *Demsetz* (*Alchian, A. A./Demsetz, H.* (1972)) Other early influential contributions include for instance *Spence, M./Zeckhauser, R.* (1971); *Ross, S. A.* (1973). Some authors subdivide agency theory into two streams, the first being labelled as positive theory of agency, the second being referred to as principal-agent-theory or mechanism design approach (*Jensen, M.* (1983); *Hart, O./Holmström, B.* (1987); *Williamson, O. E.* (1990)).

[98] See *Williamson, O. E.* (1985), p. 27.

[99] See *Arrow, K.* (1985); *Spremann, K.* (1990), p. 565ff. The fourth class with exogenously given behavior that is not susceptible to even ex post observation is generally not addressed in the literature.

[100] The first to regard the transaction as the appropriate unit of analysis in research on economic organization was *Commons, J. R.* (1934 (repr.: 1961)), pp. 4-8. However, *Coase, R. H.* (1937) was the first to explicitly analyze the issue of economic organization by comparing institutional alternatives on the basis of costs incurred. The seminal work has been published by *Williamson*, see e.g. *Williamson, O. E.* (1971);

alignments (the rules of the game), it emphasizes the difficulties associated with many transactions in concluding complete, fully contingent contracts (the play of the game). Often, only incomplete contracts may be feasible. Attention is shifted to *ex post* support institutions of contract – including consideration of their ex ante anticipation and design.[101] It is important to emphasize that these considerations are usually based on the assumption of a certain exogenously determined, underlying framework of property rights, that is, a legal environment which in itself represents an institution in the sense of the rules of the game.[102] The core of transaction cost economics is then a comparative analysis of institutional arrangements (governance structures) for the coordination of transactions on the grounds of an efficiency criterion.[103] The efficiency of these governance structures with respect to planning, adapting and monitoring completion of a task is argued to vary with certain transaction conditions.[104] Identification of these factors that are responsible for transaction cost differences is one of the

---

Williamson, O. E. (1975); Williamson, O. E. (1985). The terms "theory", "economics" and "analysis" in combination with "transaction cost" are used synonymously in this work. For a brief overview of TCA see e.g. Picot, A./Dietl, H. (1990).

[101] See Williamson, O. E. (1985), p. 29; Williamson, O. E. (2000), p. 599.

[102] Exceptions that explicitly consider this interaction include Henisz, W., J./Williamson, O. E. (1999); Skarmeas, D. A./Katsikeas, C. S. (2001). Picot, A. (1981) accounts for such influence by referring to the "infrastucture" as an additional influence. This covers mainly the general framework in terms of legal and technological conditions. The relations between the different "layers" of institutions that a transaction is embedded in have recently been outlined by Williamson, O. E. (1998); Williamson, O. E. (2000).

[103] This comparison actually rests on the sum of production and transaction costs (Williamson, O. E. (1985), p. 61). Due to their previous neglect, Williamson's analysis focuses mainly on the effects of transaction costs. Efficiency can be defined and applied in many different theoretical contexts and at many levels. Milgrom, P./Roberts, J. (1992), p. 22, for instance, define efficient choices generally as "...ones for which there is no available alternative that is universally preferred in terms of the goals and preferences of the people involved." It, hence, represents a relative concept which is contingent on the considered group of people and also on the particular set of available alternatives. Depending on the precise assumptions regarding information and knowledge, the definition could be shaped to fit neoclassical as well as neoinstitutional settings. With respect to the latter, Williamson, O. E. (2000), p. 601f, has developed the "remediableness criterion". According to this criterion, a particular governance structure is regarded as efficient if no superior feasible alternative exists that could be implemented with net benefits. For intensive discussion on various ways of defining efficiency with particular focus on neoinstitutional settings see Furubotn, E. G. (1999).

[104] This analytical focus is characteristic for the governance branch of TCA which is often treated as equivalent to transaction cost economics. Williamson, however, considers it to be only one of two parts of TCA, the other concept being a measurement branch that emphasizes the difficulties of measuring inputs and outputs to economic activities. His research emphasis within TCA is nevertheless on governance problems. See Williamson, O. E. (1975); Williamson, O. E. (1985). While the earlier work considers only two alternative governance structures (market and hierarchy), Williamson later takes the framework further to also incorporate hybrid governance structures such as, for instance, relational contracting.

main merits of *Williamson's* work.[105] Two different, though closely related streams of research within transaction cost analysis (TCA), can be identified on this basis.[106] The measurement branch focuses on the quantification of economic inputs and outputs and the cost incurred by this. The governance branch is primarily concerned with the consequences from idiosyncratic investments.

An assessment on which of the various concepts within the NIE framework is most appropriate for structuring transactions in industrial markets should be based on a distinctive understanding of marketing in the first place. An early, though very influential view stresses the relationship between "marketing" and "transaction": *Kotler* (1972) regards marketing as "specifically concerned with how transactions are created, stimulated, facilitated, and valued"[107] and claims that "the core concept of marketing is the transaction."[108] This emphasis on marketing's preoccupation with the transaction has subsequently been supported by authors linking marketing and NIE. *Kaas* (1992, 1995), for instance, defines marketing as primarily dealing with fostering market transactions in a world of imperfect information and foresight, thereby sticking to the "transactional perspective" but at the same time restricting marketing's domain to a certain kind of transaction, namely market transactions.[109] Stressing that some sort of transaction lies at the heart of marketing is also in line with the above definition of marketing: the comparative advantage over competition (CAC) can ultimately constitute itself

---

[105] *Williamson, O. E.* (1985), p. 4; for discussion see *Domrös* (1994), p. 65.

[106] See for instance *Williamson, O. E.* (1985), p. 24 ff.; *Erlei, M./Leschke, M./Sauerland, D.* (1999), p. 67ff. *Williamson's* work is mainly concerned with governance issues.

[107] *Kotler, P.* (1972), p. 49

[108] *Kotler, P.* (1972), p. 48. Although later distinguishing between the notions of exchange and transaction based on whether agreement has already been achieved or not (see *Kotler, P.* (2003), p. 12), *Kotler, P.* (1972), p. 48, originally defined transactions broadly as "...the exchange of values between two parties." Further, he argues these values to include things typically exchanged through markets such as goods, services and money but also other elements such as time, energy or even feelings. *Kotler's* view has been challenged for instance on the basis of lacking a clear focus on market transactions (*Luck, D. J.* (1969); *Tucker, W. T.* (1974)). Yet, it still constitutes an influential perspective that has produced many important insights. With its explicit focus on the notion of value, it has stimulated the development of many publications on the value approach to marketing. The notion of exchange, on the other hand, facilitates the establishment of links to microeconomic theory.

[109] See *Kaas, K. P.* (1992), p. 7; *Kaas, K. P.* (1995a), p. 21. See also *Webster, F. E. J.* (1992), p. 5.

only in the concrete transaction, i.e. the bilateral act of agreement on the terms of performance and related counter-performance between a seller and a buyer.[110]

Property rights theory with its emphasis on patterns of ownership, hence, does not reflect the key research objectives in (industrial) marketing. Neither does agency theory: its focus on incentive structure design by a principal (i.e. the buyer, if transferred to the world of marketing) does not adequately capture the active role of the seller implied by marketing theory. Moreover, the implicit assumption of general feasibility of contingent contracts runs contrary to many problems that an applied industrial marketing science must address. Nevertheless, TCA with its focus on the transaction as unit of analysis offers a well-suited dock element for many areas of research in marketing.[111] According to *Williamson* (1985) transactions are defined to occur "...when a good or service is transferred across a technologically separable interface. One stage of activity terminates and another begins."[112] This definition is somewhat more technology-oriented but basically in accord with the interpretation of the term in marketing, particularly since the rather broad notion of transaction in TCA has been argued, for instance by *Alchian/Woodward* (1988), to include both the notions of exchange and contract.[113] Exchange in this sense simply refers to "...the transfer of property rights to resources that involves no promises or latent future responsibility."[114] A contract, on the other hand, is defined to imply a promise of *future* performance. The significance of this "pledgual" nature of contracts becomes particularly evident in cases where one party makes an investment the profitability of which hinges on the future behavior of the other party. Its value is dependent on the fulfillment of the other party's promise. This

---

[110] With its focus on the ultimately desired output of marketing activities ("purchase by potential buyer"), the interpretation of marketing as management of CAC's implicitly incorporates an interpretation of marketing that has been advanced by several authors within the context of NIE, that is marketing as management of information and uncertainty in order to promote transactions. See e.g. *Kaas, K. P.* (1992), p. 6; , p. 5; *Kleinaltenkamp, M./Jacob, F.* (2002), p. 150.

[111] That the focus on the transaction itself may constitute an important corner stone for strategic structuring of industrial marketing and even for the analysis of dynamics shifts was demonstrated by *Mathur*, albeit not building on TCA, nearly 20 years ago in an interesting, but little noticed paper (see *Mathur, S. S.* (1984)).

[112] *Williamson, O. E.* (1985), p. 1. The notion of a "technologically separable interface" remains somewhat vague as it has later been recognized by *Williamson* himself. Essentially, he assumes that the available (production) technology requires some activities, namely those that are nonseparable, to be coordinated hierarchically (*Williamson, O. E.* (1999b), p. 1089).

[113] See *Alchian, A. A./Woodward, S.* (1988), p. 66, on the following line of argument.

[114] *Alchian, A. A./Woodward, S.* (1988), p. 66.

definition of a transaction in the terminology of TCA allows the term to cover a whole spectrum of transactions: it ranges from discrete spot exchanges, where the contractual dimension of the transaction has virtually no significance at all – reflected in their reliance on the general legal provisions for such exchanges – to relational transactions that involve large, long-term investments and corresponding promises and are governed through contracts which are particularly designed for the specific case.[115] Also, it encompasses the transfer of material goods as well as services and rights.

TCA has meanwhile been applied in a wide range of research areas in marketing including, for instance, supplier-manufacturer cooperations[116], pledges by manufacturers and distributors[117], stability of unsatisfying business relationships[118], aspects of hybridity and transition in channel relationships[119], and other key issues[120] and has, thereby, produced considerable insights both conceptually and empirically. It is argued to have emerged as "one of the major frameworks in the literature on marketing exchange relationships."[121] Moreover, the interaction perspective inherent to transaction cost analysis fits with the emphasis on interaction as developed in the industrial marketing literature since the 1980's.[122]

---

[115] See for an interpretation of marketing that also relates to this spectrum of transaction for instance *Hunt, S. D.* (1983), p. 9; *Dwyer, R. F./Schurr, P. H./Oh, S.* (1987), p. 11; *Plinke, W.* (1997); *Day, G. S.* (2000). Basically, the whole industrial marketing literature on NIE-based structuring of industrial markets and large parts of the relationship marketing literature recognize the importance of transactions from this spectrum (see chapter 2.1.1.2). In this analysis, only transactions between vertical partners, i.e. sellers and buyers in the classical sense, will be regarded. Horizontal transactions are not covered by the examination (for intensive discussion on these see e.g. *Bucklin, L. P./Sengupta, S.* (1993)). First, the constraint here allows for a tighter focus and second, quantification of the values traded in legal exchange processes between such horizontal partners is even more difficult than in vertical exchanges.

[116] See e.g. *Heide, J./John, G.* (1990).

[117] See e.g. *Anderson, E./Weitz, B.* (1992).

[118] See e.g. *Backhaus, K./Büschken, J.* (1999).

[119] See e.g. *Rangan, V. K./Corey, E. R./Cespedes, F.* (1993).

[120] See e.g. the global approach *Ghosh, M./John, G.* (1999), p. 131, who intend to extend TCA into a "... governance value analysis (GVA) framework to address marketing strategy decisions...".

[121] *Joshi, A. W./Stump, R. L.* (1999), p. 38; see also e.g. *Dahlstrom, R./Dwyer, R. F.* (1992); *Heide, J. B.* (1994); *LaBahn, D. W.* (1999).

[122] See *Kirsch, W./Kutschker, M.* (1978); *Gemünden, H. G.* (1981); *Hakansson, H.* (1982); *Backhaus, K.* (1998), p. 3; *Reid, D. A./Plank, R. E.* (2000), p. 43; *Homburg, C./Schneider, J.* (2001), p. 599ff; *Kleinaltenkamp, M./Jacob, F.* (2002), p. 150.

However, there is also a considerable caveat: while the criterion generally underlying analysis in transaction cost economics is efficiency in the sense of economizing on production and transaction costs, the literature on industrial marketing usually draws a distinction between an efficiency and an effectiveness dimension which are proposed to jointly determine the maxim for the behavior of the economic actors.[123] Efficiency, in that perspective, can be defined as a measure of the relation between output and input or resources utilized to achieve this output.[124] Effectiveness can be regarded as a measure of how well some external requirement (e.g. customer needs) is met.[125] Although some authors have argued efficiency to be a broad enough concept to serve as a more general purpose for economic behavior[126], thereby *implicitly* including ideas that are typically referred to as effectiveness-related in the industrial marketing literature, a potential divergence between the two perspectives must be stated from the literature.[127] Nevertheless, even if TCA-efficiency, in sum, should include the same aspects as efficiency and effectiveness, from a marketing perspective, a more differentiated view seems appropriate when it comes to deriving recommendations for marketing practice. Full in-depth examination of (strategic) marketing issues, based on a TCA-based structuring of industrial transactions, may, therefore, require additional considerations that *explicitly* account for the effectiveness dimension.[128]

---

[123] The divergences in perspective result from the different theoretical backgrounds, economics on the one hand and business management on the other hand. On the efficiency position see e.g. *Williamson, O. E.* (1985), p. 241; *Williamson, O. E.* (1991c). Contributions that explicitly distinguish between efficiency and effectiveness include e.g. *Abell, D. F.* (1980) *Varadarajan, P. R./Clark, T.* (1994), p. 95; *Ford, D./Gadde, L.-E./Hakannsson, H., et al.* (1998), p. 92ff; *Anderson, J. C./Narus, J. A.* (1999), p. 172ff; *Kim, K.* (1999), p. 218f; *Plinke, W.* (2000), p, S. 82ff. The distinction between both motivations can be traced back to arguments advanced e.g. by *Barnard, C. I.* (1938), p. 19f.

[124] See e.g. *Barnard, C. I.* (1938), p. 19 *Peffer, J./Salancik, G. R.* (1978), p. 11; *Plinke, W.* (1998), 183.

[125] See e.g. *Barnard, C. I.* (1938), p. 55f; *Peffer, J./Salancik, G. R.* (1978), p. 11; *Plinke, W.* (1998), 183.

[126] See in particular, albeit arguing from different angles, *Williamson, O. E.* (1991c); *Williamson, O. E.* (1999b); *Foss, N. J.* (2003). An important reason for the lack of an explicit distinction between efficiency and effectiveness can be seen in the fundamentally different positions of the research streams: with firms as players in a multi-actor "game", the concern through an economics lens is with the game itself, its outcome and the behavior of the players as players, while the management perspective focuses on the particular play and performance of individual players as player XY, player Z, and so on (see *Nelson, R. R.* (1991), p. 61).

[127] See related *Burr, W.* (2003), p. 121ff, who points to the lack of explicit consideration of transaction benefits in traditional TCA and discusses approaches that have been advanced in the literature in order to account additionally for this aspect.

[128] Related is the argument that TCA – in its current state – rather attempts to explain why firms exist and possibly even why there is a multitude of firms (as opposed to one large firm), but does not offer much to

2.1.2.3   Essential elements of transaction cost theory

2.1.2.3.1   Focal Concept

Theoretical recognition of the phenomenon that, in practice, some transactions are coordinated through markets while others are coordinated through organizations, with firms being the most prominent ones, has led to the identification of specific costs associated with using the market mechanism which are held responsible for the existence of various coordinative institutions: transaction costs.[129] The use of alternative coordination mechanisms such as hierarchy, however, is not without costs either.[130] As a result, the term transaction cost has been further developed to capture the costs of using some coordinative mechanism in general. Specifically, transaction costs include the *ex ante* costs that are incurred for searching appropriate transaction partners, for subsequent "...drafting, negotiating, and safeguarding an agreement."[131] They also refer to the *ex post* costs due to (1) maladaptation in case a transaction drifts out of alignment, (2) bilateral attempts to correct ex post misalignments, (3) setup and running costs of governance structures for solution of disputes, and (4) bonding in order to effect secure commitments. Both categories include direct transaction costs as well as indirect transaction costs that are opportunity costs in nature.[132]

---

illuminate the reasons for differences between these firms (*Mahoney, J. T./Pandian, J. R.* (1992), p. 370; *Williamson, O. E.* (1998), p. 48; *Nickerson, J. A./Vanden Bergh, R.* (1999), p. 2) and their different success in terms of rent seeking (*Mahoney, J. T.* (2001), p. 655ff). The latter issue, though, emerges as a primary issue in marketing strategy if means for achieving CAC's are sought. For a recent discussion of the resulting need for complementation by another framework see *Madhok, A.* (2002), who examines the relation between TCA and the rescource-based view. Essentially, he interprets them as two sides of the coin called "strategic management". The potential value of integrating the impact of firm particularities (due to path dependencies, learning processes, etc.) on the organization of transactions has recently also been pointed out by *Williamson, O. E.* (1999b), p. 1105.

[129] See *Coase, R. H.* (1937).

[130] Market governance is associated with coordination through prices, whereas hierarchical governance proceeds through directives (see e.g. *Williamson, O. E.* (1991b), p. 164; *Domrös* (1994), p. 63). Transaction costs are also referred to as organization or firm transaction costs or bureaucratic costs (*Richter, R./Furubotn, E. G.* (1999), p. 53; *Williamson, O. E.* (1999b), p. 1090).

[131] *Williamson, O. E.* (1985), p. 20.

[132] See *Williamson, O. E.* (1985), p. 21; *Rindfleisch, A./Heide, J. B.* (1997), p. 31, 46; related *Sanchez, R.* (2000), p. 320f. Despite the substantial progress that has been made regarding the measurement of transaction costs since their first introduction in the literature, the broad definition of the term still results in difficulties concerning their operationalization, particularly on the grounds of traditional concepts of cost and efficiency (see e.g. *Heide, J. B.* (1994), p. 73, fn 6; *Milgrom, P./Roberts, J.* (1992), p. 34).

Meanwhile, some authors have explicitly analyzed the research consequences of two alternative perspectives on these economic costs.[133] The first view, which is closer to neoclassical theory, has been labeled **economic natural selection**, the second **managerial choice**. The economic natural selection approach is considered to be primarily adopted by evolutionary theorists who focus on whole populations of organizations, their development in the long run, based on a selection mechanism like, for instance, transaction cost economizing. Probably most important in this context, they adopt an ex post perspective on economic costs by interpreting them as objective, that is, as results from choice.[134] On the other hand, the managerial choice stream that is mainly present in the work of *Williamson*, has rather been adopted by decision-oriented theorists. It treats those costs as relevant that are anticipated ex ante and, thereby, influence choice. These subjective costs could equate the objective costs only in general equilibrium. The actual time frame of analysis is, though, relatively short-term. With its focus on managerial decisions, this second stream seems more promising for examining issues of strategic marketing management and will, therefore, be adopted in this work.

2.1.2.3.2 Behavioral assumptions

Broadly speaking, the activities that are responsible for the emergence of transaction costs are required due to information deficiencies and the possibility of strategic "abuse" of non-ubiquitous, that is asymmetrically distributed, information. The behavioral assumptions of bounded rationality and opportunism capture this argument.[135] A third, though less explicit assumption concerns the actors´ risk attitude, which is taken to be characterized by risk neutrality.[136]

---

[133] See *Chiles/McMackin* (1996), p. 76 ff for extensive discussion.

[134] Proponents of this view are, for instance, *Ulrich, D./Barney, J. B.* (1984); *Hill, C. L.* (1990).

[135] See *Williamson, O. E.* (1985), p. 44ff. for extensive discussion and derivation of these assumptions.

[136] See *Williamson, O. E.* (1985), p. 388f; *Williamson, O. E.* (1998), p. 30. This aspect is more of a working assumption in order to facilitate the analysis. *Williamson* explicitly describes it as a "patently counterfactual" assumption (*Williamson, O. E.* (1985), p. 388), but nevertheless defends its application, in particular with regard to industrial markets. Recently, some authors have attempted to develop a conceptual framework to additionally incorporate the modelling of other risk attitudes in TCA (see *Chiles/McMackin* (1996)). Contrary to the classical definition of risk as "…the variance of the probability distribution of

Bounded rationality recognizes that there are limits to human cognitive competence. Although economic actors are assumed to intend to act in a rational, maximizing way, they are only to a limited degree able to do so.[137] The assumed far-sightedness refers to an ability to anticipate conditions of dependence (as created by idiosyncratic investments), but does not include the ability "to specify complete decision trees"[138] ex ante. Hence, it represents a semistrong form of rationality. Bounded rationality becomes critical in combination with uncertainty, whether its sources may be environmental (i.e. circumstances surrounding an exchange cannot fully be specified ex ante) or behavioral (i.e. problems of ex post verification of performance and ensuring compliance).[139] The latter phenomenon is essentially due to the second decisive behavioral assumption in TCA: **opportunism** refers to "...self-interest seeking with guile"[140] which is the strongest form of self-interest. It includes all blatant as well as subtle forms of meaningful deceit to satisfy that self-interest, whether they may occur ex ante or ex post and whether they take place in terms of active or passive behavior. The assumption of opportunism does, however, not require all actors to opportunistically exploit every given opportunity to the same (full) degree.[141] In a world of uncertainty and bounded rationality, the knowledge or conjecture that at least some actors (may) act opportunistically some of the time, suffices to establish the (subjective) need for safeguarding which in turn

---

possible gains and losses associated with a particular alternative" (*March, J. G./Shapira, Z.* (1987), p. 1404) (i.e. as an objective phenomenon) that might possibly have been implied by *Williamson*, they define risk in line with *Yates, J. F./Stone, E. R.* (1992) as "the possibility of loss" and an "inherently subjective construct" (*Chiles/McMackin* (1996), p. 80).

[137] See *Simon, H. A.* (1961), p. xxiv; *Williamson, O. E.* (1985), p. 45f. Neurophysiological limits on the ability to receive, store, retrieve, and process information without error, and language-related limits on the ability to impart information are responsible for this (see e.g. *Day, G. S./Klein, S.* (1987), p. 47). In this interpretation, bounded rationality is treated as an exogenous variable rather than as an endogenous variable.

[138] *Williamson, O. E.* (1975), p. 23; see also *Rindfleisch, A./Heide, J. B.* (1997), p. 48.

[139] Adaptation is identified as the primary problem of environmental uncertainty, performance evaluation as an outcome of behavioral uncertainty (see *Klein, B.* (1980), p. 356; *Rindfleisch, A./Heide, J. B.* (1997), p. 31).

[140] *Williamson, O. E.* (1985), p. 47. Refinements to the opportunism construct have recently been proposed by *Wathne, K. H./Heide, J. B.* (2000).

[141] The assumption of opportunism has frequently been criticized in the literature for being overly pessimistic (and unrealistic) as to the motivations of human actors (see e.g. *Granovetter, M.* (1985); *Heide, J. B./John, G.* (1992), p. 41; *Morgan, R. M./Hunt, S. D.* (1994), p. 25; *Lambe, C. J./Wittmann, C. M./Spekman, R. E.* (2001); recently, *Burr, W.* (2003), p. 115ff, discusses the issue in a general review of TCA). However, it has meanwhile be argued by proponents of the opportunism assumption that not all parties necessarily have to exhibit the same degree of opportunism for the condition to be of general relevance (see *Williamson, O. E.* (1985), p. 48; *Barney, J. B.* (1990); *Rindfleisch, A./Heide, J. B.* (1997), p. 48; *Williamson, O. E.* (1998), p. 31).

causes transaction costs.[142] Opportunism in this sense refers to a *potential* rather than requiring its ubiquitous *realization* in the behavior of economic actors.

2.1.2.3.3 Transaction determinants

The magnitude of transaction costs has been identified by *Williamson* to depend on certain, decisive transaction dimensions, namely asset specificity, uncertainty, and transaction frequency.[143]

Asset specificity relates to (durable) idiosyncratic investments.[144] These are defined as investments that are undertaken to support a particular transaction with a specific transaction partner, and that are not redeployable in alternative uses without considerable loss of value. The result of this condition is that the identity of the parties crucially matters and that the continuity of the relationship is valued – at least until amortization of the specific investment has been achieved.[145] Thus, the loss potential due to idiosyncratic investments arises in an

---

[142] For instance, a game theoretic approach to determine the critical number of actors that must be assumed to behave in a particular way for a particular equilibrium to prevail has been proposed by *Haltiwanger, J./Waldman, M.* (1991) in their "responder/non-responders framework". Relative to the numbers of agents, they examine whether the equilibrium in their analysis will more closely resemble one or the other type of agent in a population with two types of agents (responders and non-responders).

[143] See *Williamson, O. E.* (1979), p. 239; *Williamson, O. E.* (1985), p. 52ff also regarding the following discussion. In his earlier conceptualizations, *Williamson* associates uncertainty with complexity (see e.g. *Williamson, O. E.* (1975)). Some authors have identified additional determinants, e.g. supplemented the proposed dimensions, e.g. frequency with duration and uncertainty with complexity (*Milgrom, P./Roberts, J.* (1992), p. 30; *Masten, S. E./Meehan Jr, J. W./Snyder, E. A.* (1991), p. 7; *Blois, K. J.* (1996), p. 167). While the underlying considerations may indeed be relevant for an efficiency assessment of governance modes, it will later be argued that an alternative and more parsimonious way to account for such aspects is to analyze their indirect impact via the original key determinants as identified by *Williamson*. See also chapter 3.2.3.

[144] Throughout this examination, the terms "idiosyncratic" and "specific" will be used synonymously. Note that this definition encompasses but is not restricted to technological idiosyncrasies. Contractual specificity which has much less intensively been explored by the literature so far is also included. In fact, the framework proposed here builds to a large degree on the latter phenomenon and its relation to the fomer (see also chapters 2.1.2.6 and 3.2.3).

[145] While definitions of amortization in investment analysis often include just the recovery of the investment (break-even), the term is understood here in broader sense to also include a calculated profit, i.e. the opportunity cost of not having put the according capital (be it money, time or effort) to an alternative use, in markets where this is appropriate (no perfect competition). TCA related support for this interpretation can be drawn from *Alchian, A. A./Woodward, S.* (1988), p. 66, who emphasize that the critical issue is that the *profitability* of an investment may depend on the particular transaction partner. The interpretation is theoretically stringent regarding the above made definition of transaction costs to include opportunity costs.

35

intertemporal context. Its existence is conditional upon a divergence in the timeframes for the fulfillment of the mutual obligations (investment and its compensation). In principle, different types of assets can be designed to fit a particular transaction.[146] These include (but are not restricted to):

- **physical asset specificity** that can be defined as "... investments in equipment and machinery that involve design characteristics specific to the transaction."[147]

- **site specificity** that refers to transacting parties in successive stages of the production process locating in a way that is characterized by "...a "cheek-by-bowl" relationship [...], reflecting *ex ante* decisions to minimize inventory and transportation expenses. Once sited the assets in question are highly immobile."[148]

- **dedicated asset specificity** that prevails when a supplier makes a general investment which he would not otherwise make "...but for the prospect of selling a significant amount of product to a particular customer"[149], and which leaves him with significant excess capacity in case of premature contract termination. Although not explicitly developed by *Williamson*, a buyer-side analogy to this is likely to exist when a buyer relies on a single supplier for an "excessively" large volume of a product.[150]

For an investment analysis perspective see e.g. *Adam, D.* (2000), p. 117ff, *Altrogge, G.* (1996), p. 275f. However, some considerations from business management and investment analysis also offer support for the broad interpretation (see e.g. *Altrogge, G.* (1996), p. 284f)

[146] *Williamson* first identified four types of asset specificity (see e.g. *Williamson, O. E.* (1983), p. 526). Later, additional types were identified, for instance brand name capital specificity and temporal specificity, suggesting that even the most recent listing may not be a complete and definitive one (*Perry, M. K.* (1989), p. 213; *Williamson, O. E.* (1989), p. 143; *Williamson, O. E.* (1990), p. 68; *Williamson, O. E.* (1999b), fn 2). This conceptual ambiguity may be regarded as supporting the view expressed by *Joskow, P. L.* (1987), p.170, fn 14, with reference to *Tirole*, that the different types of specific investment are "simply different instances of the same phenomenon." The focus here is, hence, on the functional characteristics of specific assets, with the above categorization being interpreted as illustrative rather than as theoretically distinctive. Less well-established forms of asset specificity as e.g. brand name capital specificity or temporal specificity (see e.g. *Masten, S. E./Meehan Jr, J. W./Snyder, E. A.* (1991), p. 9; *Erlei, M./Leschke, M./Sauerland, D.* (1999), p. 181), thus, will not be discussed here explicitly.

[147] *Joskow, P. L.* (1987), p. 170.

[148] *Joskow, P. L.* (1987), p. 170.

[149] *Joskow, P. L.* (1987), p. 170; see also *Williamson, O. E.* (1985), p. 96.

[150] *Joskow, P. L.* (1987), p. 170; the term "excessively" refers to a volume that is so large that replacement of the particular supplier may be difficult and costly. Determinants are the market volume for the product as

- **human asset specificity** that arises from adaptation of human assets to a particular transaction (partner), e.g. through specific training, learning-by-doing or communication economies.[151]

Asset specificity establishes a lock-in: switching to another transaction partner is feasible only at the cost of incurring a substantial loss. *Shapiro/Varian* (1999) have elaborated this argument in great detail in the context of information technology.[152] They identify different types of lock-in ranging from durable purchases to information and databases, and loyalty programs that, essentially, can be traced to various realizations of asset specificity. The establishment of a lock-in, typically through contract conclusion between the two parties and the implied specific investment, is associated with the occurrence of a "fundamental transformation"[153]. This transformation turns the assumed bilateral ex ante large numbers bidding competition (or unconstrained bargaining situation, as characterized by *Graham/Peirce* (1989)) into an ex post monopoly situation.[154] This monopoly may be unilateral if the contract implies specific investments by only one party, or bilateral in case both partners invest specifically in each other. From the point of view of the specifically investing party, perfect ex ante substitutability of a multitude of potential transaction partners is replaced by a condition of severe constraints on substitutability. These constraints arise from the danger of economic losses from non-redeployable assets. Therefore, the degree to which a transacting party is tied to a relationship hinges on the magnitude of the loss that it incurs with premature termination and which is associated with the term "quasi-rent"[155]. The

---

well as the underlying technology. The latter influences the speed with which other suppliers may be able to increase their capacity and the degree to which these investments are subject to lagged adjustment.

[151] See *Williamson, O. E.* (1979), p. 230.

[152] See *Shapiro, C./Varian, H. R.* (1999), p. 103ff.

[153] *Williamson, O. E.* (1985), pp. 55, 61ff. It is important to note that this view of the fundamental transformation implicitly resides in a theoretical fiction, namely that of simultaneity of contract conclusion and investment. Essential for the establishment of a lock-in is the investment. However, one could argue that divergences from the letter of the contract might be least likely in the early stages of the period which the contract relates to. Therefore, this fiction can well be regarded as a plausible analytical tool. Nevertheless, some investments will certainly lag behind the contract more than others. Obvious candidates are all sorts of human asset specificity (see e.g. *Williamson, O. E.* (1985), p. 242f; *Kaas, K. P./Schade, C.* (1993)).

[154] See *Graham, D. A./Peirce, E. R.* (1989).

[155] See, for instance, *Klein, B./Crawford, R. A./Alchian, A. A.* (1978), p. 298; *Kaas, K. P./Schade, C.* (1993), p. 78; *Richter, R./Furubotn, E. G.* (1999), pp. 145, 333f; *Burr, W.* (2003), p. 130ff. A very illustrative

term as such ca be traced back to *Marshall* (1938; first edition 1890).[156] Its most influential definition in TCA has been provided by *Klein/Crawford/Alchian* (1978) who consider a quasi-rent to be the "…excess of its value over its salvage value, that is, its value in its next best use to another rent."[157] In their tradition, but with a more explicit focus on the underlying idiosyncrasy of the investment, a quasi-rent is here defined to capture that part of income resulting from the specific investment that is conditional upon realizing the transaction with that very transaction partner.[158] Due to this conditionality, the quasi-rent construct is always, and without any regard as to which of the partners invests specifically, a composite one: it is subject to (bargained) division between the parties. Two factors are regarded to determine the size of the quasi-rent[159]: first, there is the **magnitude** of the first-best-value (e.g. 100). Second, there is the **relation** between the loss when being forced to turn to the second-best-use (which would be valued e.g. at 40, resulting in a loss of 60) and the first-best-use (60/100 = 0.6) which may be interpreted as the degree of specificity of the investment.

What might be regarded as a "fair" distribution that the parties would agree on ex ante in the initial contract could, for instance, be one where the future quasi-rent is specified to be

---

delimination of the terms „rent" and „quasi-rent" has been provided by *Milgrom, P./Roberts, J.* (1992), p. 269f., who consider the difference between rents and quasi-rents to arise "…from the presence of costs that must be incurred to enter the market but that cannot be salvaged by an existing firm that chooses to exit."

[156] See *Marshall, A.* (1920 (repr.: 1938)). He distinguishes explicitly between the terms "quasi-rent" ("…the income derived from machines and other applicances for production made by man", p. 74, as opposed to "rents" which refer to "…income derived from the free gifts of nature…", p. 74) and "composite quasi-rent" ("…divisible among the different persons in the business by bargaining, supplemented by custom and by notions of fairness…", p. 626). The idea of the composite quasi-rent is developed in the context of relationships between employers and employees and with explicit reference to employees´ specialization of skills as an underlying cause for the emergence of the composite quasi-rent (p. 627). In that tradition, *Alchian, A. A./Woodward, S.* (1988), p. 67, distinguish between a a pure quasi-rent which is defined as "…the excess above the return necessary to maintain a resource´s current service flow, which can be the means to recover sunk costs" and a composite quasi-rent ("…that portion of the quasi-rent of resources that depends on continued association with some other specific, currently associated resources.", p. 67). No such distinction is made here since the analytical focus rests on the impact of asset specificity. Therefore, the notion of quasi-rent is used in this paper soely in the meaning of a composite quasi-rent.

[157] *Klein, B./Crawford, R. A./Alchian, A. A.* (1978), p. 298.

[158] *Williamson, O. E.* (1985), p 52ff. It, hence, includes the notion of "sunk costs" that are irrecoverable once incurred (*Williamson, O. E.* (1989), p. 142), but is more comprehensive in that it incorporates opportunity costs as well.

[159] For a similarly differentiated view on the quasi-rent construct see *Crocker, K. J./Masten, S. E.* (1988), p. 338.

38

distributed in proportion to the parties' specific investments.[160] These parts of the composite quasi-rent that are attributed to the individual parties are from now on referred to as quasi-rents, for instance as A's quasi-rent or as B's quasi-rent. For each party, the value of this quasi-rent, its piece of the composite quasi-rent-pie, represents the "amount at stake" which is lost in case of premature termination of contract.[161] By definition, there is no amount at stake in cases of unspecific investments, because all assets are redeployable in alternative uses without loss. That is not to say that no values are traded in such cases. Only, they are not the least dependent on the identity of the other party. However, the realized ex post division may differ substantially from the one that has been provided for by the contract, particularly if both parties' valuation of the continuation of the relationship differs, that is, if unequal idiosyncratic investments have been undertaken.[162] The partner that has less to lose will be tempted to act opportunistically and exploit the other party's greater valuation of continuing

---

[160] In general, terms such as "fairness" are no integral element of economic models of voluntary exchange that imply anticipated gains to all transactors. Nevertheless, its use in the above sense is in line with *Klein, B.* (1980), p. 356. It is meant to cover exactly the described kind of voluntary exchange in a situation of bilateral ex ante large numbers bidding. This understanding of fairness is similar to *Blau's* "fair exchange" in social exchange relations (*Blau, P. M.* (1964), p. 156) and even more so to *Homans'* "distributive justice" (*Homans, G. C.* (1961), p. 75), and also finds support in literature on incomplete contracts as shown by *Foss, N. J.* (1997), p. 181. For an extensive discussion on the role of fairness in business relationships and the distinction between distibutive and procedural fairness see also *Kumar, N./Scheer, L. K./Steenkamp, J.-B. E. M.* (1995).

[161] The amount at stake in business relationships and its effects on the emergence and stability of business relationship have extensively been examined e.g. by *Söllner, A.* (1993); *Plinke, W.* (1997). The outcome-oriented understanding of the amount at stake which is implied here, is closer related to the original understanding of the term in the literature on perceived risk (see e.g. *Cox, D. F.* (1967b), p. 34ff) *Söllner*, instead, focuses on input values as determinants of the amount at stake. Furthermore, he distinguishes between the amount at stake and the degree of specificity (ranging from completely specific to totally unspecific). He claims that the higher the degree of specificity for a given amount at stake, the greater the bonding that results from it. However, this understanding of "amount at stake" differs from what is implied by focusing on the quasi-rent construct as defined above: in this analysis, the value of the amount at stake is inseparably tied to its specificity. Supportive for this position are *Backhaus, K./Aufderheide, D./Späth, G.-M.* (1994), p. 38, fn 81.

[162] The question remains as to whether this inequality relates to unequal *absolute* amounts of investment or to unequal *relative* investments (considering the ratio of the investment to some other characteristic variable of that party, e.g. its total sales; for similar considerations see *Joskow, P. L.* (1987), p. 180). Most contributions emphasizing the significance of the difference between symmetric and asymmetric relations of specific investment do not specify whether they focus on absolute or relative terms. In case they emphasize the subjectively perceived amount at stake, a tendency towards relative assessment can be presumed (see e.g. *Preß, B.* (1997), p. 95ff.; *Plinke, W./Söllner, A.* (2000), p. 70; *Kleinaltenkamp, M./Kühne, B.* (2003), p. 20). Here, the assessment on equality or inequality will rest on relative terms, accounting for the subjective perception of the parties with respect to the difficult-to-quantify, non-monetary investments. Arguably, in a world of bounded rationality, subjective perception could cause divergences even in conditions of an ex ante bilateral large numbers bidding. However, if conditions at the outset deviate from this assumption (e.g. supply oligopoly), it is even more likely that the same absolute amount of investment causes an impaired perception of the amount at stake.

the relationship by appropriating a larger share of the composite quasi-rent than initially agreed on. This is also referred to in the literature as the hold-up problem.[163] In terms of the absolute amount of potential loss that the "victim" will rationally accept before leaving the relationship, the relevant extent is determined by the complete quasi-rent share that was supposed to accrue to it and, therefore, represents the full hold-up potential.

This idea has been captured in *Fig. 2*, which shows the complete range of feasible *ex post* allocations of the composite quasi-rent generated by two transaction partners A and B, with only one of them (A) investing specifically.[164] A is assumed to invest in transaction-specific assets so as to result in the creation of an ex post composite quasi-rent valued by both A and B at 100 monetary units. Now, after the investment has been made, all (ex post) distributions on the line between ($Q_A=0$, $Q_B=100$) and ($Q_A=100$, $Q_B=0$) are pareto-efficient in the sense that no other allocation is available that would put one party in a better position without placing the other in a worse position. In the same sense, all distributions below the line (e.g. P) are not pareto-efficient. There is, though, one crucial difference between the two extreme points on the axes: while the worst feasible allocation from the point of view of B ($Q_A=100$, $Q_B=0$) is equivalent to the value that B could realize from an alternative use of its assets, the worst distribution in $A's$ perspective ($Q_A=0$, $Q_B=100$) that would still be accepted due to its pareto-efficiency would result in losing the specific part of the value of its investment. It is not rational for A to terminate the relationship even if B appropriates more than the contractually agreed part of the composite quasi-rent, as long as the exploitation does not extend to the nonspecific parts of $A's$ investment.[165] In other words: once the specific asset has been created, A can only lose, whereas B can only win.

---

[163] See, for instance, *Klein, B.* (1980), p. 356f.; *Alchian, A. A./Woodward, S.* (1988), p. 67.

[164] See *Backhaus, K./Büschken, J.* (1999), p. 250.

[165] However, the rationale favoring the acceptance of such exploitation may not always hold. In analogy to the game theoretic literature on entry deterrence (e.g. *Dixit, A.* (1980); *Kreps, D. M./Wilson, R.* (1982); *Milgrom, P./Roberts, J.* (1982)), conditions can be modelled under which it may be rational for the victim to accept only much lower levels of exploitation (in absolute terms, referring to *Fig. 1*) and, in extreme cases, none at all. This inference centers around long-term profit potentials and the notion of reputation building (regarding possible follow-up transactions with the same transaction partner or transactions with other business partners). With repeated games and incomplete information or with infinitely repeated games it may be rationale to forego some short-term profit in order to build a long-term reputation for not allowing oneself to be exploited. On the other hand, an analogous reasoning refers to B, reducing its incentives for exploitation (see the fundamental treatment of self-enforcing contracts by *Telser, L. G.* (1981), p. 43f; also: *Heide, J. B./Miner, A. S.* (1992); *Backhaus, K./Büschken, J.* (1999), p. 253ff).

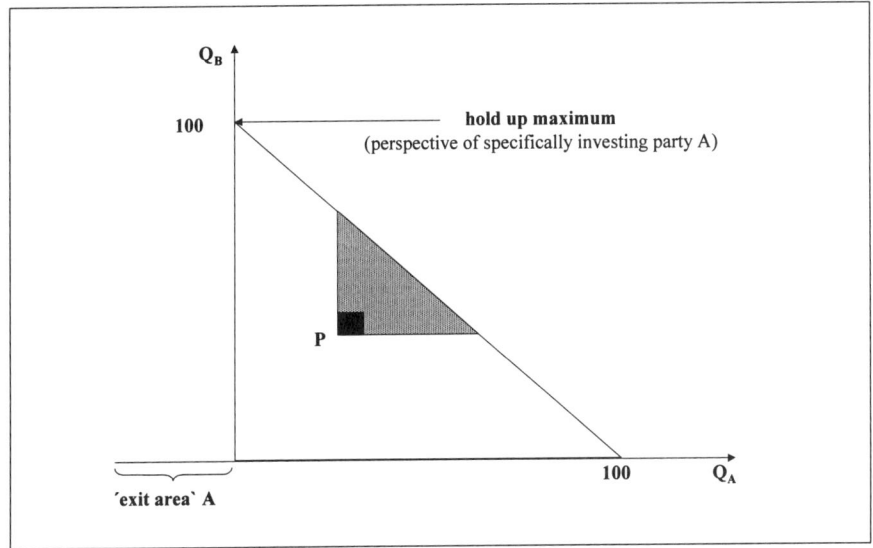

Fig. 2: Pareto-improving (ex post) distributions of quasi-rent Q between A and B[166]

This obviously puts B in a much stronger position for ex post (re-) bargaining over the composite quasi-rent.

Against this background of possible exploitation, the question arises as to why any idiosyncratic investment should be undertaken at all. The answer lies in the productivity enhancement associated with "special purpose investments" or, more precisely, "specific investments"[167], which may translate either into production cost advantages or into

---

[166] Close adaptation from *Backhaus, K./Büschken, J.* (1999), p. 250.

[167] The term "special purpose technology" has been coined by *Williamson, O. E.* (1985), e.g. p. 32. However, one could further distinguish between "special purpose" in the sense of specific tailoring to a particular transaction partner (hereafter referred to as specific or idiosyncratic as opposed to unspecific) and "special purpose" in the sense of being tailored to be applicable to some relatively narrow spectrum of technologically defined uses (hereafter referred to as specialized as opposed to not specialized). With respect to the technological domain, a similar distinction has recently been put at the center of an analysis on demand uncertainty and asset flexibility by *Sanchez, R.* (2000), p. 319ff. He distinguishes between flexible-use assets on the one side, and specific-use assets on the other side. Consequently, following *Aufderheide, D.* (2000), (p. 78), a terminological distinction is made here between the economic term "specificity" which is defined as above, and the more technological term "specialized", when relating to an investment. Note that the idea of "specialized governance structures" is nevertheless in accord with the original technological meaning, although the concrete textual design of such structures is indeed likely to be specific as well.

41

differentiation (i.e. revenue or "design") advantages for the specifically investing party.[168] An example may clarify the interrelations between specific investments and associated productivity advantages on behalf of the involved transacting parties.[169]

> Company *A* (seller) produces and sells fork-lifts to industrial buyers. It offers its customers two alternative fork-lift solutions for their material handling problems. The first offer relates to a sortiment of different-sized standard pre-fabricated trucks. The second offer involves the specific design and production of a fork-lift for a particular customer after the contract has been concluded. On behalf of the seller company, the second offer involves idiosyncratic investments that are likely to increase production costs for these trucks as compared to standardized trucks of the same size (cost disadvantage; stage 1). However, relatively higher revenues may also be expected by *A* because the customized product is likely to fufill the buyer's needs to a higher degree and, hence, may be able to extract a higher price (differentiation/ design or revenue advantages; stage 1). The buyer company *B*, on the other hand, is likely to be willing to pay a higher price, because the customized truck allows it to serve its own customers better, e.g. by being able to make offers for handling delicate goods they would otherwise not be able to deal with (differentiation or revenue advantages; stage 2). Or, alternatively, the customized truck may be able to handle the transport of components to the production process faster and, thereby, reduce idle times of the production facilities or it may need a lower counterweight and, as a result, less operating space (cost advantages that may or may not be translated into price reductions for *B*'s customers; stage 2).

The downside is, however, that these productivity advantages will only be realized by a transacting party that invests specifically *and* cares about safeguarding this investment.[170]

The second determinant is argued to be **uncertainty**, which rests crucially on the above behavioral assumptions and can be divided into parametric (environmental) uncertainty and strategic (behavioral) uncertainty.[171] Environmental uncertainty results from the existence of a large number of possible future paths that the development of environmental contingencies may take. Due to bounded rationality, neither their complete spectrum can be predicted nor can their attached probabilities be known for sure. The result is the appearance of

---

[168] See *Riordan, M. H./Williamson, O. E.* (1985), who refer to the latter as "design benefits" (p. 374); *Williamson, O. E.* (1989), p. 145; *Backhaus, K./Aufderheide, D./Späth, G.-M.* (1994), p. 42ff.; *Plinke, W./Söllner, A.* (2000), p. 69.

[169] For details on standardized and customized truck-lifting offers by the same seller see e.g. *Warmbold, J.* (1996).

[170] See *Williamson, O. E.* (1979), p. 241; *Williamson, O. E.* (1985), p. 32; *Rangan, V. K./Corey, E. R./Cespedes, F.* (1993), p. 456f.

[171] See *Williamson, O. E.* (1985), p. 56ff.

unanticipated changes in the surroundings of a transaction. When bounded rationality and opportunism are combined, behavioral uncertainty arises. It captures the danger of opportunistic exploitation by other transaction parties by means of behavior that can be characterized in terms of the agency notions of hidden characteristics, hidden intention or hidden action. By definition, parametric uncertainty has impacts (albeit to a different degree) on transactions involving both unspecific and specific investment. Behavioral uncertainty, on the contrary, is only relevant in case of transactions which are supported by idiosyncratic investments. [172]

Finally, the third attribute as proposed by *Williamson* is transaction **frequency**.[173] Its effects on the magnitude of transaction costs are twofold. First, higher frequency of transactions between two parties is argued, through higher associated volumes, to allow for easier recovery of the costs of specialized governance structures needed to support specific investments. Second, transactions with high frequency are associated with a sanction mechanism in the form of threatening the other party to withdraw and cut it off from the expected stream of future revenues.[174] Consequently, higher frequency is associated with favoring idiosyncratic investments by c.p. lowering transaction costs attached to it. Conceptual discussion about this attribute, as well as empirical evidence on its importance, has, however, been quite ambiguous.[175]

Together, the identified determinants form the basis of the discriminating alignment hypothesis. It holds that transactions "...which differ in their attributes, are aligned with

---

[172] See *Williamson, O. E.* (1985), p. 59ff; 242. Recent refinements of the uncertainty construct (e.g. *Joshi, A. W./Stump, R. L.* (1999)) will be discussed later (see chapter 3.2.3).

[173] See *Williamson, O. E.* (1985), p. 60; *Milgrom, P./Roberts, J.* (1992), p. 31. The theoretical as well as empirical significance of the frequency criterion has been subject to criticisms (see e.g. *Picot, A./Dietl, H.* (1990), p. 180f; *Erlei, M./Leschke, M./Sauerland, D.* (1999), p. 180; *Aufderheide, D.* (2000), p. 90; related: *Gadde, L.-E./Snehota, I.* (2000), p. 311f). *Boerner, C. S./Macher, J. T.* (2001) point to different operationalizations of the construct as potential causes for uneven empirical evidence.

[174] This latter argument implicitly assumes the presence of specific investments and by that illustrates the ambiguous nature of the frequency argument.

[175] See e.g. *Picot, A./Dietl, H.* (1990), p. 180, who does not consider frequency to be an independent criterion of its own but rather reinforces given tendencies.

governance structures, which differ in their cost and competence, so as to effect a (mainly) transaction cost economizing result."[176]

2.1.2.4   Transfer to industrial marketing: the transaction cost analysis way of structuring

Transaction processes on industrial markets should be particularly susceptible to an economics-based analysis.[177] This surmise has been illustrated by the growing body of literature on the development of concepts for structuring transactions on business markets on the basis of TCA reasoning by identifying distinct groups of transaction or business types. Usually, the transaction or business type construct is rather implicitly characterized as a (theoretically-derived) category that is distinct from the other categories with regard to certain criteria. The combination of all types advanced within a framework is argued to allow for categorization of real business transaction processes so that (a) the processes grouped together within a type are rather homogeneous regarding the underlying categorization criteria and, hence, the resulting marketing program recommendations, and (b) there exists a high degree of heterogeneity concerning these elements between processes that are attributed to different types.[178]

Importantly, in the spirit of the efficiency and effectiveness-oriented CAC, these concepts should take up a market-sides balancing perspective. To date, essentially three distinct TCA-based approaches have been proposed in the literature by different researchers.[179] Although slightly differing in terms of their conceptual focus, their terminology, and the number of distinct transaction or business types that are identified, these concepts arrive, in essence, at very similar conclusions.[180]

---

[176] *Williamson, O. E.* (1998), p. 37.

[177] See chapter 2.1.1. Also, *Williamson's* seminal work is grounded in the examination of transactions on markets for intermediate goods and services (*Williamson, O. E.* (1985), p. 389).

[178] See, for instance, *Kaas, K. P.* (1995b); *Backhaus, K.* (2003), p. 299.

[179] See, for instance, *Backhaus, K./Aufderheide, D./Späth, G.-M.* (1994); *Backhaus, K.* (2003) as well as *Kaas, K. P.* (1995b) and *Plinke, W.* (1997). On an overview of approaches see e.g. *Kleinaltenkamp, M.* (1994); *Kleinaltenkamp, M./Jacob, F.* (2002). The terms "transaction type" and "business type" will be used synonymously throughout the analysis.

[180] This inference is also drawn by *Kaas, K. P.* (1995b), p. 24f. Consequently, the three presented concepts will be linked by means of supplementary consistent terminology.

First, starting with empirical observations of particular marketing problems in the field of integrational technologies[181], *Backhaus/Aufderheide/Späth* (1994) have developed a concept strictly building on transaction cost reasoning by integrating measurement and governance issues.[182] Their focus is on the asset specificity and the degree of uncertainty associated with a particular transaction. Broadly speaking, they propose an algorithm for distinguishing business types that implies the following five analytical criteria:

(1) existence of *information deficiencies*?

(2) existence of *quasi-rent*?

(3) *verifiability*, i.e., is verification (i.e. observation and legal evidence) of performance results feasible by third parties?

(4) *observability*, i.e. are performance results ex post susceptible to unambiguous observation by third parties?

(5) *integration of production activity* possible?

By further distinguishing cases with positive assessment on criteria (3) and (4) on the basis of whether the quasi-rent arises, at least partially, on the seller-side, they identify three superordinate and five subordinate types of market transactions that are to be observed in the marketplace plus an additional, utopian business type which reflects the neoclassical perspective. The structured application of these criteria in the form of an algorithm for identifying business types on industrial markets is illustrated in *Fig. 3*. The five subordinate business types, all marked as white boxes with gray frames, are governed by three different kinds of contracts, each being matched to the corresponding superordinate business type.[183]

---

181 A central characteristic of integrational technologies is that they "glue" different components together so that they work together synergetically, resulting in a unified system architecture (see e.g. *Backhaus, K./Aufderheide, D./Späth, G.-M.* (1994), p. 9).

182 See *Backhaus, K./Aufderheide, D./Späth, G.-M.* (1994). The distinction between verifiability and observability in establishing different types is inspired by *Holmström, B.* (1979).

183 This systemization refers to the categories of contracts as used by *Williamson, O. E.* (1985) (pp. 69ff, 79) in reference to *Macneil, I. R.* (1978) (p. 73 ff). Hence, it differs from the terminology used by *Backhaus, K./Aufderheide, D./Späth, G.-M.* (1994), p. 55, fn 105.

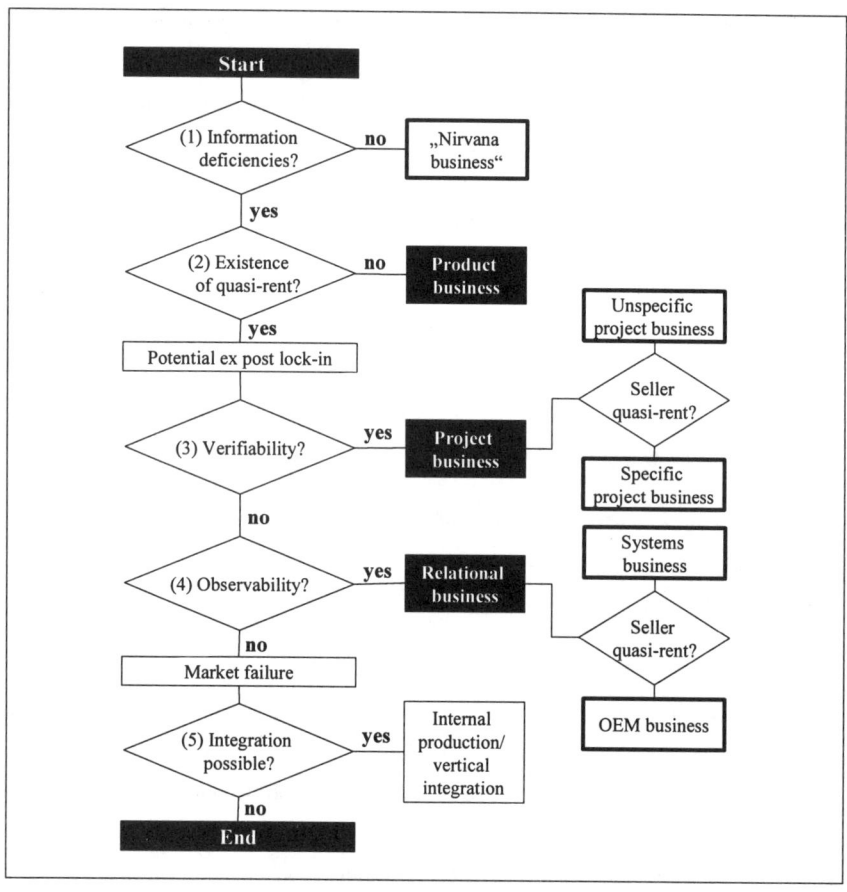

Fig. 3: Algorithm for identification of business types in industrial markets[184]

The superordinate types are depicted as gray boxes with darker shades in *Fig. 3*:

- classical contracts (market governance) in the sense of "sharp in by clear agreement; sharp out by clear performance"[185] are relevant for transactions that are characterized by (*ex ante*) information deficiencies which can, in principle, be reduced completely or below a critical threshold (at an acceptable cost) prior to the transaction and that involve no quasi-rents (**product business**),

---

[184] Taken from *Backhaus, K./Aufderheide, D./Spāth, G.-M.* (1994), p. 73.

- neoclassical contracts (trilateral governance) including contingency clauses for uncertain future eventualities, are relevant in the case of transactions implying a significant quasi-rent, for which performance can unambiguously be verified, and information deficiencies (in the above sense, but also *ex post* information deficiencies due to the quasi-rent) (**project business**, specific and unspecific)[186], and

- relational (or incomplete) contracts (bilateral governance) apply to transactions involving both kinds of information deficiencies and a significant quasi-rent, for which unambiguous performance verification is not feasible, yet observation is (**relational business**, OEM and systems business).[187]

Over the past few years, this framework has continuously been modified and applied to a variety of issues in industrial goods marketing by *Backhaus* and colleagues.[188]

Second, *Kaas* (1992, 1995) has developed a typology of transaction relations on the basis of a TCA, but makes extensive use of information economics and principal-agent-theory for derivation of marketing conceptions.[189] He identifies three distinct types of transaction relations based on different kinds of underlying contract. In particular, the first type of transaction relation (which is similar to the idea of product business expressed by *Backhaus/ Aufderheide/Späth* (1994)) refers to **exchange goods** that are characterized by standardized production prior to marketing and standardized procurement from the buyer's perspective. **Contract goods** are transferred when at least one party invests specifically and the goods' production takes place only after conclusion of a (contingent) contract, whereby the focus lies

---

185 *Macneil, I. R.* (1974), p. 738.

186 In *practice*, most transactions in project business will arguably be governed by contracts which exhibit, to some extent at least, certain characteristics of incomplete contracts in the sense of contract law. These have been described as contracts that either fail to specify performance obligations for all contingencies or even the nature of the performance (*Perry, M. K.* (1989), pp. 221ff.).

187 Relational contracts in the business types system are apt to be moderated by a rather strong notion of discreteness. They do not refer to unified governance, which is not accounted for in the above grouping (see *Williamson, O. E.* (1985), p. 79). Neither are they expected to never end, an expectation that is characteristic for many contractual relationals (see *Macneil, I. R.* (1978). Instead, by incorporating the element of investment amortization, their (potential) ending is explicitly taken into account.

188 See e.g. *Aufderheide, D./Backhaus, K.* (1995); *Reinkemeier, C.* (1998); *Heffner, M./Mühlfeld, K.* (2001); *Backhaus, K.* (2003). The underlying empirical concept has been developed by *Backhaus* as early as 1982 (*Backhaus, K.* (1982)) and has constantly been modified (e.g. *Backhaus, K.* (1995); *Backhaus, K.* (1997)).

189 See *Kaas, K. P.* (1992); *Kaas, K. P.* (1995b).

on this one transaction (and, hence, strong resemblance to project business as characterized by *Backhaus/Aufderheide/Späth* (1994) prevails). **Relational goods**, finally, are elements woven into a chain of connected transactions, which are traded using relational contracts to govern a long-term-oriented business relationship (thereby resembling relational business as described by *Backhaus/Aufderheide/Späth* (1994)). Usually, both transacting parties are assumed to invest specifically to some degree.

The **third** framework that explicitly builds on transaction cost reasoning has been advanced by *Plinke* (1997).[190] His approach uses as discriminating criteria all three classic transaction dimensions, that is transaction frequency, uncertainty, and asset specificity. In case they are all on a low level, the appropriate type of industrial marketing is regarded to be transaction marketing. For high levels of all three variables, relationship marketing is suitable. In both cases, depending on the volume traded (low or high), two further types of marketing (type 1 and type 2) are distinguished.

Recently, the approaches by *Backhaus* and *Plinke* have been modified and further developed by *Backhaus/Plinke/Rese* (2004).[191] The result is an approach rooted in transaction cost theory that, at the same time, attempts to refine existing categorizations from TCA with particular regard to the problem of structuring industrial market transactions. The focus shifts to asset specificity as sole criterion for the identification of business types.[192] At the same time, the analysis takes the understanding of asset specificity further by conceptualizing it as a *multidimensional* construct.[193] Three dimensions are distinguished: first, the *focus* of the idiosyncratic investment is considered, i.e. whether the investment relates to a single

---

[190] See, for instance, *Plinke, W.* (1997).

[191] See *Backhaus, K./Plinke, W./Rese, M.* (2004), (particularly p. 71ff) on the following sketch of the approach. Parentheses are used throughout this whole work when referring to forthcoming contributions/ yet unpublished manuscripts. They are likely not to coincide with the page numbers in the final publication.

[192] This approach could possibly be interpreted in terms of a heuristic reduction of the uncertainty construct which has been used as a categorizing criterion in the *Backhaus/Aufderheide/Späth* (1994) concept in order to achieve a more dense delimitation of the types. In the literature on TCA there is als evidence for a strong emphasis on the decisive role of asset specificity can, (see e.g. *Alchian, A. A.* (1984); *Riordan, M. H./Williamson, O. E.* (1985); *Nickerson, J. A./Vanden Bergh, R.* (1999). Supporting secondary literature includes *Foss, N. J.* (1997), p. 181; *Nickerson, J. A.* (year not indicated); *Kleinaltenkamp, M./Jacob, F.* (2002), p. 151.

[193] Based on content analysis, *Lohtia, R./Brooks, C. M./Krapfel, R. E.* (1994) also emphasize the multidimensionality of transaction specific assets. They identify six relevant dimensions of transaction specific assets, namely specificity, importance, magnitude, value-in-use, durability, risk.

transaction partner or whether it is targeted at a complete market segment. Second, the *degree of specificity* forms part of the analysis, ranging from completely unspecific, resulting in a 0%-loss if the investment is put to an alternative use, to totally specific, in which case the complete investment is lost (100%). Third, the *nature of investment amortization* is part of the complete asset specificity picture.[194] The danger of exploitation and the available relational provisions are strongly influenced by the distinction between investments that are supposed to be recouped within the course of one transaction (even though this may cover a long period of time as e.g. in the case of building power stations), and investments for which amortization is intended to be achieved in the course of a chain of transactions (with an initially undefined number of elements).[195] Interpreting all three of these dimensions, the authors arrive at a continuous three-dimensional cubic space for identifying the extent of governance problems associated with a transaction. It is depicted in the following *Fig. 4.*

---

[194] This idea actually finds indirect support in some early remarks by *Williamson, O. E.* (1985), p. 340.

[195] Admittedly, though, realizing an intended recovery is c.p. afflicted with greater uncertainty if the time horizon is long. This assertion holds no matter if the long time horizon results from a large number of transactions or from a large period of time between contract conclusion and complete fulfillment of all parties' obligations. Other authors have captured this idea by explicitly introducing a time dimension "duration" for long-term contracts (see e.g. *Köhl, T.* (2000), p. 130f; *Backhaus, K./Plinke, W./Rese, M.* (2004), (p. 91). The basic problem has already been discussed e.g. by *Kaas, K. P./Schade, C.* (1993); *Schade, C.* (1996) in the context of consulting business and by *Schade, C./Schott, E.* (1993a) regarding complex contracting goods. In this view, an important feature of long-term contractual agreements is that lock-in positions of parties may vary over time so as to lead to highly different distributions over time of (in total) equally high quasi-rents of the parties.

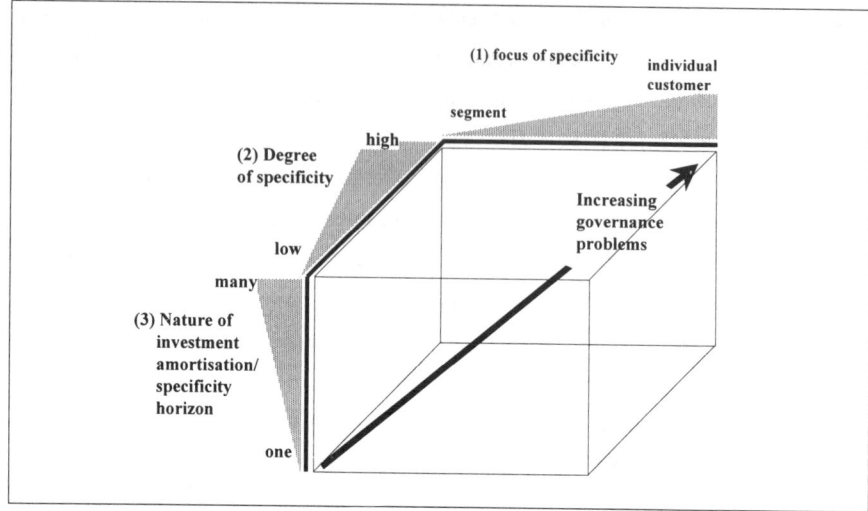

Fig.4: Characterizing dimensions of specific investments and accompanying governance problems[196]

This space is reduced to a structure composed of a few distinct types (see *Fig. 5*).[197]

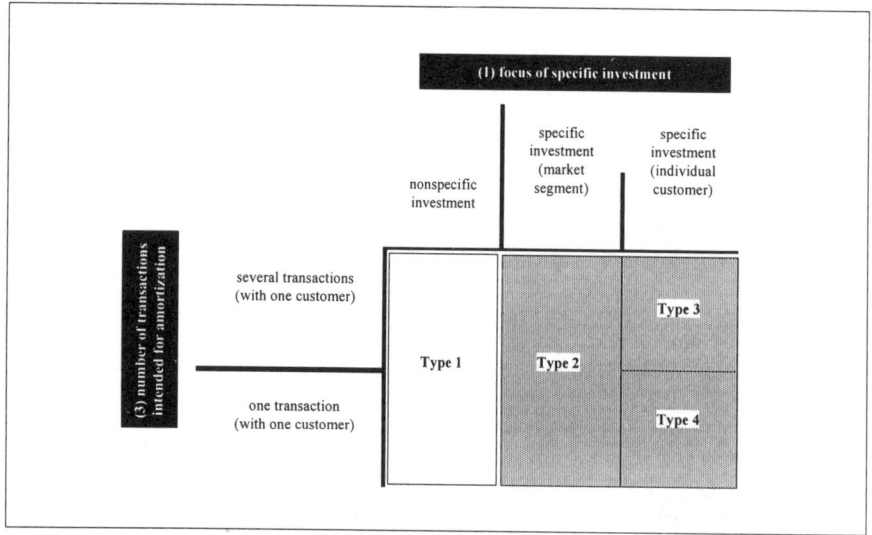

Fig. 5: Specific and nonspecific investment options and marketing types (seller perspective)[198]

[196] *Backhaus, K./Plinke, W./Rese, M.* (2004), (p. 72).

[197] See *Backhaus, K./Plinke, W./Rese, M.* (2004), (p. 73f).

Regarding the **first** dimension (focus of investment), it is argued that three cases have a discriminating impact on structuring industrial transactions: (1a) investments can be of a non-idiosyncratic nature, thereby being directed towards an anonymous market (type 1 in *Fig. 5*), or they can be specific. Then, a further distinction is made: (1b) they can be specifically targeted to a group of transaction partners, that is the investments are specific regarding a certain market segment (type 2 in *Fig. 5*), or, (1c) they are idiosyncratic with regard to a single transaction partner. The **second** dimension (degree of specificity) is essentially reduced to its extreme poles by focusing on the worst case scenario in case of premature contract termination: the result is complete loss if the investment was specific, and no loss at all if it was unspecific. Finally, the **third** dimension (nature of amortization of investment) is split into two basically different situations, that is, the investment is either recovered in one transaction (2a; type 4 in *Fig. 5*), or in several transactions (2b; type 3 in *Fig. 5*).[199] Together, these modifications allow *Backhaus/Plinke/Rese* (2004) to identify four types of investment options that an actor faces. In essence, such a matrix could be drawn for each transaction partner (buyer or seller). The relevance of the various types may, however, differ depending on the perspective. Often, the buyer's contribution to a transaction ("money") will be found to be less specific by nature – although specificity may arise then from specific investments in terms of time and effort (opportunity costs). *Backhaus/Plinke/Rese* (2004) then derive distinct marketing recommendations for the proposed typology.

Also, some considerations on dynamic aspects of managing these business types are advanced, in the sense that concrete actions are outlined as part of a marketing program which could be interpreted to result in a change in business type.[200]

Since the *Backhaus/Plinke/Rese* (2004) framework has evolved from the initial propositions by *Backhaus* and colleagues (1994) and by *Plinke* (1997), the assessment on which approach should form the basis of this examination essentially rests on a comparison between *Backhaus/Plinke/Rese* (2004) and *Kaas* (1992, 1995). In choosing between these approaches,

---

[198] *Backhaus, K./Plinke, W./Rese, M.* (2004), (p. 74).

[199] This attribute with its two fundamentally distinct levels bears some resemblance with occasional operationalizations of transaction frequency as a dichotomous variable (one-time vs recurring transactions) in some of the empirical literature on TCA (see e.g. *John, G./Weitz, B. A.* (1988)).

[200] See *Backhaus, K./Plinke, W./Rese, M.* (2004), (p. 68).

two criteria emerge as primarily important for the theoretically guided examination of strategy shifts between business types. **First**, the degree of stringent specification on theoretical TCA grounds is regarded as a major factor. This is because this examination aims at taking utmost advantage of the explanatory and normative potential of the TCA while at the same time remaining as parsimonious as possible.[201] **Second**, the examination's explicit focus on a dynamic perspective favors that concept that has already been explored, at least to a certain extent, regarding dynamic issues.[202] Both of these characteristics make the approach by *Backhaus/Plinke/Rese* (2004) seem more promising with regard to the research objective pursued here. As basis for the following investigation, the *Backhaus/Plinke/Rese* (2004) approach is chosen. First, it might allow for a more parsimonious analysis because it refers to TCA as the sole basis for structuring and development of type-specific marketing programs, while the approach by *Kaas* (1992, 1995) rests to some degree on related theoretical concepts such as information economics and principal-agent theory.[203] Second, the *Backhaus/Plinke/Rese* (2004) approach has been furthest developed to date with respect to an exploration of dynamic issues. In addition, the approach by *Kaas* (1992, 1995) is not targeted primarily at industrial goods marketing.[204]

2.1.2.5   Derivation of a modified structure based on a selected typology: the idea of "business types constellations"

Although representing a suitable starting point, the *Backhaus/Plinke/Rese* (2004) concept will be subject to some modifications that seem helpful for the analysis as intended here. The first modification refers to the multidimensionality of the specificity construct. The second

---

[201] Despite obvious problems, for instance related to the subjective nature of transaction costs, transaction cost theory is generally regarded as a theoretical concept with significant normative potential. See for discussions e.g. *Aufderheide, D.* (1993); *Pies, I.* (1993). Contributions mentioning the issue in passing include *Rindfleisch, A./Heide, J. B.* (1997), p. 43; *Stump, R. L./Joshi, A. W.* (1998), p. 36; *Silverman, B. S.* (1999), p. 1109; *Williamson, O. E.* (2000), p. 610.

[202] TCA is in fact rather comparative-static in nature. This implies the examination of different points in time, but needs to be supplemented by considerations which explain the evolution from one point of analysis to the other. More detailed discussion on this topic and identification of the Austrian Economics framework and related concepts as appropiate theoretical supplement is provided by *Foss, N. J.* (1997). See also chapter 3.3.3.2.

[203] For discussions of the value of parsimony for theoretical models see e.g. *Dubin, R.* (1969), p. 21ff.; *Whetten, D. A.* (1989), p. 490f.

[204] See *Kaas, K. P.* (1995b), p. 39.

modification rises from the aggregation of idiosyncratic investments undertaken by different market sides in three business types. In particular, these remarks are that

(1) the proposition of market segment specific investments as one of three discriminating levels of investment focus will not be followed here, resulting in only three different business types (types 1, 3, and 4 in *Fig. 5*[205]) (exclusion of market segment specific investments), and

(2) a more explicit differentiation between the point of view of the seller and the buyer is to be made here, resulting in three distinct business type from *each* perspective (explicit differentiation between seller and buyer perspective).[206] As will be argued, the actual transaction situation is then determined by the *combination* of buyer and seller business type. Basically, these combinations could be implicitly covered by a three-business-types framework. However, this could only be achieved by a reduction in the analytical precision regarding the formal description of certain transaction situations.

Ad 1) Exclusion of market segment specific investments

While agreeing on the proposed multidimensional understanding of asset specificity, in principle, the first element, focus of specificity, is argued not to constitute a precise discriminating criterion. Essentially, the investments that are labelled *market segment specific investments* are questioned to be idiosyncratic investments as originally defined in TCA. Instead, it is proposed that a specific investment in the sense of TCA can only arise in the transaction between two contracting parties This requirement is likely not to be met in the case of investments in market segment. The argument involves a sharper description of the properties of situations that might qualify as involving market segment specific investments and evaluation of the investment characteristics with regard to their idiosyncrasy. As starting point, specific investments are understood here to imply a fundamental transformation: an ex ante large numbers bidding situation with complete replacability of individual actors on the

---

[205] See p. 68.

[206] Although specific investments undertaken by buyers are also explicitly considered by *Backhaus, K./Plinke, W./Rese, M.* (2004) (p. 50ff), the authors abstain from formally depicting the identified business types on each side of the market and combining them subsequently. The significance of explicitly considering both perspectives due to the potential divergence in perceived dependence has recently also been emphasized by *Kleinaltenkamp, M./Kühne, B.* (2003), p. 14ff.

seller as well as on the buyer side is transformed into a (uni- or bilateral) monopoly situation.[207] In the case of potential market segment specific investments, by definition, at least the seller ex post faces a lock-in. The line between ex ante and ex post is drawn by the fundamental transformation that occurs due to the idiosyncratic investment and with the associated contract, i.e. specific investment and contract are regarded as "glued together" in a theoretical fiction.[208]

The following have been identified as constituting characteristics of these specific investments[209]: first, the significance of the identities of the transacting parties due to the idiosyncratic tailoring of the investment, and, second, as a result, the related advantages (productivity gains) and drawbacks (potential exploitation, dependence). A market segment specific investment may be, in analogy to those investments that are specifically designed to fit one transaction partner, described here as being tailored to the needs of the target buyers within the market segment. An important implication is that the smallest common denominator of their requirements (taking into account their reservation prices) defines the properties of the investment.[210] This means that the investment fits the needs of each member of this segment: either equally well in case of homogeneous preferences within the segment or, to a certain degree, above some minimum threshold in case of heterogeneous preferences

---

[207] See *Williamson, O. E.* (1985), p. 12. The large-numbers condition at the outset will arguably not be met in many markets, particularly in case of (close) oligopolistic market structures or even monopolies. This idea, however, is situated outside the core principals of TCA and has only recently been explicitly considered in conjunction with TCA (see e.g. *Argyres, N. S./Liebeskind, J. P.* (1999), p. 58). It is hence not yet clear, whether or to what extent the analysis of such situations would require additional reference to theories that place more emphasis on structural properties of the competitive situation at the outset.

[208] See e.g. *Foss, N. J.* (1997), p. 181. Bidding costs incurred in selling large facility construction are a notable exception. Here, unlike in most cases, the specific investment precedes the (formal) contract and not vice versa. However, two qualificatory remarks seem appropriate: first, in some cases, the seller may be able to extract from the potential buyer an agreement on payment for and prior to detailed elaboration of a fully specified bid (*Backhaus, K./Plinke, W./Rese, M.* (2004), (p. 63). Or else, second, the costs incurred for bidding may be interpretetd in analogy to general investments in anonymous markets. The resoning behind this idea is that these costs usually constitute necessary conditions for staying in the particular business. Careful selection of relevant requests for quote can be expected, yet final assessment on output from bidding (costs) is likely to involve the sum of bids in comparison to total profits.

[209] See *Williamson, O. E.* (1985), pp. 31, 54f. See also chapter 2.1.2.2.

[210] In essence, on the grounds of this arguably rigid inference, the productivity gains usually associated with any specific investment (and justifying it) have to be questioned, at least in relative terms. Lower or no derived productivity gains (stage 2, that is, on behalf of the buyers) at all (case 1 and case 2, respectively) seem feasible. If all members of the segment buy the same product, by definition, they cannot gain any advantage from it over each other (case 2). If some portion x of the segment buys the same product,

within the segment. In each case, all potential buyers within the segment will be offered the identical market offering at the same price and, thereby, become perfectly substitutable to each other with respect to the amortization of the investment. At the same time, the investment is considerably less suitable for second best uses outside this segment, that is, when selling to other segments. For the sake of simplicity, it will be assumed that each potential buyer seeks to purchase one unit of the good.[211] Situations involving a market segment specific investment by a seller can now be grouped into two classes. They are presented in *Fig. 6* together with the cases of unspecific investments and transaction partner specific investments.

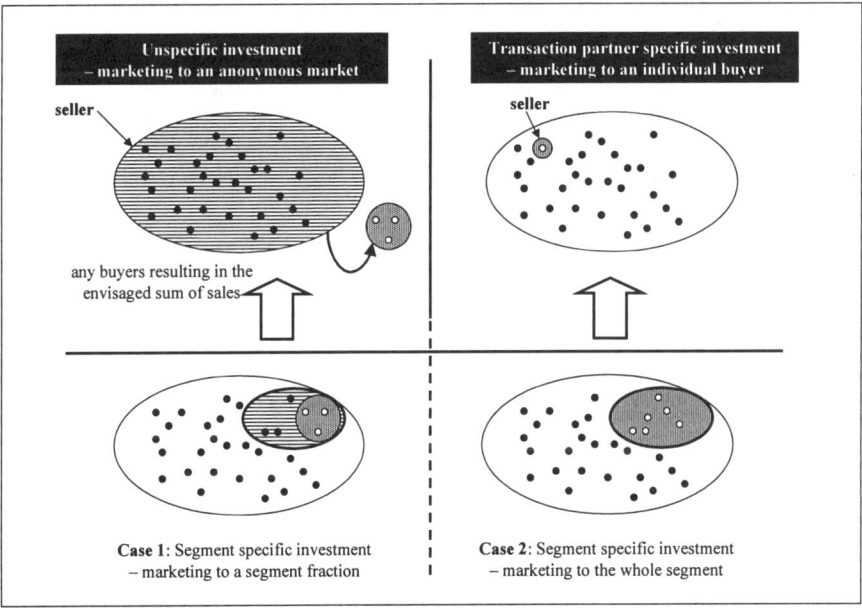

Fig. 6: Unspecific, transaction partner specific, and market specific investments

The buyers which are needed for achieving the intended amortization of the investment are marked as whites spots in dotted gray regions.

---

productivity gains may only (and even this not unconditionaly) be achieved compared to the remaining *n-x* buyers within the segment.

[211] This is, however, only a working assumption. Relaxing it in order to allow for variable quantities per buyer does not change the essence of the argument.

Case 1: for amortization of the investment, only some portion x of the whole number n of the members in the segment are required to buy from the seller.[212] The seller will make a contract only with these x buyers prior to making the investment (for instance, a special purpose machinery for production of components to aircraft construction). In case of premature termination of the contract with one of these x buyers, e.g. any $buyer_i$, the freed production capacity of the machinery can, by definition, be brought to a use just as well as the one lost, by selling to one of the $(n-x)$ segment members that are not yet customers of the seller. The first and the second best use do not differ in value to the seller. Hence, the situation is very similar to one of unspecific investment in an anonymous market. Essentially, this case is a question of delimitation of the relevant market, rather than of establishing a new category of specific investment. For $(n-x)$ getting an ever smaller number, we are approaching the second case.

Case 2: the seller will only be able to recover the investment and make the expected profit, if all n members of the segment buy from him.[213] In this case, each member needs to buy the quantity as assumed in the seller's calculations. Two contractual alternatives emerge in such a situation as consistent with economic rationale.

First, the seller could conclude just one general contract with a focal buyer, who is acting on behalf of all segment members. This general contract would cover the whole quantity of product to be delivered in the quality and with the exact specifications that are agreed on in the negotiations with this one buyer. This focal buyer in turn concludes (sub-) contracts with the other $(n-1)$ members of the market segment. From the seller's perspective, the risk of opportunistic exploitation is, hence, concentrated in a single contractual relationship. The investment is also customized to the specifications defined by one transacting party. This argument does not ignore the necessity of (sub-) contracts between the focal buyer and the other segment members determining performance specifications as well as quasi-rent distributions. However, from the viewpoint of the seller, the situation is equivalent to one where he invests specifically in an individual buyer that acts solely on his own behalf.

---

[212] This implies that the other members of the segment still have to be served by other sellers, i.e. there are more than one seller serving the market segment, ex ante as well as ex post.

[213] This is equivalent to an ex post market share of 100%, even though there may have been ex ante bidding competition. The other (if existent), losing bidders are assumed to turn away and serve other market segments. This situation's relevance, although it can be constructed in theory, is arguably low in practice.

Second, the seller could make a contract with each segment member individually. It can be shown that each of these n agreements, essentially, possesses the same qualities as in the case where the seller contracted with an individual buyer for a specific investment customized for this buyer alone. Each of the n contracts would relate to a buyer-specific quantity (here: one unit per buyer) of a product with segment-specific quality or specifications. Since the seller seeks complete amortization of its investment, each contract includes elements of calculation that are originally related to the whole segment and that are (artificially) broken down to the individual buyer's level. If one of these contracts, say with buyer$_i$, is prematurely determined, amortization of a certain portion of the segment-specific investment is endangered. However, this does not change the fact that the cap on opportunistic exploitation is determined by the individual contract and the expected returns from it, whatever their composition is in terms of buyer- and segment-specific elements.

Now, what remains to be considered is the case that the segment members (whether or not all of them are needed for amortization) collude after contract conclusion/seller investment in order to achieve lower prices.[214] This case is conditional upon a certain degree of market transparency and accordingly non-prohibitive coordination costs on behalf of the buyers. Such a condition does not appear suddenly but will already have prevailed ex ante to contract conclusion. As a boundedly rational, yet far-sighted economic actor, the seller will have taken this possibility into account, realizing two things.[215] (1) At worst the whole of (the individually contracted portions of) the segment-specific investment is potentially endangered. In terms of this amount at stake, there is no quantitative difference compared to the case of contracting with one buyer who absorbs the complete number of units produced. (2) The danger of being exploited is rather moderated than aggravated by the fact that (equivalent) exploitation requires agreement among the colluding buyers. This issue directs the seller's attention towards aspects of preventing or hindering collusive buyer behavior.[216] However, collusive tendencies on the demand-side constitute a challenge for the seller which is not exclusive to cases of specific investment. In fact, it is a general phenomenon which is also

---

[214] Collusion is here primarily understood in terms of the formation of cartels, although, strictly speaking, a second kind of collusion (merger) exists (see *Telser, L. G.* (1971), p. 179)

[215] On the notion of far-sightedness in combination with bounded rationality see *Williamson, O. E.* (1998), p. 42.

[216] See *Backhaus, K./Plinke, W./Rese, M.* (2004), (p. 79).

relevant when marketing efforts are targeted at anonymous markets. Recent examples for the latter case include group purchases of such unspecific goods as computers or energy.[217] Cartel-like buyer behavior and appropriate, feasible seller reactions are important aspects to explore, also in relation with specific investments. However, they do not call for the introduction of a distinct category of specific investments labelled market segment specific.

If one agrees with the above arguments, the result is a three-types-structure as shown in *Fig. 7(a)*. There are two grouping criteria.

First, the *degree of specificity* is used on a superordinate level. Regarding this criterion, an additional point has to be made in order to better suit the analysis of business type shift phenomena: instead of the very strong distinction between complete and nonexistent specificity, the dimension is reinterpreted in *Fig. 7(b)* to discriminate along the line of insignificant and significant levels of specificity, set apart from each other by some subjectively perceived threshold. [218] Within each of the two business types that are characterized by significant degrees of specificity, further nuanciation is allowed for.

Second, the number of transactions with a particular buyer calculated for amortization (with the two levels "1" or "> 1") which is relevant only in cases with significant asset specificity at work, is used as subordinate criterion. Since calculating the recovery of an investment is inseparably linked to undertaking it, the second aspect can also be interpreted as the nature of intended amortization of the investment, or *specificity horizon* as it will be referred to hereafter. Hence, it would figure as element of a multidimensional construct "asset specificity" that is put in concrete terms in the specific investment. Two levels are

---

[217] See for more detailed presentation and further examples e.g. *Baumeister, C.* (2000), p. 2ff.

[218] Transactions that are completely free from specificity represent the purest form of discrete exchange. An example of a transaction that comes very close to this has been given by *Dwyer, R. F./Schurr, P. H./Oh, S.* (1987), p. 12. Implicitly elaborating on *Macneil, I. R.* (1974), p. 720, they describe "… a one-time purchase of an unbranded gasoline out-of-town at an independent station paid for with cash." Arguably, this kind of transaction, isolated from all present, past and future relations, will be rare if at all existent in reality (*Macneil, I. R.* (1978), p. 856; *Granovetter, M.* (1985), pp. 489f., 495; *Dwyer, R. F./Schurr, P. H./Oh, S.* (1987), p. 12ff.). However, including it as an "ideal type" in the above typology, the truly discrete exchange transaction (as described by *Macneil*), that is one which is based on (completely) unspecific investment, provides a sharp notion of discreteness (*Macneil, I. R.* (1978), p. 856; *Webster, F. E. J.* (1992), p. 6; *Heide, J. B.* (1994), p. 74). Thus, it seems very useful as an analytical baseline that distinguishes transactions with significant levels of asset specificity from those, where the level is so low (i.e. below a certain "threshold"), that it has no consequences for the choice of governance structure and is, hence, "practically discrete" (*Dwyer, R. F./Schurr, P. H./Oh, S.* (1987), p. 25).

distinguished in the model as presented in *Fig. 7(a)* + *(b)*: first, amortization is intended to be achieved in only one transaction, and second, it is calculated over a whole chain of transactions and, by that, also implies a chain of separate contracts. This means that the initial investment points beyond the first contract towards some future transactions that are more or less accurately envisaged, yet, still lie in contractual uncertainty. Moreover, despite the fact that the investment analysis may result in fixing a (likely) number of chain links necessary for amortization, the real number may reveal itself only in the course of time. The planning horizon remains in this sense indeterminate. Any attempt to formulate something that comes close to contingency clauses is doomed to failure from the very outset.[219]

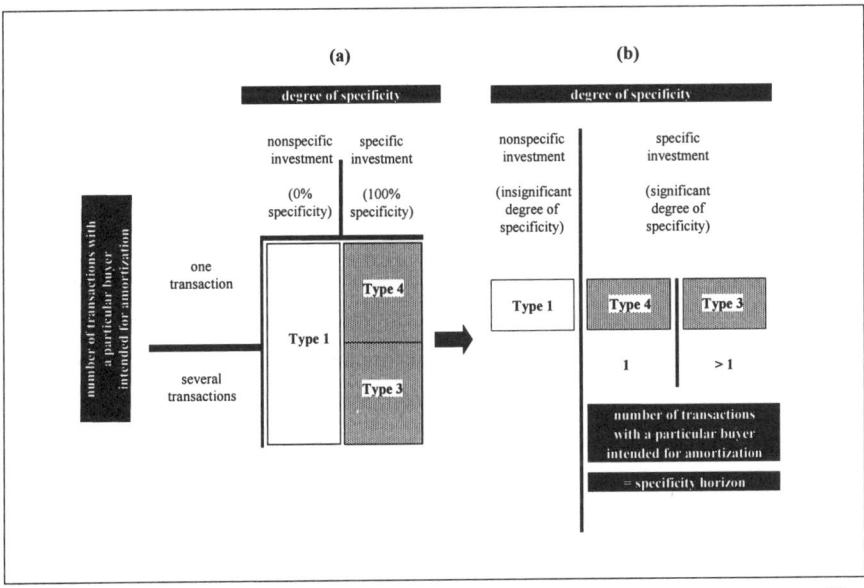

Fig. 7: Three-types-structure of industrial marketing transactions in different depictions (seller perspective)[220]

In this view, both criteria are related to TCA's central construct, namely asset specificity. This strong focus on asset specificity is arguably debatable. However, it receives support both from

---

[219] A close resemblance between the amortization criterion and the uncertainty criterion as used by *Backhaus/Aufderheide/Späth* (1994) emerges from this description. As a result, the typology which forms the basis of this investigation can clearly be interpreted in terms of an evolution from the earlier concept to which it is strongly linked. The subsequently outlined explicit distinction between seller and buyer perspective represents an important refinement with respect to this analysis.

[220] Following *Backhaus, K./Plinke, W./Rese, M.* (2004), (p. 44).

theoretical and empirical literature on transaction cost theory and its applications.[221] For instance, *Williamson* (1985) frequently characterizes asset specificity as the most critical transaction attribute in his seminal work on TCA.[222] With regard to the research question of this work, asset specificity becomes an even more suitable candidate for a discriminating variable in a structuring approach when its interpretation as a choice variable in agreeing on the terms of exchange is considered.[223] In such terms, it can (and will) be shaped by the transaction parties, and could, thereby, serve as an appropriate basis for the analysis of shifts as intended here. At this point, it should be emphasized that the advanced three types are ideal types in the sense that they represent (theoretically-derived) simplifications of more complex real world phenomena, guided by the objective of identifying those elements of a particular phenomenon that are decisive for its nature.[224] The concrete result of this identification procedure is determined by the particular lens through which a phenomenon is examined. The above structure, for instance, follows from a transaction cost-oriented view on the marketing problems that industrial sellers face.

Ad 2) Explicit differentiation between seller and buyer perspective

For the analysis of shifts between business types, it seems promising to explicitly differentiate between the seller and buyer perspective already at the stage of (static) structuring of industrial transactions. The reason is that two transaction partners do not necessarily invest specifically in each other to the same degree. And while this can, in principle, be captured by a three-types-framework, formalization of the argument facilitates the analysis and add to its clarity.

For instance, there may be a market with a large number of companies selling fruit-packaging machines. Company *A* is one of these suppliers and may produce for an anonymous market by offering each potential buyer the same range of 50 pre-fabricated machines, each of a different size or functionality. No

---

[221] For conceptually-oriented discussions see *Klein, B./Crawford, R. A./Alchian, A. A.* (1978); *Alchian, A. A.* (1984); *Riordan, M. H./Williamson, O. E.* (1985); *Nickerson, J. A./Vanden Bergh, R.* (1999); *Plinke, W./Söllner, A.* (2000); *Madhok, A.* (2002). For empirical support see e.g. *Masten, S. E.* (1984), p. 411. Criticism of such strong focus on asset specificity in TCA has been advanced e.g. by *Alston, L. J.* (1987), p. 317ff.

[222] See e.g.*Williamson, O. E.* (1985), pp. 30, 56.

[223] For a similar understanding of asset specificity as a decision variable see e.g. *Riordan, M. H./Williamson, O. E.* (1985); *Aufderheide, D.* (1993).

[224] See *Heide, J. B.* (1994), p. 81, on a similar structuring problem.

idiosyncratic investment is undertaken by A. The customer company B may now have to reorganize its production process by coordinating the interfaces between the surrounding process and fruit-packaging machine. In as far as A's machines are proprietary, that is, that their interfaces differ from those of other seller's fruit packaging machines, the buyer's reorganizing efforts represent a specific investment.

The resulting divergences in lock-in positions of buyer and seller, respectively, can formally be made explicit by applying the above outlined three business types to *each* market side separately. After formally separating buyer and seller-side, they are brought together again in the particular *constellation* of buyer business type and seller business type and associated lock-in's, that characterizes a particular transaction situation.[225] A constellation in this sense will be defined as any combination of a seller business type and a buyer business type that emerges as framework for a transaction between the two parties. Congruent and disgruent lock-in constellations are both feasible and may be identified as distinct (motivational) starting points for a strategic shift.[226] This idea of separation and subsequent combination of buyer and seller business types is depicted in *Fig. 8*. In total, nine feasible constellations result (each represented by the combination of two shaded small boxes). With the identification of disgruent constellations, there seems to be no longer a clear match of business type and one of the three types of contract as identified by *Macneil* (1978) (e.g. product business => classical contract).[227] The answer to this problem lies in the distinct understanding of the term "business type" as the *result* from technological, organizational and contractual elements of the transaction, as it will be elaborated in detail in the next chapter.

---

[225] *Schade, C./Schott, E.* (1993a) have outlined similar ideas by referring to the concept of *reciprocity of specific investments*, though, without drawing explicit formal inferences (p. 495).

[226] See chapter 3.3.2.

[227] See for related argumentation *Heide, J. B.* (1994), p. 81.

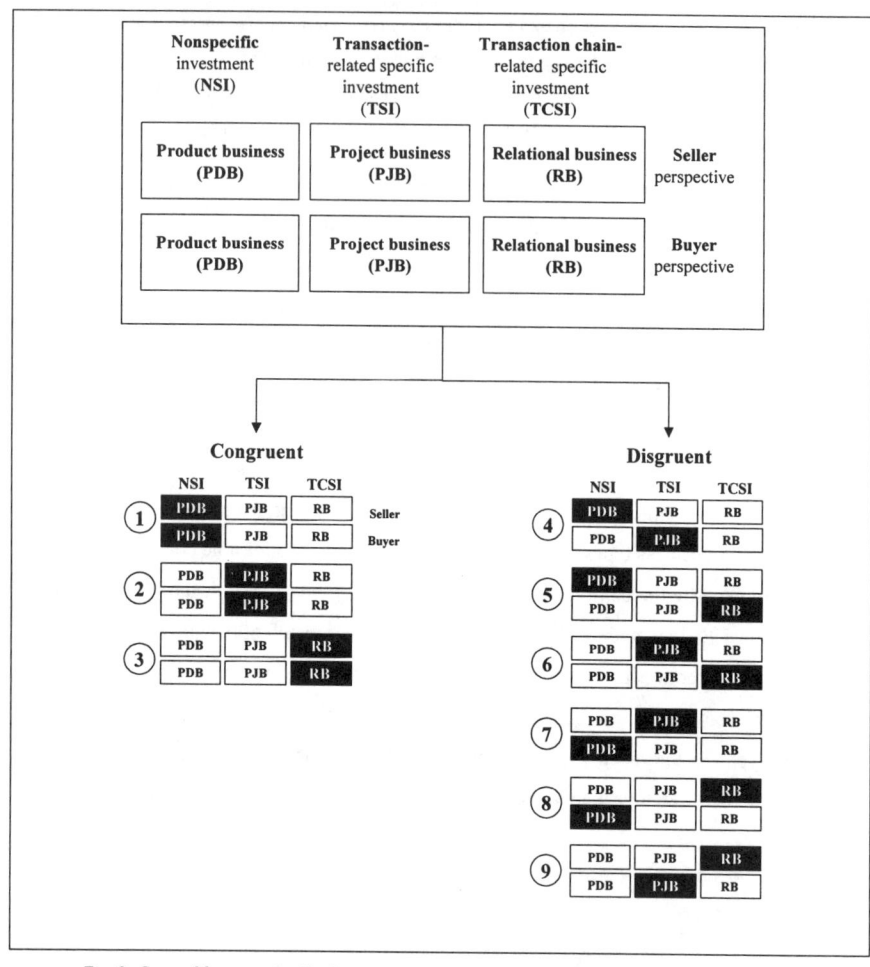

Fig. 8: General buyer and seller business types and resulting congruity (1-3) and disgruity (4-9) constellations[228]

The conceptual significance of such explicit modelling of different constellations finds support not only in the TCA literature but also in ideas advanced in research on power relations (symmetry and asymmetry) and (inter-) dependence of parties to an exchange.[229]

---

[228] The terms congruity and congruence, and disgruity and disgruence are used interchangeably through-out this work.

[229] The emphasis on the necessity to explicitly consider distinct buyer and seller positions in classification systems has a long tradition in the marketing literature as well (e.g. *Enis, B. M./Roering, K. J.* (1980),

Seminal work in this area has been provided by *Emerson* (1962) and *Blau* (1964) who are therewith regarded to have developed the earliest conceptualizations in social exchange theory (SET) and resource dependence theory.[230] Links between this stream of research and TCA have already been established, for instance, through the idea of replaceability, and potential complementarities have been demonstrated, illustrating that research in TCA could potentially gain interesting insights from considering ideas that have so far been discussed with emphasis on power relations.[231] However, heterogeneity of theoretical roots and core assumptions could be seen as a potential obstacle for incorporating ideas from research on power and dependence. While TCA ultimately stands in the classical (micro-) economic tradition, research on power relations, social exchange and resource dependence is grounded in

---

p. 187; *Plinke, W.* (1997), p. 11; from a supply management/marketing perspective e.g. *Kaufmann, L.* (2002)). Often, however, in combining both perspectives, *disgruent* constellations are not explicitly accounted for (see e.g. *Enis, B. M./Roering, K. J.* (1980), pp. 187ff.) although the potential fruitfulness of such an approach is highlighted by *Heide, J. B.* (1994)'s statement on "...unilateral dependence to undermine bilateral governance..." (p. 81) that addresses the very problem of disgruent constellations. An ealy account in marketing research has been provided by *Dwyer, R. F./Walker Jr., O. C.* (1981) who also draw on research on power-dependence relations and investigate the bargaining processes and outcomes in asymmetrical power structures against balanced power structures by means of a gaming experiment.

[230] See *Emerson, R. M.* (1962); *Blau, P. M.* (1964). Important early contributions to the analysis of power and dependence from a socioscientific perspective have also been made by *Thibaut, J. W./Kelley, H. H.* (1959), p. 100ff. At the heart of SET lies the analysis of relational interdependence of exchange partners that develops over time through interaction (*Lambe, C. J./Wittmann, C. M./Spekman, R. E.* (2001)). Resource dependence theory focuses on interfirm governance as a strategic response to conditions of uncertainty and dependence (*Peffer, J./Salancik, G. R.* (1978); *Aldrich, H. E.* (1979)). Conceptual discussions of SET and resource dependence theory in relation to TCA can be found e.g. with *Heide, J. B./John, G.* (1988); *Söllner, A.* (1993); *Heide, J. B.* (1994); *Jung, S.* (1999); *Lambe, C. J./Wittmann, C. M./Spekman, R. E.* (2001) or, briefly, *Argyres, N. S./Liebeskind, J. P.* (1999), p. 58.

[231] *LaBahn*, for instance, combines TCA with research on power and dependence for examining periods between equilibrium states, which he defines as milestones in a transaction relationship when both parties have brought their transaction specific invstments in line (*LaBahn, D. W.* (1999)). Though this view of TCA as an equilibrium theory, predicting the most efficient long-term solution to an exchange, may be debatable and stands more in the tradition of the economic natural selection view than of the managerial choice perspective taken up in this work, it nevertheless illustrates the potential fruitfulness of integration of power relations based-ideas in TCA-based analysis. Further theoretical support for the proposed relatedness of TCA, on the one hand, and research on power relations, resource dependence or SET, on the other hand, comes, for instance, from *Heide, J. B./John, G.* (1988), pp. 21, 23; *Rindfleisch, A./Heide, J. B.* (1997), p. 31, fn2; *Plinke, W./Söllner, A.* (2000), pp. 57f, 74f. Empirical research that demonstrates potential complementarity by drawing on a blend of TCA and power relations theory includes *Anderson, E./Weitz, B.* (1992); *Heide, J. B./John, G.* (1992); *Stump, R. L./Joshi, A. W.* (1998); *Skarmeas, D. A./Katsikeas, C. S.* (2001). The development of the so-called political economy framework, in essence, constitutes an attempt to bring both perspectives together (*Stern, L. W./Reve, T.* (1980); *Achrol, R. S./Reve, T./Stern, L. W.* (1983); *Day, G. S./Klein, S.* (1987)). At its core lies the interpretation of a marketing channel dyad in terms of its internal structure and external environment with both of these systems consisting of two subsystems, a polity (or power and control) system and an economy system (*Day, G. S./Klein, S.* (1987), p. 43).

sociology and behavioral research.[232] Though, it is maintained here that as long as ideas are inspired by research in other fields, but can be justified on TCA grounds these ideas might be drawn on as thoughtful impetus or support without extensive analysis of theoretical compatibility of both research streams. This is particularly interesting since TCA and research on power and dependence both deal in part with the same or at least related problems as is illustrated, for instance, by the analysis of the commitment construct. *Söllner* (1993) examines it mainly through a transaction cost lens. His concern is the theoretically-guided identification of explanatory variables for the emergence of close business cooperations. In order to capture the associated benefits and inputs, he establishes the commitment construct in a dominantly organizational transactional perspective.[233] *Brown/Lusch/Nicholson* (1995), for example, analyze commitment in the context of power relations and focus on the impact of use of power by one transacting party on the other one's commitment. In particular, they hypothesize links between different types of power and different types of commitment and transaction partner performance.[234]

Specifically, certain conceptual as well as empirical arguments from research on power relations and dependence can be identified to support the outlined TCA-grounded framework of constellations for description of transaction situations, although the term power does not form part of TCA in the same sense.[235] It can, be interpreted in transaction cost analytic terminology if referring to feasible *ex post* conditions.[236] Dependence emerges as a descriptive

---

[232] For discussion of TCA's origins see e.g. *Williamson, O. E.* (1985), p. 2ff; *Picot, A./Dietl, H./Franck, E.* (1997), p. 53 ff. The origins of research on power relations are outlined e.g. by *Emerson, R. M.* (1962); *Blau, P. M.* (1964) or recently *Lambe, C. J./Wittmann, C. M./Spekman, R. E.* (2001). Potential for a certain degree of complementarity is outlined by the fact that contributions to SET also refer to contract theory as elaborated by *Macneil, I. R.* (1978) (see e.g. *Dwyer, R. F./Schurr, P. H./Oh, S.* (1987)).

[233] See *Söllner, A.* (1993).

[234] See *Brown, J. R./Lusch, R. F./Nicholson, C. Y.* (1995).

[235] See, for instance, *Williamson, O. E.* (1990), p. 61 and fn 1. Nevertheless, the notion of power has previously been brought to seminal use by researchers that explicitly build on TCA (see e.g. *Malone, T. W./Yates, J./Benjamin, R. I.* (1987), p. 495). Economic power as defined by the availability of alternative options has also been discussed in the context of early institutionalist theories (see *Rutherford, M.* (1983), p. 725).

[236] Ex ante, large numbers bidding is a standard assumption in TCA. It largely excludes from the analysis issues of potential ex ante dependence due to factors such as ex ante market structure which may cause ex ante deviation from a bilateral large numbers bidding condition. Here, however, such issues will have to be considered as potential motivators of strategic shifts. Their incorporation in the analysis will later be substantiated later (see chapter 3.2.3).

factor in the form of specificity-contingent lock-ins and lock-in differentials in various constellations of business types[237]: the particular exchange partner is irreplaceable or replaceable only at cost.[238] This creates dependence. Power that one party possesses over another may then be regarded as a result of the other party's dependence and as a potential to exploit this dependence through opportunistic quasi-rent appropriation.

On the conceptual side, characterizations of power and dependence in the SET differ from their understanding in TCA, yet, exhibit some common traits. In the tradition of *Weber* (1947), several definitions have been advanced in research on social exchange.[239] Among the most influential has been *Emerson* (1962) who stresses that power is not an attribute of a certain actor but a property of the (social) relation between actors. He defines it as a *potential influence*, or, more precisely, as "...the amount of resistance on the part of B which can be potentially overcome by A."[240] Power is, hence, conceptualized as a relative phenomenon and is considered to be the result of the dependence of one party on the other. Dependence of an actor A upon an actor B in turn is defined by *Emerson* as "... (1) directly proportional to A's *motivational investment* in goals mediated by B, and (2) inversely proportional to the *availability* of those goals to A outside of the A-B relation."[241] The picture is completed by the consideration of the power-dependence relation between the two exchange parties, which may either be balanced or unbalanced. If it is balanced, though, even if it is at a high level, (mutual) power is not neutralized.[242] Exchange conditions with balanced dependence are, thus, distinct from unbalanced ones by some "net-dependence" criterion. Also, balanced

---

[237] *Bonus, H.* (1987), p. 90ff, basically refers to transaction cost economics as "economics of dependence"; see also e.g. *Williamson, O. E.* (1985), p. 62; *Heide, J. B./John, G.* (1988), p. 23.

[238] See *Heide, J. B./John, G.* (1988), p. 23; *Heide, J. B./John, G.* (1992), p. 35; *Heide, J. B.* (1994), p. 73. Another interpretation has been proposed by *Söllner, A.* (1993); *Plinke, W./Söllner, A.* (2000), p. 62, who focus on idiosyncratic inputs to a relationship as sources of dependence, instead of expected output from the relationship.

[239] *Weber, M.* (1947), p. 152, defines power as "...the probability that one actor within a social relationship will be in a position to carry out his own will despite resistance." Two alternative streams of research examining power issues have conceptualized it not as a potential but (1) as a process and (2) as a result or outcome. For an overview see *Lawler, E. J.* (1992), p. 20.

[240] *Emerson, R. M.* (1962), p. 2.

[241] *Emerson, R. M.* (1962), p. 2.

[242] This notion runs contrary to the understanding of power as elaborated by *Blau, P. M.* (1964), p. 117f, who defines power as the "...*net* ability of a person to withhold rewards from and apply punishments to other...". The distinctive effects of various absolute magnitudes of power get lost in this definition and make it less suitable for illustrating parallels with TCA.

relations characterized by high levels of power are set apart from those that are balanced on low levels.[243] Imbalanced situations, in particular, have been posited to constitute a central force in driving change[244], thereby illustrating the need for careful identification of the dependence relations in an exchange. *Thibaut/Kelley's* (1959) treatment of power is similar in its emphasis on the relation between power and dependence. They particularly focus on power as a means to alter someone else's outcome from a relationship, not only his behavior.[245] Such emphasis fits well with a central concern expressed by TCA. One party may opportunistically exploit the other (dependent) party by partially or completely appropriating its quasi-rent: this clearly represents an alteration in expected outcome.

Reference to economic principles and treatment of issues from the business sphere are frequent in research on power and dependence.[246] *Emerson* (1962) himself explicitly hints at the connection between his definition and economic conditions of supply and demand. An interpretation that is even more focused on transaction cost reasoning and on the above typology seems possible[247]: *availability* of alternatives prevails with large numbers bidding condition, the fundamental transformation due to idiosyncratic investments sharply reduces the space of alternatives to a monopoly condition. Realization of the envisaged benefits from the transaction now depends on the other party's identity and its abstaining from opportunistic exploitation. These benefits are c.p. predicted to be higher, the more specific the investment. They are, therefore, regarded to move in line with the above mentioned motivational investment.

The outlined emphasis on power and (mutual) dependence as relative concepts, thus, lends support to the proposed focus on constellations as characteristic for particular transactions[248]:

---

[243] See also *Thibaut, J. W./Kelley, H. H.* (1959), p. 113ff; more recently, *Gundlach, G. T./Cadotte, E. R.* (1994), for instance, build on this idea by defining the magnitude of interdependence as an impact in market channel relationship.

[244] See e.g. *Aldrich, H. E.* (1979), p. 265.

[245] ""...the power of A over B increases with A's ability to affect the quality of outcomes attained by B." *Thibaut, J. W./Kelley, H. H.* (1959), p. 101.

[246] See, for instance, *Blau, P. M.* (1964), p.168ff; *Aldrich, H. E.* (1979), p. 269.

[247] See *Emerson, R. M.* (1962), p. 3.

[248] Discussion of aspects associated with different business types constellations, yet in the power relations tradition can, for instance, be found with *Buchanan, L.* (1992), p. 67f.

each party's business type on its own makes only part of the picture. Only when combined and put in relation to the other party's position can definitive inferences be drawn. Consider a large specific investment undertaken by a buyer in relational business, for instance an initial investment in a complex, expandable production control software, which requires considerable adaptive investments within the buying firm that, in sum, creates a significant quasi-rent and dependence. The "net-dependence" will, however, be very different if the seller's position is product business, resulting in a highly disgruent constellation, or whether the seller's position is relational business, resulting in a congruent "balance of terror"[249], where both parties are highly dependent on each other. This latter situation, although potentially balanced, differs from an exchange that involves no specific investment by either party.

Empirical research in the power relations tradition provides additional support for the proposed focus on the constellation of buyer and seller business types. Examples include *Brown/Lusch/Nicholson*'s (1995) study on the impact of power usage on commitment and on performance or *LaBahn*'s (1999) study of investment options for component suppliers in order to circumvent power advantages of large customers which is based on explicit identification of congruent or disgruent power constellations (balance versus disequilibrium).[250]

From the proposed constellations framework, nine distinct combinations of seller and buyer business types can be identified. The first three refer to congruent constellations (see *Fig. 7*), while the other six represent disgruent constellations. Brief general characterizations are given for these nine constellations and short examples are sketched in an stylized and simplified manner. Quite likely, some will be more intuitive than others and may be found more frequently in business practice.[251] Full specification would require detailed description of the underlying calculations for investment recovery and of the corresponding contracts. Companies *A* and *B* represent seller and buyer, respectively.[252]

---

[249] The term here refers to the exploitation potential associated with a large and highly idiosyncratic investment.

[250] See *Brown, J. R./Lusch, R. F./Nicholson, C. Y.* (1995); *LaBahn, D. W.* (1999).

[251] Potential reasons and determinants will be elaborated in the next chapter.

[252] No provision will be made for the role of intermediaries in business marketing. Instead, the examples build

(1) Congruity: product business (PDB / PDB)

Neither party undertakes a specific investment. Premature termination as, for instance, cancellation briefly prior to the arranged time of exchange implies no significant losses for either party: each will, without incurring much effort/cost, be able to find an alternative transaction partner that sells a comparable unspecific good (seller) or holds comparable requirements (buyer). Also, subsequent buying and selling processes are unaffected by the transaction.

Actor A produces and later sells typing paper that is standardized according to DIN. Actor B buys DIN-standardized typing paper approximately once a month and frequently changes the supplier.

(2) Congruity: project business (PJB / PJB)

Both parties undertake idiosyncratic investments in each other. Premature termination as, for instance, termination during the phase of construction of the customized good implies significant losses for both parties[253]: each would incur significant efforts/costs in case it had to find an alternative transaction partner that sold an at least partially comparable specific good (seller) or that would hold at least partially comparable requirements (buyer). However, subsequent buying and selling processes are not predetermined to the least degree by investment undertaken in this transaction.

Particularly prevalent in construction and systems engineering: actor A sells water power stations that are subject to make-to-order production. After drawing up a bid that is fitted to the potential customer's specific needs and, after winning the contract, a customer-specific design for the facility is elaborated and its elements are subsequently produced and assembled at the customer site. Actor B in turn engages in the construction of some infrastructure, e.g. a berth, that is optimized to fit the supplier's shipping requirements. The power station is constructed as a completed project.

(3) Congruity: relational business (RB / RB)

Both parties undertake idiosyncratic investments in each other that point beyond the initial transaction, i.e. refer to a whole chain of intended transactions with each other. Premature termination here means termination of the relationship before the envisaged number of transactions has taken place. Until this number has been reached, each would

---

on the simplifying fiction of a direct transaction between seller and buyer independent from the underlying business type. This is only assumed for the sake of simplicity of argument, since the grouping itself does not depend on a such direct exchange.

[253] In the case of large projects, the period beween contract conclusion and complete fulfillment of all parties' obligations is sometimes characterized by severe imbalances in dependence. These changes in lock-in positions over the course of time covered by *one* contract arguably pose considerable challenges. Their detailed presentation is beyond the scope of this work. They have been addressed extensively and through a transaction cost lens e.g. by *Köhl, T.* (2000); *Backhaus, K./Plinke, W./Rese, M.* (2004), (p. 87); *Kleinaltenkamp, M./Kühne, B.* (2003), p. 16f.

incur significant efforts/costs in case it had to switch to another transaction partner: continuation of the chain with another partner would require costly adaptation with the alternative being to make a new initial investment in order to start a new chain. Hence, after the initial investment, subsequent buying and selling processes within the envisaged chain are predetermined.[254]

Actor A sells a Computer Integrated Manufacturing (CIM) software to actor B that, after contract conclusion, is tailored to B's specific needs. In later stages, actor A provides customized updates and service covered by subsequent contracts, i.e. in separate transactions, in order to achieve full investment recovery including opportunity costs, i.e. full realization of intended profits. Actor B fits the software into its existing data processing system and gets its staff trained on the CIM-system.

(4) Disgruity: seller product business & buyer project business (PDB / PJB)

While the seller undertakes no specific investment, the buyer does. Premature termination of contract would imply a significant loss for the buyer but not for the seller who would not have significant difficulties in marketing the same good to an alternative buyer. However, both subsequent buying and selling processes are unaffected by the transaction.

Actor A sells a prefabricated house of a certain type to a tax consulting agency (actor B). Actor B chooses and orders furnishings to fit the particular design and ground plan of the house.

(5) Disgruity: seller product business & buyer relational business (PDB / RB)

While the seller undertakes no specific investment, the buyer does and this investment points beyond the initial transaction. From the buyer's perspective, premature termination of the transaction chain would imply a significant loss, but not so for the seller. And while the seller faces no constraints regarding further sales, the buyer is affected in subsequent purchases through its calculation which refers to the whole chain.

Actor A sells a preprogrammed Business Intelligence (BI) software for integration of corporate information to actor B. Installation at actor B involves customization to the existing elements of the information system and subsequent staff training that is provided either by actor A or a third company (IT-consultancy). Extensions to link with or replace other parts of actor B's data processes are bound to be bought from actor A due to incompatibilities of the initial BI with software from other sellers.

(6) Disgruity: seller project business & buyer relational business (PJB / RB)

Both parties undertake idiosyncratic investments in each other. However, while the seller expects amortization from just one transaction, the buyer's calculation refers to a chain of

---

[254] This predetermination can vary in strength from limiting choice in subsequent transactions to completely determining choice (see e.g. *Beinlich, G.* (1998); *Backhaus, K.* (2003)).

related investments with only the first of them being realized at this moment. Premature termination here has two different meanings: from the seller's view, it describes termination before completion of the initial contract. The buyer, however, would incur losses as long as the chain ends before the envisaged element.

Similar to case number 3. The difference lies in the calculation of actor A. Here, the contract that refers to the programming and installation of the CIM-system is based on a full amortization calculation. Actor B in turn faces the same lock-in spreading over a chain of related transactions as above.

(7) Disgruity: seller project business & buyer product business (PJB / PDB)

While the buyer undertakes no specific investment, the seller does. Premature termination of contract would imply a significant loss for the seller but not for the buyer who would not have significant difficulties in purchasing the same good from an alternative seller. Nevertheless, both subsequent buying and selling processes are unaffected by the transaction.

Actor B has obtained a large one time order that relates to the customized production and successive delivery of difficult-to-transport components for airplane construction during the course of a certain period of time. Time-critical transportation will proceed via several shippings. Therefore, actor B orders a number of shipping containers that have to be designed and fabricated to fit the particular components. Recipients of the container order are companies A_1, A_2, and A_3.[255] With each of them, a contract is concluded covering a certain number of ships. No further orders in this context are intended by actor B.

(8) Disgruity: seller relational business & buyer product business (RB / PDB)

While the buyer undertakes no specific investment, the seller does and this investment points beyond the initial transaction. From the seller's perspective, premature termination of the transaction chain would imply a significant loss, but not so for the buyer. And while the buyer faces no constraints regarding further purchases, the seller is restricted in subsequent sales through its calculation which refers to the whole chain.

Actor B is an automobile manufacturer launching a new model. Seats need to be specifically designed to fit the model and are additionally intended to include seat covers made from a new heat-resistant material, thus requiring more than usual design efforts and also investments in some new production technology on behalf of the seat producing supplier A_i. Actor B concludes contracts with suppliers A_1, A_2, A_3. Each specifies terms of delivery for a certain period of time which is likely to be much shorter that the anticipated life cycle of the model and may not be sufficient for complete amortization of supplier investments in development and production.

---

[255] Arguably, this order splitting (also referred to as multiple sourcing) is likely to result in production diseconomies of scale. However, conditions may be such that the loss from these diseconomies is outweighted. This kind of argument will be elaborated in detail in the next chapter.

(9) Disgruity: seller relational business & buyer project business (RB / PJB)

Both parties undertake idiosyncratic investments in each other. However, while the buyer expects amortization from just one transaction, the seller's calculation refers to a chain of related investments with only the first of them being realized at the moment under consideration. Premature termination here again means two different things depending on the perspective: from the buyer's view, it describes termination before completion of the initial contract. The seller, however, would incur losses as long as the chain ends before the envisaged element.

Actor A constructs a sewage plant for the chemical producer (actor B) that is customized to the specific sewage being generated at the particular production site. The contract refers to this one project only. However, they also agree for actor B to act as a reference customer for a certain period of time, implying that actor A will not achieve complete realization of otherwise intended profits from the plant itself but only from inclusion of anticipated positive reference effects. Although, from actor A's perspective, identity of the transaction partner does not matter in the same sense as it does matter in the other examples presented above, it still does and makes full amortization of the specific investment contingent upon further successful interaction with actor B.

With some of these examples featuring very similar goods or services being traded in different constellations, the question remains how to determine precisely which business type (constellation) a particular transaction would appropriately be associated with.

2.1.2.6   Constitutive elements of a business types constellation

This issue requires closer scrutiny of those factors that underlie and, by that, define a particular business types constellation. In order to arrive at a more detailed characterization, it seems helpful to start with some clarifying definitions. The fundamental level in a transaction is taken here to be represented by the *functionality* of the exchanged object, with the term *market offering* referring to the detailed design of the good or right that is transferred in the particular transaction.

In the tradition of TCA, a very broad understanding of functionality is adopted. *Williamson* (1985), for instance, develops his basic contracting scheme based on the assumption that "...a good or service can be supplied by either of two alternative technologies. One is a general purpose technology, the other a special purpose technology."[256] Due to the use of different technologies for its production, some properties of the good or service concerning either its

---

[256]   *Williamson, O. E.* (1985), p. 32.

cost or quality position are likely to vary but not so its basic functionality. The interpretation also finds support in the marketing literature. *Anderson/Narus* (1999), for instance, define it as what "...the core product or service does, such as a white pigment providing whitening, brightening, and opacifying when it is added to a coating."[257] This allows for variations in usage across business markets and customers. It is indeterminate as to the concrete "face" of the exchanged object, or in marketing terms, the market offering. This latter refers to the concrete form in which the functionality can be purchased by the customer. It is only the market offering that includes fixing the particular business types constellation, and also goes beyond. Marketing a specific functionality in a certain business types constellation can follow a variety of ways, for instance, regarding the details of communication policy. The concrete realization of one path is the market offering. Functionality, on the contrary, is indeterminate regarding all this, and, in particular, regarding the business types constellation within which it is exchanged.[258] It can be seen in analogy to the good or service that can either be supplied by a general purpose or a special purpose technology, or, in economic terms: accompanied by unspecific or specific investments.

More detailed examination of the link between functionality on the one hand and business types constellation and market offering on the other hand rests on the identification of those mechanisms that turn an indeterminate functionality into a particular business types constellation and further into a market offering.

The decisive factor that distinguishes different business types from each other is asset specificity. Degree and horizon of asset specificity define *what* business type prevails in a particular situation. From a managerial perspective, the question *why* exactly this degree and horizon of asset specificity (i.e. business type) prevails, is explained as the outcome from a choice made by the parties involved. In such understanding, asset specificity is viewed as a

---

[257] *Anderson, J. C./Narus, J. A.* (1999), p. 34, fn 4. As a core product they regard "...the fundamental, functional performance a generic product provides that solves a customer's basic problem" (p. 161). This definition helps to stress the central point about functionality. It draws on an understanding of the concept of a "core product" as it has been advanced already in 1980 by *Kotler, P.* (1980); *Levitt, T.* (1980). Similar considerations on general functionality can be found with *Adner, R.* (2002), p. 670f.

[258] For similar argumentation, though not based on NIE reasoning, see *Mathur, S. S.* (1984).

choice variable which is subject to the parties' deliberate design, and not a given environmental factor.[259]

In this paper, the interpretation of asset specificity is a very fundamental one: it is defined by its essential consequence, namely that the transaction partner's identity matters.[260] This connection is regarded as constitutive for asset specificity to be existent. Moreover, the importance of an intertemporal context as a necessary precondition for asset specificity to represent a problem is emphasized.[261] The underlying idiosyncratic investment may refer to an investment in either money, time or effort.[262] Dependence in the sense that identity matters and exploitation is to be feared is created by the fact that the specifically investing party produces and delivers value in advance of receiving the expected countervalue. It arises from the divergence between fulfillment of agreed performance (usually provided by the seller in the form of a good or service or a combination of both) and counterperformance (usually provided by the buyer in the form of payment).[263] Therefore, the degree and horizon of asset specificity and the business types constellation on the one hand, and the magnitude of the amount at stake on the other hand, jointly determine the degree of dependence which could be operationalized via the quasi-rent construct. Due to its explicit relevance in the above argumentation, attention has to be paid to the value construct. Its interpretations in the literature are varied.[264] The value perspective on business-to-business marketing, for instance, has extensively been covered by *Anderson* et al.[265] They define value in business markets as

---

[259] For explicit consideration of asset specificity as a decision variable see e.g. *Riordan, M. H./Williamson, O. E.* (1985); *Aufderheide, D.* (1993); *Aufderheide, D.* (2000), pp. 75, 99; for explicit interpretation as environmental factor see e.g. *Picot, A./Dietl, H.* (1990). Detailed examination of the impacting factors of the choice is presented in chapter 3.2.3.

[260] See *Williamson, O. E.* (1985), p. 32.

[261] See e.g. *Domrös* (1994), p. 70. Intertemporality has been argued to be, in general, a central topic of TCA (*Williamson, O. E.* (1999b), p. 1101). Theoretically, the exchange of a highly customized good could be constructed in a way as to cause no asset specificity problem if it involved no time gap between performance and counterperformance.

[262] Despite quantification problems, time and effort could likely be translated in monetary terms.

[263] A particular form of this problem is discussed by *Tirole, J.* (1986) in a game theoretic context as "pre-performance investments". See also *Picot, A./Dietl, H.* (1990), p. 181.

[264] See e.g. *Bowman, C./Ambrosini, V.* (2000), p. 2f. *Makadok, R.* (2002), p. 10f. provides an extensive discussion for illustrating the terminological confusion.

[265] See e.g. *Anderson, J. C./Jain, D., C./Chintagunta, P. K.* (1993); *Anderson, J. C.* (1995); *Anderson, J. C./Narus, J. A.* (1995); *Anderson, J. C./Narus, J. A.* (1998); *Anderson, J. C./Narus, J. A.* (1999)). *Anderson, J. C./Narus, J. A.* (1999).

"...the worth in monetary terms of the economic, technical, service, and social benefits a customer receives in exchange for the price it pays for a market offering."[266] A more comprehensive and more theoretically-guided definition of value which some recent work on the linkages between strategic management and TCA builds on, is developed by *Brandenburger/Stuart* (1996).[267] Referring to a whole vertical chain which consists (in the simplest case) of a supplier, a firm (here referred to as the seller) and a buyer, they base their definition on two components:

- the buyer's reservation price (willingness-to-pay, i.e. the maximum price he is willing to pay), and

- the supplier's "opportunity cost" which includes his factual costs and could, in analogy, be referred to as "willingness to supply", that is, the minimum price at which he is prepared to supply the good.

From these ingredients they calculate first the "value created" by the whole chain as "buyer's willingness-to-pay – supplier's opportunity cost" and, second, the "added value" of each player as "... the value created by all the players in the vertical chain minus the value created by all the players except the one in question."[268] This, essentially, refers to that quantity which the player takes with him if he leaves the "game arena".

For the purpose of this analysis, the terms "value", "value created" and "added value" will be treated and defined as separate constructs. In line with some influential early definitions[269] and current interpretations[270], **value** is taken as the worth in monetary terms of the economic, technical, and service benefits which an actor receives in exchange for certain sacrifices. These include, but are not restricted to the price paid. Thus, value refers to a gross quantity, that is, to a quantity before deduction of price and other sacrifices (such as transaction costs)

---

[266] *Anderson, J. C./Narus, J. A.* (1999), p. 5f.

[267] See *Brandenburger, A. M./Stuart Jr., H. W.* (1996). See for application e.g. *Foss, N. J.* (2003).

[268] See *Brandenburger, A. M./Stuart Jr., H. W.* (1996), p. 6, who see this definition as consistent with another seminal definition of "added value" provided by *Davis, E./Kay, J.* (1990), p. 10. In refining such interpretations, research has recently addressed the issue of buyer valuation methodology (see e.g. *Plank, R. E./Ferrin, B. G.* (2002)).

[269] See e.g. *Zeithaml, V. A.* (1988).

[270] See e.g. *Simpson, P. M./Siguaw, J. A./Baker, T. L.* (2001), p. 121.

for obtaining the desired benefits. The term "value" is used equivalently to the notion of performance. On the other hand, following *Brandenburger/Stuart* (1996), **value created** (VC) is interpreted as a net quantity, although the focus is somewhat narrower here in that the dyad serves as baseline of the analysis.[271] "Shortening" their definition to suit the dyad results in defining the "total value created" in the dyad as the buyer's reservation price (willingness-to-pay) minus all costs that have accrued to the seller (including opportunity costs). The buyer's willingness-to-pay is interpreted as a net quantity after additional costs of acquisition that the buyer incurs have been deducted. Also, it is conceived as independent from competitive influences. These enter in the form of the price that is actually paid. This price hinges on bargaining between buyer and seller and is, consequently, influenced by their individual bargaining power which in turn depends on competition and resulting availability of substitutes. The buyer's value created (VC^B) covers its willingness-to-pay minus the actually paid price. The seller's value created (VC^S) is defined as the actually received price less the seller's costs. **Added value** (AV) accordingly refers to that part of the value created which the particular player (seller/buyer) takes with him if he quits the game.

This triad of definitions covers all relevant quantities required for the subsequent analysis. The notion of value serves as a general quantity for characterizing the exchanged objects while the distinction between value created and added value allows for the explicit examination of issues related to creating, dividing and protecting value which are only touched at in the following consideration, but elaborated in some more detail in subsequent chapters.

In case the act of advance delivery – undertaken by whatever party – cannot (1) be reversed at an insignificant cost and, (2) the performance cannot be transferred to another use where it is (almost) equally valued, the (full) realization of the actor's purposes attached to the transaction is contingent upon the original partner. Such a condition can be caused by various mechanisms inherent to the transaction. Their identification can be derived from the exchange agreement that can be regarded to cover three areas of issues to be specified:

---

[271] An alternative way to put it is that the perspective is also comprehensive in that it implicitly includes all previous stages of production. Yet, apart from the dyad in question, the rest of the chain remains in the shadow and enters just as a global input cost figure in the seller calculation.

(1) **what is exchanged** (content of performance/counterperformance)? Example: the object is a standardized automobile of a certain type. The parties agree to exchange the object for 20,000 € in cash.

(2) **how are these objects exchanged** (structure or mode of delivery of performance/ counterperformance, particularly payment terms)? Example: counterperformance (payment) will be provided following a leasing scheme.

(3) **what means is** are taken in order to care for mutual **compliance of the contract** and for **conflict solution (safeguards)**? Example: reference to the relevant place of jurisdiction for the settlement of possible disputes.

The relationship between the three areas of specification on the one hand, and their proposed relationship regarding the constellation and market offering construct, on the other hand, is depicted in *Fig. 9*. The design of the first two fields (part I) is constitutive for the particular constellation: they specify the ex ante *intended* creation and distribution of a potential value that arises in the coalition of seller and buyer.[272] Part I splits into two elements: first, there are technological features of the exchanged good, organizational and human capital related measures for its integration and use, and similar features that are primarily covered by specifications of content of performance and counterperformance. Since these are directly related to the good or service concerned, they are referred to as *product-related* mechanisms causing asset specificity. They contrast with the second element, *mode-related* mechanisms, which is formed by contractual provisions that specify the structure or mode of delivery, with payment conditions representing as a major element.[273]

---

[272] The importance of considering these issues simultaneously has recently been emphasized by *Foss, N. J.* (2003) based on the argument that bargaining involves transaction costs as well and the distribution of the "pie", thus, having feedback effects on its size. See for further support e.g. *Brandenburger, A. M./Stuart Jr., H. W.* (1996), p. 10.

[273] This argument represents a key element in a dynamic perspective on the business types approach (see chapter 3.2.3).

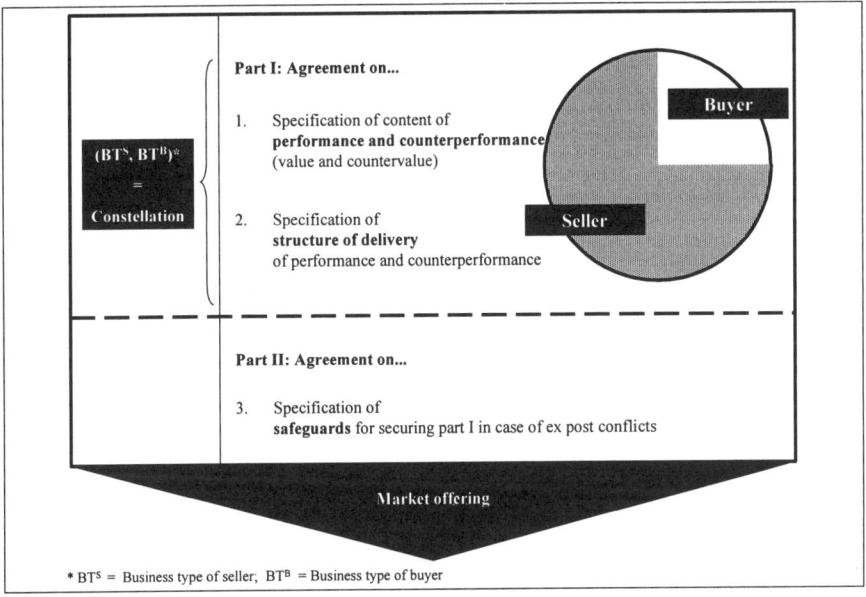

Fig. 9: Relationship between business types constellation and market offering based on different areas of specification in the contract

The relationship between the two mechanisms is additive in nature.[274] The final horizon (transaction-related or transaction chain-related) and degree of specificity in a transaction can only be assessed on the basis of the interplay between the two mechanisms. For instance, from a buyer´s perspective, telecommunication via mobile phones represents a highly unspecific good/service on the product-related side. Particular design of payment conditions like two-part-tariffs, e.g. a two-year contract with a provider, consisting of a fixed monthly rate and variable costs for each call, can, however, imply considerable specificities built up by the buyer that are based on the mode-related properties of the transaction(s).[275]

---

[274] As a result, in case of opposite signs, they have compensatory effects, a property with significant effects for the analysis of shifts in business types. The assertion is supported by claims made by *Williamson, O. E.* (1985), that "...technology and organizational modes ought to be treated symmetrically; they are decision variables whose values are determined simultaneously" (p. 89). In principle, a particular design of one mechanism may be used in order to compensate for the specific design of the other and may shift quasi-rents positions between the involved parties.

[275] On such assessment of two-part tariffs see e.g. *Katz, M. L.* (1989), p. 699; *Rubin, P. H.* (1990), p. 125. For a general overview on pricing methods in order to enhance customer retention and loyalty see *Simon, H./Tacke, G./Woscidlo, B., et al.* (2000). Seminal analysis of two-part tariffs is provided by *Lewis, A.* (1941); *Oi, W. Y.* (1971); *Büschken, J.* (1997); *Possmeier, F.* (2000).

Even contractual arrangements such as frequent-flyer programs have been argued to generate some kind of seller-specific investment, although rather in the form of opportunity costs.[276] In summary, each party's business type is understood as the contracted "package"[277] of specifications covering contents and delivery structures of value and countervalue.

The third area (part II), here referred to as safeguards, covers those elements of the agreement that make provisions for the case that ex post conflicts arise which endanger the fulfillment of the intentions (part I). They are therefore concerned with issues of value protection. These part II-safeguards do not directly deal with the definition of the business types constellation, although they exert an indirect influence since the availability of better safeguards is assumed to encourage an actor's willingness to invest specifically.[278] In sum, the realized market offering covers the concrete design of all of these areas.[279] It is this market offering that is finally assessed by the potential buyer in its cost-benefit-calculus.[280]

---

[276] See *Lieberman, M. B./Montgomery, D. B.* (1988), p. 46; on opportunity costs in such context see *Plinke, W.* (1997), p. 44f.

[277] This understanding of the package notion draws on *Backhaus, K.* (2003), p. 321. See for further reference e.g. *Schade, C./Schott, E.* (1993a), p. 503, or *Blois, K. J.* (1996), pp. 169, 171. Related from a TCA angle: *Heide, J. B./John, G.* (1988), p. 33. The line drawn between the two elements of the contract is, however, somewhat artificial since both may flow into each other. For instance, a considerable downpayment by the customer during the early stages of a customized power station construction arguably belongs to those contractual specifications dealing with payment conditions. Because it reduces the gap between completion of performance and counterperformance, it serves at the same time as a safeguard for (at least parts of) the customer-specific investment undertaken by the supplier (see *Kaas, K. P.* (1992), p. 52ff; *Backhaus, K./Plinke, W./Rese, M.* (2004), (p. 96f).

[278] Any consideration on the availability of safeguards will necessarily imply an evaluation of the costs at which they are available. Generally, the availability of safeguards may vary with institutional conditions that influence the degree of security of property rights, such as stability and quality of legal and political environment (see briefly *Williamson, O. E.* (1985), p. 155; extensive discussions are found with *Henisz, W., J.* (1998); *Henisz, W., J./Williamson, O. E.* (1999); in an international marketing context, the problem has been explored e.g. by *Gatignon, H./Anderson, E.* (1988)). The availability of safeguards is, on the other hand, determined by a second component, that is, characteristics inherent to the particular transaction situation (e.g. attributes of the exchange parties, accessible technologies or properties of the particular markets), which may, for instance, render certain kinds of contracts infeasible (see *Williamson, O. E.* (1985), p. 179; recently: *Argyres, N. S./Liebeskind, J. P.* (1999); *Argyres, N. S./Liebeskind, J. P.* (2000)). As an example for the latter case consider a buyer seeking to purchase a complex information and data processing system based on a new technology. Actually, the buyer might prefer to invest in the whole system at a time, but not all functionalities of the system may alreday be fully developed to date. These circumstances force the buyer to delay the purchase of certain functionalities and unavoidably leads to entering into a relational contractual relationship. (Cases like this example have been characterized as "forced relational purchases", see e.g. *Reinkemeier, C.* (1998), p. 35f.)

[279] It should be noted that the notions of asset specificity and safeguards as adopted here with reference to the business types constellation framework differ to a certain extent from those advanced in the traditional TCA literature on organizational economics. While the understanding of asset specificity seems broader, the term

Yet, having described the fundamentals of the business construct, the question of what kind of contract (classical, neoclassical or relational) would now govern a disgruent business types constellation remains unanswered.[281] In fact, it is plausible that in such situations, each actor would still favor that kind of available contract that offers him the best relation of costs and benefits, taking into account the safeguards against opportunistic exploitation of idiosyncratic investments. Contractual preferences are, hence, imbalanced for disgruent constellations. The final agreement is not adequately suited to at least one, or, in case of a contractual compromise, both parties' business type. This surmise does not come as a surprise if one considers the emphasis on the properties of the three types of contracts flowing into one another, as expressed by *Macneil* (1978).[282] In many cases, one will find a hybrid kind of contract which has been, more or less extensively, negotiated prior to its conclusion and which specifies claims and obligations of the two parties. While in congruent constellations, claims and obligations of each party refer to the same business type and, by doing so, make the contract as a whole susceptible to clearer classification. For disgruent constellations, each party is expected to formulate its own claims and obligations according to its envisaged business type. Negotiations over these contractual elements may lead to concessions although not inevitably to the same degree by both parties. The result is a contract that, contingent on the concessions that have been made, specifies more or less disgruent "packages" of claims and obligations. Unambiguous categorization of the resulting contract is, therefore, not feasible. The example of a supplier of office furniture, taken from *Backhaus* (1999), serves to illuminate the point[283]:

---

safeguard is considerably narrower than what is often conceptualized in the TCA literature, for it excludes specific investments that directly relate to the value or countervalue component and also excludes aspects concerning the mode of delivery. Mainly responsible for this terminological divergence is the drawing of the line in order to define the business types constellation to include the structure of delivery of performance and counterperformance. As a result, mode-related mechanisms, such as payment terms that may be used intentionally as safeguards do not to qualify as part III-safeguards because, at the same time, they impact on the degree and horizon of asset specificity of the party concerned and, hence, on the final business type (constellation) of the transaction.

[280] See *Williamson, O. E.* (1985), p. 89f, for support on the need for simultaneous consideration of technological and contractual/organizational aspects. Thus, not only "...economics comes closer to being a "science of contract" than a "science of choice"." (*Buchanan, J. M.* (1975), p. 229), but aspects of contractual agreements are strengthened for the domain of marketing as well.

[281] See also *Heide, J. B.* (1994), p. 81.

[282] See *Macneil, I. R.* (1978), p. 887.

[283] See *Backhaus, K.* (2003), p. 599f.

S is a supplier of office furniture and sells furniture that can only be bought from this company and will, therefore, in the following be regarded as relying on so called "type specifications".[284] The pre-fabricated components sold by S each belong to one of the v offered product lines. Within one line, all components are suited to fit the other elements technically (mainly regarding connections between elements, fitting heights and sizes, etc.) and also from an aesthetic point of view. The supplier clearly seeks to sell the products in product business while potential customers are locked in after the purchase and would, therefore, buy in relational business. Usual payment conditions such as payment on delivery do not lead to a change in overall business type on either side. Buyers remain to a large degree substitutable during the period of time before the seller has received the full countervalue (payment). Buyers, on the other hand, will find it difficult to replace the seller without incurring considerable cost during the period of time until the envisaged value has been fully delivered, because this point in time refers not to the delivery date of the furniture but to the moment of its complete depreciation – including considerations regarding potentially necessary replacements of individual parts due to damages or concerning future extensions (additional furniture in already equipped rooms or furnishing additional rooms). The appropriate contract type would therefore imply (a) formulations of both parties´ rights and duties in the form of a classical contract (from the seller perspective), and (b) formulations of both parties´ claims and obligations in the form of a relational contract (from the buyer´s point of view). The realized contract is likely to be found somewhere in between. Long-term availability guarantees, for instance, represent an element that extends the seller´s duties and the buyer´s rights above purely "sharp in by clear agreement; sharp out by clear performance"-terms.

2.1.2.7   Type-specific marketing problems and management focus

What could be expected from the theoretical reasoning underlying the business types approach, has consequently been shown by the literature linking marketing and TCA: different degrees and forms of information asymmetries, specific investments, and opportunism associated with the various business types and constellations call for type-specific marketing

---

[284] Along with *Kleinaltenkamp*, this kind of technical product specification is referred to as "type" (specifications of products, systems or components that refer to one particular seller or user), as opposed to "standards" and "norms" (see *Kleinaltenkamp, M.* (1990), p. 2ff.; *Kleinaltenkamp, M.* (1993), p. 19ff also on the following definitions). "Standards" are product specifications that are defined by the market process, that is, they are characterized by their acceptance through a large number of actors (sellers and buyers) in a market. Usually, they have originally been developed by individual companies or groups of companies and have been adopted by other participants in the course of a diffusion process. Often they are also called "de-facto-standards". "Norms" (e.g. DIN) are product specifications that have been defined by a legislative body or by some other public institutions specifically concerned with the definition of specifications.

programs. Several authors have identified elements of marketing programs which can generally be regarded as imperative for particular business types and constellations.[285]

Product business

Without the danger of subsequent lock-in, the main problem parties which transact in this business type face is one of efficient *ex ante* information gathering in order to reduce environmental uncertainty.

Buyers who purchase an object in product business seek information on whether, and to what degree, the product or service is likely to fit their needs. The seller's marketing program has to address this need for information, focusing on communication and information policy (e.g. advertising, promotions or at trade fairs). Relatively good replaceability of suppliers from the customer's point of view implies that the traded values are to a certain degree interchangeable. Depending on how pronounced this situation is, various forms of information will be most important ranging from directly product-related information, in the case of very high exchangeability, to such information at the other end of the spectrum that has more the character of a surrogate as, for instance, branding. Rather high degrees of comparability in the case of buyer product businesses are likely to lead to a high significance of the pricing policy as well.

On the other hand, a supplier selling in product business also faces an information problem. Despite the relatively high interchangeability of the individual buyer, information on the market as a whole is important: it is on this level that the supplier invests and seeks amortization. Market research based on relatively large numbers of respondents from the relevant market(s) is used to satisfy the seller's information need in order to, for instance, derive price-demand functions. Communication tools that are designed, for example, to encourage customer feedback are also targeted towards mass markets.

---

[285] Seminal contributions which form the basis for the following outline include *Backhaus, K./Aufderheide, D./Späth, G.-M.* (1994); *Aufderheide, D./Backhaus, K.* (1995); *Kaas, K. P.* (1995b); *Plinke, W.* (1997); *Reinkemeier, C.* (1998); *Backhaus, K.* (2003).

Project business

The most critical issue in project business is to efficiently ensure a high probability of realizing the envisaged profit – despite the danger of opportunistic exploitation which arises from behavioral uncertainty, possibly combined with environmental uncertainty.

Due to the lock-in associated with their idiosyncratic investment, buyers who purchase a good in project business face considerable *ex post* uncertainty which could not (even at a very high cost) fully be eliminated by ex ante information gathering. However, due to the well-defined horizon of the transaction, rather detailed specifications of exchanged value and countervalue are feasible and usually include reference to some arbitral institution. Primarily, formal safeguarding in terms of extensive design of contracts (design of incentives and control mechanisms) becomes important. Definition of environmental contingencies and resulting consequences, in case they actually occur, is done as completely as efficient in order to protect the parties against both kinds of uncertainty. Additionally, various means with regard to product, pricing or, to a lesser extent, communication policy are at the seller's hands for credibly signalling to the buyer his competence (as a safeguard against environmental uncertainty) and good will (as a safeguard against behavioral uncertainty). Examples include the management of references (referee customers) or installation of competence centers.

Specific investments undertaken by suppliers that sell in project business result in an analogous need for safeguarding. Measures that the seller can actively take are mostly related to appropriate contract design. Examples include bringing the payment structure in line with the time horizon and structure of the specific investment ("split tariffs"), defining the buyer's obligations and consequences for various eventualities, or active claim management.[286] Outside these contractual options, the seller's means for safeguarding are, albeit existent, fairly limited to careful selection of customers. Also, there may, for instance, be a situation where an oligopolistic market is generally characterized by unilateral specific investments on behalf of the sellers. They could – depending on legal restrictions – seek to establish

---

[286] See *Backhaus, K./Köhl, T.* (1999); *Köhl, T.* (2000) on claim management in industrial marketing.

provisions for coordinated action against "bad buyers" in case one of the sellers is faced with opportunistic exploitation.[287]

Relational business

A party transacting in relational business undertakes a specific investment that reaches beyond the initial purchase or sale, respectively. Efficient safeguarding of the expected profits against opportunism remains the most pressing concern, however, aggravated now by an ill-defined horizon for intended amortization. Contractual design becomes less effective in safeguarding, raising the importance of informal credible commitments and credible signalling mechanisms such as reputation even more.[288] Reputation has been characterized in this context as the sum from individual expectations and experiences regarding both the criteria of competence, and of behavioral reliability or trustworthiness.[289] What makes reputation so very suitable as a safeguard is the asymmetric nature of its development: while it takes many individual events and a long time to build a (good) reputation, its destruction can, under extreme conditions, be achieved in a single act of misbehavior. Therefore, reputation can serve as an effective hostage – unless the expected (short-term) returns from exploitation are greater to the potentially opportunistic party than the expected (long-term) gains from behaving according to the reputation.

In the case of buyers purchasing in relational business, the seller's prime effort lies in the management of buyer perceived uncertainties. This requires influencing the buyer's perception of the danger of not achieving the goals attached to the transaction. In the literature, basically two ways of having an impact have been distinguished[290]: first, establishing a seller-side counterbalance, and, second, reducing the buyer lock-in. While the latter path, essentially, leads to a change in business type and will, hence, not be regarded as belonging to the set of type-specific marketing tools, the establishment of a seller-side counterbalance can take place either with respect to a particular relationship (where it would also constitute a change in business type), but also on a more general level with regard to the market as such. In that

---

[287] See *Backhaus, K./Büschken, J.* (1999) for related considerations on the industry level.

[288] Seminal contributions to the analysis of reputative effects include *Klein, B./Leffler, K. B.* (1981); *Telser, L. G.* (1981); *Kreps, D. M./Wilson, R.* (1982);*Weigelt, K./Camerer, C.* (1988).

[289] See *Backhaus, K.* (2003), p. 688.

[290] See e.g. *Reinkemeier, C.* (1998); *Backhaus, K.* (2003), p. 631ff.

respect, it can be established, for instance, by means of contractual elements such as guarantees or of credible commitments. Credible (because costly) signals referring to the seller's competence include test installations, engaging in reference relationships, or the installation of a service network. All these features may also contribute to the establishment of a reputation or corporate brand.[291] The decisive factor in its building up is, however, the corresponding delivery of performance and behavior in the individual situation concerned. Communication is important in order to support "spreading the news" of these cases.[292] Relevant activities include encouraging articles in specialist journals, or establishment and support of user groups. Communication in impersonal, seller-controlled mass media is likely to have a lesser effect on creating credibility.[293] Nevertheless, it may be used to generally enhance buyers' awareness of the seller company and underline a certain desired image. Seller marketing management will also include considerations on balancing prices over time, for instance, low initial investment requirements coupled with high prices for follow-up transactions or vice versa.[294] Decisions in this area will be influenced not only by what degree of initial lock-in is accepted by customers but also by the potential for discriminating between initial and follow-on customers.

In case of a seller business type relational business the considerations outlined for seller project business, essentially, remain valid. Reliance on formal contractual safeguards is reduced due to the nature of the business type. Ensuring investment amortization rests more than elsewhere on the promotion of potential-oriented capabilities such as innovativeness or flexibility in order to sustain the competitive advantage. Under certain circumstances, vertical marketing or multi-stage-marketing, respectively, can represent an additional way of safeguarding by reducing the seller's replaceability: if successful, a pull-effect stemming from following market stages (e.g. from end users as in the case of automobile tires) is provoked

---

[291] On the relationship between reputation and branding, and on the risk reduction related importance of branding in industrial marketing contingent on product complexity, maintenance intensity, etc. see *Hutton, J. G.* (1997); *Mudambi, S.* (2002), p. 527.

[292] A comprehensive analysis of the communication mix in such costellations has been provided by *Bergmann, H.* (1995) who focuses on the marketing of CIM systems, in particular.

[293] See e.g. *Cox, D. F.* (1967c), p. 605ff.

[294] Se e.g. *Simon, H./Tacke, G./Woscidlo, B., et al.* (2000), p. 327f.

that stimulates demand of direct customers.[295] Particularly well known examples of such brands include Kevlar and Teflon (Dupont), Pentium and Celeron (Intel), Styroforam (Dow), and Thisulate (3M).[296]

2.1.2.8 Interpretation of the business types concept as a typological theory

Having outlined the structuring approach which forms the analytical basis for this paper, a few words remain to be said about its interpretation in the direction of a typological theory. This relies on three requirements to be satisfied.

First, two kinds of constructs, ideal types as well as first-order constructs, would have to be identified.[297] It is proposed here, that the TCA-based business types may well represent such ideal types which can hardly be found in practice in their purest form. Each business type or constellation, respectively, is argued to be optimal, that is, it is expected to result in a maximal level of some dependent variable, for instance, efficiency, given a certain set of antecedents.[298] These factors represent the first-order constructs for description of each ideal type and can be summarized in the (degree and horizon of) asset specificity associated with that type. They can be found in conditions such as environmental uncertainty or potential productivity gains from specific investments, and, further, in attributes of each type such as marketing problems and programs, as identified on the basis of TCA reasoning.[299] However, a divergence between the business types approach and the "classical" ideal type properties exists in the sense that the business types only represent focal points, that is, extreme cases of a continuous spectrum of

---

[295] For general discussions of multi-stage marketing see *Kunkel, R.* (1977); *Jackson, D. M./Krampf, R. F./Konopa, L. J.* (1982); *Rudolph, M.* (1989); *Baumgarth, C.* (1998b); *Kemper, A. C.* (2000), p. 306ff., *Kleinaltenkamp, M./Rudolph, M.* (2000) and the literature on ingredient branding in general (e.g. *Norris, D. G.* (1992); *Oelsnitz, D. v. d.* (1995); *Baumgarth, C./Freter, H./Schmidt, R.* (1996); *Baumgarth, C.* (1998a).

[296] See *Mudambi, S.* (2002), p. 532.

[297] See on the following *Doty, D. H./Glick, W. H.* (1994), chapter 2.1.1.2 and the literature referred to there.

[298] The general efficiency criterion has been refined into the remediableness criterion which "...holds that an extant mode of organization for which no superior *feasible* alternative can be described and *implemented* with expected net gains is *presumed* to be efficient."(*Williamson, O. E.* (2000), p. 601; see also e.g. *Williamson, O. E.* (1999a), p. 316)

[299] See chapters 2.1.2.6 and 3.2.3. For similar argumentation but with regard to the original modes of governance in TCA see *Williamson, O. E.* (2000), p. 606.

feasible and optimal governance modes.[300] Its continuity prevails not only in "muddy reality" but is also acknowledged within the theoretical concept. This is evident from incorporating different degrees of asset specificity, ranging form slightly above 0% to 100%, in project business as well as in relational business. Thereby, variations in the levels of the antecedents are accounted for. And while these "hybrid" modes are not explicitly depicted in the model, they are argued to still be potentially optimal if they fulfill the second requirement which is outlined in the following paragraph.[301]

Second, the typological theory is required to stress the internal consistency among the first-order constructs of each type and then hypothesize the consequences of a consistent pattern for the level of a dependent variable. Such reasoning can be provided on the grounds of the business types framework. Transaction situations which resemble less closely one of the consistent combinations of factors as described for the ideal types, are postulated to be less efficient or effective, respectively.[302] For instance, a marketing program which lacks a strong emphasis on reputation in a situation with high environmental uncertainty and high potential gains from specific investments on behalf of the buyers is postulated to be less successful.

Third, predictions associated with the approach should be susceptible to testing and disconfirmation. For TCA in general, the significance of falsifiability has explicitly been acknowledged by many scholars.[303] Implicitly, it has been acknowledged through the existence of a large body of empirical literature concerned with the very issue.[304] Several authors have assessed the state of empirical research and theory testing in TCA and concluded

---

[300] *Doty, D. H./Glick, W. H.* (1994), p. 237, briefly hint at ideal types within a continuum as a special but little promising case.

[301] For support on such view of ideal types see e.g. *Campbell-Hunt, C.* (2000), p. 130.

[302] For governance mode-related argumentation based on internal consistencies of attributes see e.g. *Williamson, O. E.* (1991a), p. 271, who argues that "... each viable form of governance ... is defined by a syndrome of attributes that bear a supporting relation to one another. Many hypothetical forms of organization never arise or quickly die out, because they combine inconsistent features." Viable governance forms in this sense would correspond to the proposed ideal types.

[303] See e.g. *Masten, S. E.* (1995), p. xi; *Williamson, O. E.* (1998), p. 35f; *Williamson, O. E.* (2000), p. 604.

[304] See e.g. *Masten, S. E.* (1984); *Leffler, K. B./Rucker, R. R.* (1991); *Masten, S. E./Meehan Jr, J. W./Snyder, E. A.* (1991); *Heide, J. B.* (1994); *Poppo, L./Zenger, T.* (1998); *Stump, R. L./Joshi, A. W.* (1998); *Nickerson, J. A./Hamilton, B. H./Wada, T.* (2001). Comprehensive overviews and syntheses have been provided e.g. by *Boerner, C. S./Macher, J. T.* (2001); *Geyskens, I./Steenkamp, J.-B. E. M./Kumar, N.* (2003).

that it was in rather good shape.[305] The business types approach itself has not yet been explicitly tested. However, the above arguments may be transferred in principle since the concept builds on TCA. They might be interpreted as providing promising hints that the falsifiability criterion might be fulfilled here as well. If an interpretation of the business types framework as typological theory is considered to be plausible, the framework should be particularly well-suited for the derivation of (marketing) strategies. These could serve to establish internal consistency regarding antecedents and attributes, such as, precisely, marketing programs. In any case, however, the combination of the business types framework with a strategic management perspective requires first of all a detailed outline of meaning and implications of the strategy notion in this respect.

2.2   Defining the notion of strategy

2.2.1   A framework for organizing the "strategic variety"

Notions of the term strategy are as numerous and as varied as the spectrum of theoretical and practical fields that draw on it and interpret it for the particular context.[306] Based on dispersed outlines of criteria in the literature and drawing on some more complete alternative frameworks, the variety is structured here according to several criteria which limit the scope of the specific definition and which are depicted in *Fig. 10*.[307] In particular, the criteria included in this framework allow for relatively parsimonious, yet meaningful delimitation of the strategy notion within this research context.

---

[305] See e.g. *Williamson, O. E.* (1998), p. 39f.; *Joskow, P. L.* (1991), p. 81; *Masten, S. E.* (1995), p. xi; *Masten, S. E.* (1997), p. 43ff. This point has, however, not gone undebated. For opposing positions see e.g. *Simon, H. A.* (1991), p. 27. Based on empirical evidence, *Rangan, V. K./Corey, E. R./Cespedes, F.* (1993), for instance, have identified a need for broad conceptual modification of TCA.

[306] Examples include military science, biology and ecology, psychology, economics, and business/management (*Sudharshan, D.* (1995), p. 21). For a recent review of the history of business strategy see *Kay, J./McKiernan, P./Faulkner, D. O.* (2003).

[307] See for related systematizations *Venkatraman, N.* (1989), p. 946ff, who uses scope, hierarchical level, domain and "intentions vs realizations" as criteria; *Chakravarthy, B./Doz, Y.* (1992), who categorizes on the basis of underlying focus, theoretical foundations and methodology. An alternative structure has, for instance, been advanced by *Mintzberg, H. T.* (1987), who identifies five different definitions of strategy (plan, ploy, pattern, position, perspective). Overlappings and differences with this latter concept will briefly be sketched where appropriate.

The three main discriminating criteria refer to the decision theoretic orientation[308], the analytical focus, and the subject area which may, if necessary, be further subdivided in order to arrive at a more narrowly defined subject matter. Supposedly, the three criteria are not completely independent of each other: certain subject areas or particular analytical foci may well be associated with typical research methodologies.[309] Methodology could then implicitly establish a link between these criteria and restrict the scope for selection.

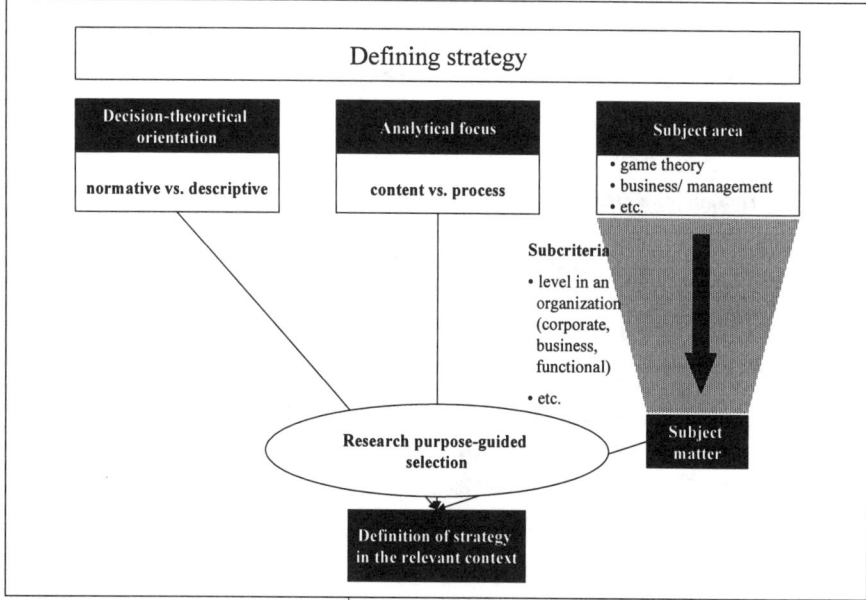

Fig. 10: Criteria for structuring the variety of definitions regarding the notion of strategy[310]

2.2.1.1   Decision theoretic orientation as organizing criterion

Definitions of strategy can be distinguished according to their (implicit or explicit) **decision theoretic orientation**. Interpreting two basic schools of thought with regard to decision

---

[308]   This notion is related to the criterion "purpose" as advanced by *Huff, A. S./Reger, R. K.* (1987), p. 213.

[309]   See e.g. *Chakravarthy, B./Doz, Y.* (1992), p. 6, who propose this for research on strategy content and strategy process, respectively.

[310]   The level in an organization is also sometimes referred to as "locus of strategy" (see *Varadarajan, P. R./Clark, T.* (1994), p. 93).

theory, a prescribing (normative) and a describing (descriptive) view, respectively, can be identified.[311] The *normative* perspective rests on an ex ante assessment and regards strategies as rationally or, at least, consciously planned bundles of actions.[312] In order to arrive at some superordinate goal, a number of individual actions has to be coordinated and this is achieved by means of a strategy. This strategy is the result of a deliberate or conscious and purpose-guided intellectual process that *precedes* the actions. In establishing this view in the business literature *Chandler's* (1962) definition of strategy as "...the determination of the basic long-term goals and objectives of an enterprise, and the adoption of courses of action and the allocation of resources necessary for carrying out these goals..."[313] has been seminal. The *descriptive* approach views strategy as "...a pattern in a stream of decisions/ actions..."[314] or, in other words, as a "...*consistency* in behavior, *whether or not* intended..."[315], which can only be identified as such from an *ex post* perspective. This position has mainly been advanced by *Mintzberg* and co-researchers. In their analysis on the development of strategies, they argue against the idea that strategies can always be planned ahead of the actions being taken, and also challenge the surmise that they can always be consciously and intentionally developed.[316] This is not to deny that some *intended* strategies may in fact be carried out and

---

[311] See on the following ideas the seminal work by *Schreyögg, G.* (1984); also *Baumgarth, C.* (1998b), p. 26ff; *Macharzina, K.* (1999), p. 197ff (also for a general overview on the topic). A choice between both of these approaches necessarily rests on the concrete research purpose. *Macharzina, K.* (1999), p. 202, suggests the normative concept to be more appropriate for ideal-type considerations and the descriptive view to be more suitable in the context of empirical research. The latter proposition has been challenged, for instance, by *Baumgarth, C.* (1998b), p. 27 (fn 68), on the grounds of normatively-oriented empirical research. Comprehensive surveys on decision theory can be found with e.g. *Meyer, R.* (2000); *Bamberg, G./Coenenberg, A. G.* (2002).

[312] Recent contributions in this tradition include *Chakravarthy, B.* (1997); *Teece, D. J./Pisano, G./Shuen, A.* (1997); *Eisenhardt, K. M./Sull, D. N.* (2001); *Tarlatt, A.* (2001), p. 14; *Ambrosini, V./Jenkins, M.* (2002), p. 264; *Montaguti, E./Kuester, S./Robertson, T. S.* (2002). The normative view essentially coincides with what has been labelled "strategy as plan" by *Mintzberg, H. T.* (1987), p. 11f. He includes in this category, however, a particular form of strategy as a plan, which he names "strategy as a ploy" in order to describe a "...specific "maneuver" intended to outwit an opponent or competitor" (p. 12). Explicitly referring to *Porter, M. E.* (1980) and *Schelling, T. C.* (1980), he argues that this form mainly relates to market signals and actions to preempt competitive responses. Relating to the concrete *content* of a strategy, the argument will be discussed in the according context (see chapter 2.2.1.3).

[313] *Chandler, A. D.* (1962), p. 13. Other influential contributions include *Ansoff, H. I.* (1965); *Learned, E. P./Christensen, C. R./Andrews, K. R., et al.* (1965); *Andrews, K. R.* (1971).

[314] *Mintzberg, H. T.* (1978), p. 935; A decision is defined as "...a commitment to action, usually a commitment of resources"; also see *Mintzberg, H. T./McHugh, A.* (1985), p.161; *Mintzberg, H. T./Waters, J. A.* (1985), p. 257.

[315] *Mintzberg, H. T.* (1987), p. 12.

[316] See *Mintzberg, H. T.* (1978), p. 935; *Mintzberg, H. T./McHugh, A.* (1985), p. 162.

will later be found as parts of the pattern which includes all *realized* strategies. However, this pattern also comprises actions that have simply emerged without any underlying conscious ("strategic") planning. Such purely *emergent* strategies are, though, expected to be just as rare as purely deliberate ones. In sum, the predominant role of hybrids is emphasized.[317]

2.2.1.2 Analytical focus as organizing criterion

The second criterion, here referred to as **analytical focus**, relates to the distinction between the content-oriented and the process-oriented perspective.[318] Although this separation has not gone undisputed, it still represents a generally accepted structure in the literature on strategic management.[319] Research on *strategy content* focuses on the "What", the substance of the strategy. With regard to the above normative characterization, the question would be *what actions* should be taken in order to get closer to a given goal, *what* should their *timing* be, and *what resources* should be allocated to each, under varying environmental contexts.[320] *Process*-oriented approaches to understanding strategy, in general, deal with the "How's" of strategy and consequently center around the processes related to strategy formulation ("finding strategy") on the one hand, and to strategy implementation ("using strategy"), on the other hand.[321] Sometimes, strategy evaluation and strategy control are added as further

[317] See *Mintzberg, H. T./Waters, J. A.* (1985), p. 258. Recent empirical research building on this tradition includes *Yetton, P. W./Johnston, K. D./Craig, J. F.* (1994); *Kowalczyk, S. J./Giusti, G. W.* (1998); *Burmann, C.* (2001); *Burmann, C.* (2002b).

[318] See *Ginsberg, A.* (1988), p. 560; *Chakravarthy, B./Doz, Y.* (1992), p. 5; *Varadarajan, P. R./Jayachandran, S.* (1999), p. 120f; *Rühli, E./Schmidt, S. L.* (2001), p. 532ff. Recently, *Varadarajan, P. R.* (1999) focuses on three aspects at the interface of content and strategy formulation. The terminology ("analytical focus") draws on *Chakravarthy, B./Doz, Y.* (1992). The proposition of a distinction between "strategy" and "implementation" (see *Sudharshan, D.* (1995), p. 5), is not unambiguously supported by the literature.

[319] See e.g. *Huff, A. S./Reger, R. K.* (1987) or *Pettigrew, A. M.* (1992), p. 7, who states the widespread acceptance of the distinction but calls for more integration. *Schendel, D.* (1992), p. 3, concludes that, at least regarding business practice, both perspectives are inseparable.

[320] *Mintzberg, H. T.* (1987), p. 15ff, subdivides the content-related perspective into „strategy as position" and "strategy as perspective". While the first notion refers to strategy as a means of locating the organization in the environment, the second concept interprets strategy as an "ingrained way of perceiving the world" (p. 16). The emphasis is on its conceptual nature: essentially, it only exists because of, and in the mind of the relevant person(s).

[321] See *Schreyögg, G.* (1984), p. 84; *Van de Ven, A. H.* (1992), p. 170; *Al-Laham, A.* (1997); *Varadarajan, P. R./Jayachandran, S.* (1999), p. 121. The process-oriented view can be traced back to *Barnard, C. I.* (1938) and *Simon, H. A.* (1945). Seminal contributions to strategy formulation include *Bower, J. L./Doz, Y.* (1979); *Schreyögg, G.* (1984), p. 89ff; *Burgelman, R. A.* (1991); contributions to strategy implementation are provided e.g. by *Schreyögg, G.* (1984)p. 124ff; *Hrebiniak, L. G./Joyce, W. F.* (2001); *Tarlatt, A.* (2001).

subprocesses.[322] Recently, attempts have been made to better integrate these perspectives that have traditionally been treated as separate streams.[323] Research on strategy formulation is largely concerned with (organizational) decision-making processes and underlying rationality assumptions, analytical tools which provide the informational input for these processes, planning methods, formal management systems and the impact of power and politics.[324] Analysis of strategy implementation refers to the way in which some strategy (content) is put into practice and covers the structures and control mechanisms that are needed in order to realize a specific strategy content.[325] This includes examination of the organizational structure and culture, environmental conditions and their feedback effects on the strategy.

2.2.1.3   *Subject area and subject matter as organizing criteria*

The third criterion for categorizing definitions of strategy refers to the relevant subject area. Among the multitude of fields that have drawn on the idea of strategy, the most relevant in the context of this work are economic and business/management approaches.

2.2.1.3.1   *Subject area I: the economic domain*

The **economic perspective** on strategy has decisively been shaped by game theory. *Von Neumann/Morgenstern* (1944) who are generally regarded as its founders have been particularly influential in defining strategy as "... a complete plan: a plan which specifies what choices he [the player] will make in every possible situation, for every possible actual information which he may possess at that moment in conformity with the pattern of information which the rules of the game provide for him for that case."[326] Strategy in a game

---

[322] See *Schendel, D. E./Hofer, C. W.* (1979), p. 16ff.

[323] *Pettigrew, A. M.* (1992), p. 6; *Varadarajan, P. R./Jayachandran, S.* (1999), p. 139.

[324] For an overview, see *Al-Laham, A.* (1997), p. 136ff. Also see *Huff, A. S./Reger, R. K.* (1987); *Ginsberg, A.* (1988), p. 560; *Day, G. S.* (1990), pp. 45ff, 33ff; *Eisenhardt, K. M./Zbaracki, M. J.* (1992); *Rajagopalan, N./Rasheed, A./Datta, D. K., et al.* (1997) extensively on strategic decision making; *Varadarajan, P. R./Jayachandran, S.* (1999), p. 121.

[325] See *Al-Laham, A.* (1997), p. 174ff; *Varadarajan, P. R./Jayachandran, S.* (1999), pp. 121, 140.

[326] *von Neumann, J./Morgenstern, O.* (1944), p. 79. *Rasmusen, E.* (2001), p. 16, summarizes that a player's strategy "...is a rule that tells him which action to choose at each instant of the game, given his information set." An action refers to a choice the player can make (p. 13), and a strategy set or space is defined as the set of strategies available to a player (p. 16).

theoretic perspective is, however, constrained in its *direct* applicability to other fields (1) by its often strong assumptions, for instance concerning the information structure, (2) by the need to formulate rather abstract models with only limited numbers of parameters in order to be able to handle the formal complexity, and (3) by the frequent ambiguity of results due to situations with multiple equilibria.[327] Despite the fact that the resulting contexts are often highly stylized, if the decisive elements of a problem are captured, important lessons can be learned from the core ideas of game theoretic strategy analysis due to its focus on interaction, that is, on the interdependency of players actions. Other players' (e.g. competitors) reactions and changes in the rules of the game (e.g. legal environment) are explicitly considered. *Brandenburger/Nalebuff* (1996), for instance, have devoted a whole book on outlining how game theoretic reasoning can be applied to business practice – stripped of its mathematical "disguise".[328]

The game theoretic perspective has also had a strong impact on what is often referred to as strategizing in TCA – despite admittedly covering only a fraction of what makes part of business strategy in sum.[329] This TCA view on strategy has mainly been shaped by *Williamson*. He has outlined his ideas briefly in a number of publications and has also made them the explicit issue of two articles.[330] Very fundamentally, he distinguishes between two broad approaches to business strategy which are set apart by their underlying economic *motivations*.[331] The first approach, referred to as *"strategizing"*, is seen to rely on (structural

---

[327] See e.g. *Wambach, A.* (2001).

[328] See *Brandenburger, A. M./Nalebuff, B. J.* (1996). Other positive assessments and illustrations on the applicability of game theoretic reasoning to business practice in general and marketing strategy in particular include *MacMillan, J.* (1992); *Sudharshan, D.* (1995), pp. 21f, 53ff; *Varadarajan, P. R./Jayachandran, S.* (1999), p. 126f; *Jost, P.-J.* (2001); *Wambach, A.* (2001); *Regan, S.* (2002). A more sceptical view has been outlined, for instance, by *Dolan, R. J.* (1981).

[329] See *Williamson, O. E.* (1991c), p. 75.

[330] See for brief sketches e.g. *Williamson, O. E.* (1985), p. 373ff; *Williamson, O. E.* (1998), p. 47f. In his articles "Strategizing, Economizing, and Economic Organization" and "Strategy research: Governance and Competence Perspectives", he extensively explores the analytical potential of TCA for the subject of business strategy (see *Williamson, O. E.* (1991c); *Williamson, O. E.* (1999b)).

[331] Recently, attempts have been made to better integrate both perspectives (see *Nickerson, J. A./Vanden Bergh, R.* (1999)). The research purpose is to obtain a more complete picture of governance mode choice. See *Riordan, M. H./Williamson, O. E.* (1985) for the first model to explicitly consider asset specificity as a choice variable. The main merits of the *Nickerson/Vanden Bergh* (1999) model can be seen in further developing an optimization calculus in TCA and also in the integration of game theoretic reasoning. Yet, their model also lacks an explicit notion of effectiveness.

market) power reasoning and limitations on competition like deterring and disciplining actual and potential rivals.[332] Characterized as "clever ploys and positioning"[333], game theory is considered the appropriate theoretical concept to tackle the relevant issues which could be summarized illustratively in the words of the headings of a seminal article by *Milgrom/Roberts* (1982): "Predation, Reputation, and Entry Deterrence".[334] The choice of words as well as the understanding of this branch suggests a close similarity with *Mintzberg's* (1987) "strategy as ploy". The fact that *Mintzberg* (1987) considers this form of strategy to represent just a small element of the whole picture supports the surmise that only a fraction of business strategy is captured by this form of strategizing. The remaining significant rest of business strategy considerations are referred to as elements of the second, (more fundamental) *"economizing"* approach to business strategy. Adopting a very broad interpretation, this part encompasses all issues that are concerned with "value realization"[335], which is regarded as equivalent to efficiency reasoning targeted at both production costs and governance costs, or, as other scholars have put it, equivalent to "lower costs or, [...] higher quality of product performance"[336]. Such interpretation has recently been taken up by OO3) who conceptualizes strategy as "...the creation, appropriation and protection of value"[337] and argues that transaction costs play a fundamental role in all of these processes. In fact, he claims that it is only in the presence of positive transaction costs that strategic problems evolve and bases this assertion in a comparison with a zero-transaction-cost setting based on the *"Coase theorem"*.[338]

---

[332] See also *Teece, D. J./Pisano, G./Shuen, A.* (1997), p. 528, who argue though from a resource-based perspective.

[333] *Williamson, O. E.* (1991c), p. 75.

[334] *Milgrom, P./Roberts, J.* (1982). Other seminal articles on this topic are *Dixit, A.* (1980); *Kreps, D. M./Wilson, R.* (1982).

[335] As opposed to strategizing which, supposedly, does not create value (see *Williamson, O. E.* (1999b), 1103).

[336] *Teece, D. J./Pisano, G./Shuen, A.* (1997), p. 513, in outlining models of strategy that emphasize efficiency.

[337] *Foss, N. J.* (2003), p. 139ff.

[338] See *Foss, N. J.* (2003), drawing on *Coase, R. H.* (1960).

Despite subscribing to the surmise that "...transaction cost economics deals with many of the key issues with which business strategy is or should be concerned"[339], three additional points have to be made on this perspective, if it builds on a strict distinction between "economizing" and "strategizing" as proposed by *Williamson*.

The **first** argument refers to the terminology: the notion of strategizing is reserved by *Williamson* for a rather small fraction of what may be the motivations underlying a business strategy as it is treated in the marketing literature. Therefore, the use of this terminology in a marketing context could potenially be hampered by misunderstandings. This point is emphasized by the fact that other authors who draw on the same dichotomy propose a fundamentally different understanding – despite explicitly referring to TCA.[340] Moreover, the line between the two different motivations may sometimes be blurry, as suggested by *Williamson* (1991) himself.[341]

The **second** issue concerns the idea that strategizing is mainly relevant for only a few firms possessing market power.[342] Structural market power is understood in this work in terms of unequal *ex ante* market power of potential transaction partners. This differs from power which arises as a result of the fundamental transformation. Since this latter issue concerns those two parties that have already engaged in a transaction relationship, it will not be referred to as market power in the following analysis, but rather as bargaining power.

Taking up the above surmise, from a marketing point of view, three arguments can be advanced in favor of a more differentiated assessment: first, (potential) entrants in a market are likely to find considerations based on game theoretic analysis of predation, reputation, or entry deterrence just as important as the incumbent. Second, if strategizing is a power issue, the definition of power and the identification of its sources become crucial for its significance. For instance, power resulting from knowledge might render strategizing relevant in a large

---

[339] *Williamson, O. E.* (1991c), p. 90; similarly: *Rumelt, R. P./Schendel, D./Teece, D. J.* (1991), p. 14; *Foss, N. J.* (2003); *Nickerson, J. A./Hamilton, B. H./Wada, T.* (2001), p. 251. Linkages between TCA and strategic management have already been discussed previously e.g. by *Day, G. S./Klein, S.* (1987).

[340] See *Kim, K.* (1999), p. 218ff. Again others have described the synthesis of market positioning and governance issues as "positioning – economizing perspective" (see *Nickerson, J. A./Hamilton, B. H./Wada, T.* (2001), p. 253).

[341] See *Williamson, O. E.* (1991c), p. 75.

[342] See *Williamson, O. E.* (1991c), p. 75.

number of situations, e.g. in case a firm obtains temporary market power due to an innovation.[343] Third, market structure-based divergences in power are an issue, once deviations from the idea that "...the two parties can be presumed [...] roughly, to be dealing with each other on a parity..."[344] are explicitly introduced.[345] If one agrees with these arguments, the scope for "strategizing" behavior widens.

Third, it has recently been argued that even such issues that have been regarded as primarily related to strategizing in the traditional TCA literature may actually be grounded in transaction cost reasoning.[346] Whether or not this view is shared, the general a priori discard of such issues does not seem appropriate for this analysis.

Another seminal contribution to the relationship between TCA and strategic management that is related in its arguments to transaction cost reasoning has been provided by *Mahoney/Pandian* (1992).[347] Along with *Bowman* (1974), they define the essence of strategy to be a "continuing search for rent"[348] with rent being the excess return from a resource above the owner's opportunity costs, that is, an above-normal rate of return.[349] Different types of such rents are subsequently identified. *Ricardian* rents are earned due to the ownership of scarce, valuable resources (e.g. patents or copyrights). *Monopoly* rents are seen to stem from barriers to entry whether due to government protection or collusive arrangements and the alike. *Entrepreneurial* rents are achieved by risk-taking and entrepreneurial insight, and quasi-rents, finally, are derived from idiosyncratic (use of) resources. In the tradition of *Porter* (1985), they consider the generation of such rents as the core issue of striving for competitive

---

[343] On the relationship between knowledge and power see e.g. *Stigler, G. J.* (1961). These issues are discussed in more detail in chapter 3.3.4.2.

[344] *Williamson, O. E.* (1998), p. 30.

[345] See e.g. *Heide, J. B./John, G.* (1992), p. 41, drawing on *Stinchcombe, A. L./Heimer, C. A.* (1985).

[346] See *Foss, N. J.* (2003).

[347] See *Mahoney, J. T./Pandian, J. R.* (1992) on the following argumentation. On an assessment of their work regarding TCA see e.g.*Williamson, O. E.* (1999b), p. 1095

[348] *Bowman, E. H.* (1974), p. 47.

[349] See *Tollison, R. D.* (1982), p. 575ff. The definition is similar to what *Alchian, A. A./Woodward, S.* (1988), p. 67, refer to as a "pure quasi-rent" which they define as "...the excess above the return necessary to maintain a resource's current service flow, which can be the means to recover sunk costs".

advantages.[350] Thereby, *Mahoney/Pandian* (1992), essentially, define strategy as the search for competitive advantages. Although their classification does not focus on the relationships between different types of rent (for instance, regarding the impact of knowledge as power), it nevertheless offers valuable insights into what economic aspects could be considered in examining the search for competitive advantages.

2.2.1.3.2   Subject area II: the domain of (industrial marketing) management

The second subject area which has to be considered in this context is **management** and **industrial marketing management** in particular. From a very broad perspective, some authors have proposed a general definition for strategy in this area. *Hunt* and colleagues (2000), for instance, define business strategy "…as the match a business makes between its internal resources and skills and the opportunities and risks created by its external environment."[351] Most scholars, however, adopt a narrower interpretation and, hence, apply a further structuring criterion which is the *level of an organization* at which strategy takes place. Generally, the following three levels are distinguished[352]: *corporate strategy* takes place at the highest decision-making level in an organization and is regarded to define and coordinate the portfolio of business arenas in which a company competes. *Business (unit) strategy* defines the concrete way in which each particular business unit competes in its marketplace. According to *Varadarajan/Clark* (1994), it is concerned with "the achievement and maintenance of competitive advantage in specific product-market domains."[353] *Functional strategies* refer to the activities and decisions taken in order to generate the required competencies in the relevant functional area (production, finance, controlling, human resources etc.). Over and above that, there is some debate on the conceptualization of functional strategies in the literature. A particular issue is whether functional strategies are

---

[350] See *Mahoney, J. T./Pandian, J. R.* (1992), p. 364; *Porter, M. E.* (1985) (2nd ed. with a new introduction: 1998); *Teece, D. J./Pisano, G./Shuen, A.* (1997) also examine the relationship between rents and strategy from different perspectives.

[351] *Hunt, S. D./Lambe, C. J.* (2000), p. 17; see also *Hunt, S. D.* (2000), p. 67.

[352] See for categorization and subsequent characterization *Vancil, R. F./Lorange, P.* (1975); *Hofer, C. W./Schendel, D. E.* (1978); *Varadarajan, P. R./Clark, T.* (1994), p. 94; *Hax, A. C./Majluf, N. S.* (1996), p. 5ff; *Backhaus, K.* (2003), p. 213; *Macharzina, K.* (1999), p. 203ff; *Varadarajan, P. R./Jayachandran, S.* (1999), p. 120. Recently, interdependencies among strategy at the different levels have explicitly been analyzed (see e.g. *Varadarajan, P. R./Jayachandran, S./White, J. C.* (2001)).

[353] *Varadarajan, P. R./Clark, T.* (1994), p. 94.

primarily guided by an efficiency or effectiveness orientation or by a synthesis of both objectives and, furthermore, whether the answer may depend on the concrete functional area.[354]

Yet, the question remains how *marketing* strategies fit in this picture.[355] The general expectation is that marketing reasoning exerts a certain influence at all three levels and that overlappings and feedback effects will be observed.[356] However, *strategic* marketing is held here to represent an issue predominantly at the business unit level.[357] This argument follows from an understanding of (industrial) marketing as primarily concerned with generating and managing CAC's – which is the core of business unit level strategy. Admittedly, for a concrete case, the assignment of strategic marketing may deviate to some extent depending on such factors as the particular organizational structure, or range and nature of products and markets.[358] A second subcriterion that is frequently used in management and marketing, respectively, is the *direction*, that is the question of who is addressed. Customers, competitors, suppliers, distributors, and other stakeholders (e.g. employees) are usually regarded as relevant target groups.[359]

---

[354] For instance, *Hofer, C. W./Schendel, D. E.* (1978) argue in favor of an efficiency orientation, while *Wheelwright, S. C.* (1984) advocates an effectiveness perspective. *Varadarajan, P. R./Clark, T.* (1994), p. 95, suggest that, at least with regard to marketing as a functional area, both objectives are relevant. This latter position is adopted here: it seems reasonable that functional strategies should be guided by the same basic goals as the superordinate levels, e.g. business unit strategy. If, for the latter, the CAC is the guideline, effectiveness and efficiency have to be considered on both levels.

[355] Among the earliest, yet rather undifferentiated, contributions to an explicit strategic orientation of marketing management is *Lyon, L., S.* (1926) (see for instance p. 3).

[356] See e.g. *Hutt, M. D./Speh, T. W.* (2004), p. 232ff, who draw on *Webster, F. E. J.* (1992).

[357] See e.g. *Meffert, H.* (1994), p. 24; *Brierty, E. G./Eckles, R. W./Reeder, R. R.* (1998), p. 220; *Varadarajan, P. R./Jayachandran, S.* (1999), p. 121; *Meffert, H.* (2000), p. 233. *Sudharshan, D.* (1995), p. 9, distinguishes marketing strategy from corporate strategy, but makes its relation to the functional level less clear. *Varadarajan, P. R./Clark, T.* (1994), p. 94ff, hold that marketing strategy is primarily identified on the functional level, although some overlappings with business strategy are acknowledged (p. 98). See also *Lorange, P.* (1980), p. 19f.

[358] See *Jarrat, D./Fayed, R.* (2001), p. 62.

[359] See *Meffert, H.* (1994), p. 33; *Nalebuff, B. J./Brandenburger, A. M.* (1996), p. 16f; *Meffert, H.* (2000), pp. 269, 282, 288, 296;

2.2.2 Proposing a definition of strategy for the business types concept

The definition of strategy which is adopted in this work rests on the research objectives of analyzing strategic shifts between business types. In that context, the formal frame is characterized by a normative, content-oriented perspective that is grounded in the relevant subject areas that constitute the foundations of this research, namely economics (TCA) and (marketing) management.[360] By characterizing strategies as normative, they are understood here as consciously planned. Yet, to account for the chosen subject matters, limitations to cognitive capacity are acknowledged implying a deviation from the requirements of full rationality.[361]

Further delimitation associated with the actual content of the strategy results in focusing on industrial marketing management combined with economic reasoning. Therefore, strategy is understood here as positioned at the business unit level and concerned with generating and sustaining competitive advantages. In combining this idea with economic considerations, strategy is generally defined as *the long-term oriented decisions and activities that enable a business unit to achieve and sustain a CAC and to maintain or improve its performance by continuously searching for rent.*[362] As such, it is mainly directed at the customer whose purchase is the ultimate target. However, this transaction-oriented view implicitly and necessarily also encompasses a competitor orientation.[363] In the context of the proposed interpretation of business types (constellations), this search for rent is taken as equivalent to attempting to create, appropriate and protect (added) value from choosing and pursuing *a particular business types constellation.*[364] Each business types constellation is, therefore,

---

[360] Positive assessments on the application of economic reasoning to strategy content issues are widespread (see e.g. for very general discussions *Montgomery, C. A.* (1988), p. 3; *Rumelt, R. P./Schendel, D./Teece, D. J.* (1991), p. 18).

[361] A characterization of the rational school in comparison with learning orientation and cognitive orientation has been provided in the context of strategic change by *Rajagopalan, N./Spreitzer, G. M.* (1996).

[362] See for foundations of this definition *Bowman, E. H.* (1974), p. 47; *Mahoney, J. T./Pandian, J. R.* (1992), p. 364; *Varadarajan, P. R./Jayachandran, S.* (1999), p. 120. Such definition possesses a considerable potential for establishing links between this research and resource based theory (see e.g. *Mahoney, J. T.* (2001), p. 656). Yet, this linkage is not explored here, but is left to future research.

[363] Impulses for changes in these strategies may, however, come from other actors in the market as well (see chapter 3.3.4).

[364] See on similar understanding of strategy, though without reference to business types and in a more differentiated view on rent seeking, *Foss, N. J.* (2003).

interpreted as a generic strategy in the sense of *Porter* (1980), giving the particular understanding of strategy for the subsequent analysis.[365] It should be noted that this definition is neither restricted to *any particular* form of searching for rent, nor, specifically, not to either one of the two motivations (economizing and strategizing) that may underlie business strategy according to the TCA perspective. That is not to say that the distinction is insignificant. In fact, both motivations will be elaborated in detail subsequently.[366]

---

[365] See *Porter, M. E.* (1980); adopting the same interpretation of "generic strategies" e.g. *Brandenburger, A. M./Stuart Jr., H. W.* (1996), p. 21.

[366] See chapter 3.3.

3 Dynamic perspective I: fundamental considerations on strategic shifts between business types constellations

3.1 Motivations for a dynamic view on the business types concept

In view of the empirically observable dynamics of the market place and theoretical assertions like *Hayek's* statement that "...economic problems arise always and only in consequence of change..."[367] it seems worthwhile to reach beyond a static typology of transactions and explore the potential of the business types concept to explain some of these dynamic issues. Such a view necessarily implies that the discriminating criteria for categorization are no longer regarded as data but as variables which are susceptible to deliberate design by the involved actors. The need for such further investigation and, at the same time, for its potential fruitfulness arises from two different perspectives, as indicated above, namely from a theoretical and from an empirical point of view.

3.1.1 Arguments from a theoretical perspective

First, conclusions on the incompleteness of a purely static approach to structuring industrial marketing can be drawn from a **general perspective on strategy in marketing**. Essentially, strategy deals with guiding the activities of economic actors. With respect to these activities in general, it has been held, albeit with different emphasis, by such scholars as *Hayek* (1945) and *Barnard* (1938), and supported by *Williamson* (1999) for the TCA perspective that "...adaptation to changes in the particular circumstances of time and place"[368] is the central problem of economic organization.[369] If one subscribes to this view, strategy will also necessarily have to be concerned with adaptation.[370] Consequently, it has been concluded that

---

[367] *Hayek, F.* (1945), p. 523. Note that *Hayek, F.* (1945) actually refers to decentralized, spontaneous adaptation of autonomous actors in the marketplace to changing circumstances. This differs, for instance, from intentional, consciously coordinated adaptation particularly whithin hierarchies as described by *Barnard, C. I.* (1938). For an extensive discussion see *Williamson, O. E.* (1991b).

[368] See *Hayek, F.* (1945), p. 524.

[369] See also *Barnard, C. I.* (1938); *Williamson, O. E.* (1999b), p. 1088.

[370] Actually, against the background of the understanding of strategy as adopted in this work, adaptation is probably more accurately reflected by *Barnard's* (1938) description.

"...strategic management is fundamentally concerned with environmental changes and organizational adaptation."[371] Such considerations necessarily imply a dynamic perspective when "dynamic" is understood as referring to those "...forces which bring about change or which resist change..."[372]. This inherent dynamic orientation is already illustrated by the terminology of the above strategy definition: a continuous search can only take place within the course of time. Its continuity stems from either one of two alternative properties of the search: either, that what is searched for (here: the CAC) cannot be found which would, however, deprive the search of its sense. Or, once the object (here: the CAC) of the search has been found, sooner or later a new search has to begin because of its fugitive nature in the face of changing circumstances. This emphasis on dynamics is reflected by frequent demands voiced by marketing scholars to explicitly incorporate dynamic thinking in marketing conceptualizations.[373]

Second, support for the requirement of a dynamic perspective can be gained from **properties of the business types framework itself**: a purely static structuring restricted to developing type-specific marketing programs is not exhaustive with regard to the analytic potential of TCA: several authors have meanwhile emphasized the role of asset specificity as a *choice variable*.[374] In that case, asset specificity is not fixed in a given transaction situation but subject to the parties' disposition. And so is the whole business types constellation, or, as *Heide* (1994) puts it with respect to governance dimensions in general: they are viewed as "...strategic decision variables in their own right, which can be made subject to deliberate design..."[375]. This idea is reflected in the outlined concept of business types constellations: no general tie the exchanged objects themselves (e.g. water power stations) and a particular business types constellation (e.g. water power stations are always marketed in mutual project business) is proposed to exist. On the contrary, it is maintained that, in essence, every product

---

[371] *Ginsberg, A.* (1988), p. 559, with reference to *Hofer, C. W./Schendel, D. E.* (1978); *Ansoff, H. I.* (1979).

[372] *Lewin, K.* (1945), p. 130. A related, though narrower interpretation has been advanced by *Teece, D. J./Pisano, G./Shuen, A.* (1997), who use the term in order to refer to situations characterized by "...rapid change in technology and market forces, and "feedback" effects on firms..." (p. 512).

[373] See e.g. *Sheth, J. N./Gardner, D. M./Garrett, D. E.* (1988), p. 194; *Dickson, P. R.* (1996), p. 102.

[374] See *Williamson, O. E.* (1985), p. 89ff; *Riordan, M. H./Williamson, O. E.* (1985); *Aufderheide, D.* (1993). For detailed analysis of this issue see chapter 3.2.3.

[375] *Heide, J. B.* (1994), p. 82.

– in the sense of its functionality – can be traded in each business types constellation.[376] The reason for this possibility rests on the compensatory nature of the different mechanisms that can lead to the emergence of asset specificity (characteristics of value and countervalue as well as mode of delivery). The basic technology underlying a certain functionality is determinative of the business type (constellation) only under specific conditions.[377] *Katz'* (1989) argument that certain pricing schemes may "artificially" create asset specificity can be considered as an illustration.[378] Further support can be derived from research on dependence and power relations. Ways to actively shape an exchange situation with respect to the parties' dependence positions and to change power relations in order to gain a power advantage have already been discussed by *Emerson* (1962), *Blau* (1964), or *Lawler* (1992).[379] Drawing on *Emerson* (1962), *Plinke/Söllner* (2000) have recently applied these ideas in combination with TCA reasoning in the context of managing business relationships.[380]

The theoretical arguments in favor of a dynamic extension to the present structuring approaches can be supplemented by practical reasoning. It highlights that the search for rents and CAC's does not stop at the borders of a particular business types constellation.

3.1.2 Arguments from a business practice perspective

Looking at current business practice, it has been argued by many authors that growing complexities of global market places and rapidly changing technological conditions force companies even more frequently to consider changes in strategy.[381] In fact, it has been argued that "changing strategies appears to be a major tool used by organizations in dealing with their changing environment […]."[382] Such assertions have meanwhile been supported by large-

---

[376] For conceptual support of this view in marketing see *Mathur, S. S.* (1984), p. 102; *Backhaus, K./Büschken, J.* (1999), p. 307. *Joskow*'s study of coal markets can be seen as as empirical support (*Joskow, P. L.* (1987)). This assertion provides the basis for a dynamic analysis of the business types framework.

[377] See on similar assessments with respect to the relation between technology and governance in general e.g. *Williamson, O. E.* (1985), p. 89; *Heide, J. B.* (1994), p. 83.

[378] See *Katz, M. L.* (1989), p. 698.

[379] See *Emerson, R. M.* (1962), p. 34ff; *Blau, P. M.* (1964), p. 125ff; *Lawler, E. J.* (1992), p. 23ff.

[380] See *Plinke, W./Söllner, A.* (2000), p. 74ff.

[381] *Rühli, E./Schmidt, S. L.* (2001), p. 545; *Burmann, C.* (2002b), p. 67.

[382] *Zajac, E. J./Shortell, S. M.* (1989), p. 427.

scale empirical evidence, for instance, by *Zajac/Shortell* (1989) in the context of the health care industry and with respect to a particular generic strategies framework, namely the *Miles/Snow* (1978) typology. Comparable empirical findings are not yet available regarding the business types concept. However, anecdotal evidence suggests that business practice indeed knows numerous cases in which companies have redesigned their market offerings in such a way that the business types constellation which it resembles closest significantly differs after being redesigned. Some cases that have been documented in the literature on business marketing may serve as examples.

The first example is based on the case of the company Bossard AG, Switzerland, and was first documented by *Willée* (1991) and later discussed explicitly in the context of business types constellations by *Backhaus* et al. (2003).[383]

S_1 is a supplier of connection technologies. Its customers are mainly OEMs from the mechanical engineering industry. The market offerings by S_1 have so far routinely been sold and bought in bilateral product business, that is, neither supplier nor customer were investing specifically in each other. The OEMs regard the suppliers in the market as relatively easily substitutable. The connecting elements (e.g. screws, washers etc.) sold by S_1 are seemingly simple and rather homogeneous, pre-fabricated products that usually gain obvious importance only the moment they break down. CAC positions have so far been sought by S_1 and its competitors on product-related dimensions such as quality, faithfulness to (delivery) deadlines, and, mainly, price. A market research study conducted by S_1 has now identified some key problems of customers that are associated with the business and that have not yet been addressed by any of the suppliers:

- lack of transparent, clear categorization and presentation of complete product range and, as a result, problems in selecting appropriate components,

- lack of product-related competencies and qualified overview in customer-companies and, as a result, barriers to using new, differentiated or advanced connecting elements that could better serve the customers´ purposes in construction.

In response to the detection of these issues, S_1 developed a process-related innovation in selling its products that, essentially, involves a shift in business type for its customers from product business towards relational business: S_1 offers its customers a software package (including first installation, data medium, and documentation) as an extension to its previous product range which works up the whole spectrum of S_1´s components for immediate further processing in Computer Aided Design (CAD) systems. The

[383] See *Willée, C.* (1991); *Backhaus, K./Baumeister, C./Mühlfeld, K.* (2003).

package costs 5,000 €. In addition to this purchase price, customers have to contract with S_1 for a 3-year-service-agreement which includes among others updating and maintenance of the system and adaptations to new component developments. Key features of the package are (1) a transparent, complete catalog of S_1's product range, (2) integrated links to relevant knowledge from connection technologies (e.g. information on DIN regulations), (3) a 97% guarantee for immediate readiness to deliver regarding all listed components, and (4) a software that supports new product constructions at a customer company that applies S_1's components. The claimed benefit and objective of the software package is to provide support for optimal solutions for all connecting issues that could possibly emerge with regard to the OEM's final products. The software is compatible with all usual systems software, operating systems, and hardware. After making the initial investment for the software package, its advantages can only be realized through purchasing from S_1, by that creating a customer lock-in.

Case 2 is based on changes in the market offering of the British news agency Reuters.[384]

S_2 is a global provider of news, television services, and financial information. Its customers are mainly grouped in four segments: asset management, investment banking and brokerage, treasury, corporates and media. S_2's market offerings include provision of economic and business data (real-time information, databases, and background information for a large number of stocks and shares and other financial instruments) and computer systems for related data interchanges. So far, the offerings have been based on particular "S_2-terminals" that are equipped with specific software. Customers have to install these terminals at their sites for a certain fee and subsequently lease them for a fixed monthly rate (currently on average 750 €) and, by doing so, gain access to the information services. While buyers are to a large extent substitutable from the perspective of S_2 (no specific investments), customers are required to invest specifically into a system that cannot be put to other uses and are locked-in by their investment in the terminal for a certain period of time. Recently, S_2 has, however, taken action for changing the face of its market offerings: due to the high costs incurred for the installation of the terminals, S_2 is planning to launch an offer that will be accessible via public information systems such as the internet. No initial, idiosyncratic investment would then be necessary for the customers, thus shifting their buying process from relational towards product business, with S_2 staying in product business.

The conclusion from these cases seems to be straightforward: if shifts between business types constellations can be found in practice, the theoretical structuring scheme should allow for their analysis. Otherwise, an important issue that forms part of the structuring task is not dealt with.

---

[384] Information on the case is based on the company's internet presence (http://www.about.reuters.de/) and on *Scheffler, S.* (2001); *Scheffler, S.* (2002).

3.2   Strategic shifts in the business types framework

3.2.1   Changes in strategy - a sketch from the literature

"Change [...] appears to be a permanent characteristic of modern technological societies."[385] Essentially the same could be said about the significance of changes for (marketing) strategy. Agreement on the general validity of such statements is widespread and has been reflected in a large body of conceptual and empirical research.[386] Interpretations of what exactly is meant by "change" and "change in strategy" vary nearly just as widely.[387] For instance, *Rajagopalan/Spreitzer* (1996) have proposed a very general definition of strategic change as "...a difference in the form, quality, or state over time in an organization's alignment with its external environment."[388] *Brockhoff* (1999), as another example, has recently characterized strategic change as a divergence – which requires further defining circumscription – between at least two strategies in the course of time.[389] A major reason for the conceptual variety lies in the wide spectrum of definitions of and approaches to strategy itself. For instance, the dichotomy between content- and process-oriented research on strategy in general is also reflected in the literature on strategic change. Different theoretical perspectives on and interpretative scope surrounding the idea of change contribute to the terminological proliferation. Nevertheless, attempts have been made to establish some principal systematizations.

Conceptual domain

In a seminal contribution, *Ginsberg* (1988) defines change in general as "...becoming different in some particular..."[390]. He then proceeds to make the point that exactly the definition of these "particulars" has stimulated considerable controversy. In order to structure

---

[385] *Macneil, I. R.* (1978), p. 889.

[386] See e.g. *Schendel, D. E./Hofer, C. W.* (1979); *Ginsberg, A.* (1988); *D'Aveni, R. A.* (1994); *Dickson, P. R.* (1996); *Chakravarthy, B.* (1997); *Teece, D. J./Pisano, G./Shuen, A.* (1997); *Tushman, M. L.* (1997); *Burmann, C.* (2001). An empirically-oriented review of the literature on strategic change has been provided by *Rajagopalan, N./Spreitzer, G. M.* (1996).

[387] In line with most publications in the field but unlike *Ginsberg, A.* (1988), p. 560, "strategic change" is used here synonymously for the more general notion of "change in strategy".

[388] *Rajagopalan, N./Spreitzer, G. M.* (1996), p. 49.

[389] See *Brockhoff* (1999), p. 221.

105

the variety of interpretations, *Ginsberg* (1988) develops a framework for conceptualizing "changes in strategy" which is depicted in *Fig. 11* and shows the organizing dimensions as well as an example for each category.[391] While the examples in the first row are examples from the business unit level, those in the second row are claimed by *Ginsberg* (1988) to encompass both the corporate and business unit level. Each dimension consists of two criteria for categorization, namely magnitude and pattern for the change dimension, and position and perspective for the strategy dimension. The first dimension refers to the conceptualization of "**strategy**". According to *Ginsberg* (1988), strategy as a position captures an outward looking concept with strategy being a means for locating the organization in its external environment. Strategy as a perspective is considered as looking inwards, and being focused on the "collective mind" or "culture".[392]

The second dimension refers to the properties of "**change**". The first criterion, changes in magnitude, covers first-order changes, that is, such changes that imply a variation in the intensity with which the current path is pursued. They have also been compared to the "steering movements"[393] of a bicyclist in order to maintain equilibrium. Changes in pattern, on the other hand, are characterized as second-order changes which imply a fundamental transformation, a variation in state or, in other words, choosing a new path.[394]

---

[390] See *Ginsberg, A.* (1988), p. 560.

[391] See *Ginsberg, A.* (1988). While both dimensions may provide insights for a systematic view on changes in strategy, the first may be the less universally applicable one. In case a definition of strategic change is sought for a specific context, degrees of freedom in formulating the definition exist only with respect to the change dimension if the definition of strategy is given.

[392] The distinction between strategy as position and as perspective is similar both terminologically and with regard to its meaning to *Mintzberg, H. T.* (1987), p. 15ff.

[393] *Meyer, A. D./Brooks, G. R./Goes, J. B.* (1990), p. 94.

[394] The distinction between first-order and second-order changes can be traced back to *Watzlawick, P./Weakland, J. H./Fisch, R.* (1974).

	Strategy as...	
	position	**perspective**
Change in... **magnitude**	Change in the intensity of a firm's resource deployments to functional areas.	Change in the intensity of the norms and values that determine, and are reflected in, how and why a firm chooses its business domain, production processes, and administrative systems.
pattern	Change in the configuration of a firm's resource deployments to functional areas.	Change in the configuration of the norms and values that determine, and are reflected in, how and why a firm chooses its business domain, production processes, and administrative systems.

Fig. 11: A framework for conceptualizing changes in strategy[395]

Related to this issue is the frequently made distinction between continuous (or evolutionary/ incremental) changes and discontinuous (or revolutionary/transformational) changes.[396] Continuous changes rather reinforce (or weaken) an existing strategy by taking a large number of small steps to finally result in the evolution of something new. Discontinuous changes involve considerable breaks from past strategy to take place during a rather short period of time. By definition, this requires the prevalence of more stable periods in between. This has, for instance, been outlined by *Miller/Friesen* (1980, 1984) in their "Gestaltansatz" where stable "periods of momentum" alternate with "periods of dramatic revolution".[397] Linking this distinction to the *Ginsberg* (1988) approach, incremental change could be regarded as similar to the magnitude criterion. Radical changes, on the other hand, resemble the changes in

---

[395] Closely adapted from *Ginsberg, A.* (1988), p. 561.

[396] For applications see e.g. *Mintzberg, H. T.* (1978), pp. 939ff, 945; *Teece, D. J./Pisano, G./Shuen, A.* (1997), p. 529; *Tushman, M. L.* (1997); *Beinhocker, E. D.* (1999). For conceptual discussion on the distinction see *Watzlawick, P./Weakland, J. H./Fisch, R.* (1974); *Meyer, A. D./Brooks, G. R./Goes, J. B.* (1990); *Rajagopalan, N./Spreitzer, G. M.* (1996), p. 58; *Leker, J.* (2000), p. 64ff. *Fu-Lai Yu, T.* (2001), pp. 9, 20ff, uses a similar distinction between extraordinary and ordinary entrepreneurial discoveries and associated changes in the context of the theory of entrepreneurship.

[397] See *Miller, D./Friesen, P. H.* (1980), pp. 591, 593.

pattern more closely.[398] However, criteria for unambiguous distinction have not yet been proposed within any of these frameworks. Rather, the line between the two criteria is often blurred: it has been pointed out that, particularly in the case of small or intermediate variations, the question arises whether the variation really is so fundamental as to represent a strategic reorientation towards some new strategy, or whether it had better be regarded as an adjustment to the present strategy.[399] Furthermore, if the eventual result from both kinds of change is something basically new, the distinction cannot rest on the final outcome itself, but rather on the duration until these outcomes are reached. Fixing this time horizon is a highly subjective issue.[400]

In addition, further criteria for systematizing strategic change have been proposed in the literature. For instance, quite frequently a distinction is made between (pro-) active and reactive changes.[401] In contrasting them with reactive changes, proactive changes have been characterized as occurring "...without tangible external stimulus..."[402]. Thereby, essentially, they are defined by locating the impulse for a change in the acting entity itself. However, it has been pointed out convincingly e.g. by *Hayek* (1969) and supported by many other scholars that every act of change in the economy requires some sort of stimulus or impulse.[403] As a result of an acknowledgement of this position, the distinction between external and internal impulses becomes blurred once limits to human cognition are accounted for[404]: looking at change both through a cognitive lens and an economic lens (e.g. in terms of market process theory/the Austrian school), a variation in the subjective knowledge that an actor possesses

---

[398] An interpretation of these terms, though from a learning theory perspective that allows for drawing such parallels, has been advanced by *Rajagopalan, N./Spreitzer, G. M.* (1996), p. 58.

[399] See e.g. *Snow, C. C./Hambrick, D. C.* (1980), p. 529ff.

[400] For recent attempts to find thresholds see *Brockhoff* (1999); *Leker, J.* (2000).

[401] See e.g. *Mintzberg, H. T.* (1978), p. 939; *Miller, D./Friesen, P. H.* (1980), p. 613; *Mathur, S. S.* (1984), p. 102; *Burmann, C.* (2002b), p. 71.

[402] *Mintzberg, H. T.* (1978), p. 939.

[403] See *Hayek, F. A. v.* (1969), p. 258.

[404] See in detail chapter 3.3.3. The significance of accounting for human limitations has also been acknowledged in the literature on strategic management, see e.g. *Amit, R./Shoemaker, P. J. H.* (1993), p. 34f.

becomes a necessary prerequisite for him to initiate a (strategic) change.[405] In line with such understanding of the origins of strategic change, both kinds of change can alternatively be distinguished from each other in analogy to diffusion theory via the time when action is taken.[406] Diffusion theory in general deals with the aggregation of the results from a multitude of individuals that make adoption decisions. Adoption refers to an individual's cognitive processes concerning the potential aquisition of a product which is concluded by an affirmative purchase decision. In diffusion theory, several categories of adopters are identified based on the time when they take over an innovation: first come innovators, followed by early adopters, an early majority, the late majority and finally laggards. Without stretching the analogy too much, one could compare the early reaction by innovators to proactive changes, and reactive changes to the subsequent reactions of later adopters. Yet, drawing the line between the two categories of changes remains an ambiguous issue.[407] It is tackled more explicitly by a third interpretation. The categories are then set apart by different degrees of cumulative "organization stress"[408]. The idea of cumulative stress summarizingly captures (perceived) imperfections of the current strategy. Occurrence of change at low levels of stress can be regarded as characteristic for proactive changes, whereas reactive changes can be assumed to take place only at high levels of organizational stress. Increases in organization stress have been associated with rentability erosion[409], a linkage which, if it could be reliably established, would facilitate the distinction.

Empirical domain

Compounding matters, the theoretical construct "strategic change", in fact, needs to be operationalized for empirical investigations and business practice.[410] Therefore, context

---

[405] For the cognition theory view see *Rajagopalan, N./Spreitzer, G. M.* (1996), p. 62ff; for a market process view, Austrian economics, and related concepts see e.g. *Schumpeter, J. A.* (1928); *Hayek, F.* (1945); *Mises, L. v.* (1949 (repr.: 1966)); *Lachmann, L. M.* (1956); *Kirzner, I. M.* (1973). For recent and extending interpretations in this tradition see e.g. *Foss, N. J.* (1997), p. 188; *Fu-Lai Yu, T.* (2001), p. 9; *Foss, N. J.* (2002). With a focus on evolution see *Metcalfe, J. S.* (2001), p. 569ff.

[406] See, on diffusion theory, the seminal work by *Rogers, E. M.* (1962 (repr.: 1968)).

[407] A related issue, the definition of what constitutes a first-mover, has been critically evaluated by *Lieberman, M. B./Montgomery, D. B.* (1988), p. 50ff.

[408] See *Huff, J. O./Huff, A. S./Thomas, H.* (1992), p. 57ff in particular; also *Burmann, C.* (2002b), p. 71.

[409] See *Stoelhorst, J. W.* (1997), p. 114f.

[410] See, also on the following arguments, *Burmann, C.* (2001); p. 118ff; *Burmann, C.* (2002b), p. 70f.

contingent definitions of the relevant construct and its components, namely strategy and change, have to be formulated.[411] In addition, appropriate measurement indicators have to be developed. For instance, related to the conceptual debate on incremental and transformational changes, thresholds of the extent of variation have to be identified in order to categorize a variation as strategic change, modification or adjustment. Also, the timing and, in particular, the time period following an impulse until a change takes place, warrants attention in order to be able to distinguish between proactive and reactive changes. As a result of the difficulties associated with these and other measurement issues, various researchers have developed different solutions, leading to ambiguous and often contradictory findings on the antecedents and consequences of strategic change.[412] Such unsatisfactory empirical results, for instance regarding the performance implications of a strategic change, have meanwhile provoked diverse attempts to refine the construct.[413] Based on a meta-analysis of 59 empirical studies on strategic change published in American journals between 1980 and 1994, *Rajagopalan/Spreitzer* (1996) develop a complex framework that aims at integrating both content- and process-related aspects of strategic change. It builds on theoretical synergies of a rationality, learning, and cognition perspective and takes into account empirical evidence.[414] Recently, *Leker* (2001) has identified four different types of strategic change on the corporate level based on an empirical study, namely expansionist, innovative, reallocative and, concentrative change. Also, corresponding manners of corporate performance development are distinguished.[415] Despite the significance of identifying the causes for such ambiguous empirical findings, this work abstracts from the issue because a purely conceptual path is pursued instead.

---

[411] For instance, *Snow, C. C./Hambrick, D. C.* (1980), p. 532ff, discuss four different methods for generating information with respect to measuring strategies, namely investigator inference, self-typing, external assessment, objective indicators (p. 527ff). A comprehensive overview of studies concerned with measuring strategies in empirical research has been provided by *Brockhoff, K./Leker, J.* (1998), p. 1206ff.

[412] For an extensive overview see *Rajagopalan, N./Spreitzer, G. M.* (1996).

[413] Examples include *Rajagopalan, N./Spreitzer, G. M.* (1996); *Leker, J.* (2001). See on assessments of the empirical findings e.g. *Ginsberg, A.* (1988), p. 568.

[414] See *Rajagopalan, N./Spreitzer, G. M.* (1996).

[415] See *Leker, J.* (2001). He limits his examination to such changes that have explicitly been announced by the company and credibly been presented to a third party.

So far, the discussion has centered around aspects of *formal systematization* of changes in strategy. Before turning to what is implied by "strategic change" within the business types framework, influential research dealing with the actual *contents* of strategic change in marketing will also be mentioned briefly in order to be better able to locate the view adopted here. In contrast, the process perspective on strategic change is not explicitly considered since it plays a minor role regarding this purpose owing to the strategy definition for the business types framework.

Various content-related concepts for strategic change have been proposed. Among the best known are the outpacing strategies concept by *Gilbert/Strebel* (1985), and the strategic intent approach by *Hamel/Prahalad* (1989), both of which focus on rather continuous changes, and the hypercompetition approach by *D'Aveni* (1994), and the turbulence-oriented concept by *Chakravarthy* (1997) which both focus rather on discontinuous changes.[416] *Gilbert/Strebel* (1985, 1987) advocate flexible strategies called "outpacing strategies" that are able "...to exploit market changes by making timely shifts back and forth."[417] This timely adaptation refers to switches – ahead of the competition – in the strategic emphasis between "perceived product value" and "actual process cost" as the two fundamental dimensions of competitive strategy. The switch, however, does not imply subsequent neglect of the other dimension. On the contrary, the ultimately advocated goal is the simultaneous strive for a leading position in both dimensions. At the heart of *Hamel/Prahalad's* (1989) concept is the notion of strategic intent. Strategic intent is characterized as a particularly ambitious approach to goal setting which should even be out of proportion to a company's resources and capabilities. Thereby, it implies a considerable stretch, coupled with distinct management processes aimed at proactive change. This change should be directed towards changing the (rules of) game so as to put competitors at a disadvantage instead of just striving for improvement in the way the company plays the game. Long-term orientation and relative stability of such intent are explicitly stressed. *D'Aveni* (1994), on the other hand, develops strategies for a "hyper-competitive" environment which is characterized by "...the dynamics of strategic maneuvering among

---

[416] See *Gilbert, X./Strebel, P. J.* (1985) *Gilbert, X./Strebel, P. J.* (1987); *Hamel, G./Prahalad, C. K.* (1989); *D'Aveni, R. A.* (1994); *Chakravarthy, B.* (1997) On general assessments of their impact see e.g. *Backhaus, K.* (2003), p. 294ff; the discussion by *Kleinaltenkamp, M.* (1987) focuses on the outpacing strategies concept.

[417] *Gilbert, X./Strebel, P. J.* (1987), p. 28.

global and innovative combatants [...] to create a condition of constant disequilibrium...."[418]. He focuses on the need to permanently shape the rules of the game in the relevant arena. Consequently, he favors the search for new competitive advantages with disruptive effects over attempts to sustain advantages. *Chakravarthy's* (1997) concept is targeted at turbulent environments with particular emphasis on information and communication industries ("Infocom").[419] He argues that, in order to cope with such conditions, companies are required, first, to reconceptualize strategies by constantly striving for first-mover advantages and by establishing customer networks. Second, they are required to share responsibilities for strategy by focusing on guidance through philosophy instead of more concrete tangible image and by pursuing a bottom-up approach to intra-company entrepreneurship. Third, distinct organizational capabilities directed at "...leveraging, strengthening, and diversifying [...] resources..."[420] are needed.

A less well established but in the context of this work particularly interesting approach that concentrates on industrial marketing has been proposed by *Mathur* (1984) and later been built on by *Mathur/Kenyon* (1997).[421] Focusing on a strategically determined distinction between what is traded and how it is traded, *Mathur* (1984) argues that the same functionality ("hardware") can be transacted in various forms of concrete market offerings which he labels commodity, product, system, and service. Plausibly illustrated by the example of heat exchangers, this categorization still lacks a coherent theoretical or empirical foundation. This characteristic impacts particularly on the concept of the so-called "transaction life cycle". Such cycles, as schematically depicted in *Fig. 12*, result from "transaction shifts": the nature of the "most popular" way to transact is believed to change over time. Thereby, different phases in the market process are created. According to *Mathur* (1984), (hardware) innovations are often first introduced as (relatively complex) systems, that is, as packages of hardware and software. Then, a number of developments that impact on the way the hardware is traded are

---

[418] *D'Aveni, R. A.* (1994), p. xiii.

[419] Turbulent environments are described as highly complex in terms of the number of competitive configurations that would ideally have to be considered, and, at the same time, as dynamic in the sense of a high rate of change in these configurations (see *Chakravarthy, B.* (1997), p. 69).

[420] See *Chakravarthy, B.* (1997), p. 81.

[421] See *Mathur, S. S.* (1984); *Mathur, S. S./Kenyon, A.* (1997). Despite the clear content-orientation of the approach, process-related aspects are also paid some attention (e.g. *Mathur, S. S.* (1984), pp. 105, 107).

presumed to take place: competitors introduce similar packages, customers become familiar with the hardware triggering unbundling processes (de-systematization), independent experts provide know-how on application of hardware and software. Even later, more competitors enter, often concentrating either on hardware or software. In a process of commodization, substitutability of the goods rises from the customers' perspective. In an attempt to escape the increasingly homogeneous competition, firms start modifying hardware or software components (de-commodization). Not seldom, they make them incompatible to those of their competitors or re-bundle hardware and software technically or contractually (augmentation).

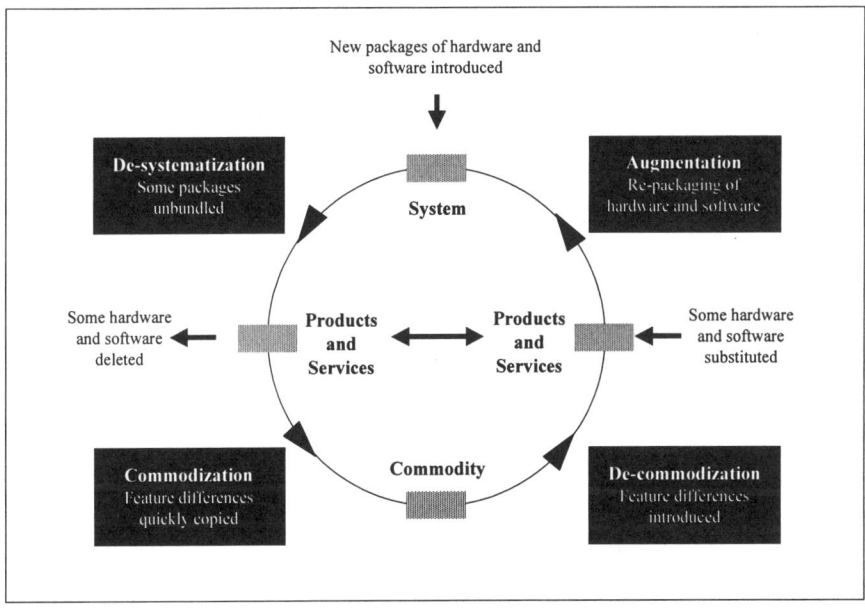

Fig. 12: The transaction life cycle[422]

Although not all customers are presumed to behave alike at any time, and despite the admitted scope for more than one successful supplier strategy at any time, a general tendency towards such cycles is claimed. Firms, therefore, face the challenge of matching the transaction shifts by appropriately adapting their strategies in order to achieve and sustain competitive advantages. In this process, the active role of strategic planning and its often discontinuous

---

[422] *Mathur, S. S.* (1984), p. 105.

nature in response to rapid transaction shifts are highlighted. Moreover, with regard to internal organization, restructuring from product divisions to transaction divisions is called for in order to account for the variety of ways in which the same hardware can be transacted.

3.2.2   Definition of strategic changes as shifts between business types constellations

Conceptual domain

None of the outlined conceptualizations is per se satisfying and sufficient as basis for the analysis undertaken here. Owing to its very fundamental nature, the definition by *Brockhoff* (1999) seems to provide a suitable starting point for narrowing down the idea of strategic change with respect to the business types framework. With the pursuit of a particular business types constellation having been defined as a strategy, strategic change appears, hence, as a divergence between two constellations in the course of time. Yet, the notion of divergence calls for further, context-guided clarification. Applying the general framework proposed by *Ginsberg* (1988), it boils down to the question of whether changes in magnitude and/or changes in pattern should be regarded as relevant "divergences" in this context.[423] The decision on which may be more appropriate or whether both should be included is based on the ideal type nature of the business types.

Due to the discrete nature of the business types in the concept, changes in pattern can be identified, namely in terms of (complete) shifts from one constellation to another.[424] For the purpose of this work, this kind of change will be referred to as "strategic shifts" between business types constellations. However, although they are not at the heart of the investigation, the possible occurrence of incremental changes or changes in magnitude is neither denied nor excluded. Although the individual business types are – conceptually – clearly delimited from each other there is still scope for an intensification or a lessening of the properties of the current business type. The incorporation of such changes in this analysis rests on the fact that

---

[423] Due to the fact that the strategy definition is already given, only one row in *Fig 9* needs to be considered. In this concrete case it is the "strategy as position"-row where the definition from chapter 2.2.2 fits in.

[424] In such cases where a shift results in altered dependence positions of the transaction partners, strategic shifts between business types constellations bear close resemblance to the power-change strategies conceptualized by *Lawler, E. J.* (1992) in drawing on previous research on power-dependence-relations (see e.g. *Emerson, R. M.* (1962); *Blau, P. M.* (1964)).

the precise degree of specificity is not fixed – apart from the distinction between significant and nonsignificant specificity. Instead, it is included as a continuous variable for those business types that are presumed to possess significant degrees of specificity, that is, project business and relational business. To sum up, there is scope for both incremental and radical changes in the business types concept, albeit taking place on different levels within the framework.[425]

In order to complete the definition of strategic change, it is positioned with regard to the distinction between proactive and reactive changes. Based on the above line of argument, the distinction is regarded here to be rooted in the timing of change in relation to the underlying impulse, not with regard to some "intrinsic origin" of the impulse. While reactive changes surely represent an important research issue as well, this investigation will be restricted to proactive changes following the idea that "…real success comes from actively shaping the game you play – from making the game you want, not taking the game you find."[426] Thereby, the original entrepreneurial act of creating something new is focused on with respect to the generation of something fundamentally new, as implied by the strategic change construct.[427] Hence, no provision will be made for changes that are brought forth by force without leaving the seller – at least in the short run – more than a single option to realize its market offering. This kind of change may be provoked e.g. by legal restrictions (e.g. obligations for standardization of technical interfaces) or customer market power. In the long run, though, firms may be expected to find ways to circumvent even such restrictions – proactive change takes place again.

With reference to the *Mathur* (1984) framework, that means that, for example, only such shifts will be examined that are brought forth by those firms which are among the first to enter a new phase and whose activity may, thus, be considered as entrepreneurial in nature.[428] In fact, the similarity between *Mathur's* (1984, 1997) approach to strategic shifts and the view

---

[425] See for other examples that integrate both kinds of change *Miller, D./Friesen, P. H.* (1980); *Tushman, M. L./Romanelli, E.* (1985); *Tushman, M. L.* (1997). Unlike in this research, *Tushman, M. L.* (1997) regards product innovations as expressions of radical changes, while process innovations are more or less equated with incremental change.

[426] *Nalebuff, B. J./Brandenburger, A. M.* (1996), p. 9.

[427] On the linkages between strategy and entrepreneurship see e.g. *Venkataraman, S./Sarasvathy, S. D.* (2001).

[428] This issue will be treated indepth in chapter 3.3.

adopted here is not restricted to terminology. His principal idea is very much what this research is based on: the focus should be on *how* to transact. *What* hardware, or, in more general terms, what functionality, is traded is not decisive for the optimal design of a market offering and the resulting way of transaction between a seller and a buyer. However, three important differences between both approaches should be highlighted: first, *Mathur's* (1984, 1997) concept is based on anecdotal evidence and plausibility arguments instead of some broader theoretical context (e.g. behavioral science or microeconomic theory) or large-scale empirical research. Second, in his approach, little emphasis is put on the role of individual economic actors and their entrepreneurial potential. Instead, some kind of automatism seems to be implied in his vision of a generally valid transaction cycle. Third, further insights could be gained from more detailed considerations on the consequences of technological indeterminism of market offerings, for instance regarding the role of contractual features, than can be found with *Mathur* (1984, 1997).

Empirical domain

Although practical concerns of operationalization of shifts between business types constellations are not a key issue of this conceptually-oriented paper, they shall not go completely unmentioned. Common measurement problems regarding strategic shifts notwithstanding, empirical investigations on shifts between business types are likely to pose some specific problems.[429] Since transactions in business reality may at best come close to one or the other of the nine constellations, instead of clearly delimited shifts, tentative steps in various forms of technology and contract-related activities, may be observable in the direction of another constellation. Such activities may, though, also be the result of considerations from other areas than marketing strategy which may create identification problems.

---

[429] Problems regarding the operationalization of strategic change have been documented extensively in the literature. Recent contributions include *Brockhoff* (1999); *Leker, J.* (2000); *Burmann, C.* (2001). Attempts to operationalize a strategic *typology* have been advanced e.g. by *Conant, J. S./Mokwa, M. P./Varadarajan, P. R.* (1990) who focus on the *Miles/Snow* (1978) typology (see *Miles, R. E./Snow, C. C.* (1978)).

3.2.3 Foundations of shifts between business types: asset specificity as a choice variable

1.2.3.1 Proposition of a framework with asset specificity as choice variable at its center

The idea of asset specificity as a choice variable has been discussed in the literature for instance by *Williamson* (1985), *Riordan/Williamson* (1985), *Aufderheide* (1993, 2000). The general proposition is that the same functionality can be delivered either through general purpose or special purpose technology, or, more to the point of this research, involving either unspecific or specific investments.[430] This basic assertion, essentially, implies that technology on its own is not fully determinative with regard to product functionalities. The general idea can be extended by combining it with the recognition that specificity can also be "artificially" created through contractual means.[431] On such understanding of asset specificity rests the definition of the business types constellation and also of shifts between constellations. It implies the idea that product-related and mode-related properties of a transaction are interchangeable in determining degree and horizon of specificity.[432]

Fig. 13 presents a framework that attempts to gain insights into the consequences of such an assertion from an individual company's management perspective by drawing on the business types framework. *Fig. 13* captures the proposed elements of these decisions as well as suggested linkages and directions of impact among them.

The framework refers to the classic transaction determinants, asset specificity, uncertainty, and transaction frequency, in a somewhat rearranged form. Transaction frequency is captured

---

[430] See *Riordan, M. H./Williamson, O. E.* (1985), p. 370; *Williamson, O. E.* (1985), p. 32; *Aufderheide, D.* (1993), p. 9ff; *Aufderheide, D.* (2000), pp. 75, 99ff, 113. Similarly, though less strictly rooted in TCA, see *Ghemawat, P./del Sol, P.* (1998), p. 35. *Sanchez, R.* (2000) draws on Riordan/Williamson (1985) in discussing the consequences from a condition which he terms "asset flexibility".

[431] See e.g. *Katz, M. L.* (1989), p. 699; *Rubin, P. H.* (1990), pp. 15,125. See also chapter 2.1.2.6.

[432] Just as the time gap between performance and counterperformance causes asset specificity to constitute a potentially dangerous property of an investment, it can also be held responsible for shifting lock-in positions between the transaction partners in case product-related effects are to be offset by mode-related properties or vice versa. Consider the following example based on the ideas of *Backhaus, K./Plinke, W./Rese, M.* (2004): supplier *A* designs and builds a customized fork-lift truck for buyer B. To the degree that the time and resources spent on this are specific, *A* is locked in due to product-related effects. Two different payment schemes could have been agreed on: (1) *B* pays on delivery. *A* is locked-in until that very moment while there is no (counter-) performance delivered in advance by B. (2) *B* engages in considerable downpayments orientated towards structure and magnitude of the specific part of *A*'s investment. Upon delivery, mainly the unspecific parts are left to be paid. *A*'s product-related specific investment is now partially offset by the particular design of the mode-related asset specificity in the opposite direction

117

implicitly in the specificity horizon and the corresponding nature of (intended) investment amortization. A further conceptual distinction concerns the asset specificity and uncertainty: they are brought together in a somewhat more hierarchical ordering of both constructs than found in most of the literature.[433] The distinction is based on the actors´ abilities to shape the particular transaction determinant according to their purposes: while asset specificity is assumed to be entirely and directly *within the game*[434] (inside the dotted line which marks the dyad; *Fig. 13*) at the disposition of the actors who are interested in transacting with each other, uncertainty is regarded to be susceptible to such influence only incompletely and rather indirectly. The most direct route to changing this factor would be to *change to another game arena* (with the game arena depicted by the gray shaded area in *Fig. 13*).[435]

Following *Fig. 13*, it is suggested that the potential transaction partners chose – in accordance with potential legal constraints[436] – the degree and horizon of asset specificity for their investments, and, thereby, the business types constellation. Their concrete choice results from the idiosyncratic investment´s inherent trade-off between its antagonistic properties, that is, between productivity gains (which are assumed to be the higher, the higher the degree of specificity) and the danger of potential exploitation. Productivity advantages result in a quasi-rent to be gained, whereas the anticipation of potential exploitation is interpreted to lead to the incurrence of transaction costs: the parties involved make provisions in order to prevent them from exploitation and from losing the amount at stake. This behavior gives rise to the emergence of transaction costs.[437]

---

[433] See as an example *Blois, K. J.* (1996). Exceptions include e.g. *Picot, A./Dietl, H.* (1990), p. 180. For a recent, structured review of traditional and modified transaction cost approaches see *Burr, W.* (2003).

[434] The term is used here in a more general, though related, sense than in game theory. It refers to the constellation between two potential transaction partners, that is, to the potential future transaction and its immediate antecedents. Competitors, suppliers and related actors are considered as parts of the game arena within which the transaction could take place.

[435] See e.g. *Ghosh, M./John, G.* (1999), p. 135, who state that such considerations which imply conscious choices by firms are largely absent from the original organizational theory literature.

[436] See for a brief discussion on this issue chapter 4.1. The inclusion of legal rules and available technologies as impacting factors which are, still, located outside the actual dyad draws, in particular, on the description of the "infrastructure" of a transaction as an influencing factor as proposed by *Picot, A.* (1981).

[437] See e.g. *Backhaus, K./Aufderheide, D./Späth, G.-M.* (1994)

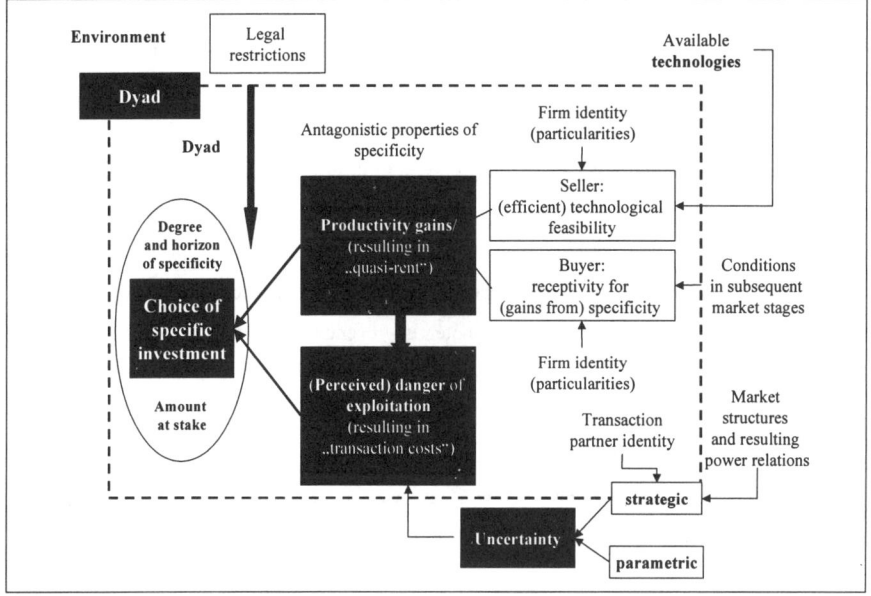

Fig. 13: A framework of asset specificity as a choice variable[438]

The potential productivity gains which could be reaped from a specific investment, that is, the extent to which a certain transaction specific investment could arise as beneficial at maximum, are influenced not only by the degree and horizon of specificity as a determinant which is directly related to the object itself, but also by (indirect) factors on the seller-side as well as on the buyer-side.[439]

---

[438] The depicted direction of impacts builds on the considerations by *Aufderheide, D.* (2000), p. 98ff, on how to avoid the circularity of simultaneous optimization of specificity, total costs and governance structure: for each considered degree of specificity, the associated parameter values have to be ascertained. The choice is based on a comparison between these alternatives.

[439] Uncertainty is not captured as an impact on productivity gains in its own right based on the following argument: it is not unlikely that the real technological feasibility and the factual gains from specificity do not coincide ex post with the transaction partners′ estimations of these parameters. However, the resulting volatility as such poses little to no safeguarding problems: absent opportunism, adaptation needs would be handled as described by *Williamson, O. E.* (1985), p. 48: "unanticipated events could be dealt with by general rules, whereby the parties agree to be bound by actions of a joint profit-maximizing kind." Hence, parametric uncertainty regarding the real levels of the variables behind the productivity gains construct is exactly what causes adaptation needs and gives rise to exploitation potential – when combined with strategic uncertainty. Therefore, uncertainty is depicted solely as an influence on the perceived danger of exploitation.

On the part of the seller, they are summarized in the issue of efficient technological realization which may, for instance, find its expression in the production costs of the specific product. Two key influences on this construct are identified: first, the seller identity, i.e. its firm particularities which are here modeled to stem from path dependencies and, second, the general technological state-of-the-art, are proposed to determine on what terms the particular seller is able to supply asset specificity.[440] On the buyer-side, influences are subsumed in the idea of receptivity for specificity which, in essence, determines what profit increase the particular buyer expects from using a specific instead of an unspecific input product. This factor, therefore, says something about potential revenue gains to the supplier of asset specificity. It captures the idea that some buyers might profit more from asset specificity (with respect to the relevant input) than others. The factors held responsible for these differences are, first, buyer identity, i.e. firm particularities that have arisen from path dependencies, and, second, conditions in subsequent market stages such as customer heterogeneity.[441] These influences can be supposed to be interrelated both on the seller-side and on the buyer-side.

The issue of potential exploitation is modeled as the perceived danger of being exploited by the other party. The perception of a potential loss of the amount at stake results in various efforts (including selection of transaction partner, contract negotiation etc.) directed towards protection against this danger. Again, determinants can be found directly rooted in the exchange object as the amount at stake, and also within its surroundings in the form of uncertainty. Each party's amount at stake has been defined as its piece of the composite quasi-rent which is, more briefly, referred to as its quasi-rent. Two factors have been proposed as determining its size, that is, the *magnitude* of the value in the first best use (hereafter referred to as "first-best-value") and the *degree of specificity* of the investment. The often only

---

[440] See e.g. *Picot, A./Dietl, H.* (1990), p. 180, on the role of technological terms as general (framework) conditions. The incorporation of path dependent firm particularities in a TCA-based strategy framework will be discussed in the following chapters. Its potential fruitfulness and, maybe, even necessity is stressed e.g. by *Foss, N. J.* (2003). On a more general level, their decisive role for strategy, together with the concept of entrepreneurship, has been pointed out e.g. by *Rumelt, R. P.* (1984), p. 560. His arguments create feedback effects for incorporation of these issues if strategy is to be examined from a TCA perspective. The restriction to firm particularities from path dependencies results from the relative ease with which they can be derived from the existing theoretical frame compared to other sources of particularities such as distinct initial endowments. Their incorporation could, at the present state of theory, at best be explained by variations in starting points of firm formation and prevailing market conditions. For further discussion see chapter 3.3.3.

[441] The seller may, though, be able to exert an indirect influence on these conditions, in which case they must be regarded at least partially as a factor within the game (as portrayed in *Fig. 13*).

implicitly captured impact of the magnitude on the perceived danger of exploitation becomes more evident if one considers the same degree of specificity (e.g. 100%) for two objects with very different magnitudes of first-best-value, such as, for instance, solder lugs for conductor boards at e.g. 15 € per 1,000 pieces and an inductive heating generator at e.g. 25,000 €. Thereby, it will also influence the efforts undertaken for safeguarding and affect the cost-benefit considerations with respect to various available governance modes. This means that although the frequency dimension as such is not explicitly incorporated in the framework, it does play a role implicitly: the magnitude of the first-best-value of a transaction or transaction chain, respectively, can be interpreted to encompass aspects similar to the classic frequency dimension. It impacts on the question of whether the costs of an elaborate, specialized governance structure are justified[442] and captures magnitude as a quantity no matter whether it is caused by a single transaction or whether it arises from a complete chain.[443]

The incorporation of (subjectively perceived) uncertainty as a variable which impacts through its influence on the perceived danger of exploitation on the choice of asset specificity can be grounded in its effects being contingent on the level (and horizon) of asset specificity.[444] It is interpreted as an antecedent to the chosen specific investment. This proposition changes the nature of the relationship between both constructs: instead of being independent influences that are simultaneously at work, they are proposed to be sequentially linked to each other with uncertainty being more of an antecedent to asset specificity.[445] Uncertainty is generally

---

[442] This reasoning has been given by *Williamson, O. E.* (1985), p. 60, in legitimating the frequency determinant. The same terminology is used e.g. by *Blois, K. J.* (1996), p. 168, who nevertheless focuses his argument at least partly on the *value* level associated with a particular transaction. Here, a different conceptualization is adopted.

[443] Arguably, for the same magnitude, there is a difference between an individual transaction and a chain with respect to the specificity choice. Yet, the difference does not stem from magnitude, but from variations in the relevant uncertainty.

[444] See e.g. *Williamson, O. E.* (1985), pp. 59, 242; *Cannon, J. P./Achrol, R. S./Gundlach, G. T.* (2000), p. 181. This conceptual argument has been challenged by empirical evidence supporting the idea of an (additional) main effect of uncertainty (see e.g. *Walker, G./Weber, D.* (1984); *Heide, J./John, G.* (1990), p. 33f; *Noordewier, T. G./John, G./Nevin, J. R.* (1990), pp. 84, 90f; for a review of empirically found positions see *Rindfleisch, A./Heide, J. B.* (1997), p. 49). The overall empirical evidence on the issue is ambiguous. Also, it has been argued that the identification of the main effect found in empirical studies may result from the fact that "...zero asset specificity is itself a hypothetical concept and all [*observable real world; added by author*] transactions entail some specific assets..." (see *Day, G. S./Klein, S.* (1987), p. 53). This work, therefore, builds on the interaction effect of uncertainty alone.

[445] See *Rangan, V. K./Corey, E. R./Cespedes, F.* (1993), p. 473; related *Picot, A.* (1991), p. 346. For the converse position, i.e. a treatment of various transaction dimensions on the same level, see e.g. *Blois, K. J.* (1996).

regarded to consist of parametric (environmental) uncertainty on the one hand, which arises in response to information deficiencies and prevails (mainly) ex ante to contract conclusion.[446] On the other hand, strategic (behavioral) uncertainty which results from the interplay of bounded rationality and opportunism is present when ex post dependencies make a transaction party vulnerable to opportunistic behavior by the partner who violates the explicit or implicit terms of contract.[447] In general, the likelihood of a party acting opportunistically may be argued to be correlated c.p. with its power over the other party, or, more precisely with respect to renegotiations, with its bargaining power.[448] Traditional TCA recognizes this idea mainly by c.p. attributing a larger likelihood of violating the terms of contract to that party which has less to loose, that is, whose lock-in to the transaction (partner) due to specific investments is weaker.[449] In fact, though, the consequences from other sources of bargaining power such as market structures in those markets which are relevant to the transacting parties are increasingly discussed in relation with TCA research and are also considered in this investigation.[450] Finally, the identity of the particular transaction partner is proposed as an indirect moderating impact on the perceived danger of exploitation. For instance, although it has been argued that inferences on future (opportunistic) behavior can be drawn only to a very limited degree from past behavior, recent empirical research increasingly points to an

---

[446] See e.g. *Williamson, O. E.* (1985), p. 57; *Backhaus, K./Aufderheide, D./Späth, G.-M.* (1994), p. 23. In incorporating the influence of uncertainty on the appropriateness of a particular constellation as impacting (indirectly) via its influence on the choice of asset specificity we draw on *Williamson, O. E.* (1985), p. 59, who already holds its influence as conditional upon the degree of specificity.

[447] See *Williamson, O. E.* (1985), pp. 49, 57ff; *Backhaus, K./Aufderheide, D./Späth, G.-M.* (1994), p. 23; for extensive investigation on various forms and outcomes of opportunism and solutions to it see *Wathne, K. H./Heide, J. B.* (2000).

[448] See *Argyres, N. S./Liebeskind, J. P.* (1999), p. 55; *Wathne, K. H./Heide, J. B.* (2000), p. 39. Bargaining power is understood here in accordance with *Argyres, N. S./Liebeskind, J. P.* (1999), p. 55, as a party's ability to impact on the terms and conditions of a contract/subsequent contracts/a chain of contracts in its own favor.

[449] On the rather recent emphasis in TCA on violations of implicit contracts see e.g. *Wathne, K. H./Heide, J. B.* (2000) and the literature cited there.

[450] See *Argyres, N. S./Liebeskind, J. P.* (1999), pp. 55ff, 58. Note that structural market power issues are understood here as a condition associated with uneven bargaining power already at the outset. Hence, the inequality is not brought about by the fundamental transformation, but already prevails *ex ante* as a result of the particular structures of the markets on the seller and buyer side (e.g. demand oligopoly). Such reasoning rests on the narrow understanding of asset specificity as adopted in this work. See also chapter 2.1.2.4 on the exclusion of market segment specific investments.

influence from past transaction history on transaction costs involved in subsequent exchanges.[451]

Against the background of the above proposed framework, the idea of shifts between business types constellations comes into play when changes in the parameter levels occur which provoke seller attempts to change the level and/or horizon of the choice variable asset specificity and, thereby, shift to another business types constellation.[452] Further investigation of such action requires a deeper understanding of the linkages between the variables in the framework. On this basis, relevant changes which induce shift considerations may be identified and implications for "screw adjustment" can be derived.

3.2.3.2   *Discussion of individual impacts and antecedents*

The discussion of individual elements of the above framework centers around the two antagonistic properties of specific investments, the related uncertainty construct, and the issue of path dependencies whose role has so far been only tentatively explored in the literature on TCA.

3.2.3.2.1   *Productivity gains*

Productivity enhancements provide the justification for idiosyncratic investments. Absent such gains there is no need to consider specific investments. The maximal extent of productivity gains which could potentially be obtained from a particular exchange is, however, suggested to vary (at least in the short and medium run) across different combinations of transaction partners.[453] Consequently, factors on both sides of the dyad are held responsible for this condition since the complete composite quasi-rent to be extracted at

---

[451]   *Stump, R. L./Joshi, A. W.* (1998), for instance, found empirical evidence for the relevance of the previous exchange history (p. 51).

[452]   What may cause such attempts, that is, the seller's motivations for considering a shift between business types constellations, is discussed in chapter 3.3. The possibility of the seller exerting an indirect impact via other variables than the specific investment is briefly hinted at in chapter 4.6 which addresses the impact of structural market power.

[453]   See *Madhok, A.* (2002), p. 541. This idea clearly deviates from the idea of perfectly competitive markets, but can be regarded as potentially compatible with the information deficient markets of TCA (see on such assessment also *Argyres, N. S./Liebeskind, J. P.* (1999), p. 58).

maximum is determined by the seller's costs of supplying the input good and by the buyer's reservation price.[454] The former influence is captured as the "technological feasibility" of efficient production of the relevant good as achieved by a certain seller. The latter issue is labelled as "receptivity" of a particular buyer for valuing (higher degrees or a different horizon of) specificity. Both influences have hitherto been awarded relatively little attention in the TCA literature, potentially owing to its strong roots in economic theory. A marketing perspective which naturally focuses more on the particularities of firms and firm strategies might, therefore, allow for valuable insights as recently demonstrated by *Gosh/John* (1999).[455]

3.2.3.2.1.1 Seller-side: technological feasibility

At each given point in time, and on an abstract level, the relevant available "state-of-the-art" technology establishes the broad frames for what degree of specificity can be efficiently supplied.[456] This level can be expected to differ for various functionalities. For a particular functionality, it is modeled as the outside-the-dyad influence of available technology. However, its impact is moderated through factors which are endogenous to the game: first, a particular supplier's access to state-of-the art technology and, second, the supplier's ability to manage the available technology and, maybe, even contribute to its further development.[457] Both determinants can be attributed to a considerable degree to firm particularities. These are proposed to result from the path dependence of past strategic choices which is held to have the potential of leading to variations in such attributes as, for instance, size of the firm, alliances with other firms, production technologies employed, learning curve respects. All of these attributes may impact on a firm's access to and ability in handling a technology at a given point in time and may influence its operating costs and costs of capital in doing so.[458] In the

---

[454] See for related ideas *Brandenburger, A. M./Stuart Jr., H. W.* (1996), p. 10.

[455] See *Ghosh, M./John, G.* (1999).

[456] This idea accords with the concept of exhaustion of technology trajectories as expressed e.g. by *Lieberman, M. B./Montgomery, D. B.* (1988), p. 48. From a business practice perspective see e.g. *Hart, C. W. L.* (1995), p. 41. See also chapter 3.3.4.3

[457] See *Pavitt, K.* (1984); for particular support on the first aspect e.g. *Ghosh, M./John, G.* (1999), p. 139f; *Madhok, A.* (2002), p. 538f. Seminal discussion of the second point has been provided by *Schumpeter, J. A.* (1928); see also chapter 3.3.

[458] See related *Williamson, O. E.* (1985), p. 378; *Ghosh, M./John, G.* (1999), p. 139; *Madhok, A.* (2002). Firm particularities could at least partly also be attributed to differences in initial endowments. See also chapter 3.3.3 for discussions on this issue.

light of these ideas, it is proposed that higher costs of the seller in supplying the productivity gains associated with specific investment will c.p. result in a seller preference for a less specific business type and vice versa. As a result, there seems to be merit in shifting the emphasis from the best constellation for organizing particular transaction to the "...best way for a specific firm – with its history, routines, resource endowments, local institutional context, etc. – to organize this transaction"[459]. The same line of argument applies, essentially, also to the buyer firm.

3.2.3.2.1.2 Buyer side: receptivity for specificity

Although this research accounts for the principal idea that specific input factors are generally associated with potential productivity enhancements, it is nevertheless held that higher degrees of specificity as expressed through higher customization, closer relationships and their alikes, "...do not necessarily mean higher performance in the eyes of the customer."[460] While the subjectivity of benefit perception by final customers stems from variations in their individual utility functions, its substantiation in the case of buyers of intermediate products is a direct consequence from the above reflections. Just as their suppliers are distinctly positioned with respect to their competitors, so are the buying companies which are also characterized by firm particularities. In particular, (path dependent) past strategic choices, coupled with, broadly speaking, the conditions in its sales markets, result in a particular position of the buying firm which impacts on its receptivity for specificity in the acquisition of a particular functionality.[461]

Several factors which may possibly influence the degree of receptivity that a buyer exhibits have recently been discussed by *Gosh/John* (1999).[462] For instance, the particular end-customer strategy of automobile producers is argued to result in differing receptivities for specific investments by either component suppliers or suppliers of machinery and software related to the firm's manufacturing processes. This kind of consideration has frequently been

---

[459] *Madhok, A.* (2002), p. 543, albeit in a more general governance context.

[460] *Cannon, J. P./Perreault, W. D. J.* (1999), p. 454.

[461] See on the relevance of positioning issues in a similar context *Ghosh, M./John, G.* (1999) who, however, adopt a more specific definition of the term (p. 135).

[462] See *Ghosh, M./John, G.* (1999), particularly pp. 137, 140f.

captured by the notion of "strategic relevance" of a certain component.[463] Input goods with high strategic relevance are likely to require use of more "specific" constellations. As an illustration consider two buyer companies that explicitly pursue brand-oriented strategies in their sales markets. One of these buyer companies (*A*) might pursue a strongly communication-based brand strategy, while the other (*B*) might have opted for a technology driven brand. Due to this difference in end-customer strategy, it seems likely that company *B* might be able to enjoy higher productivity gains from specific investments associated with a certain input factor than company *A*, and might, hence, possess a higher receptivity for specificity.[464]

Related is the issue of the extent to which end-customers value the fact that a certain component or process is supplied by a particular seller. Such a high appreciation which may be the result of successful ingredient branding, would not only per se increase that seller's bargaining power, but may also induce a higher willingness of the buyer to invest specifically in order to secure its supply with the relevant component. This argument generalizes to *Helper*'s (1991) finding that there seems to be a trade-off between more relational, i.e. specific, ways of transacting (at least with respect to buyer asset specificity) which are also more conducive to the promotion of industry technical change, and buyer bargaining power, whatever the source of it may be.[465] While buyer bargaining power is, therefore, hypothesized to reduce the buyer's receptivity for buyer specificity, the receptivity for seller idiosyncratic investments may actually increase.

Heterogeneity among end-customers is another impact that may contribute to buyer receptivity for asset specificity since the diversity of needs can be expected to get translated from one stage to another in the vertical chain, albeit potentially experiencing some attenuation. Related to this idea is *Helper*'s (1991) argumentation which points to a high receptivity for specific

---

[463] *Picot, A.* (1991) has pointed out this aspect in a general framework for deciding on vertical integration, albeit on a different systematic level: he presents "strategic relevance" of input goods, together with asset specificity, as the primary impact on transaction costs. Uncertainty and frequency are incorporated as secondary influences (p. 346). *Amit, R./Shoemaker, P. J. H.* (1993), p. 36, ascribe specificity as an inherent property to strategic assets (see also *Dyer, J. H.* (1996), p. 271ff). Further treatments of the strategic relevance issue in a TCA context include *Freiling, J.* (1995), p. 121ff.

[464] At the same time, company *B* is also likely to face a higher perceived danger of exploitation exactly due to the higher strategic relevance of the specific input good. For analytical purposes, this aspect will, however, be discussed separately in the section on the perceived danger of exploitation.

[465] See *Helper, S.* (1991), p. 789 ff. See also the following remarks on multiple sourcing strategies.

investment (both from the buyer's and the seller's perspective) when industry technical progress is called for due to a final-product market which highly values innovativeness.[466]

Sanchez (2000) points to a condition which he terms "demand-side" uncertainty about future revenues. Its presence implies that the revenues from selling specific (output) goods made from specific assets are ins in the course of time.[467] Although no such close linkage between the specificity of an input factor and the specificity of the resulting output goods is assumed here, the argument nevertheless has important consequences for the idea of buyer receptivity: in cases where such a linkage prevails and where subsequent market stages exhibit a tendency towards rapid changes in customer preferences or potentially rapid price erosion, buyer receptivity for specificity of input goods can be expected to be considerably lowered.[468] However, if the specific tailoring of the input factor supply to the needs of the buyer actually helps to reduce the demand uncertainty faced by the buyer, this may considerable enhance the buyer's receptivity for specificity.[469]

Overall, a lower receptivity of a buyer that relates to buyer-specific investment is presumed to lead, all other things being equal, to a preference for a less specific own business type. In case it refers to specific investments provided by the seller-side, c.p. a lower reservation price for such specificity is assumed. The analogous argument refers to a higher receptivity.

---

[466] See *Helper, S.* (1991), p. 789.

[467] See *Sanchez, R.* (2000), p. 318ff.

[468] See related, although from a different angle, the predictions advanced by *Sanchez, R.* (2000), p. 329, concerning options-optimizing types of economic organization in the presence of varying degrees of demand-side and supply-side uncertainty. Vague support for such proposition comes also from *Barney, J. B./Lee, W.* (2000), p. 309ff, who integrate multiple considerations from different theoretical perspectives with respect to governance choice. In particular, demand uncertainty is regarded to lead to less hierarchical governance when a real options perspective is adopted.

[469] For related argumentation see e.g. *Lurie, R. S./Kohli, A. K.* (2003).

3.2.3.2.1.3 Path dependencies[470]

Although the consequences from path dependencies, "sensitive dependence on initial conditions"[471], have long been considered in other subfields of NIE such as New Economic History[472], their impact is only recently becoming acknowledged and examined by original contributions to TCA.[473] In particular, it is argued that recognition of such influences may allow for deeper insights into the reasons for (observable) firm particularities and may, therefore, further enhance TCA's usefulness for the analysis of strategy issues. *Argyres/Liebeskind* (1999), for instance, introduce the notion of "governance inseparability"[474] as "...a condition in which a firm's past governance choices significantly influence the range and types of governance mechanisms that it can adopt in future periods."[475] They suggest that it impacts on governance choices in two ways.[476] First, it does so by constraining a firm with respect to the feasibility of switching – for the same type of transaction – from one governance mode to another. Second, governance inseparability may

---

[470] It has been argued that path dependencies represent only a cutting from the total area of "firm particularities" the general inclusion of which, as complementary factors in TCA reasoning, is increasingly advocated (see e.g. *Madhok, A.* (2002), p. 541, who therefore, advocates a better integration of research in TCA and in resource-based theories which center explicitly on firm heterogeneity). Research on incorporating firm particularities as integral parts in transaction cost theory has not yet produced many established results, even less so on other factors than path dependencies. Thus, this investigation is restricted to the consideration of path dependence issues.

[471] *Liebowitz, S. J./Margolis, S. E.* (1995), p. 205f.

[472] See *North, D. C.* (1991), p. 109, who traces the development of the idea of path dependence back to *David, P.* (1985); *Arthur, B.* (1989) who conceptualized it in order to explore paths of technological change. Other seminal contributions include e.g. *Liebowitz, S. J./Margolis, S. E.* (1995); *Liebowitz, S. J./Margolis, S. E.* (1998b).

[473] See *Argyres, N. S./Liebeskind, J. P.* (1999); *Ghosh, M./John, G.* (1999), p. 142, who focus on the marketing strategy implications of such extension; *Madhok, A.* (2002), p. 543; *Foss, N. J.* (2003); *Nickerson, J. A.* (year not indicated), p. 25f. A possible reason for the reluctance to the incorporation of path dependencies is that their inclusion arguably leads to some deviation from the original strict focus on the individual transaction as unit of analysis. However, the evaluation of trade-off between this strictness and the potential gains from considering such issues, particularly with respect to TCA's contribution to the investigation of strategic issues, seems to start shifting in favor of considering the effects of historical constraints (see related also *Williamson, O. E.* (1999b), p. 1103; *Williamson, O. E.* (2000), p. 611). Few empirical studies have yet tried to assess the effects of path dependencies or, more generally, history, in TCA-based frameworks. *Heide, J./John, G.* (1990) include "history effects" as a non-focal, but potentially important variable (p. 28f): they find a significant positive effect of historical length of the relationship on continuity expectations which in turn impact positively on the level of joint action and, therefore, favor relational governance. Other examples include *Stump, R. L./Joshi, A. W.* (1998).

[474] See *Argyres, N. S./Liebeskind, J. P.* (1999), p. 49.

[475] See *Argyres, N. S./Liebeskind, J. P.* (1999), p. 49.

[476] See on the following *Argyres, N. S./Liebeskind, J. P.* (1999).

128

constrain a firm with respect to governance differentiation. That is, it may force a firm to extend a structure which has been implemented for governing previous transactions to new transactions even though if for the latter, an alternative governance mode might be more efficient. As causes of governance inseparability, the authors identify prior contractual commitments and changes in bargaining power (over the duration of the relationship). Particularly the first effect, constraints from switching, seems to contain interesting implications for this research which outreach the general recognition that the determinants of potential productivity gains are influenced by path dependent firm particularities both on the seller and on the buyer sides.

Yet, the notion of path dependence is not an uncontroversial topic. Its use in this research, therefore, requires some more precise definition. In particular, the view by *Liebowitz/Margolis* (1995) sheds light on this issue. They identify three forms of path dependence based on their impact on the efficiency of an outcome to a dynamic process. *First-degree path dependence* implies no efficiency reduction due to an optimal path choice. *Second-degree path dependence* arises due to imperfect information. Although with better information a better path could have been chosen than was actually done, owing to the assumed limitations on knowledge, the particular outcome is not found to be inefficient. Given the available alternatives and information at the time of the decision, the choices in these cases cannot be improved on. Finally, *third-degree path dependence* is identified as a condition where the outcome is really inefficient in the sense that at some point a choice was taken which was suboptimal even then because an alternative path leading to a preferred outcome was available and known. Yet, its occurrence is shown to require the imposition of severe restrictions on prices, institutions, or foresight. The authors, essentially, dismiss the first forms based on nonexistent or non-remediable outcome consequences. While this argument may hold on a macro level, the individual company in this analysis, nevertheless, has to cope with the consequences, or, as *Helper* (1991) puts it, "past decisions affect future choices"[477]. Hence, with respect to this research, the first form of path dependence is irrelevant due to its lack of outcome relevance. While the third form may be relevant here, its occurrence hinges on very restrictive assumptions. Therefore, the main focus of this work is on second-degree path dependence. It may be relevant in that it is presumed to have an impact both on general

---

[477] *Helper, S.* (1991), p. 823. For detailed substantiation and industry evidence see also p. 789ff.

desirability and efficient assertability of a shift and are, thus, incorporated in subsequent considerations.[478]

3.2.3.2.2   Perceived danger of exploitation

The envisaged productivity gains of specific investments are brought about at the expense of an increased perception of being threatened to become a victim of opportunistic exploitation and losing the amount at stake at least partially. Emphasizing the influence of subjective perceptions in a world of bounded rationality, this factor is modeled in analogy to the perceived risk construct.[479] In order to set it apart from the distinct notion of "risk"[480], the term of "perceived danger" is coined. In line with the assumption of bounded rationality, the term implies a stronger appeal to information deficiencies than the risk construct does. Nevertheless, some analogies are implied by this terminology.

First, the emphasis on perception serves to highlight that in a world of bounded rationality the subjective state of knowledge of an actor matters.[481] Even if given with a clear conscience and determination, one party's promise to restrain from opportunistic behavior will not reduce the subjectively perceived likelihood of being exploited from the viewpoint of the other party unless this promise is credible, that is: costly in case of non-compliance.[482] Neither do events

---

[478]   See for application chapter 4.5.

[479]   See for its origins and seminal treatment *Bauer, R. A.* (1967), p. 30; *Cox, D. F.* (1967a), p. 5; *Cox, D. F.* (1967b), p. 37ff; *Cunningham, S. M.* (1967), p. 83f. *Backhaus, K./Plinke, W./Rese, M.* (2004), (p. 13), actually use the original construct in conjunction with TCA.

[480]   The notion of risk as usually applied in economics today can be traced back to *Knight, F. H.* (1921 (repr.: 1965)), esp. p. 224ff. Risk ("statistical probability") is associated with a weaker form of information deficiency, namely imperfect, yet complete knowledge, that is all possible events and related outcomes can be specified and objective probabilities can be attached to them. On the other hand, uncertainty (in a narrow sense; "estimates") prevails when at best subjective probabilities can be estimated. Bounded rationality actually represents an even stronger level of information deficiency: knowledge is imperfect and incomplete in the sense that not even all possible paths are known (see for an overview e.g. *Backhaus, K./Aufderheide, D./Späth, G.-M.* (1994), p. 19ff). Some authors refer to the first two conditions as risk and to the latter as uncertainty in a narrow sense (see e.g. *Bamberg, G./Coenenberg, A. G.* (2002), p. 77). This terminology seems, though, less suitable for an investigation which is based on TCA.

[481]   Such a position bears some similarity to the emphasis on perceived (environmental) uncertainty as prevalent in the resource dependence literature (see e.g. *Peffer, J./Salancik, G. R.* (1978); *Aldrich, H. E.* (1979)).

[482]   Messages are generally distinguished from signals due to the costliness of signals. For more detailed investigation into the requirements for a message to be credible see e.g. *Williamson, O. E.* (1985), pp. 163ff, 190ff, with emphasis on credible commitments; see also *Spence, M.* (1976), p. 593ff; from a game theoretic

130

which increase one party's affinity to act opportunistically enhance the other one's perception of danger if the party does not become aware of them. For instance, while the occurrence of severe financial difficulties may well become known to a firm's bank, it may remain concealed to a supplier that has invested specifically until prices are pushed down in renegotiations.

Second, the dichotomy of determinants from the original conception is preserved in spirit.[483] The amount at stake as maximum potential loss and maximum possible negative deviation from the goals attached to the investment represents the first determinant of the perceived danger. The second determinant is the subjective "certainty" or likelihood which is attached to the occurrence of this event – well aware of the necessary incompleteness of this estimate due to the condition of bounded rationality. Uncertainty in its various forms, combined with the ubiquitous condition of bounded rationality, forms the basis for this perceived danger of exploitation.

3.2.3.2.2.1 Uncertainty

Generally, a distinction is made between parametric uncertainty as a property of the decision environment and strategic uncertainty has been outlined above in some more detail in chapter 2.1.2.2. Yet, what remains to be discussed are the mechanisms through which uncertainty affects the perceived danger of exploitation and also its potential antecedents. In that respect, also the relation between uncertainty and complexity in the context of this investigation requires clarification.[484]

Parametric uncertainty

Increasing parametric uncertainty generally raises the perceived danger of exploitation since the probability, and potentially also the magnitude of qualitative, quantitative, schedule-

---

angle see e.g. the seminal contributions by *Kreps, D. M./Wilson, R.* (1982); *Milgrom, P./Roberts, J.* (1982); recently, including a brief overview *Prabhu, H./Stewart, D. W.* (2001).

[483] For more detailed discussion of the original dichotomy see *Cox, D. F.* (1967b), p. 37f.

[484] For different positions on this issue see e.g. *Williamson, O. E.* (1985), p. 57; *Malone, T. W./Yates, J./Benjamin, R. I.* (1987), p. 486; *Baur, C.* (1990), p. 77ff; *Homburg, C.* (1995), p. 818; *Chiles/McMackin* (1996), p. 89ff.

related or technological ex post changes in the exchange environment increase.[485] Such changes in turn endanger the validity of the decision quality and pose an adaptation problem.[486] In the case of unspecific investments, higher parametric uncertainty mainly raises the ex ante transaction costs of information gathering and worsens the relation between ideally to be gathered relevant information and actually gathered information. However, the deterioration in decision quality which can be expected is limited by the (nearly) costless substitutability in case of non-compliance.[487] For instance, a supplier of nonspecific automotive components who is unable to keep a just-in-time delivery agreement due to force majeur such as a strike or a fire in his production facilities is fairly easily replaced by another supplier. Owing to reduced substitutability, more severe consequences are likely for transactions which involve specific investments.[488] Also, achievement of (already complex) long-term contractual safeguarding of such investments is additionally hampered by growing parametric uncertainty.[489] Thus, higher levels of parametric uncertainty relatively favor nonspecific transactions over specific transactions.[490] According to the traditional TCA view on parametric uncertainty, however, in the *presence* of specific investments, higher degrees of environmental uncertainty have been argued to be more efficiently aligned with hierarchical governance than market governance.[491] Yet, the validity of this prediction in different asset

---

[485] Refinements of the construct have concentrated on its sources (e.g. volume, technology, and competition) and the information processing challenges posed by market volatility or dynamism, although this distinction has not been uniformly applied (see *Joshi, A. W./Stump, R. L.* (1999), p. 42, and the literature referred to there; also *Cannon, J. P./Achrol, R. S./Gundlach, G. T.* (2000), p. 181f). See for extensive investigation from a different, though related theoretical angle *Achrol, R. S./Stern, L. W.* (1988).

[486] See *Rubin, P. H.* (1990), p. xvi; *Heide, J. B.* (1994), p. 73; *Rindfleisch, A./Heide, J. B.* (1997), p. 31.

[487] Empirical evidence has been provided e.g. by *Anderson, E.* (1985), p. 251.

[488] See e.g. *Williamson, O. E.* (1985), p. 243; Support for such conjecture also comes from the literature on resource dependence theory (see e.g. *Peffer, J./Salancik, G. R.* (1978), p. 68).

[489] See *Picot, A.* (1991), p. 347.

[490] See *Williamson, O. E.* (1985), p. 59f, in referring to parametric uncertainty: "accordingly, market exchange continues and the discrete contracting paradigm holds across standardized transactions of all kinds, whatever the degree of uncertainty." Similarly, though only for uncertainty about obsolence of previous investments e.g. *Ghosh, M./John, G.* (1999), p. 135. *Achrol, R. S./Reve, T./Stern, L. W.* (1983) propose this mechanism only in cases, where vertical integration/cooperation fail faced with uncertainty. Recent, additional support is provided by *Argyres, N. S./Liebeskind, J. P.* (1999) who emphasize the path dependent consequences of internalization which operate in favor of market governance in uncertain environments, or *Ghemawat, P./del Sol, P.* (1998), p. 38.

[491] See e.g. *Anderson, E./Weitz, B. A.* (1986).

132

specificity contexts has also been challenged.[492] Empirical evidence on the effects from environmental uncertainty has been rather diverse.[493]

In addressing this conceptual and empirical ambiguity, the dominant explanation which emerges from the literature is the conjecture that the environmental uncertainty construct should be unbundled into its different components, with technological uncertainty, particularly in the form of technological obsolescence or unpredictability, and volume uncertainty in terms of unpredictability having been proposed as candidates.[494] Each component's effects on the choice of asset specificity could be formulated on a theoretical level even allowing for opposing directions of impact on governance choice, and could then be subject to empirical tests.[495]

However, an alternative or additional line of argument could be advanced which attempts to respond to the problem by recognizing that the direction of impact cannot be unambiguously determined due to its contingency on other factors in the framework.[496] The effects on an

---

[492] See e.g. *Walker, G./Weber, D.* (1984); *Heide, J. B.* (1994), p. 73, argues that "transaction cost theory [...] views nonmarket governance as a response to environmental uncertainty and dependence..." (p. 73). The findings by *Masten, S. E./Snyder, E. A.* (1993) have been interpreted as an illustration from business practice for more hierarchical governance in a context of high environmental uncertainty and resulting adaptation problems (see e.g. *Ghosh, M./John, G.* (1999), p. 139). However, the basic argument of *Masten, S. E./Snyder, E. A.* (1993), pp. 35f, 50, is that in a context of severe adaptation needs, leasing practices are favored over selling arrangements. Now, from the customer's point of view, leasing may represent a form of gaining access to the functionality which is associated with less specificity. Such acquisition could then resemble more a customer product business (for more detailed argumentation see e.g. *Backhaus, K.* (2003), p. 631ff)

[493] Recent comprehensive reviews of empirical literature in TCA include *Boerner, C. S./Macher, J. T.* (2001).

[494] See e.g. *Walker, G./Weber, D.* (1984), p. 376; *Balakrishnan, S./Wernerfelt, B.* (1986), p. 358; *Day, G. S./Klein, S.* (1987), p. 53; *Heide, J./John, G.* (1990), p. 27ff; *Geyskens, I./Steenkamp, J.-B. E. M./Kumar, N.* (2003), p. 15ff. For instance, *Heide, J./John, G.* (1990), p. 28, drawing on *Walker, G./Weber, D.* (1984), p. 376, define volume unpredictability as "...the inability to forecast accurately the volume requirements in the relationship..." and technological unpredictability as the "...inability to forecast accurately the technical requirements in the relationship...".

[495] For instance, it has been suggested that, while technological uncertainty might be managed more efficiently through market governance, volume uncertainty might motivate tighter interfirm linkages and, ultimately, hierarchical governance (see *Geyskens, I./Steenkamp, J.-B. E. M./Kumar, N.* (2003), p. 14). Yet, of the studies that have explicitly addressed this issue so far, not all corroborate this proposition. The evidence on technological uncertainty is, however, considerably more confirmative (see e.g. *Balakrishnan, S./Wernerfelt, B.* (1986), p. 358; *Heide, J./John, G.* (1990), p. 33).

[496] Some tentative support for this idea can be drawn from *Anderson, E.* (1985), pp. 239,251, who hypothesizes a higher combination of environmental uncertainty and specific investment to lead to a higher likelihood of a direct sales force as opposed to outside agents and finds support for this hypothesis only when a certain level of asset specificity is present.

increase in environmental uncertainty on asset specificity could be contingent on the size of the relative advantage of specific transactions over nonspecific transactions, that is, whether the previously optimal governance form was already closer to (spot) market exchange or vertical integration. Such argumentation implies the presumption of some threshold below which an increase in environmental uncertainty might lead to less specific transaction forms and above which it might work in the opposite direction, inducing closer cooperation and ultimately a shift from (specific) market transactions (e.g. relational business) towards insourcing of the activity.[497]

Finally, within the proposed business-types-framework, a third potential argument emerges which is based on asset specificity as a choice variable. From that perspective, exploring the effects of an increase in parametric uncertainty in the *presence* of specific investment (i.e. regarding the specific investment as a datum) on governance structure may distract from the central issue, that is, whether the same specific investment would be *chosen* at all. The proposition here is, therefore, that rising environmental uncertainty perceived by a party can be expected to be c.p. associated with a reduction in its chosen asset specificity. Note that this conjecture does not deny (supplementary) potential influences in the form of the first and second explanation.

In any case, given the lack of consensus on the effects(s) of environmental uncertainty and the fact that this research is concerned with exchanges over markets, albeit more or less specific, with vertical integration as the other extreme pole not included, the general expectation will be that growing parametric uncertainty (whether due to technological or volume reasons) c.p. reduces an actor's interest to invest specifically.[498] A move from project or relational business transactions towards product business is presumed to be favored by the actor.[499]

To conclude the discussion on environmental uncertainty, another issue demands attention, namely the relation between uncertainty and complexity which has been subject to

---

[497] The idea of environmental uncertainty contingently pointing in different directions of coordination has previously been expressed e.g. by *Achrol, R. S./Reve, T./Stern, L. W.* (1983), though from a different theoretical angle and with the opposite direction of impact as proposed here.

[498] See also the discussion on demand-side uncertainty in section 3.2.3.2.1.2 on buyer receptivity for specificity, and related arguments as advanced e.g. by *Barney, J. B./Lee, W.* (2000), p. 306ff.

[499] It should be noted, though, that this conjecture applies only to the actor's own business type. The actor may well have an interest in increased specific investments on behalf of the other party.

controversial debate in the literature. Yet, it still awaits unambiguous clarification. While some authors regard complexity as a distinct construct on its own, others consider it to be an antecedent to uncertainty, and still others have used it as a proxy for the degree of uncertainty.[500] For the purpose of this work, the approach proposed by *Day/Klein* (1987) which draws on *Duncan* (1972) is taken up: uncertainty is assumed to be a two-dimensional construct consisting of complexity and dynamism.[501] Each of the dimensions may relate to various parameters such as volume or technological specifications.

Strategic uncertainty

Higher strategic uncertainty also generally contributes to the perception of potentially falling victim to opportunistic exploitation, but is exclusively present in the case of transactions with idiosyncratic investments. Lacking a (costless) exit option, performance evaluation and measurement problems and issues of contractual non-compliance gain importance, since, in the case of ex post conflicts, buyer and supplier need to come together to work out a new arrangement.[502] Their exploitation lies at the heart of strategic uncertainty. The difficulty of reaching an ex post agreement varies with the severeness of the measurement problem. *Backhaus/Aufderheide/Späth* (1994) account for this by distinguishing two categories of severeness of the measurement problem which are still compatible, in principle, with transacting over markets. If the fulfillment of the agreement can at least be verified, the measurement problems are less severe than if it is only observable.[503] In general, one can assume that finite horizon transactions with only transaction specific investments may exhibit

---

[500] On the first position see e.g. *Picot, A./Dietl, H.* (1990), p. 179ff, who consider uncertainty and complexity as alternative, distinct concepts responsible for the relevance of bounded rationality. The second idea has been expressed e.g. by *Day, G. S./Klein, S.* (1987), p. 53, who identify complexity and dynamism as dimensions of uncertainty, drawing on *Duncan, R. B.* (1972), p. 315ff, who further subdivides dynamism into degree and frequency of change of the relevant environment's elements (p. 316); also: *Baur, C.* (1990), p. 77f. Complexity is regarded to result from a large number of interrelated relevant variables which can take different states. *Masten, S. E.* (1984), p. 409, finally, uses the "relative complexity of components" in an empirical study "...as a proxy for the degree of uncertainty on the production side" (p. 409).

[501] See *Duncan, R. B.* (1972), p. 315ff; *Day, G. S./Klein, S.* (1987), p. 53. *Jaworski, B. J.* (1988), on the other hand, proposes an alternative systematization with uncertainty and dynamism as constructs on the same level (p. 25)

[502] For a short summary on this issue see e.g. *Heide, J. B.* (1994), p. 73.

[503] See *Backhaus, K./Aufderheide, D./Späth, G.-M.* (1994), p. 56ff. Verifiability is associated with the conditions that are closer to risk and uncertainty in a narrow sense. Observability is subject to a severe condition of bounded rationality. Theoretical foundations are provided e.g. by *Klein, B./Leffler, K. B.* (1981).

135

c.p. less severe measurement problems than transaction chains which lack a clearly defined horizon. In default of a well-defined number of transactions and, necessarily, also of the final performance expected, the seeds for conflict are unavoidably planted from the initial contract on. The degree of specificity is also presumed to affect the extent of performance measurement problems. A higher degree of specificity necessarily implies further deviation from market-based reference points of performance and so contributes performance ambiguity and a resulting potential for conflict.[504] Finally, the extent of disgruity of the would-be constellation in terms of transaction-specific investment is likely to impact on the perceived strategic uncertainty.[505]

Although specific investments unavoidably pose problems of potential strategic exploitation, deviations from the assumed large numbers condition may c.p. aggravate them as will be discussed subsequently.

Structures of the relevant markets and resulting *ex ante* market power relations are proposed as an antecedent to strategic uncertainty.[506] While this conjecture deviates somewhat from the strict form of bilateral voluntary exchange, that is, the ex ante large numbers condition, it does not contradict the general idea of unconstrained bargaining. Also, it accounts for empirically observable phenomena like, for instance, power relations between buyers and suppliers in the automotive industry which are influenced by the (often unequal) structures on each side of the market.[507] Even further, it could be argued that the relevant market structures should extend to the seller's supply markets as well as the buyer's sales markets. *Helper* (1991), for instance, has shown that "...a buyer with market power in its final-product market can use that power to change the structure of its input markets..."[508]. Although the prime focus of this research is on the structures in the immediately relevant markets, that is, the seller with its competitors on

---

[504] In essence, the potential exploitation of performance ambiguities and adaptation needs results from an interaction effect with environmental uncertainty (see e.g. *Anderson, E.* (1985), p. 251; *Williamson, O. E.* (1985), p. 59).

[505] See for related modeling *Mudambi, R./McDowell-Mudambi, S.* (1995)

[506] Rather implictly and as a by-product in the form of bargaining power, such issues have already been implicitly featured in the discussion of buyer receptivity for asset specificity.

[507] See e.g the seminal treatment of OEM-suppliers' dependency positions with respect to automobile producers by *Freiling, J.* (1995).

[508] *Helper, S.* (1991), p. 782f.

the one side, and the buyer with its rivaling buyers on the other side as expressed by the particular intensity of competition among sellers, other influences are also acknowledged. The core idea is that even under conditions of basically unconstrained bargaining with more than one potential exchange partner, the initial bargaining power may be distributed unevenly. This is likely to be the case if the numbers of actors on each side of the market vary considerably. For instance, a large number of (small) sellers may face a choice between only two (large) potential buyers (demand duopoly). Market structure is, therefore, understood first of all in terms of the number of firms in a market.[509]

Barriers to entry which are a traditional industrial organization variable for characterization of a market's structure are captured as a further criterion.[510] Their inclusion seems particularly relevant because the potential sunk cost nature of transaction specific investments may be employed in order to erect such barriers.[511] The term "barriers to entry" is closely linked to *Bain's* (1951, 1956) investigations into the linkages between market structure, conduct of market participants and performance implications which laid, together with *Mason's* (1949) work, the foundations for the so-called "structure-conduct-performance" paradigm.[512] For the purpose of this work, it suffices to identify a suitable definition of barriers to entry without going into further details of the various theoretical positions in industrial economics which underlie the term. Influential definitions have, for instance, been proposed by *v. Weizsäcker* (1980) who regards them as "...socially undesirable limitations to entry of resources which

---

[509] For detailed presentation of various forms of markets see *Schumann, J./Meyer, U./Ströbele, W.* (1999), p. 273ff. The distinction between complete or incomplete market transparency is not relevant for this research. Intensive discussion of the implications of different market forms is also provided by *Varian, H. R.* (1999). From a strategic planning perspective, additional factors such as market growth rate tend to be included which will not be discussed here (see *Varadarajan, P. R./Jayachandran, S.* (1999), p. 126).

[510] See e.g. *Schumann, J./Meyer, U./Ströbele, W.* (1999), p. 502. The degree of product differentiation which is sometimes also referred to appears on the buyer side in terms of impacts on receptivity with the resulting consequences for bargaining power. On the seller-side, it is depicted as a direct influence by allowing the same functionality to be exchanged in various forms of market offering, and indirectly by accounting for influences such as ingredient branding. Extreme degrees of "product differentiation" are treated as innovations (see also chapter 3.3) with corresponding consequences, that is, a temporary monopoly position for the pioneer (see e.g. *Lieberman, M. B./Montgomery, D. B.* (1988), p. 41). For a comprehensive, yet brief literature review see e.g. *Karakaya, F./Stahl, M. J.* (1989).

[511] For a more detailed discussion see chapter 3.3.4. Supportive of this position is e.g. *Williamson, O. E.* (1985), p. 31, fn 26, in his discussion on the differences between the "theory of contestable markets" (see *Baumol, W. J./Panzer, J./Willig, R.* (1982)) and TCA regarding asset specificity; also *Fehl, U.* (1985) who emphasizes in his review the fact that sunk rather than fixed costs create entry barriers (pp. 37ff, 47).

[512] See *Bain, J. S.* (1951); *Bain, J. S.* (1956), also: *Mason, E. S.* (1949).

are due to protection of resource owners already in the market."[513] Drawing on *Stigler* (1968), *Baumol* et al. (1982) define entry barriers as "...anything that requires an expenditure by a new entrant into an industry, but imposes no equivalent cost upon an incumbent."[514] Owing to its less explicit normative appeal to welfare consequences, this latter definition seems more suitable for this analysis which is undertaken from an individual producer's perspective.

Finally, *transaction partner identity* is proposed to exert an impact on the perception of strategic uncertainty associated with a specific investment. A first example of such an influence is a common transaction history. The findings of a number of empirical studies suggest that a positively evaluated common transaction history might be negatively related to the perception of being endangered by opportunistic behavior on the part of the other party in subsequent transactions.[515] For example, *Stump/Joshi* (1998) have analyzed the issue of a particular transaction within an ongoing relationship with the purpose of identifying situational and contextual factors which impact on the buyer's willingness to provide specific investments in support of the new transaction.[516] Starting from the hypothesis that the intensity of the prior relationship between the transaction partners matters, they find evidence that the previous exchange history impacts on the way a new transaction is structured. Extending their result, it seems not implausible to surmise that there may be effects from past behavior in general on present expectation formation and transaction structuring – if known and relevant to the particular transaction party. For instance, a buyer who is known industry-wide to have a certain tradition of exploiting suppliers is likely to have difficulties in stimulating specific investments on the part of the suppliers even if it is a first-time business with a particular seller.[517] Analogous reasoning applies to the case of an "opportunistic" seller

---

[513] *von Weizäcker, C. C.* (1980), p.13.

[514] *Baumol, W. J./Panzer, J./Willig, R.* (1982), p. 282; see also *Stigler, G. J.* (1968 (repr.: 1990)).

[515] See e.g. *Parkhe, A.* (1993), although in the context of horizontal interfirm relations, *Stump, R. L./Joshi, A. W.* (1998), p. 51.

[516] See *Stump, R. L./Joshi, A. W.* (1998). For a related perspective accounting for the prior historical relationship of the two parties see *Heide, J./John, G.* (1990), p. 33.

[517] See e.g. *Backhaus, K./Büschken, J.* (1999), p. 254.

and a potential, new buyer. In such context, user-groups have become notable with regard to knowledge-transfer.[518]

The firms' positioning in the relevant markets as influenced by past strategic decisions are another example of such an impact on the perception of strategic uncertainty. For example consider a positioning of a buyer company in its sales market which is characterized by a high brand equity. A related discussion by *Gosh/John* (1999), for example, points to the idea that higher brand equity of a buyer in his own sales market may, in general, lead to a higher perception of strategic uncertainty associated with customized supply of input goods.[519] Such customized supply entails idiosyncratic investments by the supplier which are usually associated at least to a certain degree, and second sourcing aside, with buyer-side idiosyncrasies. The underlying reason for the buyer perception of increased danger of exploitation is that in general an established brand acts as a reputative signal to buyers because it has been costly to establish.[520] Compared to a buyer without a significant brand equity, the buyer has more to lose from quality problems and underperformance including delivery delays, his bargaining power is c.p. reduced. In case an input good is specifically tailored to the buyer's needs, the buyer's brand equity acts like a leverage strengthening his dependence on the relevant supplier. A high brand equity of the buyer is, therefore, hypothesized to be associated c.p. with a higher perceived strategic uncertainty and perceived danger of exploitation. To be sure, this is not to say that such buyers would generally decline customized products. Yet, if they purchase specific, customized input goods, they are presumed to be more likely to reduce their dependence through second- or multiple sourcing strategies, even though this clearly reduces the potential realization of scale economies at each supplier.[521]

---

[518] See e.g. *Erichsson, S. K.* (1994)

[519] See also on the following argument *Ghosh, M./John, G.* (1999).

[520] See the pertinent literature by *Klein, B./Leffler, K. B.* (1981), p. 625ff; *Schmidt, I./Elßler, S.* (1992) and the respective cited literature. In general, on signals and their costs see e.g. *Spence, M.* (1976).

[521] See for more detailed discussions of such sourcing strategies e.g. *Jackson, B. B.* (1985), p. 172ff; *Farrell, J./Gallini, N. T.* (1988); *Dutta, S./John, G.* (1995); *Homburg, C.* (1995).

3.2.3.2.2.2 Distinct modeling of buyer and seller perception

Finally, one further point needs to be highlighted, namely that divergences in the level and horizon of uncertainty may prevail between buyer and seller. Yet, since each of these parties has to make a decision on its favored degree and kind of asset specificity (i.e. on its business type), the particular characteristics of uncertainty should be specified separately for each side.

An example for this idea is provided by an empirical study by *Noordewier/John/Nevin* (1990) on the performance outcomes of purchasing agreements in OEM-vendor exchange relationships.[522] Their study is based on data from 140 OEMs concerning the acquisition of repetitively used, standardized commodity-type items. Faced with increasing environmental uncertainty (from the point of view of the buyer), buyers are found to be able to enhance their performance in acquisition cost terms through the introduction of "...more relational elements into their purchasing arrangements."[523] At first sight, this finding seems to contradict the proposition that changes in the degree of environmental uncertainty leave governance modes for nonspecific transactions largely unaffected. However, closer scrutiny of the dimensions of relationalism as used by *Noordewier/John/Nevin* (1990) reveals potential interpretations which could facilitate alignment with the proposition.

From factors such as the buyer's interest in emergency deliveries by the specific supplier as reported by *Noordewier/John/Nevin* (1990), it could be concluded that some low level of asset specificity might be present in the relationship, at least on the buyer side. In that case, changes in the contractual arrangements could be expected, though, with a tendency towards reduction of specificity. In fact, the tendency towards increased relationalism that *Noordewier/John/Nevin* (1990) find rests largely on a move towards higher specificity on the part of the supplier, much less on the part of the buyer. Some central dimensions that *Noordewier/John/Nevin* (1990) use to measure relationalism primarily entail more specificity on the part of the seller (e.g. supplier flexibility, supplier assistance). In the face of increased environmental uncertainty, the buyer seems to develop a preference for shaping the specificity differential in the transaction relation in favor of himself. The buyer's appreciation of increased supplier assistance e.g. in the form of making "...sacrifices for which there is no

---

[522] See *Noordewier, T. G./John, G./Nevin, J. R.* (1990).

[523] *Noordewier, T. G./John, G./Nevin, J. R.* (1990), p. 80.

immediate or explicit compensation..."[524] and the trend towards more specificity on the supplier-side indicate, at the same time, the (implicit) interest in certain specific investments by the seller in the relationship – as well as their (partial) appropriation by the buyer.[525] Such opportunity is arguably always valuable to the buyer, but potentially even more so in the face of high levels of environmental uncertainty since it is the very occurrence of exogenous disturbances which brings about the need for adaptations and, thereby, opportunities for exploitation.[526] The increased environmental uncertainty that the buyer encounters in the described setting thereby gets transformed into increased strategic uncertainty faced by the supplier.

As a result of these considerations, and unlike those displayed by most of the literature, an investigation of shifts between business types should account for the potential divergence in buyer and seller uncertainty and should, therefore, model them as separate impacts, with inferences on shift options drawn only on a joint consideration of both.

3.2.3.3 Implications from asset specificity as a choice variable: examples from business practice

Examples illustrating either explicitly or implicitly the idea of asset specificity as a choice variable can be found in the literature on TCA, marketing, strategic management and related fields, or may be observed from business practice. The selected examples have been documented or established in the literature without reference to the business types framework. Yet, they can be meaningfully interpreted in such direction.

3.2.3.3.1 Consequence 1: the same functionality is supplied in various business types constellations

The first example which relates to marketing a photocopying facility has been selected in order to illustrate the proposition that the same functionality can be transacted in various

---

[524] Noordewier, T. G./John, G./Nevin, J. R. (1990), p. 83.

[525] Other examples in the study are the expectation of the seller maintaining (additional) stock levels or being prepared for emergency deliveries as indicators of his flexibility.

[526] See Williamson, O. E. (1985), p. 59.

constellations of business types. In principle, all nine are possible. Yet, since *Mathur/Kenyon* (1997) who give the example use a different systematization of transactions and, therefore, refer only to four distinct ways of marketing the functionality, only these four are reinterpreted in terms of the business types framework.[527]

(1) Marketing the photocopying facility as a bilateral relational business

"The supplier, with distinctive skill, analyses a customer's requirements, recommends a configuration of equipment and environment most appropriate to those requirements, then designs, supplies, installs and maintains the specified configuration as part of a unique package."[528] In this case, seller and buyer alike are both locked-in to each other by means of idiosyncratic product-related investments. No explicit information on mode-related specific investments can be inferred. From the seller's point of view an alleviating effect could, for instance, be achieved by payments which parallel its investments in the customer-specific analysis. While this would reinforce the customer's lock-in, the opposite effect would result from shifting the lion's share of payment towards the maintenance phase.

(2) Marketing the photocopying facility as a bilateral product business

"The offering is indistinguishable from that of many competitors. Help given by the supplier may well be significant, but is no different from help given by competitors. The customer chooses whatever is cheapest to buy and use."[529] No idiosyncrasies in the product-related dimension occur on either side. Neither is there any hint of mode-related provisions taken in order to create specificity such as, for instance, ex ante paid maintenance agreements with validity tied to the use of original supplier spare parts.

(3) Marketing the photocopying facility as a combination of seller product business and buyer relational business

"Here the offering is differentiated in the merchandise dimension, but not in the support dimension. The photocopying installation is a "Rolls-Royce" installation with special

---

[527] For the original description see *Mathur, S. S./Kenyon, A.* (1997), p. 107.

[528] *Mathur, S. S./Kenyon, A.* (1997), 107.

[529] *Mathur, S. S./Kenyon, A.* (1997), 107.

features and robust quality. To the customer, it is differentiated by the way of merchandise, but undifferentiated as regards any individual support from the supplier."[530] This case can be interpreted as the seller marketing different types or designs of photocopying facilities which are likely to be (at least to some degree) proprietary in nature. The products are pre-fabricated and since no individual seller support is provided, the seller can be concluded to transact in product business. The buyer in turn invests idiosyncratically in a proprietary product. Yet, the lock-in seems to be less severe than in case 1 since maintenance can obviously be provided, although maybe at a higher price, by someone other than the original supplier.

(4) Marketing the photocopying facility as a combination of seller relational business and buyer product business

"Here the offering is differentiated as regards support, but not merchandise. The supplier acts as adviser, analysing the customer's requirements and specifying the installation from a range of standard equipment. The supplier specifies, installs and maintains the recommended configuration."[531] The seller's idiosyncratic investments result here mainly from the acquisition of buyer-specific knowledge. If the payment conditions are such that this investment amortizes only over the complete course of specification, installation and service, the seller firm faces a lock-in. Otherwise, in case it manages to receive timely compensation for its initial efforts, the lock-in would be reduced. Due to the employment of standard equipment, it is likely that the buyer could still rather easily switch to a competitor for purchase of the machinery.

3.2.3.3.2 *Consequence 2: the same functionality is supplied in various business types constellations by various firms*

The second example illustrates the impact of firm particularities, and strategic positions in particular, on the choice of asset specificity in that different buyers in a market seek to purchase items which are comparable regarding their functionality in different business types constellations. This clearly requires different producers to employ distinct constellations in

---

[530] *Mathur, S. S./Kenyon, A.* (1997), 107.

[531] *Mathur, S. S./Kenyon, A.* (1997), 107.

supplying the same functionality and, hence, emphasizes the marketing strategy implications from asset specificity as a choice variable from the point of view of an individual company. The example builds on *Gosh/John*'s (1999) illustration of varied needs for specific investments by supply chain partners from the perspective of two automobile manufacturers.[532]

There are two automobile manufacturers, B_1 and B_2. Each has positioned itself with respect to two groups of attributes in the end-customers' market, that is, reliability and fit/finish attributes on the one side, and sports car technology on the other side. While B_1 focuses on the first position, B_2 pursues the second strategy. Consequently, B_1 needs innovative assembly processes because the assembly's quality impacts heavily on the achieved level of the reliability. Innovations in production processes are, though, highly specific. B_1, thus, seeks suppliers of process modules who deliver highly customized performance. Considerable idiosyncratic investments on behalf of both exchange partners are undertaken to jointly develop the innovations. On the other hand, B_1's receptivity for specificity is much lower with respect to individual components. Such focus would, though, be decisive for other achieving high levels in other attributes that are related to sports car performance. Thus, B_2 is much less in need of innovative assembly processes. The attributes which are relevant from its perspective demand the employment and transfer of latest racing-car technology in its components. As a result, process elements will be bought on a less customized basis than in B_1's case, whereas the relationship with at least some suppliers of actual components is likely to be supported by (bilateral) highly specific investments. These manufacturer requirements provoke direct feedback effects for the suppliers of process elements on the one hand, and of components on the other hand: for each group of sellers, there is scope for at least two distinct constellations to be pursued (e.g. bilateral relational and bilateral product business, respectively), depending on which OEM is targeted.

Now that the foundations of the feasibility of shifts (in a "technological" sense) have been laid with the preceding discussion of asset specificity as a choice variable, an investigation into the motivations that lead to the consideration of such strategic behavior is called for.

---

[532] See *Ghosh, M./John, G.* (1999), p. 137, who draw on empirical evidence that *Whitney, D. E.* (1992) provides in a comparison between General Motors and Toyota.

3.3 Motivations of seller-initiated redesigns of business types constellations

3.3.1 Fundamental (entrepreneurial) objectives in transactions and the subgoals of creating, claiming, and protecting value

"...exchange itself is value creating (all parties to an exchange expect *ex ante* to increase their utility)."[533] At the heart of this statement as well as traditional economic thinking is the idea that improving one's own situation is the fundamental driver of exchange processes and transactions on markets.[534] The debate on appropriate further concretization of this objective in various theoretical contexts centers mainly around a few issues.[535] First there are questions regarding the *textual nature* of the objective and the envisaged *extent* of amelioration.[536] Inter-related are the issues of diverging *time horizons* (ranging from short- to long-term) and different *analyzed entities* (from individual actors to firms and organizations, with nearly arbitrarily fine further nuanciations among the latter) which contribute to definitional varieties.[537]

For the purpose of this research, the *extent* to which economic actors are assumed to strive for improvement of their situation is largely defined by the theoretical basis which is referred to, namely TCA. Faced with the condition of bounded rationality, actors still aim at maximizing

---

[533] *Foss, N. J.* (2003). This assertion implies a particular understanding of exchange as voluntary, mutually beneficial exchange. Other forms of exchanges exist, but do not form part of this analysis. For a discussion see e.g. *Backhaus, K./Plinke, W./Rese, M.* (2004), (p. 2 ff).

[534] See the early and famous quotation by *Smith, A.* (1789 (repr.: 1976)), p. 26f: "it is not from the benevolence of the butcher, the brewer, or the baker, that we expect our dinner, but from their regard to their own interest. We [...] never talk to them of our own necessities but of their advantages."

[535] See for general discussions on dimensions of objectives in decision theory *Bamberg, G./Coenenberg, A. G.* (2002), p. 28ff. The terms objective, goal, purpose, motivation etc. are all used interchangeably in this work (for more differentiated positions see e.g. *Scott, W. R.* (1998), p. 286ff, who provides a detailed discussion on organizational goals and various types of them serving different functions (e.g. behavioral guidance, motivation, ex post justification, evaluation) (also: *Simon, H. A.* (1964)); *Anderson, J. C./Narus, J. A.* (1999), p. 143).

[536] While the frist criterion corresponds to the notion of "Zielgröße (goal content)" as described by *Bamberg, G./Coenenberg, A. G.* (2002), p. 28f, the second covers the issue of "Höhenpräferenzrelation (preference for goal achievment)".

[537] The time horizon accords with "Zeitpräferenz" as outlined by *Bamberg, G./Coenenberg, A. G.* (2002), p. 29. The criterion of "Artenpräferenz (preference for kind of goal)" results here from the chosen entity, and the additional criterion of "Risikopräferenz (risk perference)" need not be discussed due to the risk neutrality assumption in this research.

their utility (gains).[538] Yet, they are likely to miss anything that comes close to an objectively maximal gain, but need to contend themselves with what they perceive as subjectively optimal given a certain state of information and a particular set of available alternatives.[539] The relevant *entities* in this research are firms, yet in close resemblance to individual economic actors: intra-firm exchange relations, for instance, concerning the relationships between employer and employee or between managers and shareholders are largely abstracted from. This focus impacts on the *textual nature* of the assumed objective: the aspired utility is concretized as profits, or, more generally, referred to as value.[540] The relevant *time frame* is defined in accordance with the strategic nature of shifts between business types constellations and, hence, leads to a longer-term orientation. Reference to their strategic nature also brings up another implication: starting with the associated proactivity assumption relates the strategic shift to an entrepreneurial act. Initiation and promotion of the exchange emanate from the prospective seller.[541] This interpretation in turn implies a feedback effect on the suitability of the profit (or, more generally: value) maximization goal.[542]

In this analysis, the such defined objective is assumed to be pursued by the seller within the framework of a market economy which is characterized by division of labor. The relevant firm can then further be expected to conduct transactions with at least two kinds of transaction

---

[538] See, also on the following reasoning, e.g. *Williamson, O. E.* (1985), p. 45. Utility is understood here as a general measure of subjectively perceived welfare (see e.g. *Milgrom, P./Roberts, J.* (1992), p. 22; *Schumann, J./Meyer, U./Ströbele, W.* (1999), p. 4f) and is used as a more general term than profit at this point of the argument. For further reference see e.g. the seminal discussion by *Simon, H. A.* (1969), p. 57ff.

[539] See also e.g. *Backhaus, K./Plinke, W./Rese, M.* (2004), (p. 24f). Assuming such objective is still clearly in the classic economic tradition and represents a much stronger assumption than the "satisficing" behavior as proposed by *Simon, H. A.* (1969), p. 35ff; for discussion see *Erlei, M./Leschke, M./Sauerland, D.* (1999), p. 14ff.

[540] With respect to the seller, this idea is already implied by the strategy definition in chapter 2.2.5 which focuses on the search for rent. The restriction to profits is substantiated on the buyer-side by the fact that only intermediate buyers are considered in this analysis. See for related discussions on particular aspects of profit maximization e.g. *Lieberman, M. B./Montgomery, D. B.* (1988), p. 51; *Webster, F. E. J.* (1992), p. 3f; *Dickson, P. R.* (1996), p. 105. General discussions on the profit maximization goal in economics are provided e.g. by *Milgrom, P./Roberts, J.* (1992), p. 40ff,; *Tirole, J.* (1995), p. 80 ff. For discussions of the more general value maximization principle and its prerequisites see e.g. *Milgrom, P./Roberts, J.* (1992) , p. 35ff; *Schmidt, R. H./Terberger, E.* (1997), p. 40ff. The more practice-oriented issue of how to assess firm performance in reality has been addressed e.g. by *Davis, E./Kay, J.* (1990).

[541] A more detailed discussion of the entrepreneurial nature of strategic shifts between business types constellations and the resulting necessary conditions for them to take place follows in chapter 3.3.3.

[542] See *Brandenburger, A. M./Stuart Jr., H. W.* (1996), p. 20; also chapter 3.3.3.

partners, namely suppliers and buyers.[543] This dichotomy is paralleled by the two dimensions of a market exchange which define the seller's profit from that transaction. On the one side, the seller obtains a certain revenue which results from the price paid by the customer and the involved product quantity. In marketing, this dimension is captured by the notion of effectiveness: with effectiveness as a measure of how well customers' needs are served, higher degrees of effectiveness are generally associated with the ability of extracting higher revenues. On the other side, in supplying the buyer with the offering, the seller incurs costs. This effect is at the heart of efficiency concerns. Both aspects are intertwined since buyers' assessments on how well their needs are served necessarily take into account the sacrifice they have to make in obtaining an offering.[544] While the traditional economic literature naturally lacks an explicit emphasis on the first aspect because the *particular* firm is not at the center of analysis, marketing research must explicitly confront such issues from a (potential) buyer's perspective. Suggested possibilities of integrating effectiveness considerations at least to a large degree in the efficiency notion notwithstanding, a distinction between both dimensions seems to facilitate a marketing-oriented analysis and is hence adopted here.

The principal relationship between the firm and the above groups of transaction partners, suppliers and buyers, in determining the profit/value which accrues to the firm, is depicted in the *Fig. 14*. The upper limit to the potential total value created in the depicted chain of transaction partners is given by the buyer's willingness-to-pay which does not necessarily equal the price paid under the (imperfect) market conditions assumed in this analysis.[545] The gap in between represents the buyer's share (VC^B).[546] The price obtained and the cost (including the firm's opportunity cost) incurred together determine the firm's share (VC^S). The same reasoning applies to the relation between the firm and its suppliers with the opportunity cost to the "supplier of last resort" defining the overall lower limit. The dotted

---

[543] The supplier group also includes, for instance, intra-firm "suppliers of labor". This issue is, however, not further elaborated on in this research.

[544] See also the discussion on cost and revenue/design benefits as the two potential sources of profitability enhancement resulting from specific investments in chapter 2.1.2.2.

[545] In fact, it has been argued that these very market imperfections associated, for instance, with the existence of transaction costs form the basis of those supranormal profits attached to the notion of CAC (see e.g. *Yao, D. A.* (1988), p. 59; *Foss, N. J.* (2003).

[546] *Bowman, C./Ambrosini, V.* (2000) refer to this parameter as "perceived use value", while the price actually paid is labelled as "exchange value" (p. 3f). See also chapter 2.1.2.6.

line delimits the dyad as the unit of analysis, that is, the relevant firm is explored in its seller role together with its immediate buyer(s). Nevertheless, it is recognized that actors on preceding or subsequent stages may (indirectly) impact on the seller's and the buyer's value shares. Regarding the discussion of motivations and impulses for shifts, changes in the relations with immediate suppliers and other relevant parties are, therefore, taken into account.[547]

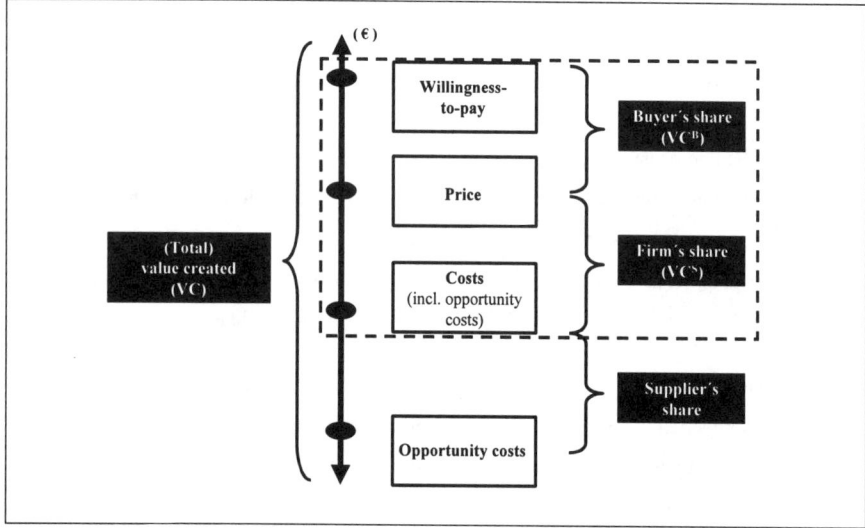

Fig. 14: Relations between the firm and its transaction partners with respect to value creation[548]

Fig. 14 also suggests that at least two ways exist for the seller in improving its value position in terms of increasing the amount of value which accrues to it (VC^S), namely

- creating (total) value, that is, extending the pie which can be divided among the transaction partners. With sole reference to the dyad, this route rests c.p. on providing the

---

[547] See chapter 3.3.3.

[548] Adapted from *Brandenburger, A. M./Stuart Jr., H. W.* (1996), p. 10. Supportive related positions include *Ghosh, M./John, G.* (1999); *Plinke, W./Söllner, A.* (1999), p. 639ff; with an explicit focus on value protection e.g. *Foss, N. J.* (2003).

buyer with an offering which increases its willingness-to-pay and, consequently, allows for extracting a higher price.[549]

- claiming value from an individual perspective which is reflected by the division of value from a joint perspective. The jointly created value of buyer and seller is subject to bargained division with the result being expressed by the price.[550]

While the productivity enhancing effects from asset specificity are captured by the first aspect, the second concern reflects (1) the issue of the particular constellation (congruent vs. disgruent; implied level of congruity/disgruity) and (2) other, structural aspects of (market) power.[551] In contrast to the first, it is likely to be, albeit necessary, associated with a reduction in total value created due to transaction costs.[552]

While the dyadic presentation of these matters seems to suggest a sequential ordering of value creation and division, both issues need to be resolved simultaneously. That is because the division impacts on the relative advantage that the players derive from the particular dyad. At the extreme, they may choose to switch to another dyad in case they expect a relatively unfavorable deal.[553] Time, though, enters in another way, in conjunction with asset specificity: an agreement on the division of value does not necessarily ensure its realization due to divergences in fulfillment timing and the related potential for (forced) renegotiation which is in sharp contrast to the initial unconstrained bargaining.[554] TCA reasoning, thus, suggests a third route which is not directly apparent from *Fig. 14*, that is

- the protection of value (from opportunistic exploitation).[555]

---

[549] See e.g. *Brandenburger, A. M./Stuart Jr., H. W.* (1996), p. 17.

[550] See *Brandenburger, A. M./Stuart Jr., H. W.* (1996), p. 9f. Other authors refer to this issue as "capturing value", see e.g. *Bowman, C./Ambrosini, V.* (2000); *Foss, N. J.* (2003). In addition to the traditional view on this process as mainly competitive in nature, recent contributions have highlighted its cooperative aspects which are argued to vary in importance in different contexts (see e.g. *Jap, S. D.* (2001)).

[551] See also chapters 3.2.3.2.1.2 and 3.2.3.2.2.1.

[552] See e.g. *Foss, N. J.* (2003).

[553] See e.g. *Brandenburger, A. M./Stuart Jr., H. W.* (1996), p. 18;

[554] See e.g. the discussion by *Argyres, N. S./Liebeskind, J. P.* (1999), p. 55ff, in a context of unexpected changes in relative bargaining power during the validity period of a long-term contract.

[555] This aspect is not explicitly discussed by *Brandenburger, A. M./Stuart Jr., H. W.* (1996), yet it deserves

More secure means of protecting value may reduce the dissipation of value in bargaining over its division and safeguarding the agreement.[556]

All three aspects, essentially, represent subgoals to the general objective of increasing value. With respect to the dyad, such efforts generally bring about either one of three possible implications for the buyer: the buyer's value situation improves as well, it stagnates or it worsens. Compatibility of the latter alternative with the idea of bilaterally voluntary exchange, in essence, relies on market imperfections associated with structurally grounded market power concerns: the relevant set of alternatives available to the buyer is defined at the decision time t_1 regardless of whether better options may have been available in t_0 if they are not on-hand anymore due to, for instance, mergers or cartelization which have reduced the (perceived) number and/or quality of substitutable offerings available to the buyer. [557]

With respect to any particular shift all three subgoals are presumed to be present, albeit with varying weightings attached. Two factors are proposed here as main determinants of this weighting: first, the *previous business types constellation*, augmented by additional bargaining power-related considerations, and, second, the *source of impulse* which sets the shift process in motion. Before discussing these impacts in detail, though, one final aspect needs to be highlighted regarding the above framework: it should be noted that a particular transaction is defined by its concrete parameter values in all three areas. However, in a context of information deficiencies and bounded rationality, all of these objectives are reduced to their *expected* parameter values, with sometimes severe constraints on the estimation of probabilities.[558]

---

particular attention from a TCA perspective as recently explicated by *Foss, N. J.* (2003). See also *Backhaus, K./Plinke, W./Rese, M.* (2004), (p. 42ff). Based on Austrian economics reasoning, they identify two fundamental ways of protecting value, namely, first, a permanent head start in terms of knowledge and its translation into market offerings, or second, successful competitor obstruction.

[556] See *Foss, N. J.* (2003). Moreover, the aspect relates to the proposed goal of sustaining a CAC as implied by the definition of marketing strategy which is adopted here, although *Foss, N. J.* (2003) suggests a clear distinction between the idea of sustained competitive advantage and "...processes of creating, capturing, appropriating, and protecting value."

[557] See e.g. *Brandenburger, A. M./Stuart Jr., H. W.* (1996), p. 19; also chapter 4.2.

[558] See e.g. *Tirole, J.* (1995), p. 80; related *Schmidt, R. H./Terberger, E.* (1997), p. 50. For applications see e.g. *Büschken, J.* (1997), p. 190.

150

3.3.2 The impact of the initial constellation on subgoal weightings and resulting strategic imperatives

As suggested by the identification of nine feasible business types constellations, the starting points for a strategic shift may differ considerably. Moreover, various initial constellations may be distinctly linked to particular subgoal weightings which in turn support different strategic orientations. This assertion draws, in particular, on arguments from research on power-dependence relations. The constructs of power and dependence are conceptualized much broader in this stream than their counterparts in TCA and within the framework of this analysis as expressed through different business types constellations.[559] Therefore, additional incorporation of market structure-based power considerations and consequences of structurally determined imbalances also becomes feasible.

The general consent in research on power relations is "...that an unbalanced relation is unstable for it encourages the use of power..."[560] as *Emerson* (1962) puts it. Such unbalanced relations are considered to accord with **disgruent business types constellations**.[561] In response to such situations, *Emerson* (1962) identifies the following "...four generic types of balancing operation..."[562] which are assumed here to each represent a feasible underlying tendency under the surface of a particular transaction relationship – whether imbalanced due to a disgruent business types constellation or due to market power asymmetries – and hint at different strategic business type responses.[563] Additionally, the balancing operations are held

---

[559] See for detailed outline chapter 2.1.2.4

[560] *Emerson, R. M.* (1962), p. 34; see also *Blau, P. M.* (1964), p. 29ff. Similar ideas are expressed also in the TCA-oriented literature (see e.g. *Heide, J. B.* (1994), who finds "...unilateral dependence to undermine bilateral governance..." (p. 81).

[561] Additionally, they are regarded to include imbalances which are founded in market structural reasons.

[562] *Emerson, R. M.* (1962), p. 35ff. He characterizes balancing processes as operating "...through changes in the variables which define the structure of the power-dependence relation as such..." (p. 35). The practical relevance of *Emerson's* (1962) propositions has recently been underscored by an empirical study by *LaBahn, D. W.* (1999).

[563] *Plinke, W./Söllner, A.* (2000), p. 74f, discuss these options as possible customer reactions to fear of opportunistic exploitation by a less dependent seller. Related to some of the aspects are e.g. *Blois, K. J.* (1996), p. 165, building on *Oliver, C.* (1990). With applicability to structurally-based imbalances, *Emerson's* (1962) ideas have recently been argued to possess great relevance in a growing number of industries such as healthcare or construction tools and supplies (see *LaBahn, D. W.* (1999), p. 24). Although beyond the scope of this discussion, it should be noted that these underlying tendencies may change over time within the course of an individual, long-term transaction such as, for instance, the construction of a power plant or water supply dam.

151

to be included as future possibilities in the ex ante expectation formation of an actor who considers entering in a new transaction relation.

(1) Cultivation of alternative relations by the more dependent party: building on the idea of a network through which the relevant actors are interconnected, an excessively dependent party may react to this imbalance by forming *additional*, new relations either with parties previously outside the network (resulting in open networks), or with previously unconnected parties within the network (resulting in closed networks).

(2) Coalition and group formation on the part of the more dependent party: whereas the first option aims at reducing the power of the less dependent party, this second response is targeted at increasing the power of the more dependent actor(s) through coalition formation.

(3) "Motivational withdrawl" on the part of the more dependent party: this operation has originally been conceptualized to imply alterations in the subjective assessment by the more dependent party, bringing forth a dampening of expectations about the relationship and ultimately fostering a move away from it.

(4) "Giving status" to the less dependent party: this option represents in many respects the opposite behavior to motivational withdrawl. The central idea is to enhance the more powerful party's motivational investment in the relation, that is, heightening the "weaker" party's relative importance for it. Both partners are drawn closer together. Particularly the previously less dependent party's expectations as to possible gains from the relation rise.

All four options can be interpreted in adaptation to the focus of this analysis on strategic shifts between business types constellations. First, such constellations are considered which are imbalanced (i.e. disgruent) to the seller's detriment (constellations 7, 8, 9)[564] before, second, constellations with excessive buyer dependence are discussed (constellations 4, 5, 6)[565].

---

[564] See *Fig. 6*.

[565] See *Fig. 6*.

Ad (1) Cultivation of alternative relations by the seller:

This idea corresponds with the phenomenon of "second supplying" on the part of the seller or, more generally, the extension of the prospective buyer base.[566] Attenuation of the dependence imbalance is sought for through enhanced substitutability of the partner, emphasizing the third subgoal (protection of value) and, to a lower degree, the first subgoal (creation of value) by reducing the associated transaction costs of bargaining and safeguarding. However, since reasoning sacrifices in terms of VC are usually encountered (e.g. because extending the potential buyer base requires increased standardization of the offering), the net effect on value creation is undetermined and may well be negative. Overall, a tendency towards seller product business is presumed.

Ad (2) Coalition and group formation on the part of the seller

In case the group formation refers to horizontal coalitions, the subgoals which may be regarded as corresponding best to this option are referred to as claiming value and protecting value. This is due to the fact that the seller's relative bargaining power increases and should allow for extracting a larger piece of the pie at a higher price actually paid and/or have better safeguards established. Possible strategic realizations run from informal or formal establishment of information-exchange "seller groups" who keep track of opportunistic behavior of individual buyers to more severe responses such as cartelization. The business types constellation as such is likely to be maintained with the subgoals being primarily pursued based on structurally determined power relations. In case vertical or lateral coalitions are entered by the seller, the subgoal of value creation is more prevalent.[567]

Ad (3) "Motivational withdrawl" on the part of the seller

This option is approached closest by the subgoal of value protection. The view that there is not much to be gained from the relation with the particular customer emerges. At the extreme,

---

[566] See *LaBahn, D. W.* (1999), pp. 5, 13, who refers to this as segment-focused product development. Note that this is fundamentally different from the idea of "second sourcing" which refers to increasing the availability of supply sources to the buyer (see also chapter 5.2.2)

[567] See for illustration the claim made by the Bossard Group on its website about the cooperation with Elesa: "Elesa and Bossard – two powerful partners: one order, one delivery, one invoice. Operating and fastening elements from one source with the familiar Bossard competence and readiness to deliver! Thanks to cooperation between Elesa and Bossard, this is now a reality for you." (*BossardGroup* (2002)).

it may lead to leaving the dyad and switching to another buyer. *Backhaus/Büschken* (1999) have described the extreme case where the switch may pertain to a whole industry.[568]

Ad (4) "Giving status" to the less dependent party (buyer)

The prime subgoal at work here is value creation which – from the perspective of the whole chain – rests on increasing the buyer's willingness-to-pay. In a purely dyadic view, reduction of the seller's (opportunity) costs evolves as a second option. Examples from business life include innovations on the part of the seller or joint R&D efforts on the one side[569], and large manufacturers helping their suppliers to get better conditions from their own suppliers on the other side. Yet, by ultimately increasing the buyer's dependence on the seller, the subgoals of claiming value and protecting value are also positively influenced. The strategic orientation points towards encouraging higher degrees or extents of buyer specific investment.

Disgruent constellations may also exhibit a power disadvantage on the part of the buyer. They are subsequently discussed with focus on their potential feedback effects on the *seller's* motivations.

Ad (1) Cultivation of alternative relations by the buyer

Second or multiple sourcing on behalf of the buyer reflects this idea. In spite of giving away economies of scale which could be gained from concentrating supply in the hands of one seller, the buyer spreads out its demand over several suppliers. Increased seller replaceability strongly supports a large weight attached to value protection, and/or to a lower degree value creation in order to "give status" to the buyer. The former option could be associated with reductions in seller specificity, hence, a move towards seller product business. The latter option, in turn, suggests an increase in buyer specificity towards buyer project or even relational business.

---

[568] See *Backhaus, K./Büschken, J.* (1999), p. 254; related *Akerlof, G. A.* (1970).

[569] See for detailed evidence from the automotive industry e.g. *Dyer, J. H.* (1996).

Ad (2) Coalition and group formation on the part of the buyer[570]

The subgoals which may be regarded as corresponding best to this option are claiming value and protecting value since the seller's relative bargaining power increases and should allow for extracting a larger piece of the pie at a higher price actually paid and/or have better safeguards established. An example from business practice are purchasing cooperatives which have a long tradition and are still very common, for instance, in the form of cooperative associations in the agricultural industry.[571] Regarding the consequential strategic orientation, the same reasoning applies as above.

Ad (3) "Motivational withdrawl" on the part of the buyer

The fundamental causes for such behavior are held to be either too low a value creation by the relevant seller or too high claims on his part. Consequently, in this case, high weights should be attached to value creation in order to increase the buyer's absolute share, if not also its relative share compared to the seller. The most likely strategic imperative is raising seller asset specificity in order to, first deliver productivity advantages, and/or, second, to provide the buyer with enlarged exploitative potential.

Ad (4) "Giving status" to the less dependent party (seller)

Such cases can primarily be linked to the subgoal of value creation due to closer cooperation as outlined above. Yet, value protection is also likely to be important since the safeguarding power gap is reduced. The strategic inferences to be drawn resemble those from the third aspect.

Congruent constellations (or balanced relations) are regarded, in principle, as more stable than imbalanced ones from the power-dependence relations point of view.[572] This would

---

[570] *Backhaus, K./Plinke, W./Rese, M.* (2004), (p. 106ff), discuss such issues as stemming from market segment specific investments. In contrast, in denial of the existence of market segment specific investments, this research links such phenomena of coalition formation (both on the buyer and the seller-side) to considerations on market structure and changes to it.

[571] As an example see the "Raiffeisen Central-Genossenschaft Nordwest eG" which emerged in 1990 from the integration of three smaller cooperatives and now represents around 180 primary cooperative associations. It acts as a gateway to both procurement and sales markets (see *Raiffeisen Central-Genossenschaft Nordwest eG* (2002)). For a brief general dicussion of cooperatives: *Milgrom, P./Roberts, J.* (1992), p. 562f.

[572] See e.g. *Blau, P. M.* (1964), p. 29f; *LaBahn, D. W.* (1999), pp. 10, 28; indirect through performance consequences from dependence-balancing: *Heide, J. B./John, G.* (1988), p. 34. *LaBahn, D. W.* (1999),

suggest that a general tendency of constellations might exist toward congruence. Yet, there is an important caveat to this idea: unless markets are perfectly competitive at all stages (which they are not, by assumption, in a world of transaction costs), that is, unless supranormal rents of all market participants are driven down to zero, and the reservation price equals the price actually paid and also equals marginal cost, some scope for bargaining over value created (VC) inevitably exists. It brings about each actor's desire to claim a larger part of this pie for his- or herself, either in the course of contract negotiation or ex post in the form of opportunistic quasi-rent appropriation.[573] Thus, all three subgoals are conjectured to prevail in congruent constellations as well with value creation being regarded as most prominent. However, if there is an opportunity to shift to a disgruent constellation which improves the seller's value position by exposing the buyer to increased dependence, it will be seized with the likely consequence of the seller making stronger claims.

Based on the above theoretical considerations, four principal suggestions regarding the seller's motivations are advanced.

Proposition 1: disgruent constellations may be stable under certain conditions.[574] Yet, since they are exposed to relatively stronger pressure, they are more susceptible to change. Sellers in such positions are c.p. expected to respond to smaller impulses.

Proposition 2: disgruent constellations which imply a relative excess dependence of the seller c.p. lead to higher weights attached to the subgoals of creating and protecting value. The effect is expected to be more pronounced with higher degrees of specificity and also with increasing time horizons until contract completion. Claiming value is particularly relevant for such disgruent constellations that are susceptible to responses other than direct constellation

---

p. 17, further tests the hypothesis that the stabilizing effect of congruence is more pronounced in constellations of high mutual levels of dependence as a result of raised costs of acting unilaterally, but finds no significant support for it (p. 24). This result is supported here based on transaction cost theoretical reasoning: first, even though congruency may result in greater stability, the level at which it might optimally settle in a certain situation is defined by the properties of that particular context, not a general rule (see *LaBahn, D. W.* (1999), p. 28; also: chapter 3.2) Second, due to the time gap between complete fulfillment of performance and counterperformance, high levels of dependence pitch in an additional element of imbalance compared to unspecific congruency. Particularly in cases of long-term contracts, inter-temporal displacements may occur in the power-dependence relation with negative consequences for stability.

[573] Actors face a trade-off between short-term gains and potential long-run losses from opportunistic behavior.

[574] For an extensive theoretically-guided substantiation in the context of automotive OEMs and their suppliers see e.g. *Backhaus, K./Büschken, J.* (1999); see also *Freiling, J.* (1995).

shifts, namely market structure-related responses. Alternatively, the indirect route via value creation may be accompanied by increased claims on value.

Proposition 3: congruent constellations are c.p. presumed to be inherently more stable and, therefore, require stronger impulses in order to experience a shift.

Proposition 4: congruent constellations are proposed to be primarily oriented towards the subgoal of value creation. In the case of a sufficiently strong impulse which supports the particular strategic direction, sellers are, however, argued to readily move towards constellations with increased buyer dependence and realign towards claiming value.

Finally, an important premise needs to be noted: the initial constellation which has just been discussed is assumed to have been perceived as the (subjectively) optimal choice at some point in time.[575] There is no reason to deviate from this choice – unless some change occurs – which, building on the emphasis on bounded rationality, must enter into the subjective perceptional space.[576] Two immediate implications follow: first, the occurrence of an impulse is a necessary condition for the initiation of a strategic shift between business types constellations. Second, the impulse must be subjectively perceived in order to become effectual and it must be translated into a (successful) redesign of the market offering in order for the process to qualify as a shift between constellations.

---

[575] See for similar assertions e.g. *Achrol, R. S./Reve, T./Stern, L. W.* (1983), p. 63; *Backhaus, K./Plinke, W./Rese, M.* (2004), (p. 30).

[576] The arrival of new information and, at some point, the translation of at least *some* of the new information into subjective knowledge is inevitable since "...the mere passage of time means experiencing events and thus gaining new information..." (see *Metcalfe, J. S.* (2001), p. 575; for similar positions e.g. *Mises, L. v.* (1940 (repr.:1980)), p. 76ff; *Lachmann, L. M.* (1977), p. 81ff). As a result, the subjective optimum is transient in nature at best. This conception bears some resemblance to the idea of "relative stability" as proposed in modern decision theory (see e.g. *Leinfellner, W.* (1987/88), p. 20).

3.3.3 Impulses as necessary conditions for shifts between business types constellations and the role of subjective increases in knowledge

3.3.3.1 The role of exogenous shocks in impulse generation

Hayek (1945) has argued that "...economic problems arise always and only in consequence of change."[577] As a result, adaptation to these changes arises as the central challenge to the behavior of economic actors.[578] The claim holds as well for the above outlined framework with asset specificity as a choice variable: a perceived (relative) optimum only holds so far as the underlying parameter values accommodate it. Not every slight change of some parameter value necessarily leads to a new optimal decision (here: constellation), that is, stability may prevail within certain boundaries.[579] Yet, in principle, it has the potential to do so. However, before turning to the question of whether a particular change in parameter value exerts a critical influence in altering the optimal business type decision[580], the very origins of the parameter value change need to be explicated.

Based on the "asset specificity as choice variable"-framework, the choice of asset specificity and business type (constellation) is regarded as the endogenous variable while the other variables (see *Fig. 13*) rather represent antecedents to this choice and are, hence, classified as exogenous whether located within the dyadic "game" or outside in the environment.[581]

---

[577] *Hayek, F.* (1945), p. 523.

[578] See *Hayek, F.* (1945), p. 524 who is, though, held as one of the originators to Austrian economics, a research stream that focuses on the (dynamic) explanation of market processes. For reference to the assertion's significance within TCA see e.g. *Williamson, O. E.* (1985), p. 8f; *Rubin, P. H.* (1990), p. xvi; *Williamson, O. E.* (1991b); *Williamson, O. E.* (1991c), p. 76ff. On the distinction between spontaneous, decentralized adaptation as implied by *Hayek* (1945) and coordinated, intentional adaptation as described by *Barnard* (1938) see *Williamson, O. E.* (1991b).

[579] For instance, while the previous constellation may be maintained in principle, changes in emphasis may be undertaken with respect to details.

[580] Chapter 4.5 provides such considerations in a simulation of a dyadic model of shifts between business types constellations.

[581] This does not necessarily imply an exogenous development or growth model. The debate about exogeneity or endogeneity of growth and technological change mainly takes place on a macroeconomic level (see e.g. *Romer, P. M.* (1986); *Lucas, R. E.* (1988); *Romer, P.* (1990); including discussion on linkages to *Schumpeterian* theory of economic development, see e.g. *Aghion, P./Howitt, P.* (1992); *Crafts, N. F. R.* (1995); *Aghion, P./Howitt, P.* (1998), p. 53ff; *Gualerzi, D.* (2001)). *Metcalfe, J. S.* (2000) recently developed an endogenous growth model that builds on a micro growth perspective. Debate on the precise notion of endogeneity and its implications feeds back on the distinction between the two streams by hampering unambiguous attribution of micro models to either of them. Moreover, from a managerial

Endogenous change in this diction could only result from changes in the preference structures/form of the utility functions of the dyad parties. This possibility is, however, excluded by focusing on the goal of profit maximization in combination with the assumptions of bounded rationality and risk neutrality. Exogenous change, hence, refers to changes in other factors than these functions. Exogenous shocks qualify for impulses within the framework exactly if *information on them* impacts on the (perceived) parameter values of the determinants in *Fig. 13* or the linkages between them (informational impulse). Examples are changing structures and related power relations in end-customer market *A* through increased formation of end-customer coalitions (demand bundling) due to improvements in available information and communication media and associated cost reduction of the coalition formation.[582] As a result, the intermediate buyer might seek reductions in specificity of its production technology in order to be able to expand its own customer basis to incorporate end-customer market *B* in a better way.

The emphasis is on the informational nature of the impulse: although usually one can expect an event to be accompanied by an according change in information status, reservations with respect to the simultaneity of both can be advanced in the sense that either information or event may lag behind. Consider, for instance, the extant literature on (product) preannouncing and its effects on competitor and buyer behavior.[583] Furthermore, information may continue to exert an influence long after the underlying referential event, and possibly even a large number of subsequent events has taken place.[584] Therefore, it is the information which is

---

perspective concerned with an individual seller company, groundbreaking technological innovations in other sectors of the economy qualify for exogenous influences, no matter what their description on a macro level may be. It should be noted, though, that at least some of the exogenous variables may be indirectly at the disposition of the parties, for instance by changing to another game arena.

[582] For detailed discussion of demand bundling in the context of new information and communication media see e.g. *Baumeister, C.* (2000); *Voeth, M.* (2002).

[583] See e.g. *Eliashberg, J./Robertson, T. S.* (1988); *Besen, S. M./Farrell, J.* (1994); *Büschken, J.* (2000).

[584] As an example consider the asymmetrical properties of reputation. Its establishment is generally held to require a large number of transactions to build up, while it can be significantly hurt by a single act of disconfirmation (see the seminal game theoretic literature on reputation *Kreps, D. M./Wilson, R.* (1982); *Milgrom, P./Roberts, J.* (1982); see also e.g. *Klein, B./Leffler, K. B.* (1981), p. 626ff; *Yao, D. A.* (1988), p. 64f; *Rubin, P. H.* (1990), p. 148ff; *Plötner, O.* (1995), p. 43f; *Prabhu, H./Stewart, D. W.* (2001)). Rebuilding is expected to take again more than one transaction. In fact, information may even have an impact although the alleged event has never occurred but may have been caused by a different event, for instance a competitor spreading false rumors (here referred to as "misleading/rumorous information") (related e.g. *Williamson, O. E.* (1991b), p. 167ff; *Williamson, O. E.* (1975), p. 36) While the earlier (game

expected to impact on asset specificity choice. The occurrence of such exogenous shocks is regarded as necessary for creating an impulse which in turn might lead to rethinking the current constellation.[585]

As such, it is, however, not taken to constitute a complete necessary condition since subjective influences have not yet been taken into account. Recent research suggests that the subjective interpretation of information, for instance, its presumed credibility, plays a critical role in determining an actor's response.[586]

3.3.3.2 The role of subjective knowledge increases and the ability to seize opportunities in impulse translation

Subjectivity throws the entrepreneurial, proactive element in the adaptation process. Subjective differences in recognizing a window of change opportunity resulting from an exogenous shock and translating it into a successful market offering are constitutive for entrepreneurial competition and allow for relating to empirically observable phenomena such as diverging firm behavior within an industry in response to impulses.[587]

Such emphasis on the diversity of economic actors is very common in, for instance, Austrian economics which decidedly focus on explaining dynamic market processes by relating them back to

- *fundamental*, i.e. inherent, differences in the nature of human actors with respect to creative abilities and creative power, and

---

theoretic) literature on "cheap talk" has been skeptical with regard to the long-term efficacy potential of such information (referred to as "bluff"; see e.g. *Rabin, M.* (1990); *Farrell, J.* (1993); *Farrell, J.* (1995)); some recent contributions are more positive (see e.g. *Eliashberg, J./Robertson, T. S./Rymon, T.* (1996)).

[585] *Lieberman, M. B./Montgomery, D. B.* (1988) hold different in attributing first-mover advantages solely to endogenous factors. In reference to the *MacMillan, I. C.* (1983) quotation that "...good generals make their luck by shaping the odds in their favor...", they claim that "...the occurrence of such an opportunity depends on the firm's own foresight, skill and luck, and that of competitors..." (p. 54). Yet, this statement leaves open the question as to how exactly "luck" can be *defined* as an endogenous factor.

[586] See e.g. *Heil, O./Robertson, T. S.* (1991), p. 416; *Prabhu, H./Stewart, D. W.* (2001), p. 63ff.

[587] *Peneder, M.* (2001), p. 39. It is also in line with the proactive understanding of strategic shifts between business types as advanced in chapter 3.2.2

160

- *radical information deficiencies* in the sense of "sheer ignorance"[588] which implies unawareness of one's ignorance and, hence, an element of surprise in its (partial) remedy, thereby reaching beyond the conditions of bounded rationality and far-sightedness as generally assumed in TCA.[589]

Within the literature on TCA, the significance of incorporating particularities of individual actors or firms, and in particular, path dependencies, has recently beginning to gain ground. In particular in recognition of the seeming importance of such issues, especially with respect to applying the TCA lens to the analysis of strategic management, TCA might be expected to profit from insights from Austrian economics. Several contributions have recently been put forth in this spirit, suggesting that despite apparent differences, on a general level, a certain compatibility of the two theoretical streams or, at least, a large potential for mutual complementation might exist.[590] Without going into further details, these assessments should justify cautious reference to a core element of Austrian economics, namely entrepreneurship.

To start with, some very tentative arguments regarding the significance of subjectivity can, however, be drawn from TCA as well. The inclusion of subjective influences is then substantiated on the grounds of three arguments that are intertwined by the underlying assumption of bounded rationality. In combination with the assumption of opportunism, some

---

[588] See e.g. *Kirzner, I. M.* (1997), p. 62.

[589] For seminal work on the foundations of Austrian economics see e.g. *Hayek, F.* (1945); *Hayek, F. A. v.* (1967); *Mises, L. v.* (1940 (repr.:1980)); *Mises, L. v.* (1949 (repr.: 1966)); *Kirzner, I. M.* (1973); *Kirzner, I. M.* (1979); related, though, sometimes held as a distinct approach ("radical subjectivist perspective"; for such assessment e.g. *Littlechild, S. C.* (1986), p. 29) see *Lachmann, L. M.* (1956); *Lachmann, L. M.* (1986); *Shackle, G. L. S.* (1972); as influential precursors see *Schumpeter, J. A.* (1928); *Schumpeter, J. A.* (1942) on entrepreneurship, on the roots of subjectivism *Menger, C.* (1871 (repr.: 1990)). For an extensive review of the field see e.g. *Vaughn, K. I.* (1994); recent discussions on various aspects can be found in a volume compiled by *Foss, N. J./Klein, P. G.* (2002). For a comparison between bounded rationality and the implied (intentional) planning element and weaker forms of rationality as assumed in Austrian economics, see e.g. *Williamson, O. E.* (1985), p. 46f. Bounded rationality comes, nevertheless, much closer to "sheer ignorance" than *Knightian* risk which represents a first basing point for comparison (see e.g. *Kirzner, I. M.* (1997), p. 64). For support on the relative proximity of the two terms refer to the descriptions of bounded rationality as incomplete knowledge e.g. by *Backhaus, K./Aufderheide, D./Späth, G.-M.* (1994), p. 19ff; *Aufderheide, D.* (2000), p. 86.

[590] See e.g. *Foss, N. J.* (1997); *Foss, N. J.* (2001); *Foss, N. J.* (2002); *Backhaus, K./Plinke, W./Rese, M.* (2004); see related the discussion *Williamson, O. E.* (1999b) on differences and similarities of governance and dynamic capabilities perspective (which draws on Austrian insights) with respect to business strategy. Referring to the managerially-oriented stream within TCA (see chapter 2.1.2.1) facilitates emphasizing the subject element within TCA. *Burr, W.* (2003) discusses the requirements for drawing on various theories in combination with TCA on a general level and also favors a pragmatic research strategy which settles for extensive consistency instead of perfect congruity of assumptions.

161

information asymmetries necessarily exist because otherwise there would be no scope for certain forms of deceit like, for instance, lying or cheating. Under such circumstances and, in particular, when combined with the condition of asset specificity which gives rise to the emergence of sunk costs, initial information asymmetries can be presumed to propagate into the future by impacting on economic behavior (path dependence).[591] Thereby, they have the potential to generate different endowments of information and also physical resources. Essentially, that means that they may create heterogeneity among the actors, both with respect to endowments with information or other resources and, as a result, diverse potential for taking advantage of given economic circumstances (hereafter referred to as "ability"[592]).

Under such conditions, it is **first** of all very unlikely if not impossible that a certain given information (here: informational impulse) is uniformly accessible. This would, in its strongest form rest on its ubiquitous availability to all actors without cost or effort.[593] In a weaker interpretation, the information might be available to all actors at the same cost. Yet, with costs as subjectively perceived costs[594] and asymmetrical information, individual actors can hardly be assumed to arrive at even cost (and effort) evaluations, thereby creating subjective differences in accessibility to the same piece of information. **Second**, even in case of uniform access at equally valued cost and effort with heterogeneous abilities, valuation of the information itself must be expected to differ. **Third**, the question of how to translate an impulse into action remains open – and offers additional potential scope for divergences. To sum up, individual actors can be expected to act differently upon the same informational impulse (including differences in strength and timing of perception). Thus, diversity in perception and translation of impulses seems, in principle, possible within a TCA-based framework.[595] This diversity is, however, only a derived condition related to path dependence,

---

[591] For similar argumentation see e.g. *Peneder, M.* (2001), p. 40.

[592] However, this notion of ability makes a weaker claim on heterogeneity than the assumption of initially heterogeneous abilities rooted in the human nature in Austrian economics (see e.g. *Hayek, F.* (1945); *Hayek, F. A. v.* (1967); *Kirzner, I. M.* (1973)). This is accompanied by an inverse relation of the assumed degrees of rationality: bounded rationality is a stronger form than process or organic rationality associated with Austrian economics (see e.g. *Williamson, O. E.* (1985), p. 46f). For a detailed comparison of the underlying assumptions of TCA and Austrian economics and resulting inferences see *Backhaus, K./Plinke, W./Rese, M.* (2004); *Foss, N. J.* (1997).

[593] See e.g. *Metcalfe, J. S.* (2001), p. 569.

[594] See chapter 2.1.2.2.

[595] The implication of past decisions affecting present choices points in the direction of path dependencies.

whereas it is a fundamental one in Austrian economics where it represents an integral part of the assumptional framework, an inherent property of the actors.

Against the sketched background, the informational impulse as such is not capable of causing a strategic shift: its transfer into a subjective factor is required. Only after this transformation has taken place does the individual actor assess his response.[596] Terminology wise, the decisive subjective parameter will be treated as distinct from the informational impulse. It is referred to as (subjective) knowledge and is expected to differ both in content and extent from one actor to another with reference to the same informational impulse.[597] From the individual viewpoint, such an increase in subjective knowledge that a shift between business types enters the actor's consideration constitutes the necessary condition for a shift in constellation to take place. It is not sufficient, however.

It is particularly with regard to further illumination of the informational impulse transformation that reference to Austrian economics seems promising. Scholars in that tradition have identified constitutive characteristics of entrepreneurs ("abilities"). To date, two fundamentally different, though, closely related conceptions of entrepreneurship have been advanced in that tradition.[598] *Schumpeter* (1926, 1928, 1942) as one of the earliest and, potentially, most influential contributors to that stream conceptualized "creativity" as the constitutive entrepreneurial characteristic and the resulting innovation through "creative

---

[596] *Fu-Lai Yu, T.* (2001), p. 9ff, has advanced a similar, subjectivist perspective and links it to to *Kirzner's* (1973, 1979) theory of entrepreneurial alertness and discovery (see also *Kirzner, I. M.* (1973), esp. p. 30ff; for related arguments e.g. *Lachmann, L. M.* (1956), p. 20ff). Such an approach exhibits considerable potential for dealing with discrepancies between TCA and Austrian Economics in their assumptions on availability of information and feasible degree of rationality. In fact, *Fu-Lai Yu, T.* (2001), pp. 27, 31ff, establishes a potential linkage by arguing that from a subjectivist point of view, "...it does not matter whether an opportunity has existed or not, the critical issue is that the actor has to perceive it..." (p. 27, fn 4). Such ideas are also implied in the above argument. For support through a cognitive lens and in the context of strategic change see e.g. *Barr, P. S./Stimpert, J. L./Huff, A. S.* (1992); *Rajagopalan, N./Spreitzer, G. M.* (1996), p. 62ff.

[597] The argument is illustrated by the assertion by *Metcalfe, J. S.* (2001), p. 569, that "...to turn information into knowledge requires prior knowledge (and beliefs)...". A recent, general treatise of knowledge, its commercialization in terms of entrepreneurial activity and the role within strategic management is provided by *Teece, D. J.* (2003).

[598] For comparisons of both approaches to entrepreneurship see e.g. *Kirzner, I. M.* (1973), p. 79ff, who considers the entrepreneur's influence in his concept as essentially equilibrating, as opposed to assigning a disequilibrating role to *Schumpeter's* (e.g. 1926, 1928, 1942) entrepreneurs; also *Kirzner, I. M.* (1979), p. 111ff; more recently *Kirzner, I. M.* (1999); *Fu-Lai Yu, T.* (2001). For a more pragmatic, management-oriented approaching of the idea see e.g. *Jenkins, M./Floyd, S.* (2002).

destruction" brought forth by entrepreneurs as the engine of market processes.[599] *Kirzner's* (1973, 1979) approach emphasizes ideas expressed by *von Mises* (1940, 1949), and, perhaps to a lesser extent, *von Hayek* (1945, 1967)[600]: based on *von Mises* (1940, 1949) concept of the "homo agens"[601] who not only possesses the ability to "...pursue goals efficiently, once ends and means are clearly identified, but also the drive and alertness needed to identify which ends to strive for and which means are available..."[602], he developed the concept of entrepreneurial alertness and discovery. These inherent abilities allow the entrepreneur to discover previously "unthought-of-knowledge"[603] which entails new opportunities for profit. That is, he identifies new ways for improving some other actor's situation (exploration) in ways that this actor will value and thereby increase its own profit (exploitation).[604] The latter aspect emphasizes that successful realization of opportunities is a crucial feature of the concept because "new ways" which are not transformed into an accepted and valued market offering will not yield any profits to the opportunity finder.[605]

Central to both of these entrepreneurial concepts is, first, the idea that entrepreneurs have a superior ability for opportunity perception and realization, and second, the active, initiating role which is assigned to the individual actor in identifying and translating the relevant

---

[599] See *Schumpeter, J. A.* (1926); *Schumpeter, J. A.* (1928); *Schumpeter, J. A.* (1942).

[600] See *Mises, L. v.* (1940 (repr.:1980)); *Mises, L. v.* (1949 (repr.: 1966)); *Hayek, F.* (1945); *Hayek, F. A. v.* (1967); *Kirzner, I. M.* (1973), p. 53ff; *Kirzner, I. M.* (1979).

[601] See *Mises, L. v.* (1940 (repr.:1980)), p. 30ff; *Mises, L. v.* (1949 (repr.: 1966)), p. 14.

[602] *Kirzner, I. M.* (1973), p. 33.

[603] *Kirzner, I. M.* (1997), p. 73.

[604] This includes both profits accrued to the entrepreneur from increased buyer willingness-to-pay and from sales due to lower actual prices which are in turn made possible through reductions in the costs incurred by the entrepreneur. Recent contributions have stressed that Kirzner's concept may encompass both (see e.g. *Fu-Lai Yu, T.* (2001), p. 11f). The aspect of opportunity exploitation has also been referred to as "economizing/ökonomisieren" (see fundamentally *Kirzner, I. M.* (1973), p. 34; see for recent reference e.g. *Backhaus, K./Plinke, W./Rese, M.* (2004), (p. 31); *Fu-Lai Yu, T.* (2001), p. 10ff). Note also that the dynamic capabilities approach (sometimes also referred to as competence approach) as developed during the past couple of years also draws heavily on Austrian insights. For a comparison with TCA see e.g. *Williamson, O. E.* (1999b), p. 1092ff. The dynamic capabilities framework centers around sources and methods of creating and capturing wealth in circumstances of rapid technological change. Seminal contributions include *Langlois, R. N.* (1992); *Langlois, R. N./Foss, N. J.* (1995); *Teece, D. J./Pisano, G./Shuen, A.* (1997).

[605] Against the marketing-oriented background of their research, *Backhaus, K./Plinke, W./Rese, M.* (2004), (p. 33), add an explicit focus on communicating the new opportunity to the prospective buyers as part of the constitutive entrepreneurial characteristics. Such communication may so far have been implicit to the opportunity's translation into profit, yet its expatiation facilitates relating to "classic" marketing issues such as communication policy.

informational impulse. These ideas supposedly reach beyond the traditional TCA framework which focuses on economizing within a given means-ends framework. Consequently, it remains rather silent as to the identification of means and ends as postulated for the entrepreneur.[606] Yet, recent research has demonstrated that this need not be an insurmountable obstacle to meaningful incorporation of Austrian insights into a TCA-based analysis.[607] Such conjecture may be even more valid in the context of this marketing strategy-oriented research where explicit additional reference to the effectiveness dimension is made.[608] In fact, the "task of identifying ends and means"[609], of operating to change the prevalent data in terms of the currently employed form of market offering, lies at the heart of this shift analysis. Shifts between business types constellations are in that sense entrepreneurial acts, the exploration of which presumably gains from considerations related to Austrian economics.

Hence, in acknowledgment of the existing divergences in theoretical perspective, the principal Austrian focus on entrepreneurship is, nevertheless, built into this analysis by considering shifts between business types constellations as the outcome of entrepreneurial activity.[610] They are held to involve activities similar to the Austrian concept of entrepreneurial alertness and discovery. A first-mover position which is accompanied by a temporary monopoly is implied.[611] Within this framework, these aspects are referred to as subjective increases in

---

[606] See for similar assessment e.g. *Foss, N. J.* (1997), p. 182.

[607] For recent illustrations of supplementary treatment or application see e.g. *Foss, N. J.* (1997); *Foss, N. J.* (2001); *Backhaus, K./Plinke, W./Rese, M.* (2004).

[608] Ecnomizing within a given means-ends framework, hence, parallels the efficiency dimension of this work, while the effectiveness dimension bears resemblance with the explorative element in discovery and alertness, although the surprise factor is less pronounced and the planning perspective ("deliberate acquisition of knowledge"; see *Kirzner, I. M.* (1979), pp. 109, 130) to a relatively larger degree forms part of strategic marketing effectiveness (for related positions see e.g. *Drucker, P. F.* (2002)).

[609] *Kirzner, I. M.* (1973), p. 34.

[610] A note on a deviation of the notion of entrepreneurship as adopted here from the understanding as usually implied in the Austrian tradition sense is appropriate. Owing to the the particular perspective of this research, that is a strategic marketing management orientation from the viewpoint of a particular company, entrepreneurship is taken to include proactive shifts between business types constellations, even if the original intention is sole hinderance of competition. Such understanding is supported by the recent literature on "strategic entrepreneurship" which is held to integrate originally entrepreneurial and strategic considerations (see e.g. *Hitt, M. A./Ireland, R. D./Camp, S. M., et al.* (2001), p. 480f; *Venkataraman, S./Sarasvathy, S. D.* (2001)).

[611] For comprehensive overviews see e.g. *Lieberman, M. B./Montgomery, D. B.* (1988); *Kerin, R. A./Varadarajan, P. R./Peterson, R. A.* (1992). Besides first-mover advantages, *Lieberman, M. B./Montgomery, D. B.* (1988) extensively discuss potential disadvantages. Among the latter, aspects of

knowledge (perception of a shift opportunity) and the ability to translate them into improvements to one's own situation (efficient assertion of shift in the market).[612] Due to the assumed strategic, long-term nature of such shifts which will frequently bring about the need for investments, for instance in research and development (R&D), the subjective increase in knowledge is held to lead to shift considerations only if lasting effects from the informational impulse are expected.[613] Furthermore, just as an informational impulse may not allude to all prospective buyers in the same way, shift considerations are not required to relate to all of them, that is, selective shifts are feasible.[614]

While the following discussion of potential impulse sources is linked to the issue of perceiving a shift opportunity, the considerations on sufficient shift conditions in the fourth chapter relate directly to the question of whether the particular firm is able to build on the

---

technological and market uncertainty (p. 47) seem particularly relevant for this research. Consider the following example: seller *A*, one of several manufacturers of standard and customized industrial vehicles, encounters an innovative new solution for its buyers' transportation problem. As a result, *A* extends its market offering to provide complete fleet management including staff responsibility (a phenomenon which has recently been referred to as "performance contracting"; for differentiated discussion and also for reference on the example see e.g. *Kleikamp, C.* (2002), p. 55ff; practice-oriented descriptions of the model include *Rühl, A.* (1997)). Since none of the other manufacturers is yet able to offer such fleet management, *A* enjoys a temporary monopoly regarding that value creating offering. However, *A*'s temporary monopoly rent is at least partly eroded exactly because of its monopolistic position. As long as no other suppliers market such an extended offer, any buyer who reduces its fleet-related personnel invests specifically in *A* (buyer relational business) and experiences a resulting lock-in which may, in turn, cause restraints to purchase. Subsequent shifts by other suppliers increase substitutability again from the buyer's perspective even with reduced personnel and leakage in fleet management know-how, presumably reducing lock-in and associated provisions.

612 Unlike the Austrian position which models these abilities as inherent characteristics of the actors, in this analysis they appear as results from diverging development paths due to bounded rationality. The notion of "asserting" a shift can be traced back to *Schumpeter, J. A.* (1928), p. 482.

613 For discussion of the more general distinction between "meaningful" and "meaningless" information in terms of price movements which is linked to the distinction between "random" and "permanent" causes, see also *Lachmann, L. M.* (1956), p. 29f.

614 For an example, see chapter 5.2.2. In such cases, additional considerations on buyer discrimination must be incorporated. Due to intersubjective differences in utility functions, an additional shift to a new constellation while simultaneously maintaining the current constellation for part of the customer base may not only be feasible, but also appropriate. As an example consider the tariff structure of German railways. Until December 14, 2002, they offered their transport functionality in principle in two different constellations: first, there is bilateral product business (independent pricing of unconnected train journeys) and, second, seller product business with buyer relational business (two part tariff which consists of a lump sum initial investment in terms of the "Bahncard" and resulting lower prices (50%) for individual train journeys). Thereby, German railways might be able to realize advantages from relational business with some customers without running into restraints to purchase due to fear of lock-in. Yet, this offer also points at potential problems with discrimination: in the case of German railways, the choice between tariffs rests completely with the prospective buyer. This is likely to give rise to self-selection bias in terms of adverse selection.

detected opportunity and assert the shift in the market at conditions which improve its situation as well.

3.3.4   Potential sources of impulses and resulting strategic imperatives

3.3.4.1   Deriving a systematization of sources

At the heart of this research is the transaction between a seller and a buyer. However, in modern industrial economies, value creation takes place through firms which are woven into complex (organizational) networks.[615] Or, as *Mattson* (1985) claims: "if we focus on a single organization we thus find that it has direct and indirect links to customers, suppliers, distributors, competitors, customers´ customers, service organisations, complementary suppliers, etc."[616] In recognition of this fact, impulses from outside the dyad are considered if and only if they impact on the business types constellation employed in the dyadic relationship under scrutiny. In principle, all members of the network as well as external constraints to its structure and evolvement in terms of legal and technological conditions come into question as impulse sources.[617] In systematizing such impacts, *Nalebuff/Brandenburger* (1996) have developed the value net which captures all players that are relevant for a firm in locating itself within the network and which are subsequently referred to as market-partners (see *Fig. 15*).[618]

---

[615] See e.g. *Morgan, R. M./Hunt, S. D.* (1994) or the IMP research on "markets as networks" (e.g. the seminal anthology by *Axelsson, B./Easton, G.* (1992); also: *Easton, G./Hakannsson, H.* (1996)), which is, however, more receptive than TCA in terms of incorporating insights from SET and behavioral science. An application of such reasoning can be found e.g. inh *Männel, B.* (1996).

[616] See *Mattson, L.-G.* (1985) cited from *Easton, G./Araujo, L.* (1992), p. 62.

[617] On the role of legal and technological constraints see also chapter 3.2.3.

[618] See *Nalebuff, B. J./Brandenburger, A. M.* (1996), p. 15ff. Its emphasis on value fits the above discussion of value oriented subgoals. Alternative systematizations have been developed, for instance, in a relationship management context by *Morgan, R. M./Hunt, S. D.* (1994), p. 21, who distinguish between the categories of buyers (intermediate and ultimate), suppliers, internal, and lateral (competitors, government, etc.) partnerships.

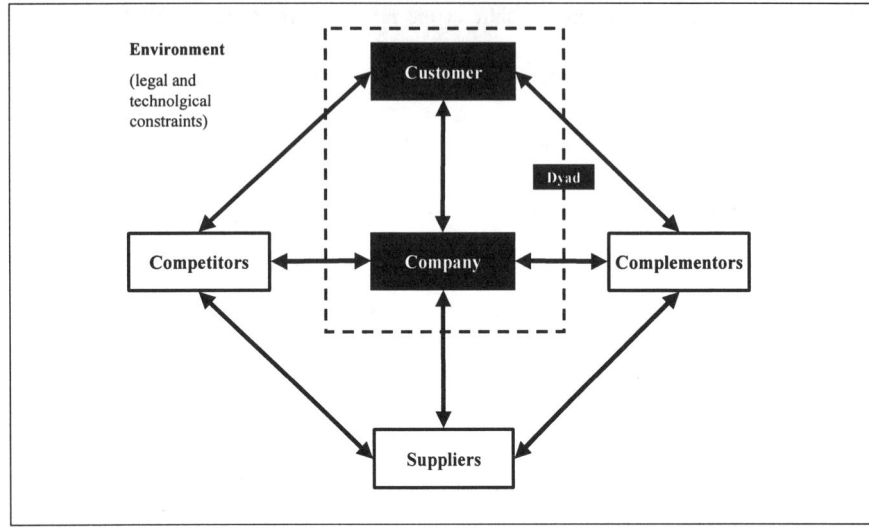

Fig. 15: The value net with particular dyadic focus[619]

Environmental factors and emphasis on the dyadic relationship are added in *Fig. 15* due to the specific focus of this research. The complementors category refers to such actors that provide products which are complementary to the company's offerings in the sense that customers valuation of its offerings is enhanced when used in conjunction with the complement like, for instance, laptop computers and beamers.[620] *Nalebuff/Brandenburger* (1996), though, point out that the different categories are interpreted as roles, not fixed properties inherent to the actors. As a result, two companies can occupy very different roles vis-à-vis each other in varying regards. For instance, Dell Computers may be a complementor to British Airways when it comes to equipping airplanes' first class with special working stations.[621] They may also be

---

[619] Adapted from *Nalebuff, B. J./Brandenburger, A. M.* (1996), p. 16.

[620] This definition includes technologically-induced indirect network effects (often: externalities) such as those, for instance, present in the case of computer hard- and software. Yet, it reaches beyond to capture purely perceptional effects as suggested by the example of the companies' Oscar Mayer (a producer of hot dogs) and Colman's (a mustard producer) products given by *Nalebuff, B. J./Brandenburger, A. M.* (1996), p. 16. For a similarly broad understanding of complements see already e.g. *Baumol, W. J.* (1977). For extensive discussion of network externalities see e.g. *Katz, M. L./Shapiro, C.* (1986) *Graumann, M.* (1993); *Besen, S. M./Farrell, J.* (1994); *Rosen, B. N.* (1994); *Liebowitz, S. J./Margolis, S. E.* (1998a); *Shapiro, C./Varian, H. R.* (1999), p. 173ff.

[621] Since spring 2004, the German Airline Lufthansa, for instance, offers its passengers on (selected) long-distance flights an onboard Internet portal based on WLAN technology referred to as "Flynet". The service

competitors with respect to videoconferencing when it becomes a substantial alternative to business trips.[622]

While the above systematization is meant to give an overview of the relevant kinds of sources, the following considerations on concrete impulses make no claim to being complete. Instead, the intention is to describe the general reasoning underlying each kind of source, to give some meaningful examples for conceivable impulses and link them to consequential seller aspirations to new business types constellations.

3.3.4.2   Discussion of individual sources

3.3.4.2.1   Market partner-related impulses

3.3.4.2.1.1 Intra-company impulses

Intra-company impulses in terms of, broadly speaking, "innovations" which are directly linked to the relevant market offering constitute perhaps the most obvious source of shift initiation.[623] Nevertheless, delimitation of the notion as understood here is necessary because the term has been used in a variety of contexts and divergent meanings.[624] Probably the most influential definition of innovation has been advanced by *Schumpeter* (1934) who characterizes it as introduction of new elements or a new combination of old elements in industrial organization.[625] In such broad understanding, the notion covers

- the introduction of new products or qualities (product innovation),
- the introduction of new production methods (process innovation),

---

results from a cooperation with the media and internet company TOMORROW FOOCUS Technologies (see *Contentmanager.de* (2004)).

[622] See related *Nalebuff, B. J./Brandenburger, A. M.* (1996), p. 17.

[623] On their role in causing first-mover positions see e.g. *Lieberman, M. B./Montgomery, D. B.* (1988), p. 43ff; *Kerin, R. A./Varadarajan, P. R./Peterson, R. A.* (1992), p. 42ff.

[624] See for such assessment e.g. *de Pay, D.* (1989), p. 8; *Hitt, M. A./Ireland, R. D./Camp, S. M., et al.* (2001), p. 484f. For examples see e.g. *de Pay, D.* (1989), p. 8, who offers a management-oriented definition of innovation as an activity which introduces new ideas into the company through research, further develops them and finally realizes them in the production process and, subsequently, in the market; *Heidingsfelder, M. M.* (1990), p. 4ff; *Domrös* (1994), p. 26f; ; *Jenkins, M./Floyd, S.* (2002), p. 250.

[625] See *Schumpeter, J. A.* (1934 (repr.: 1961)); *Schumpeter, J. A.* (1942); analogously: *Schumpeter, J. A.* (1926), p. 100ff. For according appraisal of his role see e.g. *Freeman, C.* (1987), p. 858.

- the opening up of new markets,

- the opening up of new sources of input materials, and

- the creation of new organizational structure in an industry, for instance, the creation of a monopoly situation.[626]

Furthermore, *Schumpeter* (1934) differentiates between various phases and outcomes of the complete process of some new solution appearing on the market:[627] *invention* relates the process of how a new idea is generated, while its interpretation and realization in terms of its practical and commercial use are referred to as *innovation*. *Diffusion*, finally, captures on an aggregate economy level the new solution's distribution brought forth largely by imitation through other firms.

For the purpose of this research, a narrower interpretation of what kind of "innovation" should qualify as intra-company source of impulse seems suitable. The focus is on the first two forms, product innovation and process innovation within the company that are immediately relate to the technological properties of the product.[628] Their nature is regarded in a first instance to be to a large extent rather inventional in a *Schumpeterian* sense. The reasoning behind these restrictions relies on the idea that the shift between business types constellations itself, if successfully introduced in the market, represents a superordinate form of innovation in the *Schumpeterian* nomenclature. As a consequence, the underlying impulse is treated as rather inventional, although, through its linkage to the shift, it is held to also possess some characteristics of an innovation. Further, with respect to the enumerated events qualifying as innovations according to *Schumpeter* (1934), the superordinate shift notion is open to encompass all of them. They are, however, systematized according to the framework established above. Consequently, the latter three elements are captured on the superordinate level of the shift innovation and are assigned to their according impulse sources (e.g. suppliers when it comes to the opening up of new sources of input materials). For example, the creation

---

[626] See *Schumpeter, J. A.* (1934 (repr.: 1961)); *Schumpeter, J. A.* (1942); analogously: *Schumpeter, J. A.* (1926), p. 101. for reception in the secondary literature see e.g. *Sundbo, J.* (1998 (repr.: 2001)), p. 20ff.

[627] See *Schumpeter, J. A.* (1942); *Schumpeter, J. A.* (1926); also *Rogers, E. M.* (1962 (repr.: 1968)), p. 193ff. Taking up the distinction in a marketing context e.g. *Heidingsfelder, M. M.* (1990), p. 6ff. For a brief overview see *Freeman, C.* (1987).

[628] See for applications of the distinction between product and process innovations e.g. *Teece, D. J.* (1988), p. 51ff; *de Pay, D.* (1989), p. 11; *Jarrat, D./Fayed, R.* (2001), p. 69.

of new organizational structure in an industry would qualify as a competitor-related impulse, unless the monopoly is based on a product or process innovation providing the firm with a temporary monopoly.

Against this terminological background, the concrete inventional/innovative intra-company impulse defines the resulting direction of shift considerations. Examples include

- process innovations that allow for shifting the interface between autonomous and customer-specific elements of the production process (sometimes referred to as the "order-penetration-point"[629]) closer to the customer, for instance through modularization, thereby encouraging a reduction in seller specificity, or

- product innovations that entail such utility increases from the buyers viewpoint as to warrant a (technologically and/or contractually induced) shift towards (higher) specific investment requirements by the buyer.[630]

Another aspect of intra-company impulses which is related to the seller's own supply-side is a change in the firm's **cost structure**. For instance, employment of more capital-intensive production technology, particularly when emerging as a cumulative factor over time, may – when recognized – alter the seller's preferred revenue structure in a world of risk and bounded rationality.[631] To the degree that fixed revenues, paralleling the preponderance of fixed costs to variable costs, become relatively more desirable, a shift towards buyer-side relational business gains relevance, especially when implemented with high initial investments followed by relatively low follow-up investments.

3.3.4.2.1.2 Buyers

From the variety of impulses that may be generated on the buyer side some are selected for discussion and grouped together based on their opposed directional consequences for the

---

[629] *Ihde, G. B.* (1988), p. 14; see also *Jacob, F.* (1995), pp. 138f, 191; *Kleinaltenkamp, M.* (1995), p. 2357; related *Feitzinger, E./Lee, H. L.* (1997), p. 116.

[630] On the general distinction between product and process innovations see e.g. *Utterback, J. M./Abernathy, W. J.* (1975).

[631] See, also on the following line of argument, the analysis by *Possmeier, F.* (2000).

seller's shift considerations. The first group covers impulses which result in (at least temporarily) increased **restraints to purchase**.[632] In case the present constellation requires specific investments on the part of the buyer, and even more so, if they relate to an undefined time horizon (RB^B), new information that comes to the market and calls the financial and/or technological survivability of the seller company into question has the potential to cause severe restraints to purchase.[633] Consequently, the seller may consider shifting towards buyer product business. Another example is information on impending horizontal coalition formation with the seller's participation which may result in increased perceived danger of exploitation on the part of the buyer(s).[634] As a result, either shifting towards buyer product business or increasing seller specific investment may come into question.[635]

The issue of whether the information is fundamentally substantiated or purely rumors-based is relevant solely with respect to resulting divergences in the seller's ability to credibly rebut the news. However, if this path fails and/or the relevant events actually occur and trigger lasting effects in terms of restraints to purchase, then considerations on strategic shifts in the direction of reduced buyer specificity become relevant.[636]

The second group encompasses impulses which result in an enhanced desire for **seller dependence relief** when a transaction in the current constellation would involve specific investments by the seller. The underlying reason is a concern about presumable, enduring changes (here: increases) in the buyer's inclination towards opportunistic behavior. Examples include information on

---

[632] For general discussions of contexts which are characterized by high levels of buyer restraints to purchase see e.g. *Backhaus, K./Aufderheide, D./Späth, G.-M.* (1994); *Reinkemeier, C.* (1998).

[633] In illustrating the dangers that RB^B-buyers face in case of seller bankruptcy, *Reinkemeier, C.* (1998), p. 1f, refers to the case of the software company Strässle which first became bankrupt before parts were ultimately taken over by its competitor Baan Deutschland GmbH in 1997. As a consequence, however, its proprietary PPS-system "PSK 2000" was given up medium term.

[634] This implies the integration of market structure influence, that is, small numbers conditions that may prevail due to causes other than asset specificity.

[635] On the latter possibility see e.g. *Anderson, E./Weitz, B.* (1992), p. 27, examination on the use of pledges in channel relationships.

[636] The same line of argument essentially applies as well to all subsequently discussed impulses. However, in other cases, detection of the purely rumorous character of information may be easier. Then, substantiated information would be required in order to induce shift considerations.

- opportunistic exploitation of another supplier by the relevant buyer,
- financial difficulties of the buyer which increase the probability of opportunistic exploitation, or
- coalition formation of several buyers which enhances their bargaining power.

In case of upcoming contract conclusion and the expectation of lasting effects or extended effects, for instance if the increased concerns refer to the whole industry, the seller is likely to take the possibility of shifting towards PDB^S, or at least, if feasible, towards PJB^S and to take associated contingent contracts into account.[637]

A third aspect relates to impulses associated with rising **buyer receptivity for specificity**. Changes in end-customer preferences or changes in the market structure of subsequent stages may augment the buyer's willingness-to-pay for a more specific solution (either in terms of buyer- or seller-side specificity or both). Alternatively, higher cost pressure in subsequent markets may get translated with the result that, if acceptance of higher buyer specificity would result in overall cost reduction to the buyer, he might be willing to accept this.

Sometimes, several of the effects get combined. *Thomke/von Hippel* (2002) provide an example from the specialty flavor industry where product development requires high degrees of customization and is, consequently, associated with high seller specificity.[638] As a response to increases in cost pressure from buyers, Bush Boake Allen (now: International Flavors & Fragrances, Inc. (IFF)) considered shifting some product development activities to the buyers (thereby increasing buyer specificity and simultaneously decreasing seller specificity). Concretely, they developed an internet-based tool including a database of flavor profiles which was linked to an automated machine, preferably located at the customer-site, which would produce within minutes the flavor sample that the customer had combined from the database.

---

[637] See e.g. the game theoretic analysis by *Townsend, R. M.* (1982) on the existence and nature of multi-period contracts under conditions of private (asymmetric) information. He identifies conditions for which multiperiod contracts (which could be interpreted in the direction of a PJB) are superior to a sequence of one-period contracts (which could be interpreted in the direction of a RB).

[638] See, though originally given for illustration in another research context, *Thomke, S./von Hippel, E.* (2002), p. 76f.

3.3.4.2.1.3 Suppliers

The seller's (*S*) own supply-side (S^2) may form the nutrient medium for shift impulses. The examples have been chosen again for illustration of opposed directional consequences for the seller's shift considerations. In the first case, the impulse points towards reducing the seller specificity in the relation with its buyer(s) (**seller dependence relief**). An eminent supply-side cause is information on (lasting) threats of endangered future availability of input factors required for the production of the present specific seller offerings. The concerns on worsening conditions of availability impact on the relevant dyad through the changed production cost structure. Higher prices for the particular input factor reduce the efficiency of the current technological solution and jeopardize *S*'s value created (see *Fig. 13*). The source of such threats may, for instance, be capacity destruction due to force majeure, or, alternatively, changes in market structure (e.g. coalition formation or mergers on the supply-side).[639] A second kind of impulse points in the direction of increased seller (and potentially buyer) specificity (**enhanced efficient technological feasibility**). Information on financial difficulties of the relevant S^2 supplier may trigger a process of backward vertical integration by *S* which in turn may increase its control over the critical resource.[640] This would effectively act as a price reduction for the input good, potentially facilitating the efficient provision of more specific constellations. This effect can also be seen as a result from reduced transaction costs in the relationship between *S* and S^2: *S*'s value created in the relation with its own buyers is less endangered to fall prey to extended claims by S^2.

3.3.4.2.1.4 Competitors

Although the investigation of competitor-related impulses (in particular changes of the structural market conditions) and resulting effects on governance (here: constellation) choice might have a considerable potential for enriching TCA's ability to contribute to the analysis of

---

[639] See *Ghosh, M./John, G.* (1999), p. 140, on the incentives for suppliers to extend their claims beyond the original transaction relation with a buyer to the buyer's value created in its relationship with its own customers under certain circumstances.

[640] Asymmetric access to scarce resources has been proposed as the main source of barriers to entry by Austrian economics, although their efficacy is held to be only temporary (see for recent outline *Backhaus, K./Plinke, W./Rese, M.* (2004), (p. 43f); originally Austrian contributions to the topic include *Kirzner, I. M.* (1979), p. 98f).

strategic management. This issue is, however, not uncontroversial in the recent TCA literature.[641] As outlined in chapter 3.2.3, the former view is adopted here. In particular, the threat of new competitor's entry can be interpreted as a competitor-related impulse for shifts between business types constellations.[642]

Recognizing the appearance of new competitors is by no means trivial. In fact, it "...may be difficult for an incumbent to perceive the threat and take preventative steps."[643] Together, timely recognition and adequate action in the form of a shift between business types constellations are, therefore, an entrepreneurial act.[644] Shifting to a constellation with higher specific investment by the seller, that is, a higher degree of customization in either production processes, or outcomes, or both, may serve several purposes which contribute to the **impediment of potential new competitors**: first, a higher utility to the buyer may result from increased seller specificity in terms of better fulfillment of its needs. This possibility must not run counter to the above proposition of subjective relative ex ante optimality of the previous constellation. The new information on entry threat has changed the seller's calculus to include a higher "indirect benefit component" attached to specificity which is justified on the very basis of its capacity to act as an impediment to rivals.[645] Second, and related, its replaceability diminishes since customization – aside from cases of second sourcing – usually implies adaptations and consequential dependence by the buyer.[646] Third, entry barriers may be created or elevated simply by offering the buyer a larger potential for exploitation: transaction

---

[641] For general positive assessments on incorporation see e.g. *Heide, J. B.* (1994), p. 83; *Foss, N. J.* (2003), who regards many market power-related issues to have transaction cost phenomena at their roots. The topic's relevance – at least from the viewpoint of the acting firm – is further undermined by *Milgrom, P./Roberts, J.* (1992), p. 561. Skeptical views on the relevance of market power issues for economic organization, compared to TCA have been expressed by *Williamson, O. E.* (1985), p. 124ff, who also provides a detailed conceptual discussion of the topic in the context of antitrust enforcement and transaction cost reasons for vertical integration (p. 373ff).

[642] See e.g. *Heide, J. B.* (1994), p. 83; from a marketing lens *Jarrat, D./Fayed, R.* (2001), p. 68.

[643] *Lieberman, M. B./Montgomery, D. B.* (1988), p. 48.

[644] This is not to deny that the therein implied entrepreneurship is classified as such from a managerial point of view, while it may in some cases run contrary to the idea of entrepreneurship as understood in Austrian economics tradition. For recent discussion on alternative reactions like ignorance or accomodation see *Kuester, S./Homburg, C./Robertson, T. S., et al.* (2001).

[645] See for discussion of such activities e.g. *Williamson, O. E.* (1985), p. 125ff; *Mahoney, J. T./Pandian, J. R.* (1992), p. 655f; *Williamson, O. E.* (1998), p. 48; *Mahoney, J. T.* (2001), p. 656. See also chapter 4.3 for incorporation in the analytical shift model.

[646] See e.g. *Dwyer, R. F./Schurr, P. H./Oh, S.* (1987), p. 14.

specific investments, once incurred, represent sunk costs and act, hence, as barriers to entry for potential rivals.[647] The effect is two-fold: first, all other things being equal, they discriminate the entrant by rendering rational larger price concessions in renegotiations on the part of the seller, and, second, exactly for this first effect, they can operate as (credible) signals and, thereby, deter entry completely.[648]

On the other hand, information on the occurrence of a previously unexpected exit of a competitor may influence the market structure contingent power relations between seller and buyer(s) in favor of the former. This can be expected to be particularly relevant in the presence of entry barriers, that is, when the buyer(s)´s set of alternatives is lastingly scaled down. Such an impulse may allow for shifting towards a constellation with decreased seller specificity without having to concede overcompensating price reductions. The same effect would result from shifting towards increased buyer specificity without fully compensating the buyer for the rise in perceived danger it experiences. Similar effects can be expected from information on improved conditions for taking over a competitor.

3.3.4.2.1.5 Complementors

In the presence of considerable network effects and competing (proprietary) solutions, information on changing stability or structure of the diverse coalitions may induce shift contemplation. Consider, for instance, information on the looming bankruptcy (and even more so the event itself) of an important complementor, or its switch to another "coalition". If the coalition is interpreted as some kind of self-enforcing agreement, the complementors expected gains from violating the previous, more or less formal, coalition agreement now outweigh the loss of future net benefits from abandoning the old coalition.[649] This illustrates again the prevailing condition of bounded rationality: besides the possibility that the preceding impulse

---

[647] See e.g. *Williamson, O. E.* (1985), p. 31, fn 26 in comparing the role of asset specificity in TCA and "contestability theory" (for the latter approach see *Baumol, W. J./Panzer, J./Willig, R.* (1982)); for general treatment of sunk costs as entry barriers see e.g. *Stigler, G. J.* (1968 (repr.: 1990)), p. 67; *Yao, D. A.* (1988), p. 62; *Söllner, A.* (1994); *Kuester, S./Homburg, C./Robertson, T. S., et al.* (2001), p. 1196; *Han, J. K./Kim, N./Kim, H.-B.* (2001).

[648] See the seminal literature on entry deterrence which is predominantly game theoretic in nature, e.g. *Spence, M.* (1977); *Dixit, A.* (1980); *Milgrom, P./Roberts, J.* (1982); also: *Spence, M. A.* (1984). In consideration of the case of a buyer with market power see *Mudambi, R.* (1990).

[649] See on self-enforcing agreements e.g. the seminal treatment by *Telser, L. G.* (1981).

may not have been directly relevant for the seller, but is only indirectly so, there is a second option: the seller has not recognized the impulse as such.

In both cases, a significant impact on the competitiveness of the whole network to which the seller belongs can be expected. In case lasting detrimental effects are expected, the impulse points towards the following options, depending on the number of competing coalitions: if there is only one other coalition, establishing compatibility essentially amounts to shifting towards (buyer) product business. In case of several competing solutions, the seller may also choose to stick to the current constellation, yet switch to another coalition.[650]

3.3.4.2.2 Environmental impulses

Information on changes in terms of available basic technologies and/or in the legal environment are finally considered as potential shift impulses. Availability of fundamentally different basic technology exerts an influence by potentially moving the frontier of efficient specificity provision outwards. At the heart of this idea lies the "exhaustion of technology trajectory"-hypothesis according to which there are inherent physical limits to each fundamental technology that determine the border of (efficiently) tapping its full potential.[651] In turn, the advent of a new fundamental technology opens up a new space to exploit. *Pine* (1993) describes this idea in his outline of newly emerging possibilities of efficient mass customization supply which he ascribes to progress concerning the available fundamental state-of-the-art technology.[652] The legal environment impacts on two different levels on

---

[650] An example, albeit with less pronouced impulse character, is the Ethernet case as outlined e.g. by *Markoff, J.* (1998); *von Burg, U./Kenney, M.* (2000).

[651] This idea has been captured in the managerially-oriented "s-curve"-concept as developed by *Foster, R. N.* (1986); *Utterback, J. M./Abernathy, W. J.* (1975). Examples include the replacement of commercial sailing ships by steamboats, or the substitution of electromechanic cash registers by their electronic counterparts (see *Foster, R. N.* (1986), p. 23f). In contrast to the idea of a technology's potential being exhausted before its replacement (or at least supplementation) by a superior technology, the concept of disruptive technologies has been advanced in the recent literature (see e.g. the seminal work by *Christensen, C. R.* (1992); *Christensen, C. R.* (1997); for a recent overview *Adner, R.* (2002)). Disruptive technologies are therein defined as "...technologies that introduce a different performance package from mainstream technologies and are inferior to mainstream technologies along the dimensions of performance that are most important to mainstream customers." (*Adner, R.* (2002), p. 668). Research on whether and to what extent this concept might possess relevance in a transaction cost theoretic context has not yet produced many insights. Hence, this work is confined to the traditional concept of exhaustion of technology trajectory.

[652] See *Pine, J. B.* (1993). Examples are ample, particularly regarding the consumer goods sector which was

economic decision-making, first, in very fundamental ways by defining the overall games of the rule, in particular property rights, etc., and second, by rather specific regulations relating, for instance, to individual industries.[653] The legal impacts briefly sketched in this research are found in the latter domain. An example for the domain of legal restrictions as impulse source, albeit given in a different context, can be traced to *Crocker/Masten* (1988) who analytically examine the trade-off between the design and duration of long-term contracts and then turn to evidence from natural gas production.[654]

However, information concerning the technological and legal domains is more likely to be common knowledge in nature, whereas information from market partner-related sources can be presumed to have a higher likelihood of being private information. As a result, recognizing relevant information plays a relatively minor role, thereby attributing a relatively higher weight to its transformation into a marketable offering. In any case, it is proposed that the following consequences will result if technological or legal frame are the sources of a shift impulse.

- All other things being equal, it is more likely that the whole relevant industry or a least a majority of sellers in the industry will eventually switch from one business types constellation to another.[655]

- All other things being equal, the duration of the temporary monopoly that the shift pioneer enjoys is reduced.

These propositions can be related to an idea which is generally referred to as the survivor principle[656]: Firms surviving in a competitive environment are regarded to behave

---

previously characterized by mass production to a relatively higher degree. They range from print-on-demand in the publishing industry, or customized information services over the internet, to customized jeans production in the clothing industry.

[653] See also chapter 4.1.

[654] See *Crocker, K. J./Masten, S. E.* (1988). One of their empirical findings concerns the effects from prospective deregulation subsequent to the Natural Gas Policy Act in the U.S. in 1978 which led to considerable reductions in average contract length (p. 341).

[655] The question remains what should be regarded as the appropriate time horizon for an assessment on this proposition, in particular when it comes to empirical testing.

[656] The formulation of the survivor principle is usually associated, for instance, with *Alchian, A. A.* (1950); *Friedman, M.* (1953); *Stigler, G. J.* (1968 (repr.: 1990)). An empirical test of the survivor principle which

"efficiently" at least concerning the outcome, if not regarding each individual decision process. The principle may be particularly relevant with respect to environmental impulses. Such impulses are likely to impact, at least to some degree, on all actors in the affected industry. Therefore, what is perceived as the comparatively most efficient and effective business types constellation may change for a large number of sellers in an industry at a fairly similar time. This is proposed to be relevant, in particular, when compared to cases where the shift impulse, at least originally, results from the particular relations of a particular firm in the industry with the other actor's.

---

frequently serves as basis for empirical research itself has recently been provided by *Klein, P. G./Lien, L. B.* (2003). Their findings in the context of corporate diversification are supportive of the principle's validity.

4   Dynamic perspective II: considerations on sufficient conditions for shifts between business types constellations

"...change can be seen as an outcome jointly determined by motivation to change, opportunity to change, and capability to change."[657] While generally subscribing to this assertion, application on the issue of strategic shifts between business types constellations requires some rearrangements: it is seen as an outcome jointly determined by the motivation to change, the general *perception* of a window of opportunity, and the *ability to implement* the concrete change at favorable conditions. This boils down to three central questions from the seller's perspective[658].

(1) Motivation and perceived opportunity: what is in the seller's general interest, that is: what is "desired"?

(2) Environmental/legal constraints to the concrete implementation: what are potential restrictions, that is: what is "allowed"?

(3) Ability to implement at favorable conditions: what will be accepted by the buyer, that is: what can be "asserted"?

The first issue concerns the identification of *generally* desirable new constellations and corresponding shift directions from the seller's perspective, that is motivation and perceived opportunity. This has been explored on qualitative grounds in the preceding chapter. Subsequently, it will, therefore, be assumed that a certain shift satisfies this first, necessary condition and has been assessed as potentially beneficial for the seller. Then, the second and third issues become relevant. Taken together, they are proposed to form the sufficient conditions for a successful shift. And while *general* considerations (a) on legal restrictions which represent the major impact on what is "allowed"[659], and (b) on aspects of

---

[657] *Greve, H. R.* (1998), p. 58f; see also *Miller, D./Chen, M.-J.* (1994).

[658] For similar distinction, albeit without reference to the second issue, see e.g. *Zajac, E. J./Shortell, S. M.* (1989), pp. 413, 416, who discriminate between the desire to change strategy (content perspective) and the ability to change (process perspective).

[659] See chapter 4.1.

assertability[660] may provide insights into what determines the feasibility of achieving a shift between business types, more formal analysis is subsequently added to form part of the investigation.

4.1 Legal restrictions

Legal restrictions are a central part of the institutional environment surrounding every transaction.[661] Therefore, although the investigation of their influence on the behavior of economic actors does not constitute a decisive part of this work, since they are not subject to the seller's direct disposition, some brief remarks seem appropriate[662]: legal regulations put constraints on the decisions which economic actors take. This fact has long been recognized not only in economic research but also in research on management and marketing.[663] In a systematization of legal impacts on marketing decisions, *Backhaus/Plinke* (1986) distinguish between general regulations which relate to the organization of markets (property rights regulations and contract law) and such which intervene in market processes and, thus, immediately confine the scope of marketing decisions.[664] Mainly the latter category is referred to in this section. Such legal regulations may crucially impact on how beneficial a certain

---

[660] The term assertability is inspired on the one hand by *Schumpeter's* understanding of the distinction between inventions and innovations. The latter are defined also by having successfully been introduced in the market. On the other hand, we draw on the idea that sustainable institutions (and, hence, governance mechanisms) need to be either enforceable or self-enforcing (see e.g. *Erlei, M./Leschke, M./Sauerland, D.* (1999), p. 23f).

[661] For discussion of differing impacts in an international context see e.g. *Henisz, W., J.* (1998).

[662] In business practice indirect long-term impacting through industry lobbies or even direct impacting exerted by large companies may be present. Neither is, however, subject of this investigation. The first option is excluded since this work focuses on the "adjusting screws" available to a company on its own, while the second alternative represents a special case in terms of company size and power just as well as in terms of legitimation.

[663] Early, comprehensive overviews on the impact of legal provisions on business (and in particular marketing) decisions have been provided by *Backhaus, K./Plinke, W.* (1986); *Ahlert, D.* (1988). *Howard, M. C.* (1985) presents an overview of "...basic sources of information on the legal aspects of marketing" (p. 162). The *Journal of Marketing* has had a section on "legal developments in marketing" running from the 1970's (see e.g. *Werner, R. O. E.* (1979) *Werner, R. O. E.* (1993) to 1993. In 1994, its contents were moved to the Journal of Public Policy and Marketing (see *Varadarajan, P. R.* (1994), p. v). Since that time, the issue has gained even more attention (see e.g. *Ahlert, D./Schröder, H.* (1996); *Blois, K. J.* (1996), p. 165; *Brierty, E. G./Eckles, R. W./Reeder, R. R.* (1998), p. 52; *Zerres, M./Zerres, T.* (2002)). Related to the context of this research, *Gundlach, G. T./Murphy, P. E.* (1993), for instance, explicitly focus on the relationship between the emergence of the relational exchange paradigm and attempts of formal law regulations to deal with this phenomenon.

[664] See *Backhaus, K./Plinke, W.* (1986), p. 126.

business types constellation will be perceived by the transacting parties.[665] Legal constraints, particularly in terms of governmentally-defined standards, may simply render one constellation more favorable than another, or, at the extreme, may rule out certain constellations as unlawful, or explicitly prescribe others.[666]

Note that such governmental action may, for instance, represent an attempt to specify and enforce minimum quality standards (e.g. compatibility) when otherwise performance measurement problems and conditions of high potential "...short-run profit from deceptively low quality supply..."[667] would raise the costs of supply – to a prohibitive degree at the extreme. The sketched coherences are depicted in *Fig. 16*. The diagram systematizes potential legal influences on shift considerations based on three criteria. The first criterion, termed as strength of impact, refers to the distinction between compulsory and non-compulsory legal influences. The second criterion (concerned constellation) stems from the question of whether the impact relates to the current or to the newly envisaged business types constellation. The third relevant aspect is the question of whether the product-related dimension (value/countervalue) or the mode-related dimension (structure of mutual delivery) of the business types constellation "package" is concerned by the particular legal regulation.

Owing to the inter- and intra-national variety of regulations and fast rates of change in the relevant law areas, only some general remarks for the purpose of systematizing will be advanced. They concern issues found in the lower right and left corner of the cube (dark shaded) and which can exert a particularly drastic impact on further considerations regarding a basically interesting constellation: they effectively cut them off. Yet, compulsory restrictions which simultaneously concern both package dimensions as would be required for obtaining such an effect are likely to be the exception.

---

[665] For instance, assessments on leasing (as one way of realizing a shift from one constellation to another; see chapter 5.2.1) are considerably influenced by (changes in) the taxation regulations. *Städtler, A.* (2000) describes a situation in which leasing investments increased in Germany in 1999 despite unfavorable changes in tax regulations: "die Leasinginvestitionen expandierten im Jahr 1999 [...], obwohl diverse Steuerrechtsänderungen – insbesondere der § 2b Einkommenssteuergestz – deutliche Bremsspuren bei Großimmobilien, vor allem Flugzeugen, Schiffen und Bahnen, hinterließen.." (p. 27).

[666] See in related contexts *Kleinaltenkamp, M.* (1993), p. 24; *Argyres, N. S./Liebeskind, J. P.* (1999), p. 53, and the literature referred to there; *Shapiro, C./Varian, H. R.* (1999), p. 195.

[667] *Klein, B./Leffler, K. B.* (1981), p. 635.

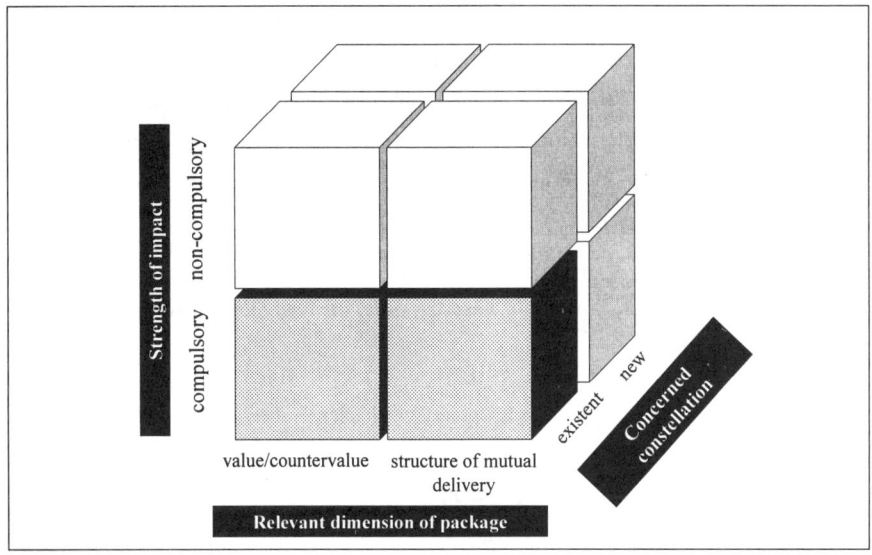

Fig. 16: Systematization of legal regulations´ impacts on shifts between business types constellations[668]

In fact, a firm may very well be able to offset legal constraints on the product-related, rather technical, side of the package by corresponding contractual, or more precisely, mode-related options and vice versa. However, shifting via redesigning one dimension may result in another cost for the seller and/or different benefits for the buyer than a shift based on the other dimension. Therefore, an explicit legal prohibition concerning one area possibly has an impact on the overall assessment of a particular shift.[669] Following from the two package dimensions, compulsory legal provisions that discriminate the new constellation may either imply direct regulation of a product´s quality or properties, e.g. norms which set standards for technical interfaces, or prohibit certain contracting or payment modes, e.g. regulations on tying and (product) bundling.[670] Finally, indirect effects which might discriminate the new constellation

[668] Similar to the differentiation between compulsory and non-complsory regulations, *Grewal, R./Dharwadkar, R.* (2002), p. 85f., distinguish between imposition and inducements as primary mechanisms used by regulatory institutions.

[669] Admittedly, this issue touches on the more operational aspects of shifting, namely possibilities of realizing a certain strategic shift. Essentially, if the dimension impacts on costs/or benefits, the considerations in the following chapters would have to be conducted for all alternative ways to realize the shift. Yet, since the argumentation is directed at presenting a general method for tackling issues of shifts between constellations, not at a concrete evaluation of a particular situation, the following argumentation abstracts from this point.

[670] See on effects of standard setting regulations e.g. *Ahlert, D./Schröder, H.* (1996), p. 156. For discussion of

may be related to the particular kind of impulse underlying the shift considerations. If the impulse is linked up to merging with a previous competitor, antitrust laws come into play.[671] Also, a product innovation which may be susceptible to patent protection might form the basis of the shift considerations. In that case, it depends on the concrete patent laws, for instance, of whether they rule out patent protection for the particular case if the impulse can profitably be translated in offering a new constellation.[672]

4.2 General considerations on asserting shifts between business types constellations

As is apparent from the reflections in the preceding chapter, it is necessary to *perceive* a shift opportunity. Yet, successful translation into a concrete market offering which is accepted by the buyer and enhances seller profit constitutes the complementary sufficient condition for a shift actually taking place. This latter condition has been referred to as "efficient assertion". In the context of voluntary exchange, the term "assertion" may surprise at first sight. Nevertheless, it might carry several implications, particularly in combination with the emphasis on efficiency, which are held to be important for this research.[673]

First, the term "assertion" reflects recognition of the idea that, from an individual firm's perspective, in principle two ways open up for realizing a shift between business types in the market. Common to both routes is the imperative of providing the buyer with a new *best available* solution to his needs – which implies the existence of an (at least) temporary monopoly power: "in the marketplace, it's the party with the power who gets to make the

---

bundling legislation see e.g. *Stremersch, S./Tellis, G. J.* (2002), p. 58f. Tying arrangements require two (or more) products to be purchased together, either simultaneously or sequentially (see *Rubin, P. H.* (1990), p. 130f). For instance, warranty on automobiles is usually maintained only if maintenance is carried out by original dealers.

[671] See e.g. the special section on "Bringing marketing insights to bear on antitrust policy and competitive conduct" in the fall 2002 issue (Vol. 21, No. 2) of the *Journal of Public Policy and Marketing*.

[672] See e.g. *Lieberman, M. B./Montgomery, D. B.* (1988), p. 42ff.

[673] Besides, it is supported by some of the basic literature: *Schumpeter, J. A.* (1928), p. 482f, for instance, uses the term "Durchsetzung" when referring to that part of the very task of the entrepreneur which is concerned with *realizing* new opportunities in the market.

rules."[674] Yet, the sources of this power may be very different and determine whether the concrete assertion is likely to possess more properties of a "cooperation" or a "conflict".[675]

The first route emphasizes the notion of a new *best* solution and centers around increases in the seller's added value from the buyer's perspective. This kind of realization is presumably what *Schumpeter* (1926, 1928, 1934) had in mind and what is focused on by the Austrian school, namely the entrepreneur who improves his own situation by ameliorating that of other economic actors – compared to their previous situation.[676] Such an approach necessarily implies extending the pie to be divided between the transaction parties. Important as it is, confining the analysis to this route would yet not adequately reflect the realities that a particular company's management faces in its shift considerations.

The second route focuses on the issue of *availability* and deviates from the requirement of pie creation.[677] Instead it allows for the seller to improve his situation by solely capturing a larger piece of the pie, that is, by altering its division.[678] The feasibility of this option crucially hinges on (*ex ante*) market power considerations and is, hence, market structure-contingent.[679] It is based on the idea that the relevant set of alternatives is contingent on the point of decision making. The set of options to choose from at decision time t_1 is defined at t_1 – irrespective of what options might have existed at the previous decision time t_0. If previously available

---

[674] *Nalebuff, B. J./Brandenburger, A. M.* (1996), p. 192.

[675] See for such terminology also *Nalebuff, B. J./Brandenburger, A. M.* (1996), p. 34.

[676] See *Schumpeter, J. A.* (1926); *Schumpeter, J. A.* (1928); *Schumpeter, J. A.* (1942). This route is implicit in large parts of research in TCA which is primarily concerned with efficiency and largely dismisses the consideration of market power reasoning with respect to the relevant research topic (see on such assessment e.g. *Ghosh, M./John, G.* (1999), p. 133; *Joshi, A. W./Stump, R. L.* (1999), p. 40f). For support on integrating market power-based considerations with TCA-based efficiency considerations see e.g. *Ghosh, M./John, G.* (1999), p. 140; *Joshi, A. W./Stump, R. L.* (1999), p. 41, referring particularly to disparities in size; *Bloom, P. N./Gundlach, G. T./Cannon, J. P.* (2000), p. 105; *Foss, N. J.* (2003).

[677] All other things being equal, it seem easier to capture a relatively larger piece of the pie from an enlarged pie since it is still possible to provide the buyer with an absolutely larger value created compared to the previous situation (on conceptual grounds see e.g. *Thurow, L. C.* (1980), p. 18; for an empirical perspective on this issue see e.g. *LaBahn, D. W.* (1999), p. 18; *Jap, S. D.* (2001)).

[678] See e.g. *Brandenburger, A. M./Stuart Jr., H. W.* (1996), p. 19ff. This refers to the ex ante agreement on the division because the shift is considered with respect to future transaction situations.

[679] See e.g. *Heide, J. B./John, G.* (1992), p. 41. See also chapters 2.2.1.3.1 and 3.2.3.

choices are no longer at hand, the buyer will accept the shift although it may imply a deterioration compared to t_0 – as long as the net value from it is still positive.[680]

Returning to the notion of "efficient assertion", the focus on efficiency reflects the surmise that, in essence, regardless of its market power, the seller could always make the buyer accept any constellation when the magnitude of the demanded countervalue is regarded as a degree of freedom. That means, it is assumed that acceptance can always be achieved – though perhaps only at the expense of being able to set a very low price. Below a certain threshold which is given by the extrapolation of the current constellation (accounting for expected changes in circumstances), this would in turn endanger the most important driver of entrepreneurial activity, namely the desire of improving one's own situation. Therefore, the sufficient condition must capture both aspects, that of the buyer opting for the seller's offer (referred to as effectiveness in marketing), and that of the rewarding consequences from this decision to the seller (referred to as efficiency in marketing).[681]

As an illustration consider the introductory case of Continental: in trying to shift from bilateral product business towards bilateral relational business, apparently, they were not able to offer sufficient increases in benefits in order to compensate the prospective buyers for the arising lock-in and still keep the resulting assertable price at a level that would ensure enhanced profitability to Continental as well. Neither did they posses the market power to assert the new constellation at efficient conditions. With respect to this example it needs to be highlighted that such an assessment is contingent: the ability to efficiently assert a particular shift may differ significantly among various firms in the same industry – as a result of path dependent firm particularities.[682]

---

[680] See e.g. *Helper, S.* (1991), pp. 786ff, who considers "involuntary commitment" by a "weak" buyer as a result of facing an oligopolistic supplier industry which is modeled to lead to reduced availability of alternatives. However, in the long run, such behavior may exert negative feedback effects on the size of the pie (for related considerations see e.g. *Helper, S.* (1991), p. 823; *Backhaus, K./Büschken, J.* (1999), p. 254f). Nevertheless, under certain conditions, such strategies may even be facilitated by reducing the size of the pie: broadly speaking, this is the case if several dyads in which the seller is involved are jointly considered and the reduction of the whole pie stems from increased scarcity of the product supplied by the seller (see e.g. *Nalebuff, B. J./Brandenburger, A. M.* (1996), p. 40f).

[681] See e.g. the conceptions of (comparative) competitive advantages as developed by *Backhaus, K.* (2003), p. 35ff; *Plinke, W.* (2000), p. 77ff.

[682] See chapter 3.3.3.2.

All of these reflections enter into the concrete parameter values of a formal approach which is subsequently proposed in order to identify sufficient shift conditions. Yet, before proceeding with the development of the model, clarification on one further issue is needed: how does the following formal analysis fit in with the explicit resistance by many Austrian scholars to mathematics-based economic analysis, and also with the, as yet, rather low extent of formalization in TCA?[683] The latter concern perhaps is less severe because it is not due to a factual reluctance towards incorporating formal methods, but rather to the awareness that TCA as a relatively young stream still awaits more formalization[684] and that many problems, such as, for instance, problems of measuring transaction costs still need to be overcome. Consequently, a growing body of formally-oriented research has emerged during the last couple of years. With respect to the former reservation, reference is made to the particular, managerially-oriented viewpoint of this research. Therefore, one of its main objectives is to provide business practice with some systematic considerations on how to approach shifts between business types. And from such a point of view, the necessity of formal considerations is not denied by Austrian scholars either.[685]

4.3   Derivation of an analytical framework for the examination of shifts between business types constellations

4.3.1   General considerations and conceptual roots of the proposed model

In proposing more formal considerations on the topic, the contributions by *Riordan/Williamson* (1985) and *Aufderheide* (1993, 2000) have been particularly inspiring from a TCA perspective.[686] Both models refer to optimization considerations. Additionally,

---

[683] For the original Austrian perspective see e.g. *Hayek, F.* (1945), p. 520; for a recent evaluation of, for instance, the relationship between Austrian economics and game theory see *Foss, K./Foss, N. J.* (2000). For assessment with respect to TCA see *Williamson, O. E.* (2000), p. 604f.

[684] See, for instance, the recent contribution by *Aoki, M.* (2001) who seeks to set on formalization of the analysis of institutions by linking it to game theory. Other contributions that adopt a formal orientation in basing on TCA reasoning include e.g. *Parkhe, A.* (1993); *Mudambi, R./McDowell-Mudambi, S.* (1995); *Jung, S.* (1999); *Nickerson, J. A./Vanden Bergh, R.* (1999).

[685] See e.g. *Schumpeter, J. A.* (1928), p. 483.

[686] See *Riordan, M. H./Williamson, O. E.* (1985); *Aufderheide, D.* (1993); *Aufderheide, D.* (2000). See also *Sanchez, R.* (2000) who integrates a real options perspective in an model that builds on *Riordan/Williamson* (1985).

the development of the model has been influenced by an approach advanced in the marketing literature, namely the TCA-based model for the evaluation of business relationships and supplier switching as developed by *Plinke* (1989, 1997). It is also included in the conceptual basis of the model presented here.[687]

4.3.1.1   The Riordan/Williamson (1985) optimization model

Riordan/Williamson (1985) formulate the choice between firm or market organization of the procurement of a good as an optimization problem with both production cost and transaction cost differences as a function of asset specificity.[688] By focusing on a "make-or-buy" decision, they take the perspective of a firm (hereafter referred to as B) which seeks to acquire some more or less specific input good either from a supplying company (hereafter: S) or through internal production.[689] With the help of this input, B produces in turn output goods which it subsequently markets to its own customers (hereafter: B^2).[690]

The authors see the novel character of the examination mainly in the proposition of a unified framework that encompasses both relevant cost categories, production costs and transaction costs, and the associated suggestions for its formalization. In their heuristic model, they hold asset specificity as primarily responsible for transaction cost differences among transactions. Internal organization or, as in the concrete case, procurement, is argued to enjoy "... a progressive governance cost advantage over market organization as the condition of asset specificity deepens."[691] On the production side, though, the firm is at a cost disadvantage in relation to the market due to its inherent incentive degradation and bureaucratic distortions, and also due to its handicaps with respect to scale and scope economies. The general conclusion drawn from the combination of these effects is that for low levels of asset specificity, market is presumably the least cost mode, while for high levels, internal

---

[687]   See *Plinke, W.* (1989); *Plinke, W.* (1997). Models with more specific focus but in in the same line of argument include *Kaas, K. P./Schade, C.* (1993); *Plinke, W./Söllner, A.* (2000).

[688]   See *Riordan, M. H./Williamson, O. E.* (1985), p. 365ff, also on the following presentation.

[689]   Asset specificity is regarded here as a continuous variable ranging from complete idiosyncrasy (100% of asset specificity) to complete standardization (0% of asset specificity).

[690]   This perspective clearly differs from the point of view taken up in this research. A more detailed discussion of the consequences follows at the end of this chapter.

[691]   *Riordan, M. H./Williamson, O. E.* (1985), p. 368.

organization is favored, and none of them enjoys a definite cost advantage for medium levels. However, these general propositions are conditional upon two assumptions: first, it is assumed that no matter which mode is chosen for procurement the same level of output (goods) is produced and, second, that the optimal level of asset specificity is identical for procurement through both modes.

Both of these assumptions can be questioned and are subsequently relaxed by *Riordan/ Williamson* (1985) in their main (formalized) model. At its core is the idea of augmenting conventional marginal demand and production analysis to include governance cost features. A profit comparison based on first-order maximizing and comparative statics properties is conducted.[692] In a first step, common production technology and associated costs are assumed for (procurement through) both modes, yielding:

$$\pi^m = R(X) - C(X, A; \alpha) - \gamma\ A - W(A))$$
$$\pi^i = R(X) - C(X, A; \alpha) - \gamma\ A - (\beta + V(A)) \tag{4.1}$$

with	$\pi^{i,m}$	= profit expressions for internal (i) and market (m) governance mode
	X	= output
	$R(X)$	= revenues contingent on output
	A	= degree of asset specificity
	α	= shift parameter: a higher value of α yields greater production cost reducing consequences to asset specificity
	$C(X, A, \alpha)$	= production costs contingent on output, asset specificity and shift parameter
	γ	= constant per unit cost of asset specificity
	$W(A)$	= market governance costs associated with a certain degree of asset specificity
	β	= (basic) bureaucratic cost parameter of internal governance costs
	$V(A)$	= asset specificity dependent internal governance costs

It is further assumed that the choice of output is optimal for each value of A. Thereby, essentially, a second optimization is implied without being explicitly formulated or elaborated on, namely an optimization with respect to B's own customers (B^2's) and the relevant price-demand-curve. The separation of the two areas of concern is expressed in (4.1) by the fact that the asset specificity condition relates to the input good alone and bears no direct consequences for B's revenues. Central findings from this first optimization are then: first, although there is a whole family of curves π^i for different values of β, which mode is favored in a certain situation does not depend on β, but only on which profit function exhibits the highest peak.

---

[692] *Riordan, M. H./Williamson, O. E.* (1985) restrict their analysis to a certain set of cost functions defined by specific properties which will not be discussed here (see p. 370).

Second, with greater cost reducing impact α of asset specificity, internal organization is progressively favored.

Subsequently, the firm's cost disadvantage with respect to internally producing the asset specific input good is incorporated in the model yielding different production cost functions for procurement through the two modes (with m representing market governance and i representing internal procurement):

$$C^m = C(X, A; \alpha)$$
$$C^i = C(X, A; \alpha) + H(X, A) \cdot X$$
$$and$$
$$M(X, A) = H_X(X, A) \cdot X + H(X, A)$$

(4.2)

with $H(X,A)$ = production cost disadvantage per output unit associated with internal organization
      $M(X,A)$ = marginal production cost advantage of internal organization per unit
      $H_X(X,A)$ = derivative of H with respect to X

As is apparent from (4.2), the surmises outlined in the first paragraph of this section regarding favored governance mode must be modified. In fact, the concrete form of the production cost disadvantage term in the relevant range of values for X and A shapes the results of the comparison. While it is assumed that $H_X<0$ and $H_A<0$ (with H_A representing the derivative of H with respect to A), $H(X,A)*X$ is assumed to be positive and asymptotically approaching zero for X and A approaching infinity. Then, *Riordan/Williamson* (1985) argue that plausibility suggests that at low levels of output (for the output good), decreasing unit cost disadvantages can be expected to be accompanied by increasing total production costs. Beyond some threshold, that is, within the large-output range where the relation of firm size to the size of the (subsequent) market increases, the total production cost disadvantage also diminishes. It finally approaches zero when B virtually serves the complete subsequent market stage. In that case, it is forced to internally produce just as many asset specific input goods as would be produced by an autonomous seller who had to serve B and a number of competitors at the same market stage. Hence, with the evolving monopoly condition, no scale diseconomies are present any more. The implication of this argument is that the general findings and results drawn from (4.1) only hold for certain in the large-output range. Below the threshold, "...the marginal production cost disadvantage of internal organization and the marginal governance cost disadvantage of market procurement operate in opposite directions."[693] In the view of *Riordan/Williamson* (1985), hence, an anomaly arises from the formalized model in the sense that a definite ordering of optimal output and asset specificity is no longer possible.

Finally, demand-side effects (in the relation between B and B^{2}'s) of asset specificity (of the good traded between S and B) are briefly considered. The analysis recognizes that asset specificity may lack (considerable) impact on production costs, but may be legitimated through yielding design benefits and consequently higher revenues in subsequent market stages (B^{2}'s). As corresponding profit expressions, the equations in (4.3) are suggested:

$$\pi^{m} = R(X, A; \delta) - C(X) - \gamma A - W(A))$$
$$\pi^{i} = R(X, A; \delta) - C(X) - \gamma A - (\beta + V(A))$$

(4.3)

with δ = demand shift parameter

Under the specific assumptions of *Riordan/Williamson* (1985) for the revenue functions ($R_A>0$, $R_{XA}>0$, $R_{A\delta}>0$, $R_{X\delta}>0$), the results for output and asset specificity relations from the main model are preserved. With growing demand enhancement effects (larger δ) of additional asset specificity (of the input good), internal procurement is increasingly favored over market organization due to increasing positive feedback effects of revenues towards procurement of more specific assets.

The orientation towards increasing formalization, the focus on the simultaneous relevance of production and transaction costs with an emphasis on the simultaneous choice on technology and governance mode, and, hence, the emphasis on asset specificity as a decision variable have been argued to constitute main strengths of the approach. Therefore, the model can be regarded to have provided decisive foundations for the analysis of the strategic shift question posed in this paper. However, it needs to be taken into account, that a marketing perspective is adopted in this analysis. From a marketing perspectives, some additional aspects warrant attention, in particular with respect to transferring the model's results. While *Riordan/ Williamson's* (1985) derivation of assumptions regarding specific properties of the analyzed cost and revenue functions is plausible, explicit consideration of how exactly such curves can come about would be helpful. The extended revenue function $R(X,A;\delta)$ may serve as an

---

[693] *Riordan, M. H./Williamson, O. E.* (1985), p. 373.

example: while the findings concerning different values of δ are fully satisfactory from a more aggregated economic point of view, from a marketing perspective, it seems also important to gain more detailed insights into the parameters' determinants. Also, from a marketing perspective, additional considerations concerning the position of the (potential) seller of the specific input good in case the buyer opts for of market procurement would be needed. This relationship and related hence questions regarding the origin of the asset specificity would be important from a marketing perspective. If the input good's idiosyncrasy is rooted in customization on the part of the seller, the assumption of asset specificity being available at the constant per unit cost of γ implicitly relies on specific seller-side conditions since customization is often viewed to cause progressively increasing production costs.[694] If the input good's specificity originates from the buyer side (e.g. internal idiosyncrasies related to adaptation of data processing procedures), there is no comparable link to seller-side specificity. Also, despite the reference to profit functions, the investigation exhibits a strong emphasis on cost-based considerations. In particular, the anomaly found by allowing for production cost differences in the main model is derived from a cost comparison. Such an approach, however, does not seem ideally suited from a marketing perspective. To sum up, since the purpose of the *Riordan/Williamson's* (1985) model is a more general one than in this research on strategic marketing management, supplementary considerations on specific marketing problems associated with asset specificity as a choice variable remain to be explored.

4.3.1.2   The optimizing approach by Aufderheide (1993, 2000)

Aufderheide (1993, 2000) proposes an alternative approach to the marginal analysis model of *Riordan/Williamson* (1985) for tackling the "paradigm problem"[695] of make-or-buy which still allows for questioning the *general* validity of TCA's original, qualitative assertions within an extended context.[696] In fact, these assertions are supposed to be encompassed as a special case of *Aufderheide's* (1993, 2000) model. In particular, he shows that the critical degree of

---

[694]   See *Adam, D.* (1997), p. 30ff.

[695]   See *Williamson, O. E.* (1989), p. 150.

[696]   See, also on the following argumentation, *Aufderheide, D.* (1993), e.g. p. 11; *Aufderheide, D.* (2000), p. 92ff. See for reference *Riordan, M. H./Williamson, O. E.* (1985); *Williamson, O. E.* (1985); *Williamson, O. E.* (1991c)

specificity as originally identified by *Williamson* (1985) below which a *relative* transactional advantage of market governance prevails and above which hierarchical governance enjoys a *relative* cost advantage may be irrelevant depending on the particular characteristics of a decision situation: with asset specificity as a choice variable, exactly that degree of specificity would be chosen that minimizes the *total* costs resulting from an integrated consideration of production and transaction costs.

At the heart of the methodology of his model is, therefore, a comparison of the *total* relevant costs of two alternative governance structures instead of a comparison of (production and transaction) cost *differentials* as adopted in much of the TCA-based literature. As sketched out, a total cost comparison allows not only for determining the least cost mode for a given degree of specificity, but also for simultaneously identifying the optimal degree of asset specificity with respect to a certain decision situation as defined by the particular properties of cost (and revenue) functions. The difference between the two approaches is depicted in *Fig. 17*, with the straight lines and arrows referring to the total cost approach as advocated by *Aufderheide* (1993, 2000), and the dotted lines and arrows giving the cost differential approach focused on, for instance, by *Williamson* (1985).

The total relevant costs are obtained from aggregating the particular production cost curve and transaction cost curve which underlie each governance alternative. In adopting a total values comparison and also with respect to a central finding, namely the need for putting some general assertions of TCA into perspective when considered in a broader context of asset specificity as a choice variable, *Aufderheide's* (1993, 2000) argumentation is in line with *Riordan/Williamson's* (1985) general model. If the make-or-buy decision refers not only to the governance mode but also to the optimal degree of specificity, the transactional advantage which internal acquisition enjoys over market procurement may become irrelevant. However, this result is derived in *Aufderheide's* (1993, 2000) model from an optimization which is based on a cost comparison, whereas *Riordan/Williamson* (1985) consider profit functions.[697]

---

[697] See *Aufderheide, D.* (1993), pp. 11, 16; *Aufderheide, D.* (2000), p. 106ff. Note that *Backhaus, K./Aufderheide, D./Späth, G.-M.* (1994), p. 45ff, include a profits-based extension to the earlier model. However, in integrating the revenue dimension, no provision is made for differences in buyer receptivity for specificity. Explicit consideration of this aspect might, though, be crucial from a marketing perspective.

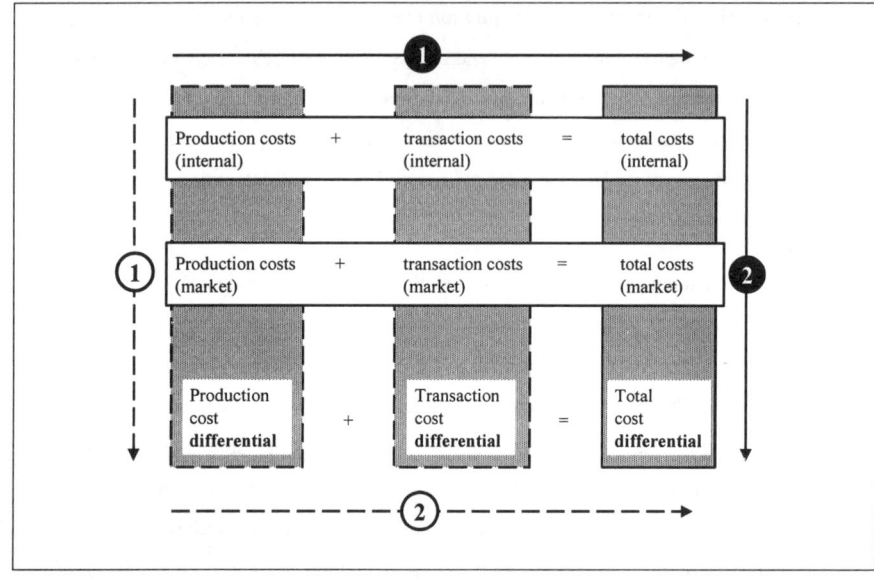

Fig. 17: Different methods for determination of total costs in alternative governance modes[698]

Aufderheide (1993, 2000), essentially, proposes the derivation of average cost per unit functions for both governance modes with the degree of asset specificity of the input good as the explanatory variable. The relevant, effective average cost per unit function over the whole range of specificity degrees ensues from the function enveloping both curves from below. Its minimum gives the optimal degree of specificity as well as the relevant mode. Again, some remarks concerning the model's impact for the analysis of strategic shifts between business types are advanced. Strong points for the model are the simultaneous consideration of production and governance costs implying a deliberate choice of asset specificity, and its emphasis on the need for a total cost comparison based on absolute values – despite the arguable measurement problems which, however, are not completely absent from the agenda in case of cost differential comparisons either. Yet, it is exactly its reduction to a cost comparison with output taken as given which represents a deficiency when marketing issues are at the center of the analysis.

---

[698] Taken from *Aufderheide, D.* (1993), p. 15; similarly *Aufderheide, D.* (2000), p. 112.

To sum up, both of the models by *Riordan/Williamson* (1985) and *Aufderheide* (1993, 2000) originate from the domain of economic theory. As such, they take an organizational buyer firm's perspective but abstract from specific marketing problems which the buyer might face regarding his own customers and also from specific marketing concerns of the input good's supplier. Hence, an investigation of shifts between business types constellations from a marketing perspective must additionally draw on complements from the marketing literature.

4.3.1.3 The approach by Plinke (1989, 1997): customer relationships as investments

Plinke's (1989, 1997) model of business relationships as investments provides such supplementary considerations.[699] While the earlier paper exclusively focuses on relationships, the later paper extends the perspective to include both basic types of market exchanges as identified by the author, namely transaction (marketing) and relationship (marketing). Transaction marketing refers to isolated transactions, whereas relationship marketing is concerned with conglomerates or sequences of non-accidentally linked transactions developing over time. In deriving these categories, he draws extensively on transaction cost ideas, providing links to the above models and also additional arguments for the approach's suitability in this context.[700] In covering a large range of associated issues, *Plinke* (1989, 1997) develops among others a formal model capturing the principal elements of a buyer's cost-benefit analysis in different relationship situations which need to be anticipated by a successful seller. He generally distinguishes between basic four types of relevant situations which are depicted in *Tab. 1*.

Properties of exchange situations/relationships	De-facto (evolving) relationship	Intended relationship
Ex ante situation	Case 1a: "Isolated transaction"	Case 2a: "Strategic decision"
Ex post situation	Case 1b: "Creeping commitment"	Case 2b: "Lock-in effect" transaction"

Tab.1: Systematization of business relationships according to calculation-relevant properties[701]

---

[699] See *Plinke, W.* (1989); *Plinke, W.* (1997).

[700] See *Plinke, W.* (1997), p. 9.

[701] Adapted from *Plinke, W.* (1997), p. 25.

In case a buyer is not bound by any previous relationship (1a in *Tab. 1*), he is argued to conduct a simple calculation based on expected direct costs and benefits from the relevant alternatives as shown in (4.4).

$$Z_{N/A} = (n_A - k_A) - (n_{AW} - k_{AW})$$
$$> 0$$

(4.4)

with $Z_{N/A}$ = preference of customer N for supplier A
   n_A ; n_{AW} = (expected) benefit from transacting with A or AW, respectively
   k_A ; k_{AW} = (expected) costs from transacting with A or AW, respectively

While the necessary condition for N buying from A is a positive expected net benefit, the sufficient condition is given by a positive evaluation faced with the best alternative AW which represents the relevant comparison level according to *Plinke* (1989, 1997).[702]

However, despite no linkage between the transactions being anticipated ex ante, in an ex post perspective, the buyer may find that over the course of several transactions a bond to the supplier has evolved (1b in *Tab. 1*). Whether this stems from experience, grown trust or increased adaptation of organizational procedures, the result is the perception of switching costs. The buyer's calculation when evaluating the offers of the in-supplier and the out-suppliers for a further transaction is enriched by considerations concerning these perceived switching costs. The modified calculus on the demand-side has to be anticipated by sellers whether they are in the position of in-suppliers or out-suppliers. For case 1b (*Tab. 1*), this translates into the terms shown in (4.5):

$$Z_{N/A} = (n_A - k_A) - [(n_{AW} - k_{AW}) - k_{A/AW}]$$
$$> 0$$

(4.5)

with $k_{A/AW}$ = direct (expected) costs of switching from A to AW

Distinct from these unintendedly evolving relationships are such relationships that are consciously entered. The difference is reflected in the proposed buyer calculations. From an ex ante view (2a in *Tab. 1*), the buyer expects a sequences of transactions to take place within some long-term relationship or cooperation. Due to this time horizon and the often associated

---

[702] This relevant comparison level corresponds, therefore, to what is called "comparison level for alternatives" by *Thibaut, J. W./Kelley, H. H.* (1959), p. 21ff (see e.g. *Plinke, W.* (1989), pp. 311, 325).

significance/volume, such decisions are categorized as strategic by *Plinke* (1997). Idiosyncratic investments in the form of adaptation of production processes, data processing systems and their alikes are frequent. The multi-period approach corresponding to the anticipation of the sequence is captured in the buyer's calculation as shown in (4.6):

$$Z_{N/A} = \left[-A_{A0} + \sum (n_{At} - k_{At}) \cdot (1+i)^{-t} - \sum k_{A/AWt} \cdot (1+i)^{-t} \right]$$
$$- \left[-A_{AW0} + \sum (n_{AWt} - k_{AWt}) \cdot (1+i)^{-t} - \sum k_{AW/At} \cdot (1+i)^{-t} \right] \qquad (4.6)$$
$$> 0$$

with $Z_{N/A}$ = preference of customer N for supplier A as net present value
$-A_{A0}$; $-A_{AW0}$ = initial investment in the relationship with A or AW, respectively, in t_0
n_{At} ; n_{AWt} = (expected) benefit from transacting with A or AW, respectively, in t
k_{At} ; k_{AWt} = (expected) costs from transacting with A or AW, respectively, in t
$k_{A/AWt}$; $k_{AW/At}$ = direct (expected) costs of switching from A to AW or AW to A, respectively, in t
i = discount rate
t = planning period

Ex post, once N has entered into a relationship with A, N is locked-in to the relationship with A who now has become the in-supplier (2b in *Tab. 1*). This provides A with a (potentially) considerable lead compared to the out-suppliers in subsequent purchasing decisions. For each transaction (within the sequence) at a time t, the question of switching arises in calculative terms which are substantially changed compared to the initial decision, and which are presented in (4.7):

$$Z_{N/A} = \left[\sum (n_{At} - k_{At}) \cdot (1+i)^{-t} \right] - \left[\sum (n_{AWt} - k_{AWt}) \cdot (1+i)^{-t} \right]$$
$$+ \left[\sum k_{A/AWt} \cdot (1+i)^{-t} \right] \qquad (4.7)$$
$$> 0$$

The outlined approach may contribute to the following analysis of shifts between business types constellations in a number of ways: First, it explicates buyer considerations and attributes them to distinct exchange situations. As these also include business relationships extending over several periods/transactions, some of the suggested formalization incorporates multi-period aspects. Finally, by drawing on TCA, the concept supplements the models by *Riordan/Williamson* (1985) and *Aufderheide* (1993, 2000) on a common theoretical basis towards a stronger focus on marketing.

4.3.2 Foundations of a simple model for evaluating shifts between business types constellations

Consistent with the objectives assumed to underlie considerations on shifts between business types, namely profit or utility maximization, a simple model is proposed here which builds on the approaches above. Following *Riordan/Williamson* (1985), asset specificity is regarded as a choice variable and an optimization is performed. In line with *Aufderheide* (1993, 2000), emphasis is laid on comparing total values instead of differentials. Furthermore, due to the specific research question of this work and the associated marketing lens, the demand perspective needs to be captured explicitly as is inspired by *Plinke* (1989, 1997). Therefore, the subsequently developed model merges, modifies, and extends the ideas from these concepts. Although real business transactions are often arguably more complex, i.e. involve a greater number and/or variety of actors, a reduced approach is chosen here: it focuses on the dyad of seller and (potential) buyer where both old and new offer and, correspondingly, old and new business types constellation have to stand the test of comparative buyer evaluation. As a first step in assessing the assertability of an envisaged shift, a basic comparison of the payoffs, that is, total utilities (on the buyer side) and total profits (on the seller-side) associated with alternative constellations, is proposed. The buyer is assumed to attempt to maximize his utility U_N – just as the seller is assumed to attempt to maximize his profits.[703] This assumption may, at first glance, seem rather strong against the background of information deficiencies and restraints to human cognition and as assumed by market process and transaction cost theory. Support can, however, be derived along three different lines: first, the maximizing *intention*, not its realizability or even realization is emphasized.[704] Second, in his attempt to reconcile *Schumpeterian* and neoclassical reasoning, *Sutton* (1998) argues that, for maximization (in the sense of an arbitrage principle) to be relevant, it is not even necessary that all actors are maximizors. In fact, "…it merely requires one firm to be smart…", that is, smart enough to fill a gap in the market if this can be done profitably.[705] Third, the models

---

[703] Seec chapter 4.3.2.3.

[704] This is illustrated by the conduct of sensitivity analyses when a numerical example from business practice is given (see chapter 4.4.2.3). This approach highlights the underlying information and cognition deficiencies and the importance to keep them in mind when "calculating" the potential for improvement from a shift (see on such role of sensitivity analysis e.g. *Adam, D.* (1996), pp. 66ff, 341).

[705] See *Sutton, J.* (1998), pp. 29ff, 44f.

that have had a particular impact on this model formulation apply maximization principles in related contexts.

The point of departure for the model follows from the idea rooted in market process theory that the seller seeks to improve his own situation and will therein succeed only by also offering a better, a new best alternative to the buyer. However, accounting for the arguments advanced in with respect to "pie division", the model also allows for incorporating market structures which deviate from those usually assumed in market process theory and TCA.[706] The core idea is to develop a conceptual frame for thinking about assertability of a strategy shift which is guided by theoretical economic reasoning. Reducing the number of elements to those factors which are decisive from a theoretical perspective may help to identify important "knobs to turn". It certainly does not allow for the development of a "recipe" when a firm should change to another constellation.

4.3.2.1   Derivation of the buyer's general utility function U_N

An important constitutive characteristic of industrial markets is the organizational nature of buyers, including firms, governmental and other relevant institutions, resulting in demand being a purely derived demand. Hence, buyers' payoffs are eventually determined by their success with the subsequent stage in the production process which is, if non-profit organizations are excluded from the analysis, equivalent to profit considerations with respect to their own customers.[707] Since only two immediately linked stages are directly captured by the dyadic perspective, the demand-side benefits from a transaction will, nevertheless, be referred to as "utility", with utility representing a measure for the individual, subjectively perceived degree of fulfillment of some need or desire (here: striving for profits).[708] Drawing

---

[706] This may be done either implicitly through the corresponding estimation of the relevant parameters, or explicitly by choosing the rules of the game correspondingly (fo the latter aspect see mainly chapter 4.5.3).

[707] See e.g. the discussion by *Besanko, D./Dranove, D./Shanley, M.* (1996).

[708] See *Schumann, J./Meyer, U./Ströbele, W.* (1999), p. 4. Despite the use of the term "measurement", issues of actual operationalization are not touched by this definition. For extensive discussion on such issues from a microeconomic perspective see e.g. *Schumann, J./Meyer, U./Ströbele, W.* (1999), p. 41ff. This definition includes all components of utility that a buyer aspires at obtaining through the transaction. No distinction is made between a direct and a derived, future-oriented utility as, for instance, proposed by *Backhaus, K./Plinke, W./Rese, M.* (2004), (p. 19ff).

on our definition of value[709], the utility accruing to a buyer from a particular transaction is a net utility and can be represented as the sum of sacrifices which he has to accept in order to obtain the relevant good or service, deducted from the object's value to him.[710] Though both elements of this "costs-benefits-comparison" are determined by the subjective perception of the buyer they are interpreted here as their worths in monetary terms.[711] The trade-off can be formalized as:[712]

$$U_{N_{ij}} = \left[V_{ij} - S_{ij} \right]$$

(4.8)

with
   $U_{N_{ij}}$ = utility to buyer i from the transaction j
    V_{ij} = value of transaction j to buyer i
    S_{ij} = sacrifice by buyer i for realizing transaction j and obtaining the implied value
    i = buyer index
    j = transaction/contract index

Each transaction is considered ("glued") together with its accompanying contract. It may involve the transfer of *more than one* exchange objects with all of them, however, being subject to *one* contract. Value and sacrifice each consist of several elements. Concerning the value construct, it follows from the business type definition that V_{ij} includes two elements, first, an "unspecific value" which the buyer derives from the underlying, indeterminate and general functionality of the product and, second, a "specific value" resulting from customization of the object to his specific needs (whether undertaken by the seller or the buyer). Deviating from the neoclassical view implies that the actual price to be paid for the object constitutes only a part of the total necessary sacrifice. From a TCA perspective, transaction costs must be taken into account as a second component in assessing the full sacrifice. Depending on the concrete nature of the transaction, the transaction costs that need to be captured in the model may take several forms which are depicted in *Fig. 18*.

---

[709] See chapter 2.1.2.6.

[710] Detailed examination of such trade-off considerations, though in a particular context (consumers as buyers; switching from an existing relationship as context) is provided by *Weiber, R./Adler, J.* (2002), p. 76ff.

[711] See e.g. *Weiber, R./Adler, J.* (2002), p. 78 in a similar theoretical context.

[712] This argumentation and, hence, also the following calculus generally applies to the buyer's utility considerations regardless of the concrete buyer business type. In the aggregation of various buyers undertaken from the seller's viewpoint the buyer business type exerts a more obvious influence on the formal model.

Directly related to the currently considered transaction (chain) are various ex ante and ex post transaction costs which are incurred, for instance, by searching for information, negotiating or setting up and running the governance structure. Despite the arguable terminological imprecision, they are subsequently and in the model referred to as "transaction costs". In case specific investments have been undertaken in the past, switching costs are also a relevant factor.[713]

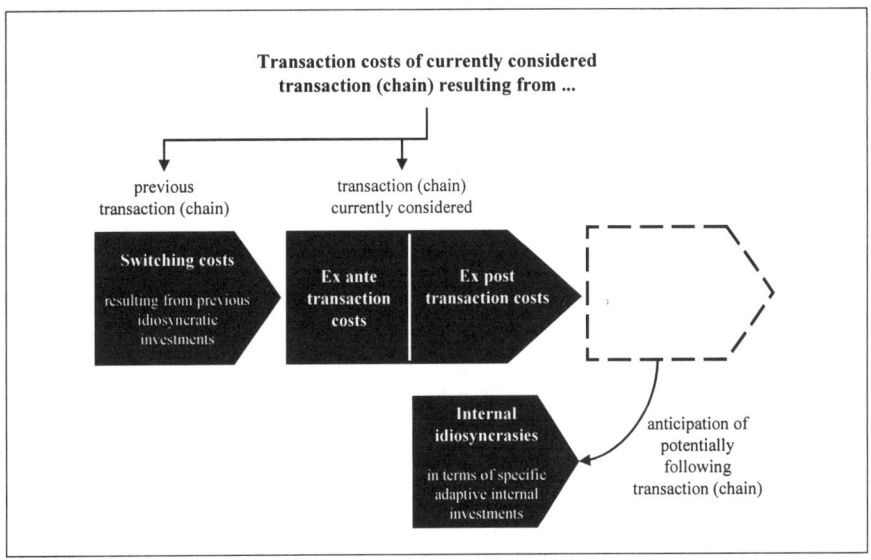

Fig. 18: Components of transaction costs in the buyer payoff function

They arise from previous idiosyncratic investments ("sunk costs") which have not yet been fully amortized and which lose their remaining value in case the existing business relationship is given up in favor of the currently considered transaction (chain). Switching costs are taken to also include opportunity costs resulting (1) from a potential common history with the previous transaction partner and implied supplier-specific learning or, (2) from contractual

---

[713] Conceptualizations and operationalizations of the switching cost construct vary widely across the literature (see for a brief overview e.g. *Benito, G. R./Pedersen, T./Petersen, B.* (1999)). *Plinke, W.* (1997), p. 44f, for instance, interprets switching costs as a superordinate category of costs which include (1) opportunity costs due to giving up some net value to still be expected from the current business relationship, (2) so-called relevant costs, that is, the "additional transaction costs" of changing a supplier, and (3) sunk costs from losing investments that were specific to the previous relationship. This interpretation is not adopted here since it deviates, if only terminologically, from the classic TCA view as present in the relevant models of *Riordan, M. H./Williamson, O. E.* (1985); *Aufderheide, D.* (1993).

arrangements which are designed to artificially create switching costs as, for instance, airline frequent-flyer programs.[714] In analogy to the above sunk costs, such opportunity costs have also been referred to as "sunk benefits"[715]. Last but not least, the transaction may involve investments in internal idiosyncrasies on the part of the buyer ("specific set up costs"[716]). These investments may take place either simultaneously with the initial investment or later during the relationship. Adaptation of administrative or production procedures, customization of software, or specific training of employees are examples. In as far as these investments are foreseen and necessary to take full advantage of the transaction object's value V_{ij} and specific to the transaction (partner), they will be incorporated in the buyer's calculation.[717] They lay the foundation stone for future switching costs with respect to subsequent transactions which are not related to the one currently being considered, and must therefore be anticipated in the current assessment of costs and benefits.[718] These considerations translate into the following equation (4.9)[719]:

$$ U_{Ni} = \left[N_{USI_{ij}} + N_{SI_{ij}} - p_{ij} \right] \cdot x_{ij} - Tr_{(N)\,ea\,ij} - Tr_{(N)ep\,ij} - M_{ij} - W_{(N)i} \qquad (4.9) $$

with $N_{USI_{ij}}$ = unspecific gross value of transaction j derived by buyer i
      $N_{SI_{ij}}$ = specific gross value of transaction j derived by buyer i
      p_{ij} = price paid to the seller for acquisition of transaction j
      x_{ij} = number of elements covered by the contract governing transaction j
      $Tr_{(N)\,ea\,ij}$ = *ex ante* transaction costs incurred by buyer i with respect to transaction j
      $Tr_{(N)\,ep\,ij}$ = *ex post* transaction costs incurred by buyer i with respect to transaction j
      M_{ij} = additional investments in internal idiosyncrasies related to transaction j
      $W_{(N)i}$ = switching costs of buyer i resulting from previous idiosyncratic investments

---

[714] See *Lieberman, M. B./Montgomery, D. B.* (1988), p. 46; *Plinke, W.* (1997), p. 44f. See *Stump, R. L./Joshi, A. W.* (1998), on the impact of a common history on transaction costs. Their findings suggest that positive experiences have transaction cost reducing effects that may be translated into monetary impacts and, thus, need to be incorporated as originally economic factors in the calculation. A somewhat differing view is proposed by *Weiber, R.* (1997), p. 300, who categorizes them as psychological influences and excludes them from the subsequent analysis of bonding in the domain of integration technologies. Seminal treatment of switching costs in general has been provided e.g. by *Jackson, B. B.* (1985), p. 42ff.

[715] *Butzer-Strothmann, K.* (1999), p. 26.

[716] See on this topic e.g. *Farrell, J./Gallini, N. T.* (1988)

[717] See *Yao, D. A.* (1988), p. 67, fn 19. This idea refers to ex ante as well as ex post considerations (see *Plinke, W.* (1997), p. 28ff). However, in practice necessity and consequences of such internal idiosyncrasies are often underestimated (see *Jackson, B. B.* (1985), p. 49f).

[718] See e.g. *Plinke, W.* (1989), p. 307; *Plinke, W.* (1997), p. 28ff.

[719] Alternative modeling of asset specificity as the product of total amount of investment and the proportion of the specific part can be found in *Mudambi, R./McDowell-Mudambi, S.* (1995), p. 422.

It should be noted that the cost and benefit elements in the equation are buyer-*perceived* costs and benefits because a large part of them will be difficult to quantify objectively (e.g. the effects of supplier-specific learning).[720] Now, since in three constellations the buyer's business type is relational business and, therefore, implies calculations covering transaction chains instead of individual, isolated transactions, adequate reformulation is required which, owing to comparative reasons, also applies to all other constellations. Thus, term (4.9) has to be summed up from all chain elements and planning periods. Furthermore, with explicit reference to several planning periods, discounting emerges as an additional aspect. The result is presented in (4.10):

$$U_{N_i} = \sum_{j=1}^{J} \sum_{t=1}^{T} \left[\frac{\left[\left(N_{USI_{ij\,t}} + N_{SI_{ij\,t}} - p_{ij\,t} \right) \cdot x_{ij\,t} \right]}{(1+r_{(N)})^{t}} - \frac{\left(Tr_{(N)\,ea\,ij\,t} \right)}{(1+r_{(N)})^{t-1}} - \frac{\left(Tr_{(N)ep\,ij\,t} \right)}{(1+r_{(N)})^{t}} - \frac{\left(M_{ij\,t} \right)}{(1+r_{(N)})^{t}} \right] - W_{(N)_{i}0}$$

$$(4.10)$$

with U_{N_i} = discounted total net benefits accruing to buyer i (present value)
       $r_{(N)}$ = discount rate for buyer i
       t = planning period (with T representing the last period belonging to the perceived chain)

Although the model could be adapted to any seemingly appropriate time structure of cost and benefits streams, the particular term (4.10) makes the assumptions that (1) if switching costs from the old chain are relevant, they are incurred in t_0, that is, together with the ex ante transaction costs and with contract conclusion, and (2) that ex ante transaction costs arise one period ahead of the other period-related costs and benefits. These are (3) assumed to be incurred at the end of each period.

$\overline{p}_{ij}$ (in equation 4.11) can be interpreted as the reservation price, that is, the critical price which the buyer is prepared to pay at maximum for a good, if two conditions are satisfied: first, and necessarily, the buyer derives a positive utility (net value) from the purchase, and second, as a sufficient condition, the (expected) utility from entering into transaction j/transaction chain ($j=1...J$) is greater than his best alternative. That available alternative which is perceived as best by the buyer represents the relevant comparison level KKo.[721]

---

[720] See *Kleinaltenkamp, M./Kühne, B.* (2003), p. 20.

[721] The term "comparison level" is used here following *Plinke* (1989, 1997), not *Thibaut/Kelley* (1959). In negotiation theory, the construct of the "best alternative to a negotiated agreement (BATNA)" captures similar ideas (see e.g. *Fisher, R./Ury, W.* (1981), p. 101ff; *Raiffa, H.* (1997)).

While, in principle, *KKo* could be modeled and will be calculated by the buyer in just the same way as the analyzed seller (*A*)'s offer, it is taken here as a "black box" which is not modeled explicitly. This assumption is in line with the modeling approach by *Brandenburger/Stuart* (1996), where "…given prices outside the vertical chain, but not inside…"[722] are assumed. They justify this abstraction on the grounds of focusing on one particular vertical chain and the bargaining problems of the players within it. Here, as a further plausibility argument in favor of this assumption, it is maintained that the true calculation by buyer *i* is unknown to the seller who can only estimate the relevant variables with respect to a particular buyer. When making the estimation concerning the buyer's best alternative, the seller's information is likely to be much worse than concerning its own offer. The term is rearranged for the (discounted) critical price $\overline{\overline{P}}_i$ of a chain or its equivalent in unrelated transactions at which buyer i is just indifferent between the supplier's offer and the best alternative, yielding (4.11):

$$\overline{\overline{P}}_i = \sum_{j=1}^{J} \sum_{t=1}^{T} \left[\frac{\left\lfloor \left(N_{USI\,ij\,t} + N_{SI\,ij\,t} \right) \cdot x_{ij\,t} \right\rfloor}{(1 + r_{(N)})^t} - \frac{\left(Tr_{(N)\,ea\,ij\,t} \right)}{(1 + r_{(N)})^{t-1}} - \frac{\left(Tr_{(N)ep\,ij\,t} \right)}{(1 + r_{(N)})^t} - \frac{\left(M_{ij\,t} \right)}{(1 + r_{(N)})^t} \right] - W_{(N)i0} - KKo$$

with

$$\overline{\overline{P}}_i = \sum_{j=1}^{J} \sum_{t=1}^{T} \left[\frac{\overline{P}_{ij\,t}}{(1 + r_{(N)})^t} \right] \qquad\qquad (4.11)$$

$$\overline{P}_{ij\,t} = \overline{p}_{ij\,t} \cdot x_{ij\,t}$$

and   *KKo*   = present value of net utility derived from the relevant comparison level/best available alternative for buyer *i*[723]

     $\overline{\overline{P}}_i$ = (discounted) critical price of a chain/ its equivalent in unrelated transactions to buyer *i*

     $\overline{P}_{ij\,t}$ = critical price for the sum of unity covered in contract *j* in period *t* to buyer *i*

     $\overline{p}_{ij\,t}$ = critical price per unit in period *t* for contract *j* to buyer *i*

With the buyer's payoff function having been defined based on the above variables, one additional point needs to be made, namely how the concrete parameter values are obtained. Unfortunately, the theoretical framework underlying this research does not allow for the derivation of definitive functional relations between the explicitly formalized elements in the

---

[722] See *Brandenburger, A. M./Stuart Jr., H. W.* (1996), pp. 9, 20.

[723] This parameter could, alternatively, be modeled on a per unit base.

buyer's payoff function and their antecedents beyond the general directions of effect as proposed in chapter 3.2.3. Nevertheless, the ideas outlined in the framework "asset specificity as a choice variable" are conjectured to provide some guidance when thinking about concrete parameter values. For instance, a positively evaluated shared transaction history is likely to c.p. reduce the buyer's perceived danger of exploitation, thereby reducing his subjectively assessed transaction costs. Unfavorable ex ante market structures are in turn presumed to increase his exploitation supposition and, hence, the transaction costs.

4.3.2.2   Derivation of the seller's general profit function π_A

If the buyer arrives at a positive assessment on the total cost/price-benefit-relation associated with the new constellation and compared with the best alternative from the set of available options, he is assumed to effectively buy from the seller. This argument leads to a fundamental assumption which the following formal analysis of shift assertability is based on: in principle, the seller is assumed to be able to make the buyer accept any constellation – acceptance is ultimately a matter of (critical) price.[724] At the extreme, the seller might have to pay the buyer to "purchase" from him. This extreme case highlights an immediate consequence from the assumption, namely that, in principle, any constellation becomes assertable. That is to say, a price p exists necessarily at which the necessary and sufficient conditions are fulfilled, this particular price p will be assessed by the seller on the grounds of its own cost-benefit-analysis. The issue is whether the *general* desirability of a certain shift translates into an efficient option for the *particular* case, that is, contributes to the seller's purpose of profit maximization.[725] In the end, it boils down to a comparison between the profit expectations from continuing with the present constellation and from a shift under the *assertable* conditions.

---

[724] See also chapter 4.2. This idea is understood in line with voluntary exchange. Support for this idea can be derived, for instance, from *Plinke, W./Söllner, A.* (1999), p. 643, who rank price as the number one reason for losing a contract. Notions of structural market power are only implicit in this basic analysis in terms of the estimates for transaction costs, and will be explicitly discussed in chapter 4.5.3.

[725] See chapter 3.1 for legitimation of assuming this overall objective for the seller. In essence, the same two conditions apply to the seller for entering into a transaction, that is, first, a positive expected net value which is, second, greater than the best alternative. This best alternative may be another buyer but in this case it may also be the previous constellation.

The seller-side profit calculations for the different seller business types are captured by equations which can be developed in analogy to the buyer calculations and will, therefore, be presented here more directly to the point. For the shift analysis, prices will be interpreted as critical prices. In project and relational business (seller business type), profit/value maximization is sought with respect to each individual buyer.[726] The calculation relates to individual transactions or transaction chains which imply specific investments by the seller. Goods ($j=1...J$) are usually or at least largely produced after contract conclusion. In these cases, the general profit function depicted in (4.12) results which can be summed up over all n buyers for a particular BT-constellation (4.13):

$$\pi_{ASi} = \sum_{j=1}^{J} \sum_{t=1}^{T} \left[\frac{p_{ijt} \cdot x_{ijt} - C_{ijt}(k_{vCijt}, K_{FCijt}, x_{ijt})}{(1+r_{(A)})^t} - \frac{(Tr_{(A)\,ea\,ijt})}{(1+r_{(A)})^{t-1}} - \frac{(Tr_{(A)ep\,ijt})}{(1+r_{(A)})^t} \right] + \frac{(a_t)}{(1+r_{(A)})^t} - \frac{W_{(A)0}}{n}$$

(4.12)

$$\pi_{AS} = \sum_{i=1}^{n} \sum_{j=1}^{J} \sum_{t=1}^{T} \left[\frac{p_{ijt} \cdot x_{ijt} - C_{ijt}(k_{vCijt}, K_{FCijt}, x_{ijt})}{(1+r_{(A)})^t} - \frac{(Tr_{(A)\,ea\,ijt})}{(1+r_{(A)})^{t-1}} - \frac{(Tr_{(A)ep\,ijt})}{(1+r_{(A)})^t} \right] + \frac{(a_t)}{(1+r_{(A)})^t} - W_{(A)0}$$

(4.13)

with $\pi_{AS\,i}$ = profit from a (chain of) transaction(s)/contract(s) ($j=1....J$) with buyer i (including $J=1$) (specific investments by the seller implied)

$\pi_{AS\,i}$ = profit from a (chain of) transaction(s)/contract(s) ($j=1....J$) with all n buyers in this BT constellation (specific investments by the seller implied)

p_{ijt} = price paid by buyer i in transaction/contract j

x_{ijt} = number of units of the good j sold to buyer i in the corresponding number of contracts of type j

C_{ijt} = production costs incurred by the seller for transaction j with buyer i

k_{vCijt} = variable production costs for the seller for transaction j with buyer i

K_{FCijt} = fixed production costs for the seller for transaction j with buyer i

$Tr_{(A)\,ea\,ijt}$ = ex ante transaction costs for the seller for transaction j with buyer i

$Tr_{(A)\,ep\,jt}$ = ex ante transaction costs for the seller for transaction j with buyer i

a_{jt} = indirect benefit component in period t

$W_{(A)0}$ = switching costs of the seller incurred due to previous investments which are not yet fully amortized)

i = buyer index (with n as the total number of buyers for a particular BT constellation)

j = index of types of transactions/contracts/goods

$r_{(A)}$ = discount rate for the seller

t = planning period (with T representing the last period belonging to the considered chain)

---

[726] Arguably, this assumption is more suitable for transactions which involve higher degrees of specificity. For analytical purposes, it will be abstracted from this, although considerations explicitly accounting for different degrees of specificity could be build into the model.

Switching costs $W_{(A)\ 0}$ result from the fact that production in a changed BT-constellation is likely to require different machinery or process handling. Shifting then implies losses in terms of sunk costs incurred for investments related to the previous constellation in so far as these investments have not yet been fully amortized. Another element to be discussed is what is referred to in (4.12) and (4.13) as an "indirect benefit component (a)". It captures difficult-to-quantify (especially regarding the individual dyad) shift motivations which may be, first, associated with the particular buyer such as general enhancement of information basis or (long-term) impact on buying decision criteria and/or, second, oriented more diffusely towards (a group of) other buyers, and/or, third, directed more generally against actual or potential competitors (e.g. entry deterrence by creating entry/exit barriers).[727]

For product business (seller business type) which requires only unspecific investments (in the market) by the seller the value function takes the form (4.14). The potential necessity to compare a series of unrelated transactions with a chain of linked transactions when considering a shift is already incorporated in the equation by allowing for $j>1$. Thereby, it is also possible to have the seller offer more than one type of good (e.g. PC-printer and PC mouse with standardized interfaces) within a series. Thus, reference will be made to *types* of transaction/contract to account for this idea.

---

[727] The first aspect in particular was important in the case study, support on the second aspect comes e.g. from *Oliver, C.* (1990), p. 246. Explicitly supportive on the first two elements, and related to the third also: *Backhaus, K./Plinke, W./Rese, M.* (2004), (pp. 21f, 42ff). The third aspect is generally associated with the literature on entry deterrence. Drawing on *Williamson, O. E.* (1979), *Mahoney, J. T.* (2001), p. 655f, regards asset specificity – in the absence of government intervention – as a necessary condition for isolating mechanisms that sustain rents. More detailed discussion of such motivations has been provided in chapter 3.3

Due to the fact that, in principle, homogeneous pre-fabricated goods are sold to anonymous buyers, demand is incorporated in the profit calculation in the form of the relevant price-demand function.[728]

$$\pi_{AU} = \sum_{j=1}^{J} \sum_{t=1}^{T} \left[\frac{\left[p_{jt} \cdot x_{jt}(p_{jt}) \right] - C_{jt}(k_{vC_{jt}}, K_{FC_{jt}}, x_{jt})}{(1+r_{(A)})^t} - \frac{\left(Tr_{(A)\,ea\;jt} \right)}{(1+r_{(A)})^{t-1}} - \frac{\left(Tr_{(A)ep\;jt} \right)}{(1+r_{(A)})^t} \right] + \frac{(a_t)}{(1+r_{(A)})^t}$$
$$ - W_{(A)0}$$

(4.14)

with

$$x_{jt}(p_{jt}) = \sum_{i=1}^{n} x_{ijt}(p_{jt})$$

$$Tr_{(A)\,ea\;jt} = \sum_{i=1}^{n} Tr_{(A)\,ea\;ijt}$$

$$Tr_{(A)ep\;jt} = \sum_{i=1}^{n} Tr_{(A)\,ep\;ijt}$$

and π_{AU} = profit from a series of unrelated (types of) transactions/contracts ($j=1...J$) with some buyers n (including the case $J=1$)
(only unspecific investments by the seller implied)

p_{jt} = price paid by each buyer i ($i=1...n$) in each (type of) transaction/contract j

x_{jt} = total number of units of the relevant type of good j sold to the n buyers in the corresponding number of transactions of type j

x_{ijt} = number of units of the relevant type of good j sold to the buyer i using the corresponding contract type

$Tr_{(A)\,ea\;jt}$ = ex ante transaction costs for the seller allocated to the sum of transactions of type j

$Tr_{(A)\,ep\;jt}$ = ex post transaction costs for the seller allocated to the sum of transactions of type j

$Tr_{(A)\,ea\;ijt}$ = ex ante transaction costs for the seller allocated to transaction j with buyer i

$Tr_{(A)\,ep\;ijt}$ = ex post transaction costs for the seller allocated to transaction j with buyer i

a_{jt} = indirect benefit component in period t

$W_{(A)0}$ = switching costs of the seller incurred due to previous investments which are not yet fully amortized

i = buyer index (with n representing the total number of buyers at a particular price)

j = index of types of transactions/contracts/goods

$r_{(A)}$ = discount rate for the seller

t = planning period (with T representing the last period belonging to the considered series)

Breaking down the calculation to the individual dyad yields (4.15):[729]

---

[728] Arguably, in industrial marketing, a dyadic approach even in seller product business often seems feasible as illustrated by and substantiated with respect to the following example. The reason lies in the fact that even (relatively) homogeneous products are usually sold at various prices to different customers due to differences in allowances and discounts on the one hand, and potential divergences in buyer bargaining power on the other hand (see e.g. *Plinke, W./Söllner, A.* (1999), p. 652).

$$\pi_{AUi} = \sum_{j=1}^{J}\sum_{t=1}^{T}\left[\frac{\left[p_{jt}\cdot x_{ijt}(p_{jt})\right]-C_{jt}(k_{vCjt},K_{FCjt},x_{ijt},n)}{(1+r_{(A)})^{t}}-\frac{\dfrac{\left(Tr_{(A)\,ea\,jt}\right)}{n}}{(1+r_{(A)})^{t-1}}-\frac{\dfrac{\left(Tr_{(A)ep\,jt}\right)}{n}}{(1+r_{(A)})^{t}}\right]+\frac{\dfrac{(a_{t})}{n}}{(1+r_{(A)})^{t}}$$

$$-\frac{W_{(A)0}}{n} \qquad\qquad\qquad\qquad (4.15)$$

with

$$\frac{Tr_{(A)\,ea\,jt}}{n}=Tr_{(A)\,ea\,ijt}$$

$$\frac{Tr_{(A)ep\,jt}}{n}=Tr_{(A)\,ep\,ijt}$$

and $\pi_{AU\,i}$ = profit from a (series of unrelated) transaction(s)/contract(s) ($j=1...J$) with buyer i
(including $J=1$)
(only unspecific investments by the seller implied)

This breaking down is somewhat artificial for this seller business type and is presented here rather for the sake of completeness. For instance, the allocation of transaction costs to each contract type j and even more so to each buyer is somewhat "artificial" in this business type and cannot rely on the principle of causation. For illustration, consider the example of a seller who develops his "General Standard Terms and Conditions" and then applies them for a certain number of periods to all types of contracts whether selling a PC-mouse or a PC-printer and certainly to all customers alike.

Given these equations, the sufficient condition for a shift between business types constellations is defined as its assertability at conditions which leave the seller with increased profit expectations compared to the previous constellation. For the concrete case, such an assessment rests on estimating the relevant variables on the seller-side and on the buyer side. From a more general point of view, it is again possible to reach beyond the above equations by examining some determinants of their elements as proposed by transaction cost reasoning. Yet, as argued, this can only rest on theoretically-guided reasoning about general impact directions of the antecedents, for the variables in the seller payoff function as well as for those in the buyer payoff function. To give an example, firm particularities are assumed to be reflected in terms of the particular production cost structures or relevant transaction costs.

---

[729] Note that this allocation of transaction costs is based on the assumption of equal "utilization" by the individual customers.

4.4   Shifts between business types constellations in business practice:
a case-study based illustration of the model

4.4.1   Applicability of the case study method for shift analysis

The use of case studies has a long tradition in management science, economics and transaction cost theory as well.[730] Nevertheless, some introductory remarks seem worthwhile in order to clarify the intentions of its use in the present context. Definitions of the term are numerous and various. This gives an impression of the variety of purposes it can be used for. *Yin* (1994), for instance, has defined case studies as investigations of "... a contemporary phenomenon within its real-life context, especially when the boundaries between phenomenon and context are not clearly evident."[731] Applied in both quantitative and qualitative research, the *individual case study* (hereafter referred to as case study) has been characterized as being located somewhere in between a concrete data collection method and a methodological paradigm, thereby representing a research approach in its own.[732] The emphasis on this distinct nature is, however, stronger when used in a qualitative research context. In essence, case studies may serve three fundamental purposes, that is, first, exploration, second, description/illustration or, third, explanation.[733] When exploration is the aim, information on important aspects and dimensions of the research topic, generation of hypotheses, and support for operationalization are sought for.[734] If a case study is supposed to be illustrative in nature, it offers an example for ideas proposed on theoretical or quantitative empirical grounds. Also, it may serve as a (non-representative) "plausibility check".[735] Finally, explanatory case studies

---

[730] See *Williamson, O. E.* (1985), p. 349f; *Perry, M. K.* (1989), p. 219; *Yin, R. K.* (1994), p. xiii; *Ghemawat, P.* (2002a), p. 41. Examples of applications are numerous and also include work which is related to this research (see e.g. *Yetton, P. W./Johnston, K. D./Craig, J. F.* (1994); *Kern, T./Wilcocks, L. P.* (2000); *Ghemawat, P.* (2002b)).

[731] *Yin, R. K.* (1994), p. 13.

[732] See e.g. *Witzel, A.* (1982), p. 78; *Lamnek, S.* (1995), p. 4.

[733] See e.g. *Lamnek, S.* (1995), p. 9 ; *Yin, R. K.* (1994), p. 3f.

[734] See *Schnell, R./Hill, P. B./Esser, E.* (1999), p. 237f.; A notable example of using case studies for the purpose of exploring new phenomena and building theory in a TCA-related context has been provided by *Rangan, V. K./Corey, E. R./Cespedes, F.* (1993) who draw on clinical field research methodology.

[735] See *Lamnek, S.* (1995), p. 13f.

aim at detecting and unfolding the underlying reasons of observed phenomena.[736] The case study approach which is adopted here is purely illustrative.

Basically, all usual quantitative and qualitative methods of data collection could be used to generate the necessary data. More specifically related to this research, though, arguments have been advanced in favor of using qualitative methods. With respect to the following illustrative case study on strategic shifts, we draw on *Chiles/McMackin* (1996) who suggest that qualitative methods such as face-to-face interviews or verbal protocols are particularly suitable for the study of TCA issues in its managerial orientation and the implied subjective dimension of transaction costs.[737] For this case study, data collection has taken the form of guided interview.[738] The major advantage of this method is an open, unconstrained line of communication which allows for capturing insights into relevance structures and potentially unexpected aspects of the topic.[739] Drawbacks such as higher requirements in terms of interviewer qualification, time, or willingness to cooperate on behalf of the interviewees, or lower comparability of results compared to standardized interviews did not represent obstacles in the particular case. Regarding the sampling strategy used to find the illustrative case presented here, a theory-based approach was chosen.[740] Such an approach is characterized by the idea of "…finding examples of a theoretical construct and thereby elaborate and examine it."[741]

---

[736] See *Yin, R. K.* (1994), p. 4ff.

[737] See *Chiles/McMackin* (1996), p. 94f.

[738] The questions are displayed in appendix I. The interview data themselves are not included for reasons of data confidentiality.

[739] See *Schnell, R./Hill, P. B./Esser, E.* (1999), p. 354ff.

[740] For an extensive overview of different sampling strategies in qualitative research see *Miles, M. B./Huberman, A. M.* (1994), p. 27ff and the literature referred to there.

[741] *Miles, M. B./Huberman, A. M.* (1994), p. 28.

4.4.2 A case from the chemical industry

4.4.2.1 Background and impulse

Chemistry Co. is a large chemical producer operating in numerous business segments.[742] One of them is Automotive OEM Coatings which is characterized by a bilateral oligopoly situation. Industrial coatings for specific use on automobiles are marketed to OEM 's as customers. These are guided in their buying decisions by three principal criteria: price, quality and delivery know-how. The buying center usually consists of members from three departments, that is, purchasing, production and process engineering. Since the power relations between these departments vary from customer to customer, so does the weighting of the three criteria.

Until not long ago, *Chemistry Co.* sold its coatings in the traditional way, that is, in the form of a bilateral product business.[743] In that constellation, neither *Chemistry Co.* nor the customer is required to invest specifically to a significant degree. On the seller-side, the same basic production technology and coating material (e.g. *Colou 55*) is used to serve all customers with needs which can be satisfied by the functions available from this material. Some customer-specific modifications are usually made, potentially leading to price variations among customers. The final product is then delivered as wet, semi-finished goods. While properties related to handling can be evaluated by the buyer for the previously delivered material, a final assessment is only feasible when the coating has been applied on the car bodywork and has dried completely. However, the customer-specific modifications are neither that time consuming nor that complicated production-wise as to prevent customers from being able to switch suppliers at a short notice if necessary, for instance, due to delivery or quality problems of the original supplier. The products of the various sellers are, therefore, in essence mutually interchangeable from the buyer perspective. Payment conditions fit the bilateral product

---

[742] The example described in the following section is based on a real business case. However, actual names of firms and products have been disguised on request of the company.

[743] Exceptions from this way of transacting have, however, already existed in the past, namely in the form of research and development (R&D) projects which are conducted in cooperation with a target customer who participates in the necessary research investments. In exchange for his investment the target customer is warranted the right to exclusive supply with the resulting products for a certain period of time.

business: contracts usually cover a certain amount of semi-finished goods based on a particular basic material, with a price x €/kg.[744]

However, *Chemistry Co.* has recently changed its strategic orientation by redesigning its offer to what is referred to as systems supply. At the core of this change lies a shift of business types constellation away from the bilateral product business. Depending on the particular design of payment conditions, the new constellation can be characterized either as a bilateral project business or as a bilateral relational business. The case, therefore, illustrates the proposition that each party's business type can only be derived from the complete package of specifications covering content and delivery structures of value and countervalue.[745] Albeit now being marketed to several customers in a similar way, the new offer could, in principle, have been designed for an individual customer.

Before describing both contractual alternatives, that is, both alternative specifications of structure of delivery, their common underlying technological basis (specification of content) is highlighted. In order to facilitate understanding of the shift, *Fig. 19* depicts the integration of a paintshop at the OEM's production site in the automobile production process and includes some general data on paint shop organization and an assignment of the relevant production process steps to more general competence areas and industries.

---

[744] The prices agreed on may just as well be expressed in $ or any other currency in a particular case. In this paper, € is uniformly used as the relevant currency.

[745] See chapter 2.1.2.6.

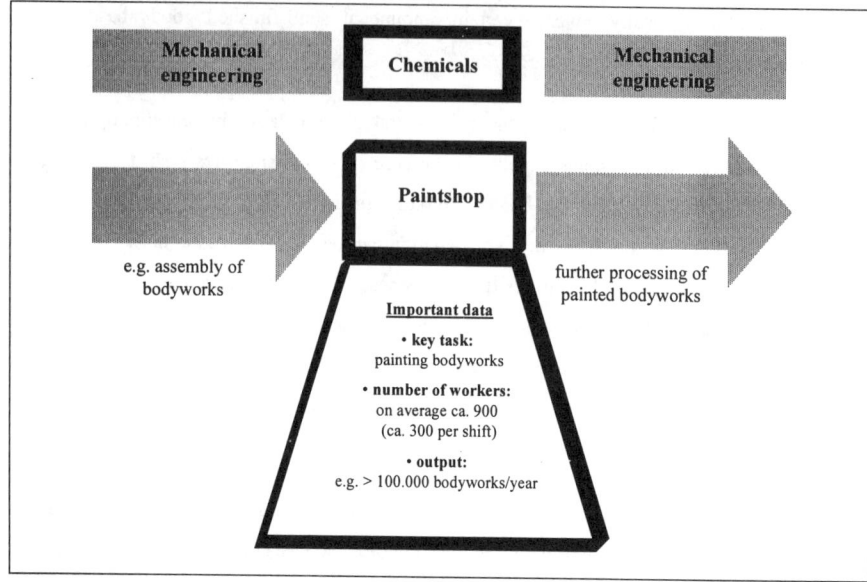

Fig. 19: Schematic presentation of paintshop integration in automobile production

While in the previous constellation, *Chemistry Co.*'s "simply" had to care for the timely delivery of the right amount and quality of wet semi-finished paint, the new offering which has been described as "paint plus extended service" implies many more far-reaching responsibilities. Essentially, it involves taking over important parts of the pro-cesses in the customer's paintshop and associated responsibilities and is, hence, closely tied to the particular transaction (partner) both factually and spatially. Idiosyncratic investments by *Chemistry Co.* in customer-specific machinery, such as fork-lifts or storage equipment, but also in human capital (usually 10 to 30 workers) are integral parts of the offering. The workers are trained by *Chemistry Co.* specifically regarding their employment with this customer. After contract termination, the responsibility for their further employment is with *Chemistry Co.*. The fundamental elements of the paintshop and most workers are, though, still provided by the customer. Consequently, the overall responsibility lies with the customer. Yet, *Chemistry Co.* takes over the responsibility for the disposition of painting materials and the compliance of planned quantity usage. If material is used in excess of the planned quantity and if this is due to inefficiencies on behalf of *Chemistry Co.*, the resulting losses (or decreases in profit) have to be borne by them.[746] Also, for instance, *Chemistry Co.*'s responsibility in terms of product liabilities vis-à-vis consumers is largely extended when compared to the traditional constellation.

Essential contractual features are (among others) duration (usually 2-3 years, owing to a legal cap at 3 years) and payment conditions. During the contract duration agreed upon, *Chemistry Co.* needs to achieve amortization of its specific investments since after that ownership is transmitted to the customer. The ease of achieving this aim crucially hinges on the payment conditions. Basically, two distinct types of these conditions are offered by *Chemistry Co.* at present.

(1) One-component-pricing: materials (semi-finished goods) and services (made possible through *Chemistry Co.*'s investments) alike, that is, variable and fixed costs, unspecific and specific investments are all being paid for by the customer in terms of a single figure agreed on which is called "cost per unit (CPU)" and includes the profit margin as calculated by *Chemistry Co.*.[747] The units referred to are painted bodyworks.

(2) Two-component-pricing: the customer's counterperformance is split into two parts: first, he pays an ex ante fixed monthly amount which covers (at least largely) the fixed costs of *Chemistry Co.* resulting from its specific investments. Paint material is paid on a cost per unit basis, with painted bodyworks as units. (This option, essentially, represents a two-part tariff with the (advance) lump-sum payment "…spread over time according to a path that is independent of the […] purchase levels."[748])

With respect to payment conditions, it has to be noted that, independent of the chosen payment mode, the initial contract provides for annual renegotiations with each re-negotiated price holding for the ensuing year. Sometimes, some price changes are, however, already explicitly covered by the general initial agreement. For instance, the framework contract may specify the distribution of efficiency gains achieved by *Chemistry Co.* in its parts of the paintshop according to some ratio. The precise contractual provision in the initial agreement

---

[746] In order to reduce the risk of ex post conflicts on whether some inefficiency has to be accounted for by *Chemistry Co.*, the framework contract specifies in detail which information has to be provided to what extent by the customer when plans are calculated.

[747] The term „cost" per unit is, therefore, not quite accurate from the seller's point of view.

[748] See *Katz, M. L.* (1989), p. 699.

impacts crucially on which business types constellation prevails. Note that the resulting distinction relates only to project and relational business because in any case, both parties invest specifically in each other: *Chemistry Co.* invests mainly in terms of specific machinery and human resources. The buyer invests specifically by giving up certain areas of competence, reorganizing production processes to fit in *Chemistry Co.* and also, by allowing them to acquire specific knowledge about the buyer's production process. Against this background, some inferences can be drawn from the agreed payment conditions.

- If unit prices are codified in the initial agreement for all three periods in advance, that is, no provision at all is made for price renegotiations, this is a clear case of bilateral project business. Amortization calculations are based on the initial agreement alone.[749]
- In case no provision was made apart from a general clause which allows for completely unconstrained price renegotiations at the end of each period, a bilateral relational business would prevail since the amortization of the specific investments is to a large degree determined at later stages.
- Finally, cases in between, for instance an agreement in terms of a 15% participation on the part of the buyer in efficiency gains achieved by *Chemistry Co.*, would fall somewhere in between (project business with tendencies towards relational business): some guide is provided for calculating the investments amortization, yet at the same time, scope for bargaining opens up: only a procedural rule is included which restricts renegotiations to some degree. However, the 15% represent a purely nominal quantity which is not linked to unambiguously observable quantities outside the dyad. The real extent of participation depends substantially, for instance, on factually achieved efficiency gains, but also on the acknowledged efficiency gains.

With respect to *Chemistry Co.'s* business type, a further nuanciation seems appropriate owing to the two possible tariff structures. If the initial agreement provides scope for future price renegotiation, the outlined effects are presumed to be more pronounced in case the transaction follows tariff structure (1): the amortization of *Chemistry Co.'s* specific investments depends to a much larger degree on payment terms which are not fully specified but are subject to

---

[749] This assessment holds irrespective of the inclusion of price escalator clauses. Such clauses tie changes in price to variations in exogenous parameters such as industry labor costs or (raw) material prices via some mathematical algorithm. They do not open up scope for price renegotiations in their original sense (for a brief sketch of calculation and application of escalator clauses see e.g. *Backhaus, K.* (2003), p. 535ff).

unknown future developments and price renegotiations. The agreements from the annual renegotiations could, therefore, be regarded as resembling "subcontracts", resulting in some kind of sequence or chain of related contracts/transactions. In case the initial contract specifies conditions (2) as relevant, the seller business type is more easily identified as a project business: the compensation of the specific investments is governed by the initial contract only, leaving just the unspecific investments part to be renegotiated.

Information on the underlying impulse has been rather sparse. Nevertheless, there is evidence that the shift has been brought about partly by customer requests for general increases in supplier responsibility takeover, and partly by (new) information available to *Chemistry Co.* on possibilities of impacting buying decision criteria. In particular, the idea is to shift the focus of buyer attention away from the price of the paint material as a dominant or at least very important criterion and towards total cost considerations (from the buyer perspective) including a stronger focus on quality and process optimization.

4.4.2.2   *Application of the analytical model in a numerical example*

For illustration, the proposed formal model will be applied to the case of *Chemistry Co.'s* shift from bilateral product business towards bilateral project (relational) business. The comparison is based on expected total profits from, first, the traditional constellation and, second, the envisaged new constellation, implying in both cases that the seller's estimates on the buyer calculations are made explicit.[750] The relevant time horizon T for the comparison is defined by that constellation which requires the longest time until the aspired amortization is achieved. In the case of *Chemistry Co.*, this is the new constellation due to the usual contract duration of two to three years, regardless of whether it tends towards project or relational business. The model is estimated for both payment modes in the new constellation separately. It is based on the assumption of a three-year-contract in the new constellation.

---

[750]   Based on company information, a scenario has been developed which captures the fundamentals of the case but deviates from it in terms of concrete numbers for reasons of data confidentiality. Also, the difficult-to-quantify indirect benefit component a has been omitted from the illustration. This seems justifiable based on the fact that according to company information its inclusion would only further favor the new constellation. Hence, no change in the qualitative findings would result from its inclusion as apparent from the subsequent calculation.

Unlike suggested in equation (4.14), owing to the particularities of the bilateral oligopoly, this case allows for consideration of an individual dyad without having to break down calculations based on general price-demand-functions to this level. Transaction costs also arise with respect to the individual dyad, while the fixed costs assigned to the transaction are still dependent on transactions with other customers. Profits are calculated on the basis of a three-year estimation in order to ensure comparable time horizons. The calculation is based on a fictive but realistic example scenario. It is assumed that of all automobiles produced by a customer company named "*Star Cars*", 200,000 bodyworks per year are painted with coating *Colou 55* from *Chemistry Co.*. On average, 12 kg of paint are applied per bodywork. These figures are held constant for the three years considered in the calculation. Contracts are concluded ex ante on an annual basis.

For the buyer side, the following further assumptions are made: *Star Cars* derives an unspecific benefit from the functionality of *Colou 55* of $N_{USI} = 5.6$ €/kg. No specific benefits N_{SI} accrue to the buyer, nor are any investments in internal idiosyncrasies by *Star Cars* necessary. Transaction costs are mainly incurred in terms of ex ante transaction costs ($Tr_{(N)\ ea} = 200,000$ €) relating to each of the three contracts. It is estimated that in t_0 (time of first buying decision within the series) the net present value (in t_0) of the best available alternative KKo is 2,860,000 calculated over the course of one year. No substantial changes are expected to occur regarding KKo during the subsequent two years. The discount rate $r_{(N)}$ amounts to 8%. Drawing on (4.11) and inserting the numbers for the variables yields, for each period, the same critical price $\overline{p} = 4.223$ € which *Star Cars* is prepared to pay at maximum per kg of paint (see (E_4.1)):

$$\overline{\overline{P}} = \sum_{t=1}^{3} \left[\frac{\left[5.6 \cdot 12 \cdot 200,000 \right]}{(1+0.08)^t} - \frac{200,000}{(1+0.08)^{t-1}} \right] - KKo,$$

with

$$\overline{\overline{P}} = \sum_{t=1}^{3} \left[\frac{\overline{P}_t}{(1+0.08)^t} \right]$$

$$\overline{P}_t = \overline{p}_t \cdot (200,000 \cdot 12)$$

(E_4.1)

With $\bar{p}_t = \bar{p} = 4.223$ € for all three periods, the seller's profit can be calculated drawing on (4.16) and modifying it according to the deviating market structure in the example. The necessary assumptions concerning cost data are given by assigned K_{FC} of 3,000,000 € each period, variable production cost per kg of wet semi-finished *Colou 55* of 2.5 €, and ex ante transaction costs per annual contract of 180,000 €. Ex post transaction costs do not rise to a significant degree. The discount rate $r_{(A)}$ amounts to 8% for the seller as well. Inserting these data yields (E_4.2):

$$\pi_{AU} = \sum_{t=1}^{3} \left[\frac{4.22 \cdot 12 \cdot 200{,}000 - (2.5 \cdot 12 \cdot 200{,}000 + 3{,}000{,}000)}{(1+0.08)^t} - \frac{180{,}000}{(1+0.08)^{t-1}} \right] = 2{,}405{,}977.7 \qquad (E\_4.2)$$

That is, based on the above data and assuming a stable competitive environment and buyer calculations, continuing to transact via the traditional constellation earns *Chemistry Co.* a net present value of approximately 2.4 million € for the next three years.[751]

4.4.2.2.2 *New constellation: bilateral project business with tendencies towards relational business*

One-component-pricing

The estimation is based on the following scenario: a three-year-contract is concluded in t_0, which specifies a price per painted bodywork (CPU$_1$) paid by *Star Cars*. It is estimated 200,000 bodyworks per year will have to be painted by *Chemistry Co.*. On average, 12 kg of paint are applied per bodywork. For both parties, transaction costs arise mainly prior to and with contract conclusion and, to a lesser, but still considerable degree at the beginning of the second and third period. They arise mainly from price renegotiations and supervisions of contract compliance, e.g. concerning information provision.

Again, the estimated buyer calculation represents the starting point with the relevant equation given by (4.11). It is assumed that the best available alternative *KKo* remains the same as for the traditional constellation (net present value for first period of 2,860,000 €) throughout all

---

[751] It should be emphasized once more that the assumptions underlying the concrete figures are only *examples* from the spectrum of possible and plausible alternatives. Hence, the results will vary quantitatively and, very likely, also in qualitative terms. Yet, this does no harm to the general *method* proposed here. This certainly applies just as well to the example calculation for the new constellation.

three periods. Let the ex ante transaction costs in t_0 equal 600,000 €, and the ex post transaction costs (including price renegotiations for each subsequent period) at the end of each period t ($t = 1,...,3$) 500,000 €.[752] Furthermore, due to depreciation of old machinery (t_l) and increasing internal adaptations throughout periods t ($t = 1,...,3$), let M_l be 640,000 €, and $M_2 = M_3 = 1,390,000$ €. No switching costs $W_{(N)}$ are incurred by *Star Cars* since the previous way of transacting was product business. N_{SI} is estimated at 57.20 € per bodywork. The critical price for the first period can be calculated following (4. 16) as demonstrated in (E_4.3):

$$\overline{p}_t = \left[\left[\frac{\left[\left(N_{USI_t} + N_{SI_t} \right) \right]}{(1+r_{(N)})^t} - \frac{\left(Tr_{(N)\,ea\,t} \right)}{(1+r_{(N)})^{t-1} \cdot x_t} - \frac{\left(Tr_{(N)ep_t} \right)}{(1+r_{(N)})^t \cdot x_t} - \frac{(M_t)}{(1+r_{(N)})^t \cdot x_t} \right] - \frac{KKo_t}{x_t} \right] \cdot (1+r_{(N)})^t \quad (4.16)$$

$$\overline{p}_1 = \left[\frac{\left[((12 \cdot 5.6) + 57.2) \right]}{(1.08)^1} - \frac{600,000}{(1.08)^0 \cdot 200,000} - \frac{500,000}{(1.08)^1 \cdot 200,000} - \frac{640,000}{(1.08)^1 \cdot 200,000} - \frac{2,860,000}{200,000} \right] \cdot (1.08)^1$$

$$= 100.00 \qquad\qquad\qquad\qquad (E\_4.3)$$

The results for the following two periods can be obtained in analogy, yielding $\overline{p}_t = 100.00$ € per bodywork for all periods t alike. *Star Cars* would, under these terms, be indifferent amongst their three purchasing options KKo, the traditional offer by *Chemistry Co.* and the new offer by *Chemistry Co.*

Now, as indicated in the real case, if *Chemistry Co.* would foresee that under their coordination of the relevant parts of the paintshop, efficiency gains could be realized, *Chemistry Co.* could easily tip the balance in favor of the new constellation by sharing these efficiency gains with the customer. For instance, *Chemistry Co.* might estimate an annual decrease on average by 1 kg/bodywork and agree to split the resulting efficiency gains between the two parties with *Star Cars* receiving a reduction in CPU of 0.835 € for each kg decrease in *Colou 55* needed per bodywork. Based on these figures, the critical price of 100 € per bodywork applies just to the first period. The prices for the second and third period then follow from the critical price in the first period as $\overline{p}_2 = 99.165$ and $\overline{p}_3 = 98.33$. Thereby, the benefits to *Star Cars* become immediately apparent since the price reduction agreement

---

[752] This incorporation of price renegotiations to the previous period is justified based on its close linkages to results from information exchanges and monitoring in that previous period.

effectively provides them with part of the seller's rent which otherwise would have been captured by *Chemistry Co.*.[753]

Taking up this situation leads back to the central question of this chapter: is the new constellation still favorable for the seller depending upon the price at which the buyer would accept the shift? Thus, what remains to be analyzed is the profitability of the bilateral project constellation from *Chemistry Co.*'s perspective. Some additional information is needed for this calculation. In particular, it will be assumed that *Chemistry Co.* faces a considerable increase in transaction costs. Ex ante transaction costs prior and associated with contract conclusion amount to 1,800,000 €, ex post transaction costs (including price renegotiations for each subsequent period) at the end of each period t ($t = 1,...,3$) 800,000 €. Unspecific production costs for the painting material will be incurred just as for the first option, that is fixed costs K_{FC} of 3,000,000 € per period, and variable production cost per kg of wet semi-finished *Colou 55* of 2,5 €. However, taking into account the anticipated efficiency gains, the quantity of material is assumed to decrease to 11 kg in t_2 and 10 kg in t_3. *Chemistry Co.* now additionally incurs specific production costs for specific machinery, employees and further related expenditures (e.g. special accident insurance policies) which amount to 7,500,000 € per period.[754] Furthermore, in order to account for the different capital requirements of the alternative strategies, the costs of capital of the differential need to be included. It is assumed that the differential is being financed at an interest rate of 8% and can be obtained from the difference between total costs in the traditional constellation and total costs in the new constellation for each period t.[755] Drawing on (4.13), supplementing it by capital costs, and inserting the data yields:

---

[753] The seller rent is defined as the difference between revenues and variable costs (see e.g. *Schumann, J./Meyer, U./Ströbele, W.* (1999), p. 217ff). In case of zero fixed costs, it is equal to the seller's profit, otherwise it exceeds the latter by the amount of fixed costs.

[754] Splitting both cost components satisfies an early call by *Williamson, O. E.* (1985), p. 54, who argues that the distinction between fixed and variable costs is "...merely an accounting distinction" and claims the distinction between redeployable and non-redeployable assets to be more relevant for the analysis when a strong focus is placed on contractual issues.

[755] Alternatively, assumptions could be made regarding supplementing investments in the traditional constellation. Due to the given sequence of both strategies coming into play, the above modeling seems, however, more appropriate.

$$\pi_{AS} = -\frac{-1,800,000}{(1.08)^0} - \frac{(1,620,000 \cdot 0.08)}{(1.08)^0} +$$

$$\frac{100 \cdot 200,000}{(1.08)^1} - \frac{(2.5 \cdot 12 \cdot 200,000 + 3,000,000)}{(1.08)^1} - \frac{7,500,000}{(1.08)^1} - \frac{(800,000)}{(1.08)^1} - \frac{(8,120,000 \cdot 0.08)}{(1.08)^1} +$$

$$\frac{100 \cdot 200,000}{(1.08)^2} - \frac{(2.5 \cdot 11 \cdot 200,000 + 3,000,000)}{(1.08)^2} - \frac{7,500,000}{(1.08)^2} - \frac{(800,000)}{(1.08)^2} - \frac{(7,620,000 \cdot 0.08)}{(1.08)^2} +$$

$$\frac{100 \cdot 200,000}{(1.08)^3} - \frac{(2.5 \cdot 10 \cdot 200,000 + 3,000,000)}{(1.08)^3} - \frac{7,500,000}{(1.08)^3} - \frac{(800,000)}{(1.08)^3} - \frac{(7,120,000 \cdot 0.08)}{(1.08)^3} +$$

$$= 4,674,781.4$$

(E_4.4)

With about 4.67 million € expected profits for the three-year-contract period, capturing a larger share of the total value chain provides *Chemistry Co.* with profits that are more than doubled compared to the traditional constellation.

Yet, the scenario does not account for potential splitting of the efficiency gains. Modifying calculation (E_4.4) by changing the prices per bodywork to $\overline{p}_2 = 99.165$ for period t_2 and to $\overline{p}_3 = 98.33$ for period t_3 reduces *Chemistry Co.'s* profits to 4,266,465.985 or approximately 4.27 million € for the three-year-contract-period, yet, still creates a win-win situation.

Two-component-pricing (two-part tariff)

The only change compared to the one-component-pricing scenario is a modification in payment conditions.[756] Again, a three-year-contract is concluded in t_0 which specifies a price per painted bodywork (CPU$_2$) paid by *Star Cars* only that this time it just relates to the paint material. *Star Cars* pays for the surrounding performance through a fixed rate at the end of each year which is, unlike CPU$_2$, not subject to annual price renegotiations.[757]

Beginning again with the estimated buyer calculation requires starting with equation (4.11). Only this time, CPU$_2$ is incorporated resulting from the traditional model as (4.223 € * 12 kg/bodywork = 50.676 €) per bodywork. The resulting critical price $\overline{p}_{t_f}$ is the critical annual rate and is calculated for the first period following (4. 17) as demonstrated in (E_4.5):

---

[756] Obviously, this change in payment conditions has severe consequences (in favor of the seller) for the risk distribution among the parties once variations in the variables, for instance, regarding the annual number of bodyworks, are taken into account (see chapter 4.4.2.3).

[757] While in reality, the buyer pays a fixed *monthly* rate, we use an annual rate here for analytical simplicity since it does not change our results qualitatively.

$$\overline{P}_t = (\overline{p}_{tf} + \overline{p}_{tv} \cdot x_t)$$

(4.17)

$$= \left[\frac{\left[\left(N_{USI\,t} + N_{SI\,t} \right) \cdot x_t \right]}{(1+r_{(N)})^t} - \frac{\left(Tr_{(N)\,ea\,t} \right)}{(1+r_{(N)})^{t-1}} - \frac{\left(Tr_{(N)ep\,t} \right)}{(1+r_{(N)})^t} - \frac{\left(M_t \right)}{(1+r_{(N)})^t} - W_{(N)_0} - KKo \right] \cdot (1+r_{(N)})^t$$

with $\quad \overline{p}_{tv} \quad = CPU_2$

$\qquad \overline{p}_{tf} \quad =$ critical price for the fixed (annual) rate

$(\overline{p}_{1f} + 50.676 \cdot 200,000)$

$$= \left[\frac{\left[(12 \cdot 5.6) + 57.2 \right] \cdot 200,000}{(1.08)^1} - \frac{600,000}{(1.08)^0} - \frac{500,000}{(1.08)^1} - \frac{640,000}{(1.08)^1} - 2,860,000 \right] \cdot (1.08)^1$$

(E_4.5)

$\Leftrightarrow \quad \overline{p}_{1f} = 9,868,000$

The results for the following two periods can be obtained in analogy, yielding $\overline{p}_{2f} = \overline{p}_{2f} = 9,766,000 \,€$ which would make *Star Cars* indifferent among the three purchasing options *KKo*, the traditional offer by *Chemistry Co.* and the new offer by *Chemistry Co.* Again, *Chemistry Co.* could include the expected efficiency gains in the calculation, granting *Star Cars* a reduction in CPU_2 of 0.835 € for each kg decrease in *Colou 55*. As a result, in t_2, CPU_2 would amount to 49.841 €, and to 49.006 € in period t_3. *Chemistry Co.*'s profits remain unchanged since only the payment *structure* is varied.

4.4.2.2.3   Comparison of the strategic options

At first sight, comparing the alternative strategic options yields an unambiguous outcome in favor of shifting towards the new business types constellation. In case the expected efficiency gains are realized and shared, a clear win-win-situation results. However, this result comes with a few, interrelated caveats.

The first concern refers to deficiencies with respect to the calculation's input. The data represent a single possible scenario. Yet, chances that the estimates will coincide with what actually happens during the course of these three years are very low. In fact, the realizations of the variables may differ considerably from their estimates.[758] This suggests that potential benefits from incorporating alternative scenarios could exist. Related is a second issue, namely that of the quality of the calculation's output as a decision criterion. Based solely on the above univalent figures, a further assessment, for instance, on the two different payment modes in the new constellation is not possible. Even though the calculated profits from the particular scenario are equal, very different risks of underachievement are attached to them. This is revealed, once more scenarios than just the one outlined above are considered. Then, the two shift options differ considerably in terms of the uncertainty faced by *Chemistry Co.*. In the case of one-component-pricing, *Chemistry Co.* bears a considerable proportion of the danger that less than the expected number of automobiles is sold and, consequently, needs to be painted. On the contrary, with the second payment conditions option, the specific investments of *Chemistry Co.* are due independent of the number of automobiles sold and bodyworks painted, respectively. The related (sales) uncertainty is to the greatest extent borne by *Star Cars* who are in this case responsible for the amortization of the paintshop. The example, hence, serves as a further example in support of the claim that environmental uncertainty (here: sales uncertainty) weighs heavier for transactions with high specificity involved. At the same time, it is evident that as soon as the strategic options (old vs. new constellation, one- vs. two-component pricing) are characterized by different probabilities of under- or overachievement in alternative scenarios, a decision should be based on more complex criteria than a single univalent profit figure.

A well-established device for responding at least to some of the associated decision uncertainties is sensitivity analysis.[759] Starting from some initial data configuration, the data are varied in such a way as to obtain answers to the following questions[760]: first, what happens if the values of one or more variables (and/or probabilities of occurrence) change? And, second, by how much can one particular variable (or probability) change without affecting the optimal decision? Such reflections will also enter into the subsequently presented, extended model.

---

[758] Not to speak of another possible scenario in the traditional constellation, namely, that *Chemistry Co.*, might be able to win the contract on efficient terms for period one, but not so for period 2 and/or 3.

[759] For recent application of sensitivity analysis in marketing see e.g. *Stremersch, S./Tellis, G. J.* (2002).

[760] See *Mathur, K./Solow, D.* (1994), p. 578; *Adam, D.* (1996), p. 221

224

4.5 Extending the concept to capture the value of flexibility and consequences of path dependencies in an interactive context

4.5.1   The necessity of incorporating issues of flexibility and path dependency

Both from an originally strategic and a TCA angle, incorporating considerations on flexibility and path dependence in the above model seems important.[761] Shifts between business types constellations have been described as strategic in nature. As such, they are per definition more long-term oriented and will frequently involve considerable investments and resource commitments which are, at least in the short run, irreversible.[762] In a transaction cost context, such irreversibility primarily stems from the specificity associated with an investment and its resulting sunk cost nature.[763] Two principal, intertwined inferences can be drawn from this brief characterization.

(1) (Past) shift decisions must be expected to affect availability and suitability of future (strategic) choices. A model of shifts between business types should account for this effect which is associated with path dependence and short-run irreversibility of strategic decisions.

(2) It is exactly these interrelations that determine the significance of strategic decisions and, at the same time, make the case for valuing flexibility. No unambiguous definition of the terms has yet emerged from the literature.[764] For the purpose of this analysis it suffices to include flexibility as a very broadly defined concept in terms of available scope of action. Drawing on *Ghemawat* (1991), flexibility is defined as the ability to revise a (strategic)

---

[761] For supportive positions in strategy research see e.g. *Ghemawat, P.* (1991); *Helper, S.* (1991); *Bowman, E. H./Hurry, D.* (1993); *Ghemawat, P./del Sol, P.* (1998), p. 26; *Ghemawat, P.* (2002a), pp. 65, 69. For argumentation from a TCA angle see the discussion on antecedents of chosen asset specificity in 3.2.3.2 and the literature referred to there.

[762] See chapter 2.2.2.

[763] See *Dixit, A. K./Pindyck, R. S.* (1995), p. 109ff, who also discuss other sources of irreversibility such as government regulations.

[764] See *Adam, D.* (1996), p. 287ff. Thus, he identifies three different kinds of notions of flexibility: first, flexibility in terms of available scope of actions, second and related, flexibility in terms of rate of adaptation, and, third, in terms of the reactions of performance measures faced with adaptation. Flexibility of the third kind, hence, presupposes the existence of flexibility of the first or second kind with resepct to the employed production technology. Different categorizations have been advanced e.g. by *Jacob, H.* (1974), p. 322; *Meffert, H.* (1994), p. 453ff.

decision as opposed to having to stick to it in any circumstances.[765] Its value is presumed to increase relatively with rising uncertainty.[766] It has been shown that, particularly under such conditions, it may be optimal to hold options open even at the expense of incurring some investment.[767] This proposition is consistent with the assertion made above that conditions of higher parametric uncertainty relatively favor unspecific transactions, that is, product businesses, because of their better chances for redeployment in alternative uses.

Obviously, both issues gain relevance only in an inter-temporal setting. A suitable model, thus, needs to be constructed from a multi-period perspective with several points of decision explicitly built in. Such an approach differs from the incorporation of multiple periods as mentioned above which centered around effects from the mere passage of time and potentially attached changes in environmental parameters (e.g. sales volume).

4.5.2 A simple interactive model of shifts between business types

4.5.2.1 Objectives of the model

The basic objective of the model developed here is to gain insights into whether a certain shift that may have been identified as (potentially) desirable on a global level is assertable, that is: accepted by the buyer, under efficient, profit-increasing conditions for a particular seller. The investigation builds on the profit comparison as outlined in chapter 4.3 and illustrated by the case study in chapter 4.4. Yet, it incorporates some additional, important issues, namely:

- path dependence/short-run irreversibility of the shift decision,
- the value implied in flexibility,
- interactivity of the dyadic transaction situation, and finally, this all in

---

[765] See *Ghemawat, P.* (1991), p. 116.

[766] See e.g. *Dixit, A. K./Pindyck, R. S.* (1995), p. 110.

[767] See e.g. *Bowman, E. H./Hurry, D.* (1993), p. 767. A whole stream of research in its own has meanwhile evolved around this topic, the value of flexibility in strategic decisions, usually referred to as the "real options approach". For seminal contributions see e.g. *Smit, H. T. J./Ankum, L. A.* (1993); *Dixit, A. K./Pindyck, R. S.* (1994); *Trigeorgis, L.* (1995); for a brief, rather qualitative discussion see *Bowman, E. H./Hurry, D.* (1993); in a neo-institutional context recently see e.g. *Sanchez, R.* (2000); *Dimpfel, M./Algesheimer, R.* (2002), p. 8ff, who particularly focus on uncertainty and irreversibility as the determinants of action flexibility; *Burr, W.* (2003), p. 129ff.

- an inter-temporal decision-making setting.

Against this background, the central objective of the model is to investigate the impact of various elements of the payoff functions proposed above on the decision of whether to shift from one constellation to another or not.[768] While the formulation of the model proceeds in such a way as to provide a general framework for thinking about shift decisions under the given assumptions, the results themselves hold in a general context only so far as they represent illustrations of behavior which is in principle possible within the model and which, therefore, can occur in general. The precise data underlying these results are only examples. However, this example nature of the particular configurations to which the model is applied to does not invalidate the model's usefulness with regard to its objectives: neither precise forecasting is intended which would require high correlation between estimates and real data, nor is the objective to establish general rules of when to shift from one constellation to another: "because strategic opportunities are by definition uncertain and connected to the possession of unique information or resources, strategy analysis must be situational."[769] Within this broad frame, some subordinate objectives are derived from the concrete research context.

Following from the dyadic orientation and in accord with the underlying strategy definition, the interaction between a seller and an individual buyer is modelled. Competition enters indirectly via its impact on the best available alternative that the buyer draws on in its evaluation of the seller's offering. Yet, with shifts between business types constellations having been interpreted as some form of entrepreneurial activities, the period of temporary monopoly until competition catches up (or even overtakes it) exerts a crucial impact on the seller's expectation about how profitable a shift will be compared to the current constellation. Hence, the model should also allow, in principle, for mapping this issue. Last but not least, the focus of the model is on value creation and protection (as expressed, for instance, through the incorporation of variables for transaction costs). The issue of value division and associated bargaining is, for the moment, analytically separated from the first two aspects and is not

---

[768] In this analysis, direct reference is made only to the pay off variables as depicted in chapters 4.3.2.1.1 and 4.3.2.2.1. The influence of the indirect determinants (chapters 4.3.2.1.2 and 4.3.2.2.2) can only be traced back via their hypothesized effects on the payoff function elements.

[769] *Rumelt, R. P.* (1984), p. 569.

explicitly captured in the model.[770] Nevertheless, the actual price paid by the customer needs to be determined within the model in order to be able to arrive at a statement concerning the (subjectively) optimal constellation decision. To ensure this, the model must contain a mechanism for solving the price issue. Furthermore, this procedure must be linked to the influence of competition outlined above, because the availability of substitutes crucially impacts on the buyer´s bargaining power and, hence, the actual price paid for the performance offered by the seller.[771] As a result, value division issues are included only in a very schematic way, but are not explicitly modelled. A brief discussion of such aspects with respect to the model is presented in the subsequent chapter 4.5.3. As apparent from the immediately following model description, this approach leads to a combination of reasoning in the spirit of (unilateral) optimization (with respect to price determination) and of reasoning in the tradition of interactive outcome determination.

4.5.2.2   Model design and underlying assumptions

Against the background of these objectives, a sequential, non-cooperative multi-period game theoretic model of interactive seller and buyer decision-making under "uncertainty"[772] is developed which results in a new business types constellation being either introduced or not.[773] In order to keep the model complexity as low as possible, the simplest case of a multi-period model was chosen: two discrete decision points are modeled and, partially overlapping with them, two discounting periods. The formal structure of the model is described in *Tab. 2*.

---

[770] For similar argumentation on analytical separation between the issues of pie creation and division see e.g. *Brandenburger, A. M./Stuart Jr., H. W.* (1996), p. 18.

[771] See chapter 3.3. Extensive discussions of this issue can be found in negotiation theory with the "best alternative to a negotiated agreement (BATNA)" (see e.g. *Fisher, R./Ury, W.* (1981); *Raiffa, H.* (1997), p. 74) having been advanced as the central construct determining a party´s bargaining strength. Moreover, the bargaining problem outside the dyad is assumed to have already been solved and is, hence, not considered at all. For a similar approach see *Brandenburger, A. M./Stuart Jr., H. W.* (1996), p. 9.

[772] This notion of uncertainty refers to its meaning in game theory which corresponds with the *Knightian* notion of risk (see chapter 3.2.3.2.2); see also the subsequent outline of information structure.

[773] Sequential games are games where the players choose their actions in a particular sequence. Instructive introductions include *Gardner, R.* (1995), p. 145ff; *Rasmusen, E.* (2001), p. 90ff; *Berninghaus, S. K./Ehrhart, K.-M./Güth, W.* (2002), p. 89ff. Most of the game theoretic literature centers around interactions

Model parameter	
Players	Seller S and buyer B (plus nature 0 making random choices).
Order of play	**Stage 0 (= decision stage)** 0 The seller decides whether or not to invest in the development of a new constellation ("inv."/ "no inv."). **Stage 1 (= decision stage / period 1 for discounting)** 1 Nature chooses between two different scenarios with $q1$ giving the probability for scenario 1_1 and $(1-q1)$ giving the probability for scenario 1_2. Probability $q1$ is known to both players. 2 The seller decides whether to offer the new or the old constellation (in case of investment at stage 0), or whether to offer the old constellation without or in conjunction with investment in the new constellation (in case of no investment at stage 0). 3 The buyer decides whether to buy immediately from the seller ("purchase") or to wait until the second stage ("wait") for potential improvements in his best available alternative. **Stage 2 (= period 2 for discounting)** 4 Nature chooses between two different scenarios with $q2$ giving the probability for scenario 2_1 and $(1-q2)$ giving the probability for scenario 2_2. Probability $q2$ is known to both players. This second nature move is assumed to be independent of the nature move at stage 1. A scenario-contingent seller action follows: in the case of scenario 2_1 the seller offers the new constellation if previous investment has been undertaken, and offers the old constellation if no investment has been undertaken. In the case of scenario 2_2 the seller offers the old constellation if no shift towards the new constellation has yet occurred, and offers the new constellation if the shift has already taken place at stage 1.
Information structure	Perfect, but uncertain (game theoretic notions).
Payoffs	Seller and buyer each receive a payoff at each of the 24 terminal nodes.[774]

Tab. 2: Model description for decision on shift between business types

Consider the following setting: in a competitive market for intermediate goods, a seller S and a buyer B are considering a transaction. There may have been previous transactions between the two explicitly considered players but not necessarily so. Competition is considered only as an implicit impact on the buyer´s evaluation of the seller´s offer. The seller has previously

---

between competitors. The body of research focusing on the interaction between a seller and a buyer is much smaller (see e.g. *Mudambi, R.* (1990)).

marketed his offer in an arbitrary business types constellation labelled as "old constellation" and is now considering to shift towards some "new constellation" which he has identified as potentially suitable for improving his profit situation based on general considerations. The seller's comparison between the two constellations which are assumed to constitute alternatives with respect to the transaction situation under scrutiny rests on two decision periods. An issue that deserves particular attention before proceeding with the model outline is that of assumed information structure. The model applied here is one with perfect but uncertain information. These are the game theoretic terms and do not coincide with those from TCA. Perfect information characterizes a condition where each player knows exactly what has happened so far at each decision point where the player had to make a decision.[775] Uncertain information reflects the idea that nature (or chance, as it is sometimes referred to) moves after some player moves have occurred. Such game theoretic uncertainty corresponds closest to the *Knightian* notion of risk (all possible future states are known and objective probabilities can be attached to them) but may also include uncertainty in a narrow sense (only estimates of subjective probabilities are possible). Hence, the actors have better information than under conditions of bounded rationality as it is usually interpreted.[776] Nevertheless, assuming this particular information structure can be justified on the grounds of considerably reducing modeling complexity while still preserving scope for the inclusion of information deficiencies. In fact, incorporating random nature moves at two stages of the model represents a relatively simple way of accounting for information deficiencies. Moreover, such an approach allows to circumvent the somewhat controversial issue of modeling bounded

---

[774] The payoffs are discounted with the individual player's discount rate to its first respective point of decision. This is stage 0 for the seller, and stage 1 for the buyer. The respective payoff functions build on those developed in chapter 4.3 and are depicted in detail in appendix II.

[775] See e.g. *Gardner, R.* (1995), p. 8; *Rasmusen, E.* (2001), p. 47ff. The game theoretic terminology already deviates in this respect from that which is usually applied in TCA and also in this research: in the latter nomenclature, perfect information is free from any deficiencies. From a game theoretic view, this model also displays symmetric and complete information.

[776] For further discussion see the recent contribution by *Williamson, O. E.* (2000), pp. 601, 605f, who holds lacking agreement on the definition of bounded rationality across different streams of research (e.g. in TCA and the property rights theory of the firm (on the latter see in particular *Grossman, S. J./Hart, O.* (1986); *Hart, O./Moore, J.* (1999))) as a main factor in the controversy about appropriate modeling of incomplete contracts.

rationality.[777] Hence, only uncertainty in a game theoretic sense is included in the form of two nature moves. Each nature move is associated with two possible scenarios occurring with different probabilities. In addition, such modeling finds support in real world phenomena such as the announcement of business data, development scenarios and corresponding probability figures (e.g. on economic trends, bankruptcy quotas, etc.) in general or in industry-specific publications.

The model structure is designed to fit the particular objectives of this research. Yet, it is flexible enough to accommodate different concerns which may be attached to shift considerations in terms of the two nature moves. The different scenarios at stage 1 and stage 2 can be interpreted according to the particular relevance of various impacts (competitor reactions, legal constraints, user groups etc.). Note also, that the model is not restricted to any particular initial or target constellation but may depict any shift consideration. Perhaps the best way to outline how the model works, is to go through the game tree which is depicted in *Fig. 20*, and explicate step by step what happens and how it relates to the above research purposes.

---

[777] See e.g. *Williamson, O. E.* (2000), pp. 601, 605f, who views controversy about the definition and appropriate operationalization of bounded rationality as a major current obstacle to further formalization in TCA which lives up to its original spirit.

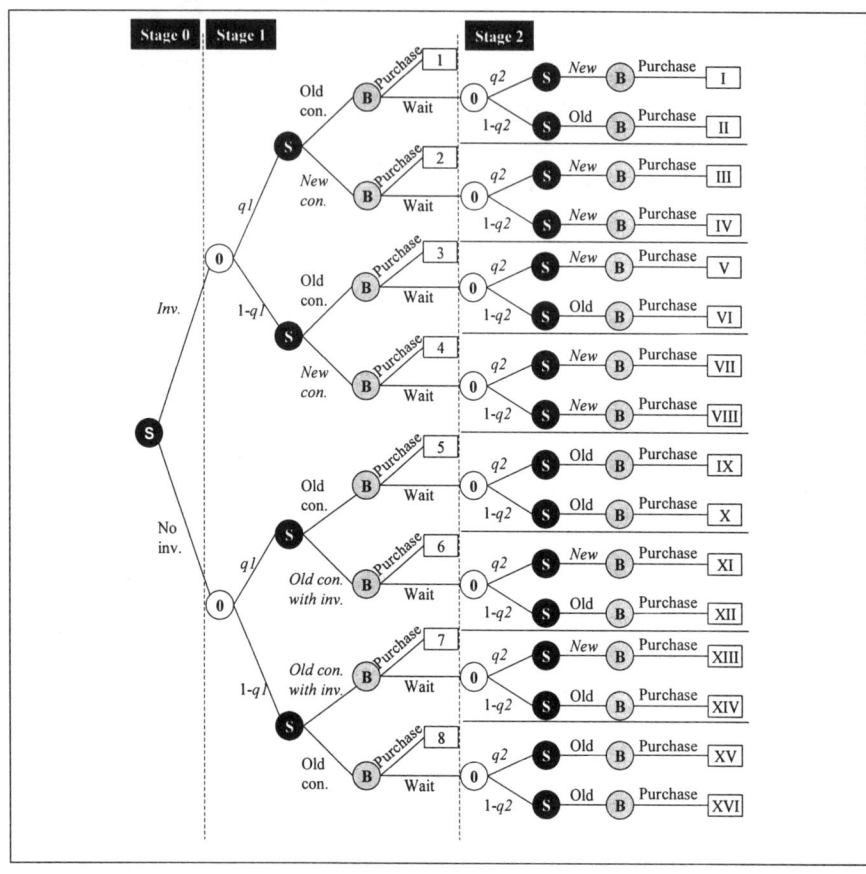

Fig. 20: Extensive form presentation of the shift decision model

At stage 0, the seller decides on whether or not to invest in R&D targeted at the development of a new market offering in a new constellation. This investment is modelled as a necessary condition prior to a potential shift. It can be interpreted as an option on the future ability to offer the new constellation and, hence, integrates considerations on the value of flexibility.[778]

At the beginning of stage 1, a nature move takes place resulting in the occurrence of either one of two possible scenarios (1_1, 1_2). Attached to each branch is a probability ($q1$ for scenario

---

[778] The particular method of solution for model also allows for circumventing this requirement if it is considered to be inappropriate for the particular case by setting the parameter value of the necessary R&D investment at 0.

1_1, and (1-$q1$) for scenario 1-2), reflecting that, in essence, nature creates a probability distribution over the two scenarios. Here, these scenarios capture two different competitive environments: in scenario 1_1, the competition soon starts to develop a new offering as well. This improved alternative offering also becomes effective with a time lag of one period, that is, at stage 2. The resulting anticipated improvement in the buyer's best available alternative is captured in the parameter δ_{1_1} which gives the expected percentage of improvement in the buyer's best available alternative at stage 2 compared to stage 1. Scenario 1_2 could in turn represent the case of relatively inactive competition where no improvement in the competition's offering takes place.[779] In each of these scenarios, the seller has two options. In case he has undertaken the R&D investment at stage 0, the seller chooses between offering the old or the new constellation. Otherwise, he chooses between offering the old constellation with or without investment in the new constellations. Then, it is the buyer's turn to choose between the two available actions of immediate purchase and waiting until the second stage. In fact, it is assumed that, although the buyer may defer purchase to the second period, he may not completely abstain from it. Eventually, he must make a purchase of a fixed quantity of the product at a point within the model's time horizon.[780] This quantity may vary with the degree of asset specificity, but it does not vary with price.[781]

At stage 2, a nature move occurs again relating to two different scenarios 2_1 and 2_2 (with probabilities $q2$ for scenario 2_1, and (1-$q2$) for scenario 2_2). These stage 2 scenarios are interpreted here to capture potential changes in the specific benefits which accrue to the buyer from the new constellation. Scenario 2_2 is modeled as one which considerably discriminates the new constellation from that stage onwards, for instance, due to new environmental laws

---

[779] As a result, unlike many comparably simple game theoretic sequential models under perfect information, this model displays some distinctive features both regarding formulation and results: holding out until the second stage may become rational for the buyer in the anticipation of increased bargaining power over the course of the game. In fact, as is apparent from the proposed model solution and the corresponding screenshot of the entry mask (see *Fig. 22*) the model also provides scope for including an explicit modeling of the alternative scenario 1_2 by allowing for the incorporation of the analogous parameter δ_{1_2}.

[780] This idea can be substantiated by considering the case of a buyer who currently uses a completely depreciated machine which should actually be replaced in the first period, but can make it through one more period at maximum.

[781] See for similar assumptions e.g. *Huber, F.* (1999), p. 162. Substantiation for this assumption can be gained from cases of fixed substitution relations between different input factors (limitational production function) (see e.g. *Adam, D.* (1997), p. 288ff).

which nearly rule out the new constellation or, at least, call for severe adaptations.[782] The resulting anticipated deterioration in the specific value that the buyer derives from the specific component of the new constellation is captured in the parameter δ. δ represents (as a percentage) the expected decrease compared to the specific value that the buyer can extract from the new constellation at stage 1. On the other hand, scenario 2_1 might represent the positive case where this development does not take place. After that, the seller makes a scenario-contingent move which has been specified prior to the start of the game: in the case of scenario 2_1, the seller offers the new constellation if previous investment has been undertaken, and offers the old constellation if no investment has been undertaken. In the case of scenario 2_2, the seller offers the old constellation if no shift towards the new constellation has yet occurred, and offers the new constellation if the shift has already taken place at stage 1. This particular twist of the model is intended to reflect the (short-term) irreversibility of shifts between business types: once the seller has undertaken the shift, he is required to stick to the new constellation until the end of the game.[783] Finally, there are 24 terminal nodes with appended payoff vectors.

In addition to the above assumptions and in line with the general assumption of this work, both actors are assumed to be risk neutral.[784] Furthermore, consistent with the modeling in chapter 4.3, the seller is assumed to always set the price in such a way that the buyer necessarily accepts the offering, that is, the seller sets the price infinitesimally below the critical price at which the buyer is just indifferent among its best available alternative and the seller's offering. The best alternative is assumed to always be either equal to or greater than zero. Hence, some form of substitute (albeit of potentially very low value to the buyer) is taken to always exist. The case of a (sustained) monopoly is explicitly excluded. This appears reasonable not only with respect to the majority of transaction situations in business reality, but considerations on efficient shift assertion derive their relevance mainly from a competitive environment.[785] The assumption represents, however, no contradiction to the proposed

---

[782] Alternatively, one could imagine the arrival of detrimental information about the new constellation's lacking suitability for certain usages as assessed by lead users or user groups.

[783] This is not to deny that, if a larger number of periods was played, it might be sensible to allow switching back after a certain number of periods.

[784] This is in line with the outlined working assumptions in TCA.

[785] See also the discussion in chapter 4.6.

temporary monopoly position of the seller in the new constellation, since such a position does not deny the persistent existence of the previously available solutions. Whether the resulting profit (or loss) from a particular path is attractive for the seller is subject to the choice of path.[786]

Faced with the incorporated uncertainty resulting from the nature moves, the players are assumed to maximize their *expected* payoffs. These payoffs, essentially, build on the model formulated in chapter 4.3, albeit supplemented by the explicit introduction of R&D investment. The payoff combination attached to the terminal node 1 at stage 2 (I) is singled out for exemplification, while the other payoff combinations can be seen in detail from appendix II.

From the particular assumed mechanism for arriving at the actual price, it follows that the total **buyer's payoff** equals its best (net) alternative which enters as a per unit quantity.

$$U_N = kko_1 \cdot x_1 \cdot (1+\delta_{1\_1}) \cdot (1+r_{(N)})^{-1} \qquad (4.18)$$

with U_N = net utility derived in total by the buyer from the seller's offering
       kko_1 = net utility derived per unit from the best available alternative at stage 1
       x_1 = number of units of the best available alternative offering needed at stage 1 in the old
                  constellation
       $r_{(N)}$ = buyer discount rate
       δ_{1_1} = percentage increase in net utility derived by the buyer from the best available
                  alternative (scenario 1_1)

The **critical price** per unit of the seller's offering that establishes the link between buyer and seller payoff can then be obtained from:

$$p = N_{USI} + N_{SI\_new1} - \left(\frac{Tr_{(N)ea\_new}}{x_2}\right) \cdot (1+r_{(N)}) - \left(\frac{Tr_{(N)ep\_new}}{x_2}\right) - \frac{M}{x_2} - \frac{W_{(N)}}{x_2} - \frac{(kko_1 \cdot x_1) \cdot (1+\delta_{1\_1})}{x_2}$$

$$(4.19)$$

---

[786] Additional insights on this issue are gained later when it is taken up in the discussion on bargaining issues (see chapter 4.5.3)

with	p	= critical price per unit of seller offering (here: in new constellation)
	N_{SI_new1}	= specific gross value derived from one unit of seller offering in new constellation (scenario 2_1)
	x_2	= number of units of the seller´s offering needed at stage 2 in the new constellation
	$Tr_{(N)ea\_new}$	= ex ante transaction costs in the new constellation relating to the whole transaction
	$Tr_{(N)ep\_new}$	= ex post transaction costs in the new constellation relating to the whole transaction

Note that, since the example refers to a $q2$-path (scenario 2_1) at the last stage, there is no potential decrease in specific value at this stage. Hence, the corresponding parameter δ does not appear in this particular equation.

Finally, the relevant total **seller payoff** on a per unit basis is derived from the following equation:

$$\pi_A = (-\frac{RD}{n\_new}) + \frac{p \cdot x_2 - C_{USI\_new} - C_{SI\_new} - \left[Tr_{(A)ea\_new} \cdot (1+r_{(A)})\right] - Tr_{(A)ep\_new} + \frac{a\_new}{n\_new} - \frac{W_{(A)}}{n\_new}}{(1+r_{(A)})^2}$$

(4.20)

with	π_{AS}	= seller payoff (profits) derived from the transaction
	RD	= total investment in research and development for new constellation (here: undertaken at stage 0)
	n_{new}	= estimated number of buyers in new constellation[787]
	C_{USI_new}	= unspecific production costs (variable and fixed) in the new constellation[788]
	C_{SI_new}	= specific production costs (variable and fixed) in the new constellation
	$Tr_{(A)ea\_new}$	= ex ante transaction costs in the new constellation relating to the whole transaction
	$Tr_{(A)ep\_new}$	= ex post transaction costs in the new constellation relating to the whole transaction
	a_new	= total estimated indirect benefit component from the new constellation
	$r_{(A)}$	= discount rate for the seller

---

[787] Inclusion of this number, admittedly, repesents a circular statement within model formulation. However, appropriate solution methods can act as a remedy (e.g. simulation of different parameter values ranging from 0 to an estimated maximum number). When considering a particular dyad, n_{new} includes this dyad already since the relevant parameters (RD, fixed costs, $W_{(A)}$, a_new) are broken down based on n_{new} only at such nodes where the buyer purchases in the new constellation. Moreover, it is the only alternative to the much less realistic assumption of R&D costs, fixed costs, etc. being incurred on a buyer specific basis. The last alternative, en-block inclusion of these parameters without breaking them down ex ante is not compatible with the research focus on the individual dyad. A similar kind of assumption, though in a different respect (willingness-to-pay), has been adopted by *Brandenburger, A. M./Stuart Jr., H. W.* (1996), p. 11f.

[788] In principle, the parameter could be underlaid with any (kind of) cost function. As is apparent from the screenshots in chapter 4.5.2.3 the cost functions employed here correspond to "typical cost functions" (see e.g. *Schumann, J./Meyer, U./Ströbele, W.* (1999), p. 159). The model is, though, not restricted to such cost functions and could easily be adapted to accommodate any other cost function.

4.5.2.3   Proposing a simulative solution method

The standard solution concept for sequential games of the above form is the (subgame) perfect Nash-equilibrium.[789] It requires each player to maximize its payoff at each point of the game including re-optimization of decisions at later stages if appropriate and including anticipation of such future re-optimization.

Based on a particular set of parameter values (hereafter referred to as configuration) and the resulting numerical payoffs, the solution to the game is obtained through backward induction using the concept of subgame perfectness. Backward induction means that the last stage of the tree is solved first, then the second-to-last, and so forth until the first stage. This method addresses the issue that "…in picking his first action, a player looks ahead to its implications for all future periods, so it is easiest to start […] where the future is shortest."[790] The result is a recommendation for every decision node of which action to choose – even if that node is not reached in equilibrium. Nevertheless, the mechanism will be illustrated on the basis of a simple numerical example in order to facilitate the understanding of the results in the subsequent chapters. The following *Fig. 21* shows the above game tree but is supplemented by example payoffs in order to demonstrate the backward induction solution as applied to the shift decision model.

---

[789] This refinement of the Nash equilibrium concept has been developed by *Selten, R.* (1975). For the original concept of Nash equilibrium refer to *Nash, J. F.* (1950); *Nash, J. F.* (1951). A strategy combination is referred to as a Nash equilibrium if neither player has an incentive to unilaterally deviate from it. Subgame perfectness requires a strategy combination to be a Nash equilibrium for the entire game, and requires its relevant action rules to be Nash equilibria for the respective subgames (for an overview e.g. *Moorthy, K. S.* (1985).

[790] *Rasmusen, E.* (2001), p. 110.

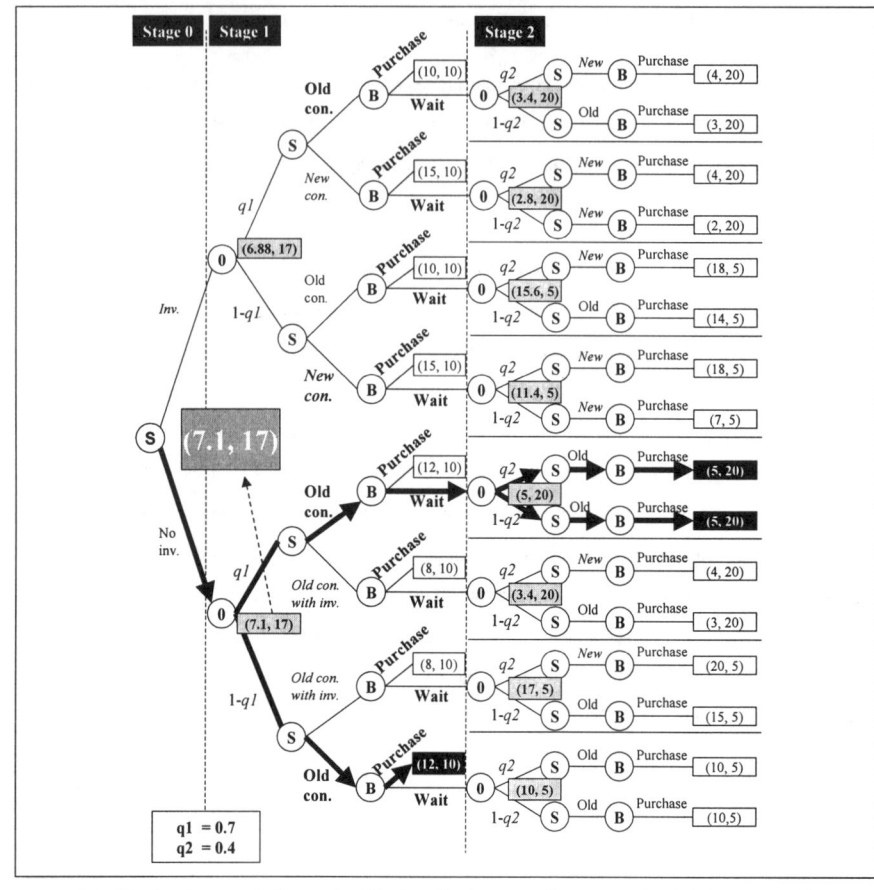

Fig. 21: Simple numerical example of backward induction with respect to the shift decision model

The terminal nodes now contain the relevant payoffs to the seller (first figure in the parentheses) and the buyer (second figure in the parentheses) instead of their numbering. Let $q1$ equal 0.7, and $q2$ equal 0.4. The solution proceeds as following: first, from each pair of terminal nodes at stage 2 that belong to the same stage 2 nature node, the corresponding expected payoffs for both players are calculated applying the probabilities $q2$ and $(1-q2)$. The expected payoff vectors are depicted in gray boxes close to the respective nature move. In the second step (stage 1), the buyer compares his expected payoff from waiting until stage 2 with the according payoff from an immediate purchase. His choice between "Purchase" and "Wait" is guided by the objective to maximize his payoff at each of the eight buyer decision nodes. In *Fig. 20*, the results from his eight decisions are marked by bold type of the corresponding

238

option. These decisions are taken into account by the seller who compares at each of his four decision nodes the payoffs that would accrue to him in case he offered the old constellation versus the new constellation (in the upper half of the tree) and in case he offered the old constellation versus the old constellation accompanied by investment in the new constellation (in the lower half of the tree). The results are four decisions for each of the possible realizations of the nature move at stage 1. Attached are four payoff vectors. The upper pair of vectors is set apart from the lower pair by the stage 0 seller decision. Again, expected payoffs are computed, this time using the probabilities $q1$ and $(1-q1)$, respectively, and are depicted in gray boxes near the underlying nature move. As a consequence, a certain expected payoff is associated with each of the two possible actions that are available to the seller at stage 0. Once again, his choice between them is guided by the objective to maximize his payoff. In the above example, this leads to the decision not to invest in the new constellation at stage 0. The complete equilibrium path is indicated by arrows in bold type, yielding an expected payoff of 7.1 to the seller and 17 to the buyer.

Reaching beyond such an individual case analysis („point solution") gives rise to the following considerations: the most obvious candidate for gaining insights which hold over a number of contexts would be a solution based on the general payoff functions. In principle, such an analytical solution can be obtained for the model above. However, some problems are associated with this approach which are not rooted in the model structure, but in the specific formulation of the payoff functions. Due to the large number of variables in conjunction with the number of stages, this procedure would bring about some complexity. More importantly, the solution's interpretation in terms of sensitivities as proposed in chapter 4.4 would rather be complicated by these factors and detection of interesting (model) behavior would substantially be hampered. In short, the derivation of the results would not be very instructive.

These problems can be circumvented by referring to a third alternative: straightforward analysis of the model can be performed by numerical simulation.[791] This solution involves

---

[791] The use of computer-aided numerical solutions and sensitivity analysis to game theoretic models has some tradition, as is apparent e.g. from *Lieberman, M. B.* (1987), p. 446; *Mudambi, R./McDowell-Mudambi, S.* (1995), p. 422ff. See related e.g. *Klein, B./Leffler, K. B.* (1981), p. 351ff; *Hauser, J. R./Shugan, S. M.* (1983); *Leinfellner, W.* (1987/88), p. 20; *Stefansson, B.* (2000); *Adner, R.* (2002). For general con-

computation of a large number of different configurations and solution of each via backward induction based on the concept of subgame perfectness. For this purpose, a computer program for solving the tree for each configuration was written.[792] The approach allows for highly flexible use of the model, easy adaptation to changes in the data and clear presentation of the results. It allows for variations of parameter values, and ascertainment of sensitivities in the shift decision with respect to any parameter of interest.

The program is equipped with an input mask (see *Fig. 22*) for entering all parameter values that constitute the basic configuration. In case sensitivity analysis is sought, additional parameters can be specified, namely the percentage increase or decrease in the buyer's best available alternative at stage 2 compared to stage 1, δ_{1_1} and δ_{1_2}, respectively (relating to the scenarios 1_1 and 1_2 and the according probabilities $q1$ and $(1-q1)$), and the percentage decrease in specific value to the buyer from the new constellation at stage 2 compared to stage 1, δ (relating to scenario 2_2). After entering the configuration of interest, the model can be solved either

- for the exact entered values ("point solution"), or

- for a range of values of a certain parameter (e.g. probability $q2$)[793], informing about the result's sensitivity with respect to this variable,

- for a range of values of two different parameters (e.g. probability $q2$ and R&D investment RD)[794], informing about the result's sensitivity with respect to these two variables.

---

siderations on simulations e.g. *Rubinstein, R. Y.* (1981); *Morgan, B. T.* (1984); on the use of (computer) simulation in social science see e.g. *Troitzsch, K. G.* (1990); regarding business administration e.g. *Adam, D.* (1996), p. 488ff;

[792] The program is in Delphi 3 Professional which is a common component-oriented language building on Pascal (in the form of Object Pascal). The source code is available from the author at request.

[793] This range has to be defined in the source code of the program where the variable itself also has to be defined as the running variable in the particular case.

[794] Again, the ranges have to be defined in the source code of the program, additionally the variables themselves must be defined as the running variables. In principle, simultaneous inclusion of more than two variables is also possible. However, from three variables onwards, graphic presentation is largely hampered. Moreover, disproportionate demands on computation are associated with an increasing number of running variables. In fact, if the time required for analyzing one running variable is t, then the time for analyzing n variables is t^n.

240

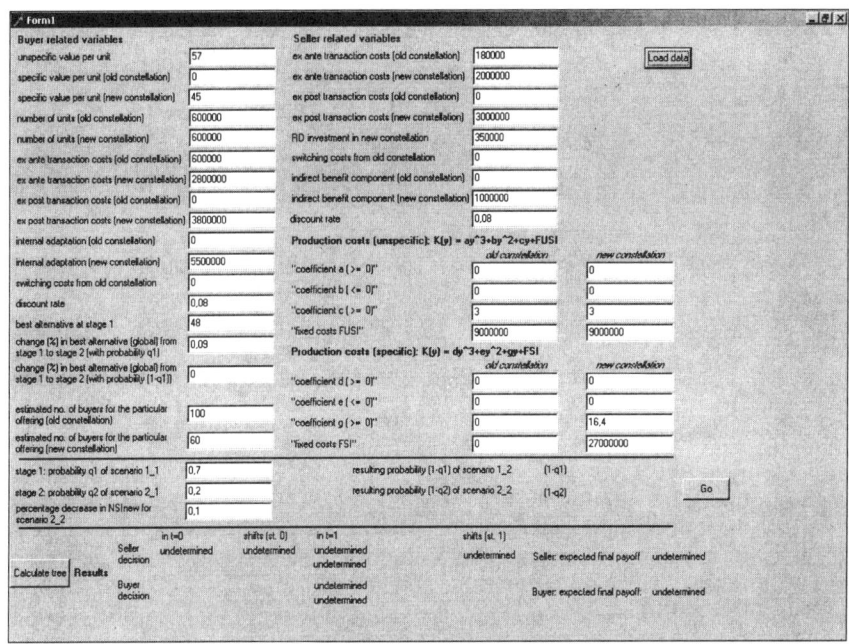

Fig. 22: Screenshot of entry mask for computer-supported model solution

The resulting equilibrium decisions of the players and the associated payoffs at all stages can be seen from the output mask which is depicted in *Fig. 23*. The upper part of the output mask contains the players payoffs at the respective terminal nodes with the discounted stage 1 payoffs on the left hand side and the discounted stage 2 payoffs on the right hand side. Below, the resulting equilibrium paths and the appended "final payoffs" are displayed. However, these "final payoffs" have to be interpreted with caution: they constitute only expected values so that the real values will generally deviate depending on the realizations of the nature moves. Also, the final payoffs do not necessarily coincide with the maximum payoffs due to the interaction between both players.

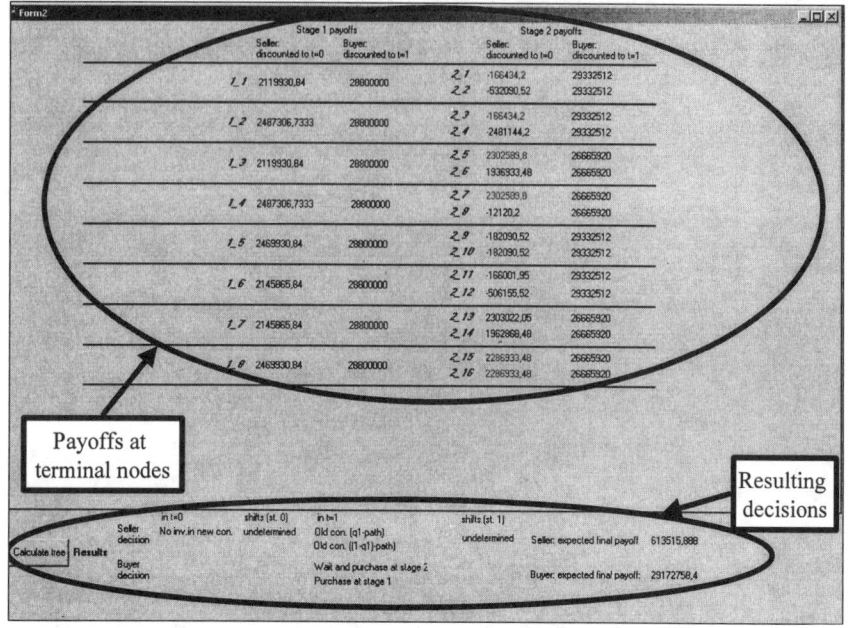

Fig. 23: Screenshot for output mask of point solution

4.5.2.4   Selected results from the model

Due to the large number of variables and possible combinations, a complete analysis of all main and interaction effects is not feasible within the scope of this work. Therefore, only some selected results are presented in the following section. The selection is based on two criteria. The first criterion is content-guided and relates to the meaningfulness of the chosen variables for a shift between business types. The second criterion is more formally oriented and is linked to the intention of presenting results which demonstrate the variableness of behavior that may emerge from the model. Based on these criteria, four results have been selected for presentation, namely, the joint impact of variations in R&D investment and probability $q2$, the joint impact of alternative R&D investments and varying improvements of the buyer's best available alternative throughout the game, the joint impact of variations in the seller's ex ante and ex post transaction costs in the new constellation, and, finally, the impact of variations in the probability $q2$. From these analyses, some interesting insights into conditions favoring or hindering shifts arise and thresholds are identified for changes in equilibrium strategies.[795] In particular, besides some intuitive results, other findings were unexpected.

4.5.2.4.1   The joint impact of the probability for an unfavorable stage 2 scenario and the R&D investment in the new constellation

The first selected result concerns the impact of different stage 2 probabilities $(1 - q2)$ for a decrease in specific benefits derived by the buyer from the new constellation compared to stage 1, and alterations in the R&D investment for the new constellation. Moreover, $q2$ is the probability of the "good" stage 2 scenario where no decrease in specific benefits derived by the buyer occurs. The complete configuration on which this result is based can be seen from appendix III.[796] The first presentation (*Fig. 24*) shows the seller's expected payoff (on the ordinate) plotted against the R&D investment (on the abscissa) with an underlying probability $q2 = 0.4$. The figure also depicts the seller's equilibrium strategies.

As can be seen from *Fig. 24*, a change in the seller's equilibrium strategy occurs at a necessary R&D investment of 290,000 €. In the left interval, the seller invests in the new constellation at stage 0, yet offers it only on the $(1-q1)$-path at stage 1 (terminal node "4"). On the $q1$-path, where the buyer's best available alternative is expected to have improved, the seller offers the old constellation instead (leading to terminal nodes I and II and expected value from both, respectively, since the buyer decides to wait and purchase at stage 2). For R&D investments over 290,000 €, no investment in the new constellation takes place, and the seller sticks to the old constellation throughout the game (leading to the terminal nodes IX and X on the $q1$-path, and to terminal node "8" on the $(1-q1)$-path). For that strategy, the seller's expected payoff is a constant since variations in the running variables leave it unaffected. The buyer's equilibrium strategy remains the same.

---

[795] The accuracy of the calculated thresholds obviously depends on the increments applied to the running variables. Particularly for large total ranges of certain parameters, the thresholds represent rougher approximations to the real threshold values. Such an approach seems, however, not too critical in view of the higher estimation imprecision that can be presumed to prevail for such parameters in business practice.

[796] See appendix III. The old constellation represents a bilateral product business, the new constellation a bilateral project or relational business.

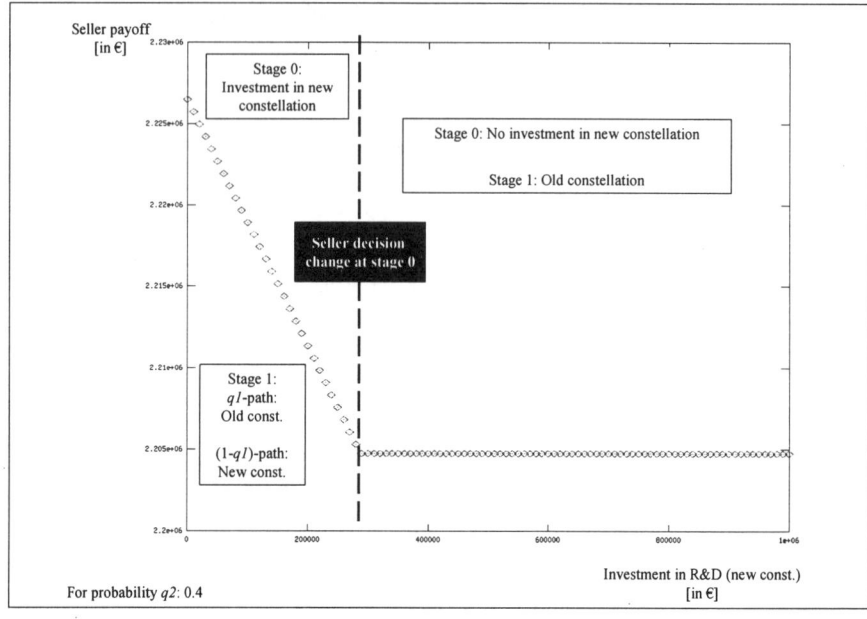

Seller payoff [in €]

Stage 0: Investment in new constellation

Stage 0: No investment in new constellation

Stage 1: Old constellation

Seller decision change at stage 0

Stage 1: $q1$-path: Old const.

$(1-q1)$-path: New const.

For probability $q2$: 0.4

Investment in R&D (new const.) [in €]

Fig. 24: The relationship between seller expected payoff and the investment in R&D for the new constellation[797]

The switch in equilibrium strategy can be observed for alternative values of $q2$, but it shifts towards higher parameter values of RD for increasing probabilities $q2$. This can be explained by the fact that higher probabilities of $q2$ (attached to the "good" scenario 2_1) relatively favor the new constellation and allow for higher R&D investments. *Fig. 25* shows this relationship. For instance, an R&D investment of 400,000 € in combination with a probability $q2$ of 0.5 yields an expected seller payoff of approximately 2.2 million €. The corresponding function is found in the plane in *Fig. 25*.

---

[797] The expected seller payoff in *Fig. 23* is given in exponential format meaning that the figure left of E is multiplied with 10 to the power of the figure on the right of E. For example, 1,000,000 is then written as "1 E 06". The same format applies to some other parameters in the following sections.

244

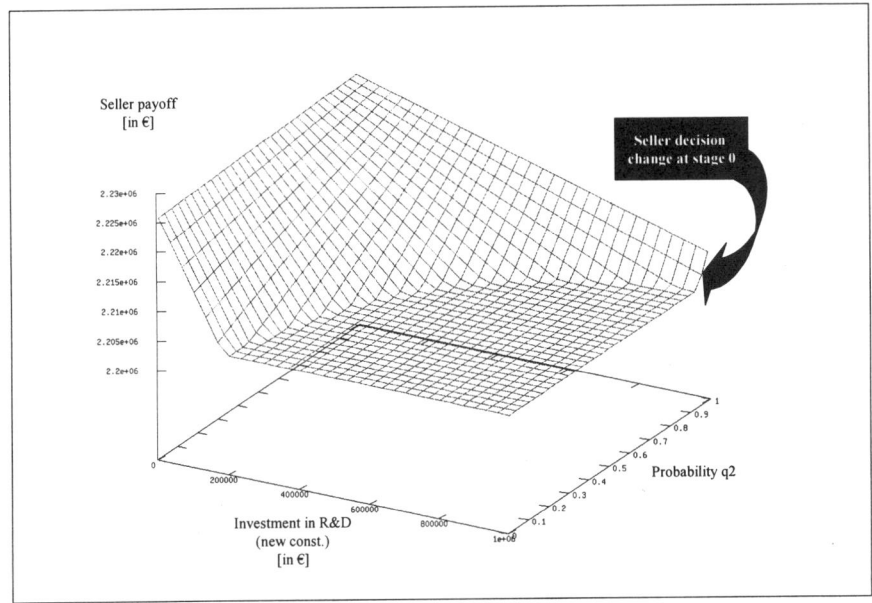

Fig. 25: The relationship between seller expected payoff, the investment in R&D for the new constellation and probability $q2$[798]

Overall, these findings support the conjecture that, above a certain threshold, R&D investments necessary for the development of the new constellation will generally prevent the seller from shifting. However, this effect is largely moderated by the impact of different scenario probabilities at later stages resulting in a considerable variance in the amount of R&D investment borne by an equilibrium strategy that supports the new constellation. Higher probabilities of a positive stage 2 scenario attach greater weight to considerations of keeping the option to offer the new constellation at that later stage.

4.5.2.4.2   The joint impact of R&D investment and improvement of the buyer's best available alternative in the course of the game

The second selection combines variations in R&D investment with different extents of relative improvement of the buyer's best available alternative throughout the game. First, the two-dimensional presentation in *Fig. 26* shows the expected seller payoff from his respective equilibrium strategies plotted against the relative improvement of the buyer's best alternative at stage 2 compared to stage 1 (δ_{1_1}). The results are based on an R&D investment of 350,000 € and a probability $q1$ of the relevant scenario 2_1 of 0.7. The complete configuration on which this result is based is available from appendix IV.[799]

For relative improvements up to 8% the seller's equilibrium strategy is to invest in the new constellation at stage 0 and to unconditionally offer the new constellation at stage 1, and as a result, also at stage 2. The buyer's corresponding equilibrium strategy is to purchase at stage 1 for $q1$-paths and $(1-q1)$-paths alike. Hence, the relevant terminal nodes are "2" and "4".

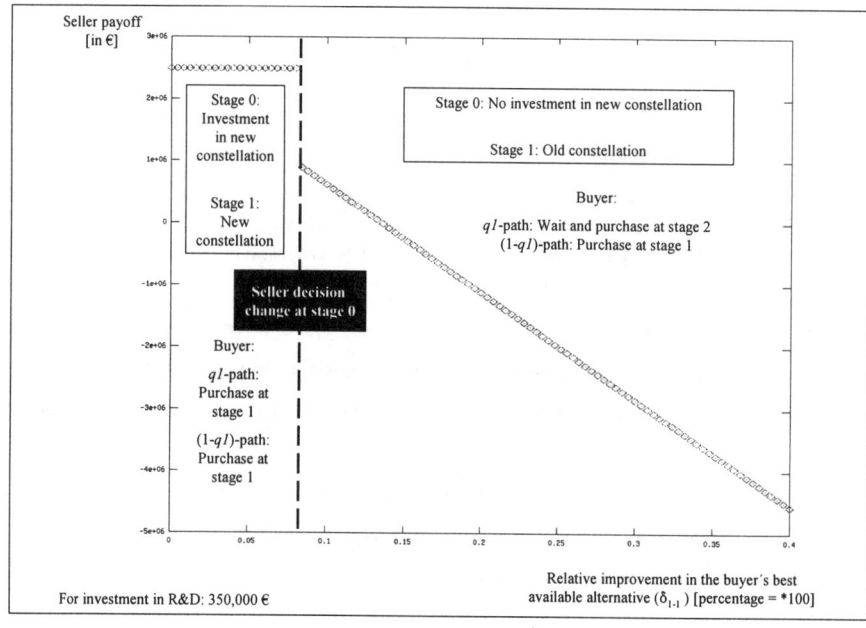

Fig. 26: The relationship between seller expected payoff and the relative improvement in the buyer's best available alternative at stage 2

With higher parameter values for the relative improvement in the buyer's best available alternative (on $q1$-paths), the buyer's equilibrium strategy changes becomes "Wait and

---

[798] The rather low variation in expected payoffs in this figure is due to the particular chosen configuration, but does not interfere with the general qualitative validity of the result that such model behavior occurs.

[799] See appendix IV. The old constellation represents a bilateral product business, the new constellation a bilateral project or relational business.

purchase at stage 2" for $q1$-paths while the optimal action on $(1-q1)$ remains unchanged. As a result, the seller is *forced* to another path where his new equilibrium strategy is not to invest at stage 0 and to unconditionally stick to the old constellation. The new equilibrium is found in the lower half of the tree where the relevant terminal nodes on the $q1$-path are IX and X, and the $(1-q1)$ path leads to terminal node "8". It is accompanied by a sudden dramatic decrease in the seller´s expected payoff.

This result fundamentally differs from the first finding. In the first case, the curve is continuous indicating that at the switching point, the seller is indifferent among his two equilibrium strategies which bring about exactly the same payoffs at this point.[800] The seller payoffs from his two equilibrium strategies converge towards each other until this point and then diverge again. Here, it is the buyer´s equilibrium strategy that changes, triggering a new equilibrium strategy on the part of the seller. No continuous convergence of payoffs takes place, resulting in the a discontinuity that is particularly evident from the three dimensional *Fig. 27*.

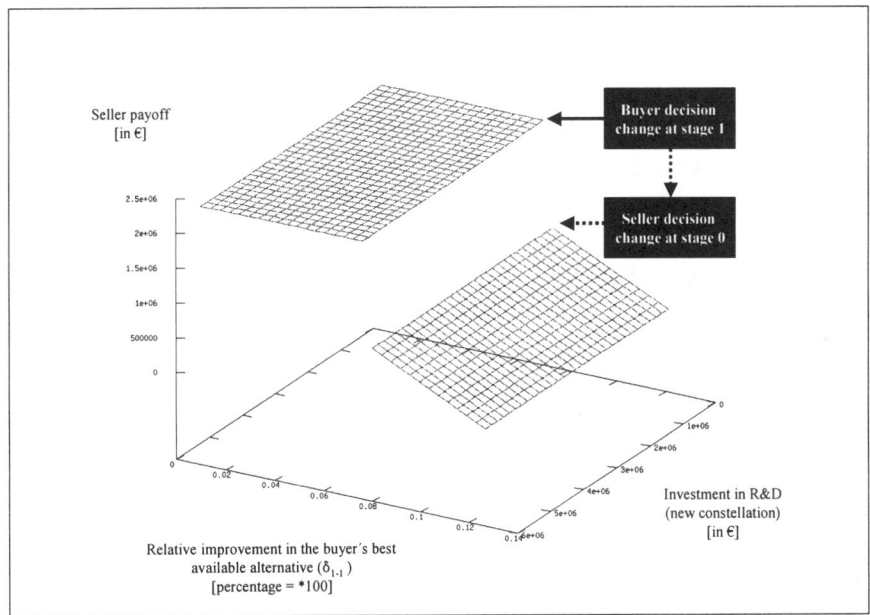

Fig. 27: The relationship between seller expected payoff, the relative improvement in the buyer´s best available alternative at stage 2 and the R&D investment

---

[800] The same reasoning underlies the third and fourth example (see chapters 4.5.2.4.3 and 4.5.2.4.4).

Both planes very slightly converge with increasing R&D investment in that the upper plane approaches the lower one.[801] Interestingly, up to a certain expected improvement, the competition's efforts to catch up do not affect the seller's expected payoff at all (upper plane), because they do not affect the buyer's unconditional choice for immediate purchase. However, for anticipated improvements in the best available alternative above that threshold, the result underscores an important assertion: namely, that competitive forces, if anticipated by the prospective buyer, may not only reduce the expected profits from an entrepreneurial shift to a new constellation, but may even completely restrain the seller from shifting.[802]

4.5.2.4.3 The joint impact of ex ante and ex post seller transaction costs incurred in the new constellation

The third selected result deals with the influence of variations in ex ante and ex post seller transaction costs for the new constellation. The two-dimensional graph in *Fig. 28* shows the expected seller payoff from his respective equilibrium strategies plotted against his ex ante transaction costs. The results are based on zero ex post transaction costs. Albeit this may seem as a very strict requirement, it does not affect the qualitative results. Moreover, it serves to highlight the whole spectrum of interesting behavior. The complete configuration on which this result is based is available from appendix V.[803]

As is apparent from *Fig. 28*, two different kinds of switch with respect to the seller's equilibrium strategies can be observed. First, at ex ante transaction costs of 2.7 million €, a decision change at stage 1 takes place. Below this parameter value, the seller's equilibrium strategy is to invest in the new constellation at stage 0, followed by offering the new constellation on both kinds of stage 1 paths. Since the buyer's equilibrium strategy implies waiting on $q1$-paths and immediate purchase on $(1-q1)$-paths, the relevant terminal nodes are III and IV for the $q1$-path, and "4" for the $(1-q1)$-path.

---

[801]   The effect is difficult to see from the diagram since it only amounts to 0.13% for the depicted range of *RD* against the background of the particular configuration.

[802]   The underlying mechanism bears some resemblance with the phenomenon of buyer leapfrogging behavior as documented both in the conceptual and empirical contributions (see e.g. *Weiber, R./Pohl, A.* (1996); *Büschken, J.* (2000); related *Tang, M.-J.* (1988), p. 87)

[803]   See appendix V. The old constellation represents a bilateral product business, the new constellation a bilateral project or relational business.

For ex ante transaction costs of 2.7 million € and above, the seller adopts a more differentiated action choice at stage 1: for $q1$-paths which are associated with a more adverse development of the competitive environment, he adopts the more cautious choice of offering the old constellation at stage 1 (which still implies the option to sell in the new constellation in case the "positive" scenario 2_1 results from the nature move at stage 2). For $(1-q1)$-paths, he keeps offering the new constellation. The buyer's equilibrium strategy remains unchanged, resulting in terminal node "4" still being the outcome of the $(1-q1)$-path. The $q1$-path, however, now leads to terminal nodes I and II.

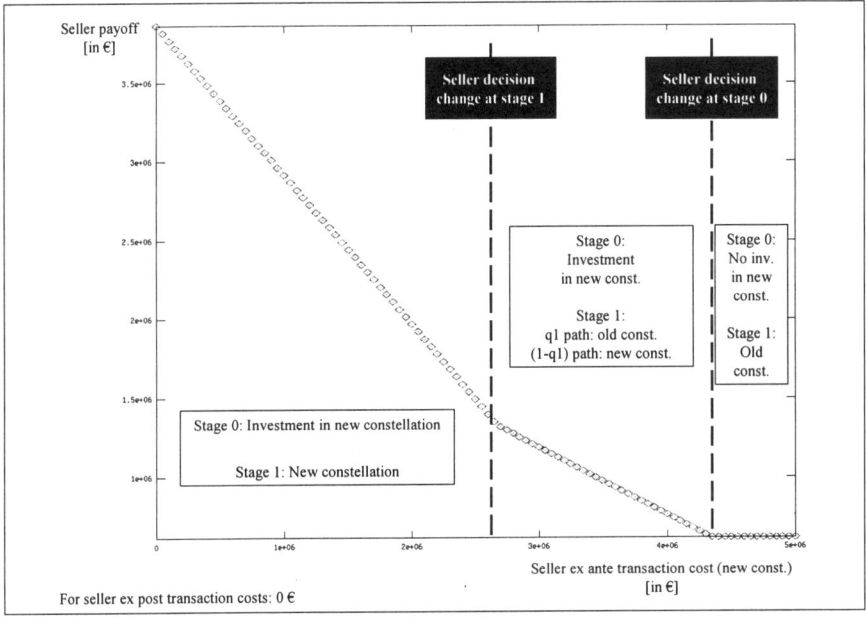

Fig. 28: The relationship between seller expected payoff and seller ex ante transaction costs in the new constellation

The seller's equilibrium strategy changes again at 4.35 million € ex ante transaction costs. Above this threshold, no investment in the new constellation occurs at any stage. The buyer's equilibrium strategy still implies waiting on the $q1$-path and immediate purchase on $(1-q1)$-path, leading to terminal nodes IX and X, and "8", respectively.

Subsequently, ex post transaction costs were added as a second running variable, resulting in the following Fig. 29. Again, both kinds of switch can be detected. A striking, albeit not

249

surprising effect, which can clearly be seen from *Fig. 29* concerns the impact of different discounting horizons for the two transaction cost categories. Both of the seller's equilibrium strategies involving an investment in the new constellation (lower and medium interval) are, all other things being equal, supported by higher thresholds for ex post transactions costs than for ex ante transaction costs.

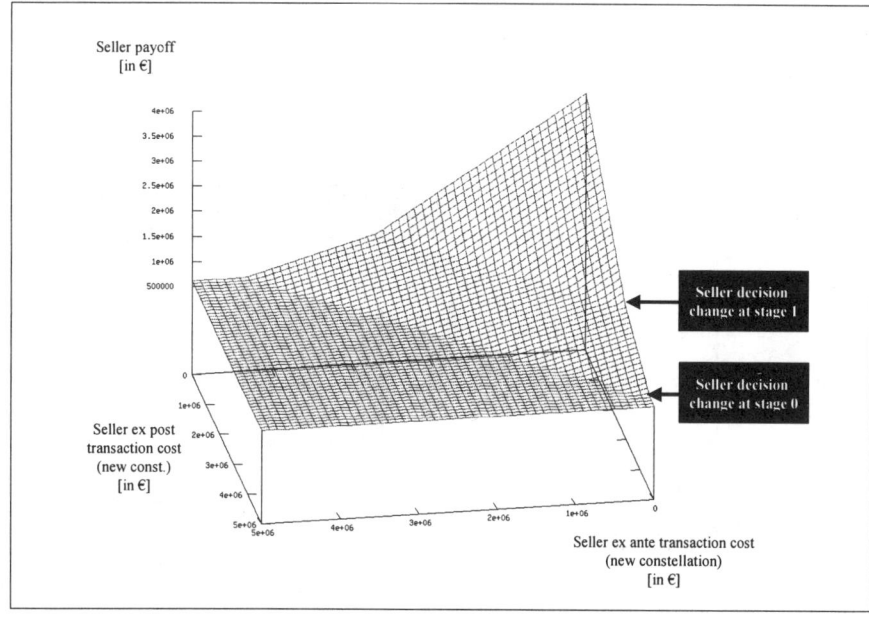

Fig. 29: The relationship between seller expected payoff, seller ex ante transaction costs and seller ex post transaction costs (both for the new constellation)

Overall, the results support the theoretically-derived assertion that rising transaction costs for the new constellation relatively discriminate it. However, they open up more differentiated perspectives: the successive "parting" from the new constellation in view of rising attached transaction costs, nicely illustrates the idea of keeping the option to offer the new constellation in case of favorable environmental conditions at stage 2. This sequence of equilibrium strategies requires at least some moderate relative improvement of the buyer's best available alternative over the course of the game.[804] Only then, the buyer's equilibrium strategy in the

---

[804] For the particular configuration, the necessary minimum percentage of improvement amounts to 9%.

relevant range includes the choice to wait until stage 2 for purchase (on $q1$-paths), making in turn the hold out choice part of the seller's equilibrium strategy in the medium interval.

4.5.2.4.4   *Some particularities of the impact of the probability for an unfavorable stage 2 scenario*

The fourth selected result relates to some particular findings with respect to the impact of different stage 2 probabilities $q2$ where $(1-q2)$ refers to the "bad" scenario of a decrease in specific benefits derived by the buyer from the new constellation compared to stage 1.[805] The complete configuration on which this result is based can be seen from appendix VI.[806] *Fig. 30* depicts the relationship between the seller's expected payoff from the decision (on the ordinate) and the probability $q2$ (on the abscissa), whereby $q2$ is the probability of the "good" stage 2 scenario where no decrease in specific benefits derived by the buyer occurs. In addition, the seller's equilibrium strategies are shown.

Over the whole range of $q2$, two stage 0 changes in the recommended shift decision can be observed.[807] First, for very low probabilities $q2$, that is, for a high likelihood of the "bad" decrease scenario, the seller's equilibrium strategy is – as one would expect – not to invest in the new constellation at either stage. Consequently, he offers the old constellation in both stage 2 scenarios which prevents the expected payoff from being influenced by variations in $q2$. This is relevant because the buyer's equilibrium strategy implies waiting until the second stage for the $q1$ and the $(1-q1)$ path alike. The terminal nodes corresponding to this equilibrium are IX, X, XV, and XVI.

---

[805]   In this particular case, a decrease of 90% is assumed. Although this decrease figure may at first sight seem rather high, it is not unrealistic in view of the dramatic consequences that may be associated, for instance, with changes in legal regulations (for a recent example consider the intended introduction of beverage can deposits by the German government and the reactions by the relevant industries). The results hold, in principle, also for lower decrease percentages down to 85%, and, for the first change down to 80%. The old constellation represents a kind of a product business, while the new constellation resembles the more specific business types.

[806]   See appendix VI. The old constellation can best be described as a bilateral product business, the new constellation as a bilateral project or relational business.

[807]   In fact, the depicted equilibrium strategies apply to the configurations just below and above the threshold. At the threshold, that is, at the very set of parameter values which marks the switch point, the seller is indifferent among both of these equilibrium strategies. Hence, there is not one but two subgame perfect Nash equilibria at this point.

As *q2* rises, that is, the probability of the "bad" scenario falls, the new constellation becomes relatively more favorable until at *q2* = 13,74% the seller´s equilibrium strategy changes. It is now optimal for him to invest in the new constellation at stage 0 and to unconditionally offer the new constellation at stage 1. Increasing expected payoffs (at terminal nodes III, IV, IX and X) are appended to this strategy.

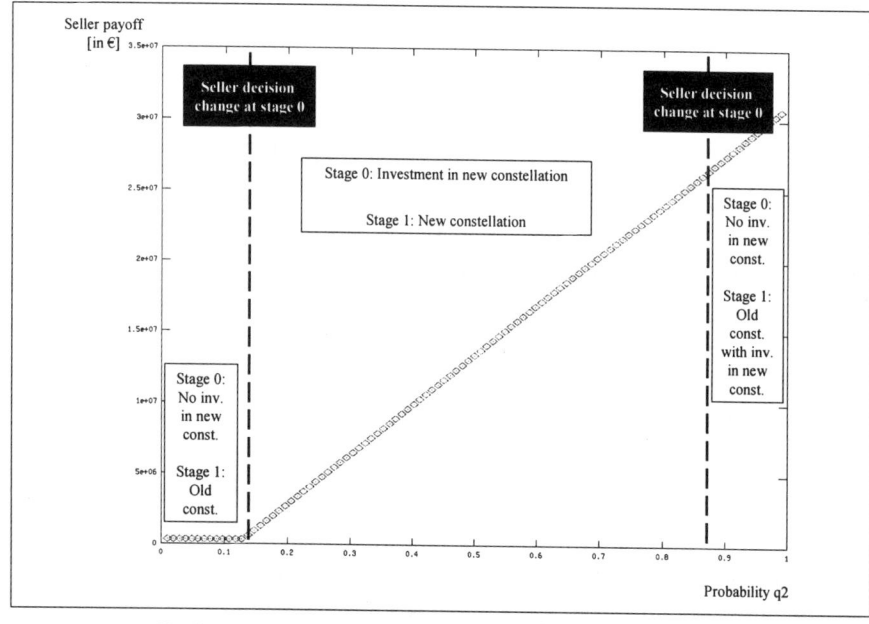

Fig. 30: The relationship between seller expected payoff and probability q2

Nevertheless, and this finding surprises at first sight, at *q2* = 87,24%, another switch in the seller´s equilibrium strategy occurs. Above that probability *q2*, the optimal seller strategy is to forgo investment at stage 0, and to offer the old constellation at stage 1. Yet, in doing so, he should (unconditionally) undertake a simultaneous investment in the new constellation at stage 1, thereby acquiring the ability to offer the new constellation at stage 2 in case scenario 2_1 occurs. This is relevant, since the buyer´s equilibrium strategy still implies waiting until the second stage for the *q1*-path as well as for the (1-*q1*)-path. The resulting terminal nodes are XI, XII, XIII, and XIV. This new equilibrium strategy is, again, associated with increasing payoffs for the seller. This increase takes place at a different, higher slope. However, due to

252

the very small difference in slope, this switch can not readily be seen from the graphic presentation, but is apparent from the underlying data.[808]

Yet, the question arises why this effect has not led much earlier to the occurrence of the third equilibrium strategy, or, even its substitution for the second one. Several factors need to come together to explain this counter-intuitive result of a second stage 0 decision switch. In essence, it can be traced back to the variations in the weightings $q2$ and $(1-q2)$ with which the individual payoffs at the terminal nodes at stage 2 enter into the computation of the expected payoffs at stage 2, because the buyer unconditionally waits until the second stage in both intervals. The postponed investment in the lower half of the tree (where the third equilibrium appears) generally favors the stage 2 terminal nodes that are associated with offering the new constellation. However, this effect is hampered in the medium interval by another offsetting effect: in the lower half of the tree, the seller offers the old constellation on $(1-q2)$-paths, unlike in the upper half of the tree where he offers the new constellation on such paths.[809] And this offering is, under the particular conditions, associated with lower profits, with the R&D investments lacking allocation being a prominent explanatory factor. This effect becomes, though, less pronounced with decreasing probabilities $q2$ that represent the weight with which these branches enter into the expected payoff calculation. The first effect, which promotes the lower half of the tree and ultimately brings forth the third equilibrium, becomes dominant.

Overall, the above results reveal an interesting model behavior for the optimal seller strategy depending on the parameter value $q2$. The weightings attached to the two possible scenarios at stage 2, hence, require careful estimation, because the seller's optimal strategy exhibits a counter-intuitive switch for high probabilities of the "good" scenario.

4.5.3   Some supplementary considerations on value division

The above results have shown that the considered shift is not always part of the equilibrium strategy, that is, it is not always assertable under efficient conditions. A further – not surprising – observation was that, depending on the particular configuration, even equilibrium

---

[808]   The increase in slope from the medium interval to the upper interval amounts to only 0.615%.

[809]   There, having shifted to the new constellation already at stage 1, the seller is required, per assumption, to offer the new constellation on $(1-q2)$-paths.

strategies may have negative expected payoffs attached to them as outcomes, irrespective of whether these strategies include solely the new, or the old constellation, or both of them (see e.g. *Fig. 26* and *Fig. 27*). With such an outcome, the seller can be expected to abstain from the transaction with that particular buyer. Yet, two additional points need to be made about this inference.

First, under a different value division regime, in particular one that would allow the seller to set a *lower* price than one just below the critical price, the seller could considerably raise his expected payoff. Roughly speaking, this means that by granting a larger piece of the pie to the buyer, a mutually beneficial result could be achieved.[810] The key to this outcome is that such a regime might allow moving to an entirely different path, that is, changing the respective equilibrium strategies. The following *Fig. 31* illustrates the principal idea based on a 15% improvement of the buyer's best alternative over the course of the game in scenario 1_1 and a likelihood of this scenario of 70%. The case refers to the issue treated in chapter 4.5.2.4.3. While the rectangular boxes mark the outcomes under the value division regime adopted above, the dashed ellipses (in the original payoff structure) indicate scope for a mutually beneficial change in division regime. The solid ellipses show how the seller could considerably push his own expected payoff by just overcompensating the buyer in case of an immediate purchase at stage 1 for the foregone benefits from waiting for the improvement of his alternatives at stage 2.[811] Specifically, in the example, the seller could move from an expected loss of approximately 250,000 € to an expected profit of approximately 1.07 million €.

---

[810] This alternative division might also be brought forth by greater bargaining power of the buyer. Hence, the result is in line with recent findings by *Iyer, G./Villas-Boas, M. J.* (2003) on channel coordination. In their game-theoretic analysis of bargaining processes between a manufacturer and a retailer, they find that different degrees of bargaining power of the parties may have a considerable effect on the size of the total pie (total channel profits) which is to be divided. In particular, they identify conditions under which greater retailer power leads to an increase in the overall channel pie which provides the manufacturer with higher profits (in absolute terms) despite a reduction in the manufacturer's share of the pie.

[811] Investigation into how precisely the rules of the game would have to be designed to support this outcome is beyond the scope of this work. In any case, the results illustrate that under certain rules and in certain configurations, players are trapped in an equilibrium that does not maximize their joint benefits. The situation somewhat resembles the famous Prisoner's Dilemma which constitutes the paradigmatic case for conditions under which a mutually unfavorable equilibrium emerges because individual and collective rationality collide. For basic discussions of this game which is generally attributed to *A. W. Tucker*, see e.g. *Luce, R. D./Raiffa, H.* (1967), p. 94ff.

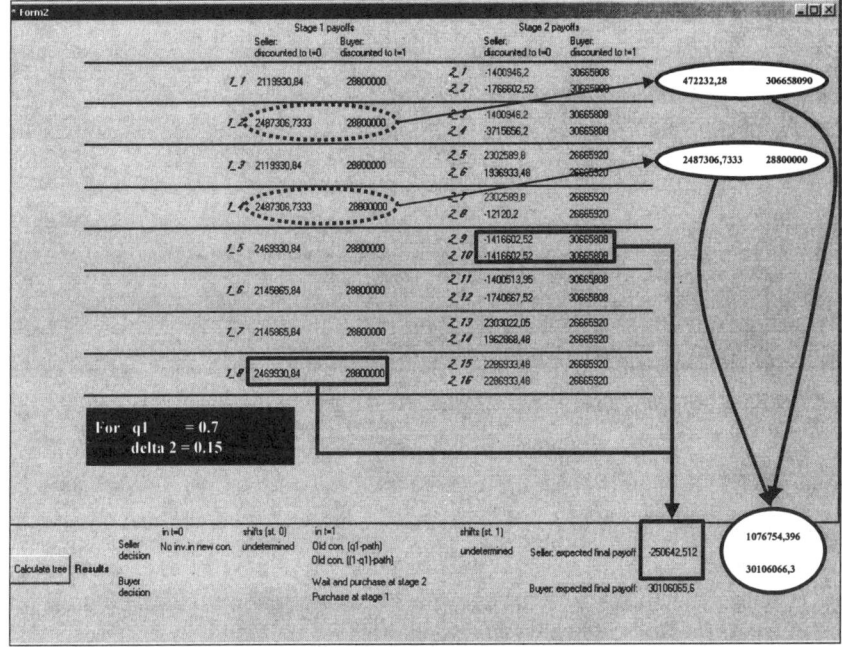

Fig. 31: Example of realizing mutual benefits from a change in pie division principle

This finding provides quantitative support for the idea that the particular adopted division principle crucially affects the potential gains to the transaction parties – either to their detriment or to their advantage. Based on an empirical study, such a position has recently been outlined by *Jap* (2001).[812] Adopting a more cooperative perspective on value division than most of the literature, she finds a significant effect from different pie sharing principles and varying characteristics of organizations and resources on relationship quality in complex collaboration contexts.

The **second** additional aspect concerns the seller's influence on the buyer's set of alternatives. If the seller was able to impact on the best available alternative to the buyer *prior to the game* and/or on its development *throughout the game*, this would significantly change both players' expected payoffs and might also alter the players' equilibrium strategies. However, unlike the first option, this option does not imply the creation of mutual benefits made possible through a

---

[812] See *Jap, S. D.* (2001).

change in the rules of the game, but rests on a unilateral improvement of the seller's situation. This is not surprising given that the key to this route is structural market power – or, more precisely, excessive ex ante market power on the part of the seller in the relation to this buyer. Changes in the structural market power can thereby let a new constellation become relevant that has previously not been accessible.[813]

4.5.4   Concluding remarks on insights from and limitations of the extended model

Based on an extended game theoretic model, various conditions were identified to be either conducive or impedimentary for the envisaged shift direction. Sensitivities of (seller) payoff and (seller) equilibrium strategy (that is, whether to shift or not) were analyzed with respect to several relevant variables. The results revealed some very distinct forms of model behavior under various conditions. Yet, the explanatory power, particularly of the concrete numerical results, must be evaluated with great care. Generally, the particular assumptions underlying the theoretical should be taken into account as well as the fact that business reality can be expected to be far from meeting these requirements. The degree of this divergence determines the model's practical applicability, which constitutes one, but not the sole criterion for evaluating its usefulness. In any case, explicit exposition of the models's limitations is helpful in creating transparency with respect to which insights can and cannot be expected to be gained from the model. Mainly two areas of limitations are discussed in the following, namely limitations resulting from the model design and such that concern the particular solution method and the use of the model.

First, consider **limitations of the model** (design). The following restrictions are particularly important with respect to an assessment of the model and the interpretation of its results.

- The information which is available to the actors has been assumed to be uncertain, yet perfect. This is a very ambitious assumption compared to the informational conditions that are likely to prevail in practice, and also with regard to the assumption of bounded rationality in TCA.

---

[813] See chapter 3.3.4; also explicitly on this issue *Heide, J. B./John, G.* (1992), p. 41.

- In line with a common working assumption of TCA, all actors have been assumed to be risk neutral. The inclusion of other risk attitudes can be expected to produce different results.

- The continuous process of business interaction has been broken down into discrete stages. The number of discrete stages that are considered is limited to two.

- Only a limited number of variables has been allowed to change from one stage to the other (namely best available alternative, specific benefits of the new constellation).

Second, limitations associated with the particular **solution and the use of the model** need to be considered. In particular, the following aspects deserve attention.

- *First*, the adopted solution method is simulative in nature. As already mentioned, an analytical solution can be derived.[814] Yet, it would not be very instructive with respect to its interpretation. In order to extract concrete, meaningful results, it would again be necessary to investigate the effects of variations in the parameter values. This is achieved in a much more illustrative way by the simulative solution which possesses the additional advantage of a highly flexible handling with respect to further research interests.

- A *second* concern relates to the general problem of input data reliability and its consequences for the use of this model. In fact, the availability of the necessary data represents a crucial concern for even the most tentative ambition to use this model as a rough indicator in a shift decision. Two main problems emerge: (1) the relevant buyer data (including information on his best alternative) are likely to be difficult if not impossible to obtain and estimates are likely to be rather vague in nature, and (2) the availability of seller data is also likely to be hampered owing to the structure and design of the firm's accounting and controlling system, and the subjective nature of many elements such as transaction costs. Hence, knowledge about the stability of the findings would be important for practical applicability.

---

[814] This would require capturing the process of backward solution in a formal system of inequality equations as it has been, in principle, realized in the program source code.

- The first way to address this issue would be to allow for all variables to vary simultaneously in the same way as provided for by the solution at hand for a maximum of two variables at a time. However, the complexity of the results and limits to the possibility of graphical depiction would represent major obstacles with respect to an interpretation.

- The second way to potentially overcome the problem would be to ascribe distribution functions to each parameter. However, this is not likely to ensure much success: first, the question of which distribution function is attributed to each parameter needs to be answered based on solid substantiation. Second, in case various distribution functions come into consideration, the question of various possible combinations with the other parameters arises. With respect to the great number and variety of parameters included in the model, the existence of a theoretical framework or empirical evidence offering unambiguous guidelines to these questions is difficult to imagine. An attempt to arrive at meaningful results based on distribution functions derived from plausibility considerations would be hampered by three additional handicaps: the computer capacities demanded would be substantial. The ultimate results would again hold at best for the particular configuration: accounting for uncertainty of its data would not help to solve the problem universally. That is, the possibility of radically different results for configurations which are structured in a fundamentally different way is not tackled. Last but not least, it would be very difficult to derive meaningful results with respect to individual influence factors from the results.

Overall, these reflections, and in particular those on the adopted solution method, support the approach chosen in this work. In general, modeling is subject to abstractions and necessarily departs from real life's variety. The above model has, despite its obvious limitations, been able to support some qualitatively-derived conjectures. Moreover, it has generated some counter-intuitive, yet meaningful findings. With just four examples having been outlined in detail, more variables of the model remain to be explored and, possibly, interesting effects remain to be discovered.

5   Conclusion

5.1   Summary

The starting point of the above analysis was the empirical observation that companies tend to change their market offerings fundamentally at times, where "fundamentally" refers to a holistically interpreted change in the way they transact with their (prospective) buyers. Against this background, it is not only relevant from the viewpoint of business practice, but also interesting from a theoretical perspective to *systematically* explore underlying motivations for and potential prerequisites of such seller-initiated redesigns of market offerings.

The investigation at hand has sought to provide some tentative insights into these issues based on a typological systematization of transactions on industrial markets which is rooted in transaction cost reasoning. Building on existing approaches in this field the business types framework adopted here constitutes the kernel of the static foundations of the shift analysis. Focusing on asset specificity as the categorizing criterion, three distinct business types (product, project and relational business) are identified. Compared to its conceptual roots, the presented concept exhibits mainly one distinguishing feature, namely a more explicit differentiation between seller and buyer perspective. Therefore, each party in a transaction is assigned one of the three business types contingent upon its asset specificity position. Merging both perspectives gives the complete picture of the transaction which is captured in the notion of a "business types constellation". Symmetric business type combinations are referred to as congruent constellations, and asymmetric ones as disgruent.

In defining the construct in detail, emphasis has been laid on the idea that technological and contractual properties of a transaction jointly determine a party's specificity position and are, at least to a certain degree, substitutable in nature with respect to creating or reducing asset specificity. Interpreting the choice of a firm to adopt a particular constellation in its selling efforts as strategic in nature, led over to a dynamic perspective that conceives the systematizing dimension asset specificity not as given, but as a variable which is susceptible to alteration by the involved parties. A substantial alteration in the level and horizon of asset specificity of either one or both parties is regarded as a change in business type (constellation), and, if it is seller-initiated, is referred to as a strategic shift in the sense of this analysis.

In terms of its *foundations*, such understanding crucially hinges on the idea of asset specificity's technological indeterminism. In terms of its *consequences*, it calls for the identification of factors that impact on the choice of specific investment. For the business types framework, these influencing factors have been derived from transaction cost theory, though involving some rearrangements and supplements. In particular, a more explicit, sequential ordering of the transaction determinants' effects has been proposed with uncertainty operating as an antecedent to the choice of asset specificity. Moreover, some factors have been integrated as impacts that are just beginning to receive noteworthy attention in conceptual discussions on transaction cost theory, like, for instance, path dependencies and (ex ante) structural market power.

Building on the so-established general feasibility of shifts between business types, motivations that may induce shift considerations or are attached to them have been discussed. Starting with value creation, claim and protection as relevant objectives, the impact of different congruent and disgruent initial business types constellations on the direction of shift considerations has been explored. Drawing on insights from research on power and dependence relations, four propositions were advanced which center around the higher stability of congruent constellations in view of potential change impulses, and around different goal weightings guiding shift considerations in different directions. In concluding this qualitative discussion of motivations and necessary prerequisites, the scope for impulses to play an important role in proactive, entrepreneurial strategic shifts has been explored. By supplementing transaction cost reasoning with arguments from Austrian economics, it was possible to identify the occurrence of subjective knowledge increases in response to informational impulses as a necessary condition for a proactive shift to take place. Based on the value net that is embedded in a particular environment and that links a firm to its customer, competitors, complementors and suppliers, relevant sources of such impulses were identified and illustrated by the presentation of various examples and their likely impact on the targeted shift direction.

However, even if these proposed necessary shift conditions were fulfilled, that is, if the seller firm under scrutiny was aiming at a particular shift, a quantitatively-oriented assessment of whether it would likely be able to profitably seize the detected shift opportunity was still lacking. This idea translated into the postulation of "efficient assertability" as a sufficient condition for a successful shift. This means that the particular seller firm characterized by its path-dependent resource access conditions and abilities must be able to make the buyer accept the new constellation at terms which are profit-enhancing from the seller's perspective. The subsequent in-depth investigation of this issue was guided by the central assumption that the buyer can always be "convinced" to purchase from the seller, because his acceptance is ultimately at matter of price. The substantiation of exchanges failing to be accomplished has, thereby, been completely relocated to the seller.

Having briefly sketched out the problem of legal constraints imposing restrictions on particular constellations or shifts, a formal economic model has been advanced for capturing the idea of "efficient assertability". First, building on three related transaction cost-based models, a model for comparative analysis of constellations was proposed. Payoff functions were derived for both parties with references to the identified influence factors on the choice of asset specificity. The application of the model has been illustrated using a case study from the chemical industry. From the example, two further issues became apparent: first, explicit consideration of variations in the data input, e.g. via sensitivity analysis, should be able to strengthen the meaningfulness of the output information. Second, explicitly accounting for the interactive transaction dimension might improve the insights to be gained from the model.

In response to these concerns, the model was extended to a simple game theoretic model of the dyadic relationship between a seller and a buyer, and data variations were integrated in the analysis. In addition, two issues of prime importance to the strategic shift decision were schematically incorporated, namely path dependency and flexibility. The extended model was developed to serve the more general objective of representing a theoretically-guided heuristic framework for reflecting on shifts between business types constellations. The second, more concrete objective was to learn about effects that may result from variations in the parameter values of the payoff function elements on the efficient assertability of a particular shift. Within the scope of this work, this second purpose was investigated by means of giving some examples. Nevertheless, based on a computer simulation, it was possible to extract some interesting results from the model and display them in an instructive way. Sensitivities of the seller's payoff and equilibrium strategy were analyzed with respect to several variables. In particular, the following exemplifying findings were gained based on specific data configurations. Whereas the first three are mainly corroborative with respect to expectations that could be formed based on the employed theoretical reasoning, the fourth result is rather counter-intuitive.

- As expected, R&D investments in the new constellation were found to prevent the seller from shifting if they exceeded a certain threshold. This effect was moderated by the impact of different probabilities for unfavorable scenarios at a later stage of the game.

- As expected, improvements of the buyer's best available alternative throughout the game that exceeded a certain threshold were found to first provoke switches in the buyer's optimal choices and, thereby, then trigger a change in the seller's best strategy. The finding supports the idea that effects from strong competition, if they are anticipated by prospective buyers, may not only reduce the profits that the entrepreneurial firm could reap from a shift, but may keep it from shifting completely.

- As expected, high transaction costs in the new constellation (here on the seller-side) were found to create conditions that are unfavorable to the shift. Starting with low transaction costs, a gradual increase of these costs was found to cause a stepwise "parting" from the new constellation. This reflects the value of maintaining some flexibility regarding the scope of possible offerings at later stages.

- The sole effect of the probability for unfavorable conditions at a later stage was found to exhibit some interesting properties. In particular, two changes in the seller's optimal decision at the first stage (investment or no investment in the new constellation) were observed. This result was explained basically on the grounds of changing weightings attached to individual payoffs at the later stage.

Finally, some supplementary considerations on value division were presented based on the observations from the simulation. The particular adopted division principle was found to potentially have an important effect on the likelihood of a shift occurrence, and issues concerning the impact of structurally-founded market power were briefly discussed.

5.2   Limitations and directions for further research

Overall, this work represents only a first tentative step in the direction of better understanding seller-initiated shifts between business types, their underlying motivations, and conducive or unfavorable conditions. In particular, the following limitations have to be taken into account when assessing the model's contribution to the topic.

- **Empirical domain:** Due to the purely conceptual nature of this work, empirical research to either support or dismiss the theoretically-derived hypotheses and results is needed. In particular, the proposed framework on asset specificity as a choice variable and the effect directions of the outlined impulses appear as suitable candidates.

- **Variations in the model:** The quantitative model necessarily implies a number of significant abstractions from business reality. The main concerns relate to the model's generalizability, the reliability of input data and the meaningfulness of the output information. While all three areas of imposed restrictions offer scope for further research, a few issues deserve to be singled out: some interesting effects were not explicitly modeled but relocated to the payoff functions and incorporated only implicitly in hypotheses concerning type specific parameter values in the payoff functions. To name just a few examples, the time structure within long-term project businesses or relational businesses could explicitly be analyzed in a next step. Investigating whether more explicit depiction of the differences between these two business types would convey valuable insights, might also be an interesting topic. Another aspect is that so far, only implicit provision has been made for the influence of structural market power which would, for instance, be reflected in a higher perceived danger of exploitation and, consequently, higher transaction costs on the part of the "weaker" transaction partner. Additionally, changes in the rules of the game, e.g. alternative assumptions on information and knowledge, on value division rules or even explicit allowance for bargaining, might reveal further interesting aspects. Related are questions about indirect influence capabilities on the part of the seller to create conducive conditions (e.g. shared history) *prior* to initiating the actual shift.

- **Theoretical domain:** Further research on possibilities of and obstacles to the integration of insights from different theoretical streams such as transaction cost theory and Austrian economics seems promising. Also, investigations into the usefulness of formal models (for instance building on game theory[815]) and their concrete design might provide valuable insights both from a theoretical and a practical perspective. Appropriate modeling of information structures and, in particular, the condition of bounded rationality pose a substantial challenge.

---

[815] See e.g. the recent work by *Aoki, M.* (2001) who adopts a game theoretcially-oriented perspective on comparative institutional analysis.

Appendices

1. Foundations of business activities and structures of relevant markets

2. Foundations of customer buying decision processes in the relevant business

3. Traditional business model (business types constellation) including payment conditions

4. New business model(s) including payment conditions

5. Evaluation of business models in terms of business types constellations

6. Supplier calculation and expectations associated with implied shift in business types constellation

7. Buyer calculation and expectations associated with implied shift in business types constellation

Appendix II: Tables of payoff functions used in the extended model

Seller and buyer payoffs at terminal nodes for transaction at stage 1

Stage 1 terminal node 1

Buyer	$U_N = (kko_1 \cdot x_1)$
Crit. Price	$p = N_{USI} + N_{SI\_old} - \dfrac{Tr_{(N)\,ea\_old} \cdot (1 + r_{(N)}) + Tr_{(N)ep\_old} + M_{old}}{x_1} - kko_1$
Seller	$\pi_A = -RD + \dfrac{p \cdot x_1 - C_{USI\_old} - C_{SI\_old} - \left[Tr_{(A)\,ea\_old} \cdot (1 + r_{(A)}) \right] - Tr_{(A)\,ep\_old} + \dfrac{a\_old}{n\_old}}{1 + r_{(A)}}$

Stage 1 terminal node 2

Buyer	$U_N = (kko_1 \cdot x_1)$
Crit. Price	$p = N_{USI} + N_{SI\_new} - \dfrac{Tr_{(N)\,ea\_new} \cdot (1 + r_{(N)}) + Tr_{(N)ep\_new} + M_{new} + W_{(N)}}{x_2} - kko_1$
Seller	$\pi_A = -RD + \dfrac{p \cdot x_1 - C_{USI\_new} - C_{SI\_new} - \left[Tr_{(A)\,ea\_new} \cdot (1 + r_{(A)}) \right] - Tr_{(A)\,ep\_new} + \dfrac{a\_new + W_{(A)}}{n\_new}}{1 + r_{(A)}}$

Stage 1 terminal node 3

Buyer	$U_N = (kko_1 \cdot x_1)$
Crit. Price	$p = N_{USI} + N_{SI\_old} - \dfrac{Tr_{(N)\,ea\_old} \cdot (1 + r_{(N)}) + Tr_{(N)ep\_old} + M_{old}}{x_1} - kko_1$
Seller	$\pi_A = -RD + \dfrac{p \cdot x_1 - C_{USI\_old} - C_{SI\_old} - \left[Tr_{(A)\,ea\_old} \cdot (1 + r_{(A)}) \right] - Tr_{(A)\,ep\_old} + \dfrac{a\_old}{n\_old}}{1 + r_{(A)}}$

Stage 1 terminal node 4

Buyer	$U_N = (kko_1 \cdot x_1)$
Crit. Price	$p = N_{USI} + N_{SI\_new} - \dfrac{Tr_{(N)\,ea\_new} \cdot (1 + r_{(N)}) + Tr_{(N)ep\_new} + M_{new} + W_{(N)}}{x_2} - kko_1$
Seller	$\pi_A = -RD + \dfrac{p \cdot x_1 - C_{USI\_new} - C_{SI\_new} - \left[Tr_{(A)\,ea\_new} \cdot (1 + r_{(A)})\right] - Tr_{(A)\,ep\_new} + \dfrac{a\_new + W_{(A)}}{n\_new}}{1 + r_{(A)}}$

Stage 1 terminal node 5

Buyer	$U_N = (kko_1 \cdot x_1)$
Crit. Price	$p = N_{USI} + N_{SI\_old} - \dfrac{Tr_{(N)\,ea\_old} \cdot (1 + r_{(N)}) + Tr_{(N)ep\_old} + M_{old}}{x_1} - kko_1$
Seller	$\pi_A = \dfrac{p \cdot x_1 - C_{USI\_old} - C_{SI\_old} - \left[Tr_{(A)\,ea\_old} \cdot (1 + r_{(A)})\right] - Tr_{(A)\,ep\_old} + \dfrac{a\_old}{n\_old}}{1 + r_{(A)}}$

Stage 1 terminal node 6

Buyer	$U_N = (kko_1 \cdot x_1)$
Crit. Price	$p = N_{USI} + N_{SI\_old} - \dfrac{Tr_{(N)\,ea\_old} \cdot (1 + r_{(N)}) + Tr_{(N)ep\_old} + M_{old}}{x_1} - kko_1$
Seller	$\pi_A = -RD + \dfrac{p \cdot x_1 - C_{USI\_old} - C_{SI\_old} - \left[Tr_{(A)\,ea\_old} \cdot (1 + r_{(A)})\right] - Tr_{(A)\,ep\_old} + \dfrac{a\_old}{n\_old}}{1 + r_{(A)}}$

Stage 1 terminal node 7

Buyer	$U_N = (kko_1 \cdot x_1)$
Crit. Price	$p = N_{USI} + N_{SI\_old} - \dfrac{Tr_{(N)\,ea\_old} \cdot (1 + r_{(N)}) + Tr_{(N)ep\_old} + M_{old}}{x_1} - kko_1$
Seller	$\pi_A = -RD + \dfrac{p \cdot x_1 - C_{USI\_old} - C_{SI\_old} - \left[Tr_{(A)\,ea\_old} \cdot (1 + r_{(A)}) \right] - Tr_{(A)\,ep\_old} + \dfrac{a\_old}{n\_old}}{1 + r_{(A)}}$

Stage 1 terminal node 8

Buyer	$U_N = (kko_1 \cdot x_1)$
Crit. Price	$p = N_{USI} + N_{SI\_old} - \dfrac{Tr_{(N)\,ea\_old} \cdot (1 + r_{(N)}) + Tr_{(N)ep\_old} + M_{old}}{x_1} - kko_1$
Seller	$\pi_A = \dfrac{p \cdot x_1 - C_{USI\_old} - C_{SI\_old} - \left[Tr_{(A)\,ea\_old} \cdot (1 + r_{(A)}) \right] - Tr_{(A)\,ep\_old} + \dfrac{a\_old}{n\_old}}{1 + r_{(A)}}$

Seller and buyer payoffs at terminal nodes for transaction at stage 2

Stage 2 terminal node I

Buyer	$U_N = (kko_1 \cdot x_1) \cdot (1 + \delta_{1\_1}) \cdot (1 + r_{(N)})^{-1}$
Crit. Price	$p = N_{USI} + N_{SI\_new} - \dfrac{Tr_{(N)\,ea\_new} \cdot (1 + r_{(N)}) + Tr_{(N)ep\_new} + M_{new} + W_{(N)} + (kkq_1 \cdot x_1) \cdot (1 + \delta_{1\_1})}{x_2}$
Seller	$\pi_A = -\dfrac{RD}{n\_new} + \dfrac{p \cdot x_2 - C_{USI\_new} - C_{SI\_new} - \left[Tr_{(A)\,ea\_new} \cdot (1 + r_{(A)}) \right] - Tr_{(A)\,ep\_new} + \dfrac{a\_new}{n\_new} - \dfrac{W_{(A)}}{n\_new}}{(1 + r_{(A)})^2}$

Stage 2 terminal node II

Buyer	$U_N = (kko_1 \cdot x_1) \cdot (1 + \delta_{1\_1}) \cdot (1 + r_{(N)})^{-1}$
Crit. Price	$p = N_{USI} + N_{SI\_old} - \dfrac{Tr_{(N)\,ea\_old} \cdot (1 + r_{(N)}) + Tr_{(N)ep\_old} + M_{old} + W_{(N)} + (kkq_1 \cdot x_1) \cdot (1 + \delta_{1\_1})}{x_1}$
Seller	$\pi_A = -RD + \dfrac{p \cdot x_1 - C_{USI\_old} - C_{SI\_old} - \left[Tr_{(A)\,ea\_old} \cdot (1 + r_{(A)}) \right] - Tr_{(A)\,ep\_new} + \dfrac{a\_old}{n\_old} - \dfrac{W_{(A)}}{n\_old}}{(1 + r_{(A)})^2}$

Stage 2 terminal node III

Buyer	$U_N = (kko_1 \cdot x_1) \cdot (1 + \delta_{1\_1}) \cdot (1 + r_{(N)})^{-1}$
Crit. Price	$p = N_{USI} + N_{SI\_new} - \dfrac{Tr_{(N)\,ea\_new} \cdot (1 + r_{(N)}) + Tr_{(N)ep\_new} + M_{new} + W_{(N)} + (kkq_1 \cdot x_1) \cdot (1 + \delta_{1\_1})}{x_2}$
Seller	$\pi_A = -\dfrac{RD}{n\_new} + \dfrac{p \cdot x_2 - C_{USI\_new} - C_{SI\_new} - \left[Tr_{(A)\,ea\_new} \cdot (1 + r_{(A)}) \right] - Tr_{(A)\,ep\_new} + \dfrac{a\_new}{n\_new} - \dfrac{W_{(A)}}{n\_new}}{(1 + r_{(A)})^2}$

Stage 2 terminal node IV

Buyer	$U_N = (kko_1 \cdot x_1) \cdot (1 + \delta_{1\_1}) \cdot (1 + r_{(N)})^{-1}$
Crit. Price	$p = N_{USI} + N_{SI\_newl} \cdot (1 - \delta) - \dfrac{Tr_{(N)\,ea\_new} \cdot (1 + r_{(N)}) + Tr_{(N)ep\_new} + M_{new} + W_{(N)} + (kkq \cdot x_1) \cdot (1 + \delta_{1\_1})}{x_2}$
Seller	$\pi_A = \left(-\dfrac{RD}{n\_new}\right) + \dfrac{p \cdot x_2 - C_{USI\_new} - C_{SI\_new} - \left[Tr_{(A)\,ea\_new} \cdot (1 + r_{(A)})\right] - Tr_{(A)\,ep\_new} + \dfrac{a\_new}{n\_new} - \dfrac{W_{(A)}}{n\_new}}{(1 + r_{(A)})^2}$

Stage 2 terminal node V

Buyer	$U_N = (kko_1 \cdot x_1) \cdot (1 + \delta_{1\_1}) \cdot (1 + r_{(N)})^{-1}$
Crit. Price	$p = N_{USI} + N_{SI\_newl} - \dfrac{Tr_{(N)\,ea\_new} \cdot (1 + r_{(N)}) + Tr_{(N)ep\_new} + M_{new} + W_{(N)} + (kko_1 \cdot x_1) \cdot (1 + \delta_{1\_2})}{x_2}$
Seller	$\pi_A = \left(-\dfrac{RD}{n\_new}\right) + \dfrac{p \cdot x_2 - C_{USI\_new} - C_{SI\_new} - \left[Tr_{(A)\,ea\_new} \cdot (1 + r_{(A)})\right] - Tr_{(A)\,ep\_new} + \dfrac{a\_new}{n\_new} - \dfrac{W_{(A)}}{n\_new}}{(1 + r_{(A)})^2}$

Stage 2 terminal node VI

Buyer	$U_N = (kko_1 \cdot x_1) \cdot (1 + \delta_{1\_2}) \cdot (1 + r_{(N)})^{-1}$
Crit. Price	$p = N_{USI} + N_{SI\_old} - \dfrac{Tr_{(N)\,ea\_old} \cdot (1 + r_{(N)}) + Tr_{(N)ep\_old} + M_{old} + W_{(N)} + (kko_1 \cdot x_1) \cdot (1 + \delta_{1\_2})}{x_1}$
Seller	$\pi_A = -RD + \dfrac{p \cdot x_1 - C_{USI\_old} - C_{SI\_old} - \left[Tr_{(A)\,ea\_old} \cdot (1 + r_{(A)})\right] - Tr_{(A)\,ep\_old} + \dfrac{a\_old}{n\_old}}{(1 + r_{(A)})^2}$

Stage 2 terminal node VII

Buyer	$U_N = (kko_1 \cdot x_1) \cdot (1 + \delta_{1\_2}) \cdot (1 + r_{(N)})^{-1}$
Crit. Price	$p = N_{USI} + N_{SI\_new} - \dfrac{Tr_{(N)\,ea\_new} \cdot (1 + r_{(N)}) + Tr_{(N)ep\_new} + M_{new} + W_{(N)} + (kkq \cdot x_1) \cdot (1 + \delta_{1\_2})}{x_2}$
Seller	$\pi_A = -\dfrac{RD}{n\_new} + \dfrac{p \cdot x_2 - C_{USI\_new} - C_{SI\_new} - \left[Tr_{(A)\,ea\_new} \cdot (1 + r_{(A)}) \right] - Tr_{(A)\,ep\_new} + \dfrac{a\_new}{n\_new} + \dfrac{W_{(A)}}{n\_new}}{(1 + r_{(A)})^2}$

Stage 2 terminal node VIII

Buyer	$U_N = (kko_1 \cdot x_1) \cdot (1 + \delta_{1\_2}) \cdot (1 + r_{(N)})^{-1}$
Crit. Price	$p = N_{USI} + N_{SI\_new} \cdot (1 - \delta) - \dfrac{Tr_{(N)\,ea\_new} \cdot (1 + r_{(N)}) + Tr_{(N)ep\_new} + M_{new} + W_{(N)} + (kkq \cdot x_1) \cdot (1 + \delta_{1\_2})}{x_2}$
Seller	$\pi_A = -\dfrac{RD}{n\_new} + \dfrac{p \cdot x_2 - C_{USI\_new} - C_{SI\_new} - \left[Tr_{(A)\,ea\_new} \cdot (1 + r_{(A)}) \right] - Tr_{(A)\,ep\_new} + \dfrac{a\_new}{n\_new} + \dfrac{W_{(A)}}{n\_new}}{(1 + r_{(A)})^2}$

Stage 2 terminal node IX

Buyer	$U_N = (kko_1 \cdot x_1) \cdot (1 + \delta_{1\_1}) \cdot (1 + r_{(N)})^{-1}$
Crit. Price	$p = N_{USI} + N_{SI\_old} - \dfrac{Tr_{(N)\,ea\_old} \cdot (1 + r_{(N)}) + Tr_{(N)ep\_old} + M_{old} + W_{(N)} + (kko_1 \cdot x_1) \cdot (1 + \delta_{1\_1})}{x_1}$
Seller	$\pi_A = \dfrac{p \cdot x_1 - C_{USI\_old} - C_{SI\_old} - \left[Tr_{(A)\,ea\_old} \cdot (1 + r_{(A)}) \right] - Tr_{(A)\,ep\_old} + \dfrac{a\_old}{n\_old}}{(1 + r_{(A)})^2}$

Stage 2 terminal node X

Buyer	$U_N = (kko_1 \cdot x_1) \cdot (1 + \delta_{1\_1}) \cdot (1 + r_{(N)})^{-1}$
Crit. Price	$p = N_{USI} + N_{SI\_old} - \dfrac{Tr_{(N)\,ea\_old} \cdot (1 + r_{(N)}) + Tr_{(N)ep\_old} + M_{old} + W_{(N)} + (kkq \cdot x_1) \cdot (1 + \delta_{1\_1})}{x_1}$
Seller	$\pi_A = \dfrac{p \cdot x_1 - C_{USI\_old} - C_{SI\_old} - \left[Tr_{(A)\,ea\_old} \cdot (1 + r_{(A)})\right] - Tr_{(A)\,ep\_old} + \dfrac{a\_old}{n\_old}}{(1 + r_{(A)})^2}$

Stage 2 terminal node XI

Buyer	$U_N = (kko_1 \cdot x_2) \cdot (1 + \delta_{1\_1}) \cdot (1 + r_{(N)})^{-1}$
Crit. Price	$p = N_{USI} + N_{SI\_new} - \dfrac{Tr_{(N)\,ea\_new} \cdot (1 + r_{(N)}) + Tr_{(N)ep\_new} + M_{new} + W_{(N)} + (kkq \cdot x_1) \cdot (1 + \delta_{1\_1})}{x_2}$
Seller	$\pi_A = \dfrac{RD}{(1 + r_{(A)}) \cdot n\_new} + \dfrac{p \cdot x_2 - C_{USI\_new} - C_{SI\_new} - \left[Tr_{(A)\,ea\_new} \cdot (1 + r_{(A)})\right] - Tr_{(A)\,ep\_new} + \dfrac{a\_new}{n\_new} + \dfrac{W_{(A)}}{n\_new}}{(1 + r_{(A)})^2}$

Stage 2 terminal node XII

Buyer	$U_N = (kko_1 \cdot x_1) \cdot (1 + \delta_{1\_1}) \cdot (1 + r_{(N)})^{-1}$
Crit. Price	$p = N_{USI} + N_{SI\_old} - \dfrac{Tr_{(N)\,ea\_old} \cdot (1 + r_{(N)}) + Tr_{(N)ep\_old} + M_{old} + W_{(N)} + (kkq \cdot x_1) \cdot (1 + \delta_{1\_1})}{x_1}$
Seller	$\pi_A = -\dfrac{RD}{(1 + r_{(A)})} + \dfrac{p \cdot x_1 - C_{USI\_old} - C_{SI\_old} - \left[Tr_{(A)\,ea\_old} \cdot (1 + r_{(A)})\right] - Tr_{(A)\,ep\_old} + \dfrac{a\_old}{n\_old}}{(1 + r_{(A)})^2}$

Stage 2 terminal node XIII

Buyer	$U_N = (kko_1 \cdot x_1) \cdot (1 + \delta_{1\_2}) \cdot (1 + r_{(N)})^{-1}$
Crit. Price	$p = N_{USI} + N_{SI\_new} - \dfrac{Tr_{(N)\,ea\_new} \cdot (1 + r_{(N)}) + Tr_{(N)ep\_new} + M_{new} + W_{(N)} + (kko_1 \cdot x_1) \cdot (1 + \delta_{1\_2})}{x_2}$
Seller	$\pi_A = \dfrac{RD}{(1 + r_{(A)}) \cdot n\_new} + \dfrac{p \cdot x_2 - C_{USI\_new} - C_{SI\_new} - \left[Tr_{(A)\,ea\_new} \cdot (1 + r_{(A)}) \right] - Tr_{(A)\,ep\_new} + \dfrac{a\_new}{n\_new} + \dfrac{W_{(A)}}{n\_new}}{(1 + r_{(A)})^2}$

Stage 2 terminal node XIV

Buyer	$U_N = (kko_1 \cdot x_1) \cdot (1 + \delta_{1\_2}) \cdot (1 + r_{(N)})^{-1}$
Crit. Price	$p = N_{USI} + N_{SI\_old} - \dfrac{Tr_{(N)\,ea\_old} \cdot (1 + r_{(N)}) + Tr_{(N)ep\_old} + M_{old} + (kko_1 \cdot x_1) \cdot (1 + \delta_{1\_2})}{x_1}$
Seller	$\pi_A = -\dfrac{RD}{(1 + r_{(A)})} + \dfrac{p \cdot x_1 - C_{USI\_old} - C_{SI\_old} - \left[Tr_{(A)\,ea\_old} \cdot (1 + r_{(A)}) \right] - Tr_{(A)\,ep\_old} + \dfrac{a\_old}{n\_old}}{(1 + r_{(A)})^2}$

Stage 2 terminal node XV

Buyer	$U_N = (kko_1 \cdot x_1) \cdot (1 + \delta_{1\_2}) \cdot (1 + r_{(N)})^{-1}$
Crit. Price	$p = N_{USI} + N_{SI\_old} - \dfrac{Tr_{(N)\,ea\_old} \cdot (1 + r_{(N)}) + Tr_{(N)ep\_old} + M_{old} + (kko_1 \cdot x_1) \cdot (1 + \delta_{1\_2})}{x_1}$
Seller	$\pi_A = -\dfrac{RD}{(1 + r_{(A)})} + \dfrac{p \cdot x_1 - C_{USI\_old} - C_{SI\_old} - \left[Tr_{(A)\,ea\_old} \cdot (1 + r_{(A)}) \right] - Tr_{(A)\,ep\_old} + \dfrac{a\_old}{n\_old}}{(1 + r_{(A)})^2}$

Stage 2 terminal node XVI

Buyer	$U_N = (kko_1 \cdot x_1) \cdot (1 + \delta_{1\_2}) \cdot (1 + r_{(N)})^{-1}$
Crit. Price	$p = N_{USI} + N_{SI\_old} - \dfrac{Tr_{(N)\,ea\_old} \cdot (1 + r_{(N)}) + Tr_{(N)ep\_old} + M_{old} + (kko_1 \cdot x_1) \cdot (1 + \delta_{1\_2})}{x_1}$
Seller	$\pi_A = -\dfrac{RD}{(1 + r_{(A)})} + \dfrac{p \cdot x_1 - C_{USI\_old} - C_{SI\_old} - \left[Tr_{(A)\,ea\_old} \cdot (1 + r_{(A)})\right] - Tr_{(A)\,ep\_old} + \dfrac{a_{\_old}}{n_{\_old}}}{(1 + r_{(A)})^2}$

275

Appendix III: Data configuration for variation of *q2* and *RD*

Buyer related variables

unspecific value per unit	57
specific value per unit (old constellation)	0
specific value per unit (new constellation)	45
number of units (old constellation)	600000
number of units (new constellation)	600000
ex ante transaction costs (old constellation)	600000
ex ante transaction costs (new constellation)	2800000
ex post transaction costs (old constellation)	0
ex post transaction costs (new constellation)	3800000
internal adaptation (old constellation)	0
internal adaptation (new constellation)	5500000
switching costs from old constellation	0
discount rate	0,08
best alternative at stage 1	48
change [%] in best alternative (global) from stage 1 to stage 2 (with probability q1)	0,1
change [%] in best alternative (global) from stage 1 to stage 2 (with probability (1-q1))	0
estimated no. of buyers for the particular offering (old constellation)	100
estimated no. of buyers for the particular offering (new constellation)	60

stage 1: probability q1 of scenario 1_1	0,1	resulting probability (1-q1) of scenario 1_2	(1-q1)
stage 2: probability q2 of scenario 2_1		resulting probability (1-q2) of scenario 2_2	(1-q2)
percentage decrease in NSI new for scenario 2_2	0,1		

Seller related variables

ex ante transaction costs (old constellation)	180000
ex ante transaction costs (new constellation)	2000000
ex post transaction costs (old constellation)	0
ex post transaction costs (new constellation)	3000000
RD investment in new constellation	
switching costs from old constellation	0
indirect benefit component (old constellation)	0
indirect benefit component (new constellation)	1000000
discount rate	0,08

Production costs (unspecific): K(y) = ay^3+by^2+cy+FUSI

	old constellation	new constellation
"coefficient a (>= 0)"	0	0
"coefficient b (<= 0)"	0	0
"coefficient c (>= 0)"	3	3
"fixed costs FUSI"	9000000	9000000

Production costs (specific): K(y) = dy^3+ey^2+gy+FSI

	old constellation	new constellation
"coefficient d (>= 0)"	0	0
"coefficient e (<= 0)"	0	0
"coefficient g (>= 0)"	0	16,4
"fixed costs FSI"	0	27000000

Load data

Go

	in t=0	shifts (st. 0)	in t=1	shifts (st. 1)	
Seller decision	undetermined	undetermined	undetermined undetermined	undetermined	Seller: expected final payoff undetermined
Buyer decision			undetermined undetermined		Buyer: expected final payoff undetermined

Calculate tree   Results

Appendix IV: Data configuration for variation of *RD* and *Kko*

Buyer related variables		Seller related variables	
unspecific value per unit	57	ex ante transaction costs (old constellation)	180000
specific value per unit (old constellation)	0	ex ante transaction costs (new constellation)	2000000
specific value per unit (new constellation)	45	ex post transaction costs (old constellation)	0
number of units (old constellation)	600000	ex post transaction costs (new constellation)	3000000
number of units (new constellation)	600000	RD investment in new constellation	
ex ante transaction costs (old constellation)	600000	switching costs from old constellation	0
ex ante transaction costs (new constellation)	2800000	indirect benefit component (old constellation)	0
ex post transaction costs (old constellation)	0	indirect benefit component (new constellation)	1000000
ex post transaction costs (new constellation)	3800000	discount rate	0,08
internal adaptation (old constellation)	0		
internal adaptation (new constellation)	9500000		
switching costs from old constellation	0		
discount rate	0,08		
best alternative at stage 1	48		

Production costs (unspecific): $K[y] = ay^3+by^2+cy+FUSI$

	old constellation	new constellation
"coefficient a (>= 0)"	0	0
"coefficient b (<= 0)"	0	0
"coefficient c (>= 0)"	3	3
"fixed costs FUSI"	9000000	9000000

change (%) in best alternative (global) from stage 1 to stage 2 (with probability q1)

change (%) in best alternative (global) from stage 1 to stage 2 (with probability (1-q1)) | 0

Production costs (specific): $K[y] = dy^3+ey^2+gy+FSI$

	old constellation	new constellation
"coefficient d (>= 0)"	0	0
"coefficient e (<= 0)"	0	0
"coefficient g (>= 0)"	0	16,4
"fixed costs FSI"	0	27000000

| estimated no. of buyers for the particular offering (old constellation) | 100 |
| estimated no. of buyers for the particular offering (new constellation) | 60 |

stage 1: probability q1 of scenario 1_1	0,7	resulting probability (1-q1) of scenario 1_2	(1-q1)
stage 2: probability q2 of scenario 2_1	0,2	resulting probability (1-q2) of scenario 2_2	(1-q2)
percentage decrease in NSInew for scenario 2_2	0,1	

Load data

Go

	in t=0	shifts (st. 0)	in t=1	shifts (st. 1)	
Seller decision	undetermined	undetermined	undetermined	undetermined	Seller: expected final payoff undetermined
Buyer decision			undetermined		Buyer: expected final payoff undetermined

Calculate tree | Results

277

Buyer related variables		Seller related variables	
unspecific value per unit	57	ex ante transaction costs (old constellation)	180000
specific value per unit (old constellation)	0	ex ante transaction costs (new constellation)	
specific value per unit (new constellation)	45	ex post transaction costs (old constellation)	0
number of units (old constellation)	600000	ex post transaction costs (new constellation)	
number of units (new constellation)	600000	RD investment in new constellation	350000
ex ante transaction costs (old constellation)	600000	switching costs from old constellation	0
ex ante transaction costs (new constellation)	2800000	indirect benefit component (old constellation)	0
ex post transaction costs (old constellation)	0	indirect benefit component (new constellation)	1000000
ex post transaction costs (new constellation)	3800000	discount rate	0,08
internal adaptation (old constellation)	0	Production costs (unspecific): $K(y) = ay^3 + by^2 + cy + FUSI$	

Production costs (unspecific): $K(y) = ay^3 + by^2 + cy + FUSI$

Buyer related variables			old constellation	new constellation
internal adaptation (new constellation)	5500000	"coefficient a (>= 0)"	0	0
switching costs from old constellation	0	"coefficient b (<= 0)"	0	0
discount rate	0,08	"coefficient c (>= 0)"	3	3
best alternative at stage 1	48	"fixed costs FUSI"	9000000	9000000

Production costs (specific): $K(y) = dy^3 + ey^2 + gy + FSI$

Buyer related variables			old constellation	new constellation
change (%) in best alternative (global) from stage 1 to stage 2 (with probability q1)	0,1	"coefficient d (>= 0)"	0	0
change (%) in best alternative (global) from stage 1 to stage 2 (with probability (1-q1))	0	"coefficient e (<= 0)"	0	0
estimated no. of buyers for the particular offering (old constellation)	100	"coefficient g (>= 0)"	0	16,4
estimated no. of buyers for the particular offering (new constellation)	60	"fixed costs FSI"	0	27000000

stage 1: probability q1 of scenario 1_1	0,7	resulting probability (1-q1) of scenario 1_2	(1-q1)	
stage 2: probability q2 of scenario 2_1	0,2	resulting probability (1-q2) of scenario 2_2	(1-q2)	Go
percentage decrease in NSInew for scenario 2_2	0,1			

	in t=0	shifts (st. 0)	in t=1	shifts (st. 1)	
Seller decision	undetermined	undetermined	undetermined	undetermined	Seller: expected final payoff: undetermined
Buyer decision			undetermined		Buyer: expected final payoff: undetermined

Load data

Calculate tree | Results

Appendix VI: Data configuration for variation of *q2*

Buyer related variables		Seller related variables	
unspecific value per unit	8	ex ante transaction costs (old constellation)	200000
specific value per unit (old constellation)	2	ex ante transaction costs (new constellation)	500000
specific value per unit (new constellation)	18	ex post transaction costs (old constellation)	0
number of units (old constellation)	2400000	ex post transaction costs (new constellation)	1300000
number of units (new constellation)	2400000	RD investment in new constellation	5000000
ex ante transaction costs (old constellation)	180000	switching costs from old constellation	0
ex ante transaction costs (new constellation)	600000	indirect benefit component (old constellation)	0
ex post transaction costs (old constellation)	0	indirect benefit component (new constellation)	150000
ex post transaction costs (new constellation)	450000	discount rate	0,05
internal adaptation (old constellation)	0		
internal adaptation (new constellation)	400000		
switching costs from old constellation	0		
discount rate	0,02		
best alternative at stage 1	4,5		

Production costs (unspecific): $K(y) = ay^3 + by^2 + cy + FUSI$

	old constellation	new constellation
"coefficient a [>= 0]"	0	0
"coefficient b [<= 0]"	0	0
"coefficient c [>= 0]"	2,5	2,5
"fixed costs FUSI"	3000000	3000000

Production costs (specific): $K(y) = dy^3 + ey^2 + gy + FSI$

	old constellation	new constellation
"coefficient d [>= 0]"	0	0
"coefficient e [<= 0]"	0	0
"coefficient g [>= 0]"	0	0
"fixed costs FSI"	2000000	9000000

change (%) in best alternative (global) from stage 1 to stage 2 (with probability q1) : 0,8

change (%) in best alternative (global) from stage 1 to stage 2 (with probability (1-q1)) : 0,3

estimated no. of buyers for the particular offering (old constellation) : 10

estimated no. of buyers for the particular offering (new constellation) : 8

stage 1: probability q1 of scenario 1_1 : 0,5 — resulting probability (1-q1) of scenario 1_2 : (1-q1)

stage 2: probability q2 of scenario 2_1 : [ ] — resulting probability (1-q2) of scenario 2_2 : (1-q2)

percentage decrease in NSInew for scenario 2_2 : 0,9

Load data

Go

	in t=0	shifts (st. 0)	in t=1	shifts (st. 1)	
Seller decision	undetermined	undetermined	undetermined undetermined	undetermined	Seller: expected final payoff: undetermined
Buyer decision			undetermined undetermined		Buyer: expected final payoff: undetermined

Calculate tree | Results

279

References

Abell, D. F. (1980), "Defining business: the starting point of strategic planning", Englewood Cliffs (NJ) 1980.

Achrol, R. S./Reve, T./Stern, L. W. (1983), "The environment of marketing channel dyads: a framework for comparative analysis", in: Journal of Marketing, 47 (Fall), pp. 55-67.

Achrol, R. S./Stern, L. W. (1988), "Environmental determinants of decision-making uncertainty in marketing channels", in: Journal of Marketing Research, 25 (February), pp. 36-50.

Adam, D. (1996), "Planung und Entscheidung", 4th ed., Wiesbaden 1996.

Adam, D. (1997), "Produktionsmanagement", 8th ed., Wiesbaden 1997.

Adam, D. (2000), "Investitionscontrolling", 3rd ed., München 2000.

Adner, R. (2002), "When are technologies disruptive? A demand-based view of the emergence of competition", in: Strategic Management Journal, 23 (8), pp. 667-688.

Aghion, P./Howitt, P. (1992), "A model of growth through creative destruction", in: Econometrica, 60 (2), pp. 323-351.

Aghion, P./Howitt, P. (1998), "Endogenous growth theory", Cambridge (MA) 1998.

Ahlert, D. (1988), "Marketing-Rechts-Management", Köln 1988.

Ahlert, D./Schröder, H. (1996), "Rechtliche Grundlagen des Marketing", 2nd ed., Stuttgart 1996.

Akerlof, G. A. (1970), "The market for "lemons": quality, uncertainty and the market mechansim", in: Quarterly Journal of Economics, 84 (August), pp. 488-500.

Alchian, A. A. (1950), "Uncertainty, evolution, and economic theory", in: Journal of Political Economy, 58 (June), pp. 211-221.

Alchian, A. A. (1984), "Specificity, specialization, and coalitions", in: Journal of Institutional and Theoretical Economics, 140 (March), pp. 34-49.

Alchian, A. A./Demsetz, H. (1972), "Production, information costs, and economic organization", in: American Economic Review, 62 (December), pp. 777-795.

Alchian, A. A./Woodward, S. (1988), "The firm is dead; long live the firm - a review of Oliver E. Williamsons's *The economic institutions of capitalism*", in: Journal of Economic Literature, 26 (March), pp. 65-79.

Aldrich, H. E. (1979), "Organizations and environments", Englewood Cliffs (NJ) 1979.

Al-Laham, A. (1997), "Strategieprozesse in deutschen Unternehmen:Verlauf, Struktur und Effizienz", Wiesbaden 1997.

Alston, L. J. (1987), "Review of Williamson, O. E. (1985): *The Economic Institutions of Capitalism*", in: Journal of Economic Behavior & Organization, 8 (2), pp. 315-327.

Altrogge, G. (1996), "Investition", 4th ed., München 1996.

Ambrosini, V./Jenkins, M. (2002), "Can multiple perspectives on strategic management inform practice?" in: *Jenkins, M./Ambrosini, V.* (Eds.), Strategic management: a multi-perspective approach, Basingstoke, New York 2002, pp. 264-267.

Amit, R./Shoemaker, P. J. H. (1993), "Strategic assets and organizational rent", in: Strategic Management Journal, 14 (1), pp. 33-46.

Anderson, E. (1985), "The salesperson as outside agent or employee: a transaction cost analysis", in: Marketing Science, 4 (3), pp. 234-254.

Anderson, E./Weitz, B. (1992), "The use of pledges to build and sustain commitment in distribution channels", in: Journal of Marketing Research, 24 (February), pp. 18-34.

Anderson, E./Weitz, B. A. (1986), "Make-or-buy decisions: vertical integration and marketing productivity", in: Sloan Management Review, 27 (Spring), pp. 3-19.

Anderson, J. C. (1995), "Relationships in business markets: exchange episodes, value creation, and their empirical assessment", in: Journal of the Academy of Marketing Science, 23 (4), pp. 346-350.

Anderson, J. C./Jain, D., C./Chintagunta, P. K. (1993), "Customer value assessment in business markets: a state-of-practice study", in: Journal of Business-to-Business Marketing, 1 (1), pp. 3-29.

Anderson, J. C./Narus, J. A. (1995), "Capturing the value of supplementary services", in: Harvard Business Review, 73 (January/February), pp. 75-83.

Anderson, J. C./Narus, J. A. (1998), "Business marketing: understand what customers value", in: Harvard Business Review, 76 (November/December), pp. 53-67.

Anderson, J. C./Narus, J. A. (1999), "Business marketing management", Upper Saddle River (NJ) 1999.

Andrews, K. R. (1971), "The concept of corporate strategy", Homewood (IL) 1971.

Ansoff, H. I. (1965), "Corporate strategy: an analytic approach to business policy for growth and expansion", New York (NY) 1965.

Ansoff, H. I. (1979), "Strategic management", New York (NY) 1979.

Aoki, M. (2001), "Toward a comparative institutional analysis", Cambridge (MA) 2001.

282

Argyres, N. S./Liebeskind, J. P. (1999), "Contractual commitments, bargaining power, and governance inseparability: incorporating history into transaction cost theory", in: Academy of Management Review, 24 (1), pp. 49-63.

Argyres, N. S./Liebeskind, J. P. (2000), "The role of prior commitment in governance choice", in: *Foss, N. J./Mahnke, V.* (Eds.), Competence, governance, and entrepreneurship, Oxford 2000, pp. 232-249.

Arrow, K. (1969), "The organization of economic activity: issues pertinent to the choice of market versus nonmarket allocation", in: *U.S. Joint Economic Committee, s. C., 1st Session*, The analysis and evaluation of public expenditure: the PPB system, Washington (DC) 1969, pp. 59-73.

Arrow, K. (1985), "The economics of agency", in: *Pratt, J./Zeckhauser, R.* (Eds.), Principals and agents: the structure of business, Boston (MA) 1985, pp. 37-51.

Arthur, B. (1989), "Competing technologies, increasing returns, and lock-in by historical events", in: Economic Journal, 99 (March), pp. 116-31.

Aspinwall, L. (1958), "The characteristics of goods and parallel systems theories", in: *Kelley, E. J./Lazer, W.* (Eds.), Managerial Marketing, Homewood (IL) 1958, pp. 434-450.

Aufderheide, D. (1993), "Spezifität, vertikale Integration und wettbewerbspolitische Implikationen: Eine Anmerkung", Volkswirtschaftliche Beiträge der Westfälischen Wilhelms-Universität, No. 187, Working Paper, Münster 1993.

Aufderheide, D. (2000), "Wettbewerb durch Regulierung?" unpublished postdoctoral thesis, Westfälische Wilhelms-Universität, Münster 2000.

Aufderheide, D./Backhaus, K. (1995), "Institutionenökonomische Fundierung des Marketing: Der Geschäftstypenansatz", in: *Kaas, K. P.* (Ed.), Kontrakte, Geschäftsbeziehungen, Netzwerke - Marketing und Neue Institutionenökonomik, Schmalenbachs Zeitschrift für betriebswirtschaftliche Forschung (Sonderheft No. 35), pp. 43-60.

Axelsson, B./Easton, G., (1992). "Industrial networks: a new view of reality", London 1992.

Bacharach, S. B. (1989), "Organization theories: some criteria for evaluation", in: Academy of Management Review, 14 (4), pp. 496-515.

Backhaus, K. (1982), "Investitionsgüter-Marketing", München 1982.

Backhaus, K. (1992), "Investitionsgüter-Marketing - Theorieloses Konzept mit Allgemeinheitsanspruch", in: Schmalenbachs Zeitschrift für betriebswirtschaftliche Forschung, 44 (9), pp. 771-791.

Backhaus, K. (1995), "Investitionsgütermarketing", 4th ed., München 1995.

Backhaus, K. (1997), "Industriegütermarketing", 5th ed., München 1997.

Backhaus, K. (1998), "Industrial marketing: a German view", in: Thexis, 15 (4), pp. 2-6.

Backhaus, K. (2003), "Industriegütermarketing", 7th ed., München 2003.

Backhaus, K./Aufderheide, D./Späth, G.-M. (1994), "Marketing für Systemtechnologien: Entwicklung eines theoretisch begründeten Geschäftstypenansatzes", Stuttgart 1994.

Backhaus, K./Baumeister, C./Mühlfeld, K. (2003), "Kundenbindung im Industriegütermarketing", in: *Bruhn, M./Homburg, C.* (Eds.), Handbuch Kundenbindungsmanagement, Wiesbaden 2003, pp. 193-221.

Backhaus, K./Büschken, J. (1999), "The paradox of unsatisfying but stable relationships - A look at German car suppliers", in: Journal of Business Research, 46 (3), pp. 245-257.

Backhaus, K./Köhl, T. (1999), "Claim-Management im internationalen Anlagengeschäft", in: *Hübner, U./Ebke, W. F.* (Eds.), Festschrift für *Bernhard Großfeld* zum 65. Geburtstag, Heidelberg 1999, pp. 17-34.

Backhaus, K./Plinke, W. (1986), "Rechtseinflüsse auf betriebswirtschaftiche Entscheidungen", Stuttgart 1986.

Backhaus, K./Plinke, W./Rese, M. (2004), "Marketing - An economic perspective", (forthcoming).

Bagozzi, R. P. (1975), "Marketing as exchange", in: Journal of Marketing, 39 (October), pp. 32-39.

Bain, J. S. (1951), "Relation of profit rate to industry concentration", in: Quarterly Journal of Economics, 65, pp. 293-324.

Bain, J. S. (1956), "Barriers to new competition", Cambridge (MA) 1956.

Balakrishnan, S./Wernerfelt, B. (1986), "Technical change, competition and vertical integration", in: Strategic Management Journal, 7 (4), pp. 347-359.

Bamberg, G./Coenenberg, A. G. (2002), "Betriebswirtschaftliche Entscheidungslehre", 11th ed., München 2002.

Barnard, C. I. (1938), "The functions of the executive", Cambridge (MA) 1938.

Barney, J. B. (1990), "The debate between traditional management theory and organizational economics: substantial differences or intergroup conflict?" in: Academy of Management Review, 15 (3), pp. 382-393.

Barney, J. B./Lee, W. (2000), "Multiple considerations in making governance choices: implications of transaction cost economics, real options theory, and knowledge-based theories of the firm", in: *Foss, N. J./Mahnke, V.* (Eds.), Competence, governance, and entrepreneurship, Oxford 2000, pp. 304-317.

Barr, P. S./Stimpert, J. L./Huff, A. S. (1992), "Cognitive change, strategic action, and organizational renewal", in: Strategic Management Journal, 13 (Special Issue Summer 1992), pp. 15-36.

Bartels, R. (1962), "The development of marketing thought", Homewood (IL) 1962.

Bartels, R. (1965), "Development of marketing thought: a brief history", in: *Schwartz, G.* (Eds.), Science in Marketing, New York 1965, pp. 47-69.

Bartels, R. (1988), "The history of marketing thought", 3rd ed., Columbus (OH) 1988.

Barzel, Y. (1997), "Economic analysis of property rights", 2nd ed., Cambridge 1997.

Bauer, R. A. (1967), "Consumer behavior as risk taking", in: *Cox, D. F.* (Ed.), Risk taking and information handling in consumer behavior, Boston (MA) 1967, pp. 23-33.

Baumeister, C. (2000), "Nachfragebündelung als Instrument der Preisdifferenzierung", Lohmar, Köln 2000.

Baumgarth, C. (1998a), "Ingredient Branding - Begriff, State of the Art und empirische Ergebnisse", Arbeitspapiere des Lehrstuhls für Marketing der Universität-GH-Siegen, Working Paper, Siegen 1998.

Baumgarth, C. (1998b), "Vertikale Marketingstrategien im Investitionsgüterbereich", Frankfurt/Main 1998.

Baumgarth, C. (2001), "Markenpolitik", Wiesbaden 2001.

Baumgarth, C./Freter, H./Schmidt, R. (1996), "Ingredient Branding", Arbeitspapiere des Lehrstuhls für Marketing der Universität-GH-Siegen, Working Paper, Siegen 1996.

Baumol, W. J. (1977), "Economic theory and operations analysis", 4th ed., Englewood Cliffs (NJ) 1977.

Baumol, W. J./Panzer, J./Willig, R. (1982), "Contestable markets and the theory of industry structure", New York 1982.

Baur, C. (1990), "Make-or-buy-Entscheidungen in einem Unternehmen der Automobilindustrie: Empirische Analyse und Gestaltung der Fertigungstiefe aus transaktionskostentheoretischer Sicht", München 1990.

Beinhocker, E. D. (1999), "On the origin of strategies", in: The McKinsey Quarterly 1999, (4), pp. 47-57.

Beinlich, G. (1998), "Geschäftsbeziehungen in der Vermarktung von Systemtechnologien", Aachen 1998.

Benito, G. R./Pedersen, T./Petersen, B. (1999), "Foreign operation methods and switching costs: conceptual issues and possible effects", in: Scandinavian Journal of Management, 15 (2), pp. 213-229.

Bensaou, M. (1999), "Portfolios of buyer-supplier relationships", in: Sloan Management Review, 40, pp. 35-44.

Bergmann, H. (1995), "Kommunikationsstrategien im Systemgeschäft: Die Vermarktung von CIM-Systemen", Wiesbaden 1995.

Berninghaus, S. K./Ehrhart, K.-M./Güth, W. (2002), "Strategische Spiele: Eine Einführung in die Spieltheorie", Berlin 2002.

Besanko, D./Dranove, D./Shanley, M. (1996), "The economics of strategy", New York 1996.

Besen, S. M./Farrell, J. (1994), "Choosing how to compete: strategies and tactics in standardization", in: Journal of Economic Perspectives, 8 (2), pp. 117-131.

Blackwell, R. D./Miniard, P. W./Engel, J. F. (2001), "Consumer behavior", 9th ed., Fort Worth 2001.

Blalock, H. M. J. (1969), "Theory construction: from verbal to mathematical formulations", Englewood Cliffs (NJ) 1969.

Blau, P. M. (1964), "Exchange and power in social life", New York (NY) 1964.

Blois, K. J. (1996), "Relationship marketing in organizational markets: when is it appropriate?" in: Journal of Marketing Management, 12, pp. 161-173.

Bloom, B. S. et al. (1956), "Taxonomy of educational objectives: the classification of educational goals. Handbook 1: Cognitive domain", New York (NY) 1956.

Bloom, P. N./Gundlach, G. T./Cannon, J. P. (2000), "Slotting allowances and fees: schools of thought and the views of practicing managers", in: Journal of Marketing, 64 (April), pp. 92-108.

Boeker, W. (1989), "Strategic change: the effects of founding and history", in: Academy of Management Journal, 32 (3), pp. 489-515.

Boerner, C. S./Macher, J. T. (2001), "Transaction cost economics: an assessment of empirical research in the social sciences", Working Paper, McDonough School of Business, Georgetown University, Washington 2001, also available from: www.msb.edu/faculty/jtm4/papers/etce.pdf.

Bonus, H. (1987), "Illegitime Transaktionen, Abhängigkeit und institutioneller Schutz", in: Hamburger Jahrbuch für Wirtschaft und Gesellschaft, 32, pp. 87-107.

Bossard Group (2002), "Elesa and Bossard - two powerful partners", Bossard Group, Date of access: November 11th, 2002, available from: http://www.bossard.com/group/en/frameset.cfm?Page=2300.

Bower, J. L./Doz, Y. (1979), "Strategy formulation - A social and political process", in: Schendel, D. E./Hofer, C. W. (Eds.), Strategic management - A new view of business policy and planning, Boston (MA) 1979, pp. 152-166.

Bowman, C./Ambrosini, V. (2000), "Value creation versus value capture: towards a coherent definition of value in strategy", in: British Journal of Management, 11 (1), pp. 1-15.

Bowman, E. H. (1974), "Epistemology, corporate strategy, and academe", in: Sloan Management Review, 15, pp. 35-50.

Bowman, E. H./Hurry, D. (1993), "Strategy through the option lens: an integrated view of resource investments and the incremental-choice process", in: Academy of Management Review, 18 (4), pp. 760-782.

Brandenburger, A. M./Nalebuff, B. J. (1996), "Mehr Geschäftserfolg - dank der Spieltheorie", in: Harvard Business manager, 18 (2), pp. 82-93.

Brandenburger, A. M./Stuart Jr., H. W. (1996), "Value-based business strategy", in: Journal of Economics and Management Strategy, 5, pp. 5-24.

Brierty, E. G./Eckles, R. W./Reeder, R. R. (1998), "Business marketing", 3rd ed., Upper Saddle River (NJ) 1998.

Brockhoff (1999), "Strategieidentifikation und Strategiewechsel", in: *Wagner, G. R.* (Ed.), Unternehmensführung, Ethik und Umwelt. *Hartmut Kreikebaum* zum 65. Geburtstag, Wiesbaden 1999, pp. 210-225.

Brockhoff, K./Leker, J. (1998), "Zur Identifikation von Unternehmensstrategien", in: Zeitschrift für Betriebswirtschaft, 68 (11), pp. 1201-1223.

Brown, J. R./Lusch, R. F./Nicholson, C. Y. (1995), "Power and relationship commitment: their impact on marketing channel member performance", in: Journal of Retailing, 71 (4), pp. 363-392.

Buchanan, J. M. (1975), "A contractarian paradigm for applying economic theory", in: American Economic Review, 65 (2), pp. 225-230.

Buchanan, J. M. (1990), "The domain of constitutional economics", in: Constitutional Political Economy, 1 (1), pp. 1-18.

Buchanan, L. (1992), "Vertical trade relationships: the role of dependence and symmetry in attaining organizational goals", in: Journal of Marketing Research, 29 (February), pp. 65-75.

Bucklin, L. P./Sengupta, S. (1993), "Organizing successful co-marketing alliances", in: Journal of Marketing, 57 (April), pp. 32-46.

Burgelman, R. A. (1991), "Intraorganizational ecology of strategy making and organizational adaptation - Theory and field research", in: Organization Science, 2 (3), pp. 239-262.

Burmann, C. (2001), "Strategische Flexibilität und Strategiewechsel als Determinanten des Unternehmenswertes. Eine Analyse aus ressourcen- und wissenschaftstheoretischer Perspektive", unpublished postdoctoral thesis, Westfälische Wilhelms-Universität, Münster 2001.

Burmann, C. (2002a), "Strategische Flexibilität und Strategiewechsel als Determinanten des Unternehmenswertes, Wiesbaden 2002.

Burmann, C. (2002b), "Messung und Wirkung von Strategieveränderungen", in: Marketing ZFP, 24 (1), pp. 67-79.

Burr, W. (2003), "Fundierung von Leistungstiefenentscheidungen auf der Basis modifizierter Transaktionskostenansätze", in: Schmalenbachs Zeitschrift für betriebswirtschaftliche Forschung, 55 (March), pp. 112-134.

Büschken, J. (1997), "Sequentielle nicht-lineare Tarife", Wiesbaden 1997.

Büschken, J. (2000), "Leapfrogging and profit maximizing new product preannouncement timing", Diskussionsbeiträge der Katholischen Univerität Eichstätt der Wirtschaftswissenschaftlichen Fakultät, No. 143, Working Paper, Ingolstadt 2000.

Butzer-Strothmann, K. (1999), "Krisen in Geschäftsbeziehungen", Wiesbaden 1999.

Campbell-Hunt, C. (2000), "What have we learned about generic competitive strategy? A meta-analysis", in: Strategic Management Journal, 21 (2), pp. 127-154.

Cannon, J. P./Achrol, R. S./Gundlach, G. T. (2000), "Contracts, norms, and governance", in: Journal of the Academy of Marketing Science, 28 (2), pp. 180-194.

Cannon, J. P./Perreault, W. D. J. (1999), "Buyer-seller relationships in business markets", in: Journal of Marketing Research, 36 (November), pp. 439-460.

Chakravarthy, B. (1997), "A new strategy framework for coping with turbulence", in: Sloan Management Review, 38 (Winter), pp. 69-82.

Chakravarthy, B./Doz, Y. (1992), "Strategy process research - Focusing on corporate self-renewal", in: Strategic Management Journal, 13 (Special Issue Summer and Winter 1992), pp. 5-14.

Chandler, A. D. (1962), "Strategy and structure: chapters in the history of the industrial enterprise", Cambridge (MA) 1962.

Chiles/McMackin (1996), "Integrating variable risk preferences, trust, and transaction cost economics", in: Academy of Management Review, 21 (1), pp. 73-99.

Christensen, C. R. (1992), "Exploring the limits of the technological S-curve", in: Production and Operations Management, 1 (4), pp. 334-366.

Christensen, C. R. (1997), "The innovator's dilemma", Boston (MA) 1997.

Coase, R. H. (1937), "The nature of the firm", in: Economica, 4 (November), pp. 386-405.

Coase, R. H. (1960), "The problem of social cost", in: Journal of Law and Economics, 3 (October), pp. 1-44.

Commons, J. R. (1934 (repr.: 1961)), "Institutional economics: its place in political economy", Madison (WI) 1961.

Conant, J. S./Mokwa, M. P./Varadarajan, P. R. (1990), "Strategic types, distinctive marketing competencies and organizational performance: a multiple measures-based study", in: Strategic Management Journal, 11 (5), pp. 365-383.

Contentmanager.de (2004), "CeBIT Highlights TOMORROW FOCUS Technologies: HPS takes off – Content Management für Lufthansa", Contentmanager.de, Date of access: May 24th, 2004, available from: http://www.contentmanager.de/magazin/news_h6803_cebit_highlights_tomorrow_foc us_technologies_hps.html

Copeland, M. T. (1923), "The relation of consumers' buying habits to marketing methods", in: Harvard Business Review, 1 (April), pp. 282-289.

Coviello, N. E./Brodie, R. J./Munro, H. J. (1997), "Understanding contemporary marketing: development of a classification scheme", in: Journal of Marketing Management, 13 (6), pp. 501-522.

Cox, D. F. (1967a), "Introduction", in: *Cox, D. F.* (Ed.), Risk taking and information handling in consumer behavior, Boston (MA) 1967, pp. 1-22.

Cox, D. F. (1967b), "Risk handling in consumer behavior - An intensive study of two cases", in: *Cox, D. F.* (Ed.), Risk taking and information handling in consumer behavior, Boston (MA) 1967, pp. 34-81.

Cox, D. F. (1967c), "Risk taking and information handling in consumer behavior", in: *Cox, D. F.* (Eds.), Risk taking and information handling in consumer behavior, Boston (MA) 1967, pp. 604-639.

Crafts, N. F. R. (1995), "Exogenous or endogenous growth? The Industrial Revolution reconsidered", in: Journal of Economic History, 55 (4), pp. 745-772.

Crocker, K. J./Masten, S. E. (1988), "Mitigating contractual hazards: unilateral options and contract length", in: RAND Journal of Economics, 19 (3), pp. 327-343.

Cunningham, S. M. (1967), "The major dimensions of perceived risk", in: *Cox, D. F.* (Ed.), Risk taking and information handling in consumer behavior, Boston (MA) 1967, pp. 82-108.

D'Aveni, R. A. (1994), "Hypercompetition: managing the dynamics of strategic manouvering", New York 1994.

Dahlstrom, R./Dwyer, R. F. (1992), "The political economy of distribution systems: a review and prospectus", in: Journal of Marketing Channels, 2 (1), pp. 47-86.

Darby, M. R./Karni, E. (1973), "Free competition and the optimal amount of fraud", in: Journal of Law and Economics, 16 (1), pp. 67-88.

David, P. (1985), "Clio and the economics of QWERTY", in: American Economic Review, 75 (2), pp. 332-337.

Davis, E./Kay, J. (1990), "Assessing corporate performance", in: Business Strategy Review, 1 (Summer), pp. 1-16.

Day, G. S. (1990), "Market driven strategy: processes for creating value", New York (NY) 1990.

Day, G. S. (1999), "Market driven strategy: processes for creating value", reprint of 1990 with a new introduction, New York (NY) 1990.

Day, G. S. (2000), "Managing market relationships", in: Journal of the Academy of Marketing Science, 28 (1), pp. 24-30.

Day, G. S./Klein, S. (1987), "Cooperative behavior in vertical markets: the influence of transaction costs and competitive strategy", in: *Houston, M. J.* (Ed.), Review of Marketing, Chicago 1987, pp. 39-66.

de Pay, D. (1989), "Die Organisation von Innovationen: Ein transaktionskostentheoretischer Ansatz", Wiesbaden 1989.

Dickson, P. R. (1996), "The static and dynamic mechanics of competition: a comment on Hunt and Morgan´s comparative advantage theory", in: Journal of Marketing, 60 (October), pp. 102-106.

Dimpfel, M./Algesheimer, R. (2002), "Action flexibility or the option to use real options: a neo-institutional perspective", Paper presented at the "6th Annual International Conference on Real Options", Paphos, Cyprus 2002.

Dixit, A. (1980), "The role of investment in entry-deterrence", in: Economic Journal, 90 (March), pp. 95-106.

Dixit, A. K./Pindyck, R. S. (1994), "Investment under uncertainty", Princeton (NJ) 1994.

Dixit, A. K./Pindyck, R. S. (1995), "The options approach to capital investment", in: Harvard Business Review, 73 (May/June), pp. 105-115.

Dodge, H. R. (1970), "Industrial marketing", New York (NY) 1970.

Dolan, R. J. (1981), "Models of competition: a review of theory and empirical findings", in: *Enis, B. M./Roering, K. J.* (Eds.), Review of Marketing, Chicago 1981, pp. 224-234.

Domrös (1994), "Innovationen und Institutionen", Berlin 1994.

Donnan, M. P./Comer, J. M. (2001), "Insights into relationship structures: the Australian aluminium industry", in: Industrial Marketing Management, 30 (3), pp. 255-269.

Doty, D. H./Glick, W. H. (1994), "Typologies as a unique form of theory building: toward improved understanding and modeling", in: Academy of Management Review, 19 (2), pp. 230-251.

Drucker, P. F. (2002), "The discipline of innovation", in: Harvard Business Review, 80 (August), pp. 95-103.

Dubin, R. (1969), "Theory building", New York (NY) 1969.

Duncan, R. B. (1972), "Characteristics of organizational environments and perceived environmental uncertainty", in: Administrative Science Quarterly, 17 (September), pp. 313-327.

Dutta, S./John, G. (1995), "Combining lab experiments and industry data in transaction cost analysis: the case of competition as a safeguard", in: Journal of Law, Economics and Organization, 11 (1), pp. 189-204.

Dwyer, R. F./Schurr, P. H./Oh, S. (1987), "Developing buyer-seller relationships", in: Journal of Marketing, 51 (April), pp. 11-27.

Dwyer, R. F./Walker Jr., O. C. (1981), "Bargaining in an asymmetrical power structure", in: Journal of Marketing, 45 (Winter), pp. 104-115.

Dyer, J. H. (1996), "Specialized supplier networks as a source of competitive advantage: evidence from the auto industry", in: Strategic Management Journal, 17 (4), pp. 271-291.

Easton, G./Araujo, L. (1992), "Non-economic exchange in industrial networks", in: Axelsson, B./Easton, G. (Eds.), Industrial networks: a new view of reality, London 1992, pp. 62-88.

Easton, G./Hakannsson, H. (1996), "Markets as networks: editorial introduction", in: International Journal of Research in Marketing, 13 (5), pp. 407-143.

Edmonds, B. (1999), "Syntactic measures of complexity", Manchester 1999.

Eisenhardt, K. M./Sull, D. N. (2001), "Strategy as simple rules", in: Harvard Business Review, 79 (January), pp. 107-116.

Eisenhardt, K. M./Zbaracki, M. J. (1992), "Strategic decision making", in: Strategic Management Journal, 13 (Special Issue Winter 1992), pp. 17-37.

Elder, R. F. (1935), "Fundamentals of industrial marketing", New York (NY) 1935.

Eliashberg, J./Robertson, T. S. (1988), "New product preannouncing behavior: a market signaling study", in: Journal of Marketing Research, 25 (August), pp. 282-292.

Eliashberg, J./Robertson, T. S./Rymon, T. (1996), "Market signaling and competitive bluffing: an empirical study", Marketing Science Institute Working Paper, No. 96-102, Cambridge (MA) 1996.

Emerson, R. M. (1962), "Power-dependence relations", in: American Sociological Review, 27 (1), pp. 31-41.

Engelhardt, W. H./Günter, B. (1981), "Investitionsgütermarketing", Stuttgart 1981.

Enis, B. M./Roering, K. J. (1980), "Product classification taxonomies: synthesis and consumer implications", in: *Lamb, C. W. J./Dunne, P.* (Eds.), Theoretical developments in marketing, Chicago 1980, pp. 186-189.

Erichsson, S. K. (1994), "User Groups im Systemgeschäft: Ansatzpunkte für das Systemmarketing", Wiesbaden 1994.

Erlei, M./Leschke, M./Sauerland, D. (1999), "Neue Institutionenökonomik", Stuttgart 1999.

Etzioni, A. (1975), "A comparative analysis of complex organizations", New York (NY) 1975.

Farrell, J. (1993), "Meaning and credibility in cheap-talk games", in: Games and Economic Behavior, 5 (October), pp. 514-531.

Farrell, J. (1995), "Talk is cheap", in: American Economic Review, 85 (May), pp. 186-190.

Farrell, J./Gallini, N. T. (1988), "Second-sourcing as a commitment: monopoly incentives to attract competition", in: Quarterly Journal of Economics, 103 (November), pp. 673-694.

Fehl, U. (1985), "Das Konzept der Contestable Markets und der Marktprozess", in: *Bombach, G./Gahlen, B./Ott, A. E.* (Eds.), Industrieökonomik: Theorie und Empirie, Tübingen 1985, pp. 29-49.

Feitzinger, E./Lee, H. L. (1997), "Mass customization at Hewlett-Packard: the power of postponement", in: Harvard Business Review, 75 (January/February), pp. 116-121.

Fisher, R./Ury, W. (1981), "Getting to yes", Boston (MA) 1981.

Ford, D. et al. (1998), "Managing business relationships", Chichester 1988.

Foss, K./Foss, N. J. (2000), "The kowledge-based approach and organizational economics: how much do they really differ? And how does it matter?" in: *Foss, N. J./Mahnke, V.* (Eds.), Competence, governance, and entrepreneurship, Oxford 2000, pp. 55-79.

Foss, N. J. (1997), "Austrian insights and the theory of the firm", in: Advances in Austrian Economics, 4, pp. 175-198.

Foss, N. J. (2001), "Misesian ownership and Coasian authority in Hayekian settings: the case of the knowledge economy", in: Quarterly Journal of Austrian Economics, 4 (4), pp. 3-24.

Foss, N. J. (2002), "Whither economic organization?" in: Zeitschrift für Betriebswirtschaft, (Ergänzungsheft 2), pp. 57-66.

Foss, N. J. (2003), "The strategic management and transaction cost nexus: past debates, central questions, and future research possibilities", in: Strategic Organization, 1 (2), pp. 139-169.

Foss, N. J./Klein, P. G., Eds. (2002). "Entrepreneurship and the firm: Austrian perspectives on economic organization", Cheltenham 2002.

292

Foster, R. N. (1986), "Innovation: Die technologische Offensive", Wiesbaden 1986.

Franke, N. (2002), "Realtheorie des Marketing: Gestalt und Erkenntnis", Tübingen 2002.

Frederick, J. H. (1934), "Industrial marketing", New York 1934.

Freeman, C. (1987), "Innovation", in: *Eatwell, J./Milgate, M./Newman, P.* (Eds.), The New Palgrave: a dictionary of economics, London 1987, pp. 858-860.

Freiling, J. (1995), "Die Abhängigkeit der Zulieferer", Wiesbaden 1995.

Freytag, P. V./Clarke, A. H. (2001), "Business to business market segmentation", in: Industrial Marketing Management, 30 (6), pp. 473-486.

Friedman, M. (1953), "The methodology of positive economics", Essays in positive economics, No. 328, University of Chicago Press: Chicago 1953.

Fu-Lai Yu, T. (2001), "Firms, governments and economic change: an entrepreneurial perspective", Cheltenham 2001.

Furubotn, E. G. (1999), "Economic efficiency in a world of frictions", in: European Journal of Law and Economics, 8 (3), pp. 179-197.

Furubotn, E. G./Pejovich, S. (1974), "The economics of property rights", Cambridge (MA): 1974.

Furubotn, E. G./Richter, R. (1998), "Institutions and economic theory: the contribution of the new institutional economics", Ann Arbor 1998.

Gadde, L.-E./Snehota, I. (2000), "Making the most of supplier relationships", in: Industrial Marketing Management, 29 (4), pp. 305-316.

Gardner, R. (1995), "Games for business and economics", New York (NY) 1995.

Gatignon, H./Anderson, E. (1988), "The multinational corporation's degree of control over foreign subsidiaries: an empirical test of a transaction cost explanation", in: Journal of Law, Economics and Organization, 4 (Fall), pp. 305-336.

Gemünden, H. G. (1981), "Innovationsmarketing: Interaktionsbeziehungen zwischen Hersteller und Verwender innovativer Investitionsgüter", Tübingen 1981.

Geyskens, I./Steenkamp, J.-B. E. M./Kumar, N. (2003), "Make, buy, or ally: a meta-analysis of transaction cost theory", unpublished Working Paper, Tilburg 2003.

Ghemawat, P. (1991), "Commitment: the dynamics of strategy", New York (NY) 1991.

Ghemawat, P. (2002a), "Competition and business strategy in historical perspective", in: Business History Review, 76 (Spring), pp. 37-74.

Ghemawat, P. (2002b), "Global vs. local products: a case study and a model", Harvard Business School Working Papers Series, No. 02-059, Boston (MA) 2002.

293

Ghemawat, P./del Sol, P. (1998), "Commitment versus flexibility?" in: California Management Review, 40 (4), pp. 26-42.

Ghosh, M./John, G. (1999), "Governance value analysis and marketing strategy", in: Journal of Marketing, 63 (Special Issue), pp. 131-145.

Gilbert, X./Strebel, P. J. (1985), "Outpacing strategies", in: IMEDE - Perspectives for Managers, 9 (2).

Gilbert, X./Strebel, P. J. (1987), "Strategies to outpace the competition", in: Journal of Business Strategy, 8 (1), pp. 28-36.

Ginsberg, A. (1988), "Measuring and modelling changes in strategy: theoretical foundations and empirical directions", in: Strategic Management Journal, 9 (6), pp. 559-575.

Graham, D. A./Peirce, E. R. (1989), "Contract modification: an economic analysis of the hold-up game", in: Law and Contemporary Problems, 52 (1), pp. 9-32.

Granovetter, M. (1985), "Economic action and social structure: a theory of embeddedness", in: American Journal of Sociology, 91 (3), pp. 481-510.

Graumann, M. (1993), "Die Ökonomie von Netzprodukten", in: Zeitschrift für Betriebswirtschaft, 63 (12), pp. 1331-1355.

Greve, H. R. (1998), "Performance, aspirations, and risky organizational change", in: Administrative Science Quarterly, 43 (1), pp. 58-86.

Grewal, R./Dharwadkar, R. (2002), "The role of the institutional environment in marketing channels", in: Journal of Marketing, 66 (July), pp. 82-97.

Grossman, S. J./Hart, O. (1986), "The costs and benefits of ownership: a theory of vertical and lateral integration", in: Journal of Political Economy, 94 (4), pp. 691-719.

Gualerzi, D. (2001), "Endogenpous and exogenous factors in growth theory", Paper presented at the "Old and New Growth Theories: An Assessment" Conference, Pisa, Italy 2001.

Gundlach, G. T./Cadotte, E. R. (1994), "Exchange interdependence and interfirm interaction: research in a simulated channel setting", in: Journal of Marketing Research, 31 (November), pp. 516-532.

Gundlach, G. T./Murphy, P. E. (1993), "Ethical and legal foundations of relational marketing exchanges", in: Journal of Marketing, 57 (October), pp. 35-46.

Hakansson, H. (1982), "International marketing and purchasing of industrial goods: an interaction approach", New York (NY) 1982.

Haltiwanger, J./Waldman, M. (1991), "Reponders versus non-responders: a new perspective on heterogeneity", in: Economic Journal, 101 (September), pp. 1085-1102.

Hamel, G./Prahalad, C. K. (1989), "Strategic intent", in: Harvard Business Review, 67 (May/June), pp. 63-76.

294

Hamel, G./Prahalad, C. K. (1994), "Competing for the future", in: Harvard Business Review, 72 (July/August), pp. 122-128.

Han, J. K./Kim, N./Kim, H.-B. (2001), "Entry barriers: a dull-, one-, or two-edged sword for incumbents? Unraveling the paradox from a contingency perspective", in: Journal of Marketing, 65 (January), pp. 1-14.

Hart, C. W. L. (1995), "Mass customization: conceptual underpinnings, opportunities and limits", in: International Journal of Service Industry Management, 6 (2), pp. 36-45.

Hart, O./Holmström, B. (1987), "The theory of contracts", in: *Bewley, T. F.* (Eds.), Advances in Economic Theory: Fifth World Congress 1987, Cambridge (MA) 1987, pp. 71-102.

Hart, O./Moore, J. (1999), "Foundations of incomplete contracts", in: Review of Economic Studies, 66 (1; Special Issue: Contracts), pp. 115-138.

Hauser, J. R./Shugan, S. M. (1983), "Defensive marketing strategies", in: Marketing Science, 2 (4), pp. 319-360.

Hax, A. C./Majluf, N. S. (1996), "The strategy concept and process: a pragmatic approach", 2nd ed., Upper Saddle River (NJ) 1996.

Hayek, F. (1945), "The use of knowledge in society", in: American Economic Review, 35 (4), pp. 519-530.

Hayek, F. A. v. (1967), "Studies in philosophy, politics and economics", Chicago 1967.

Hayek, F. A. v. (1969), "Der Wettbewerb als Entdeckungsverfahren", Tübingen 1969.

Heffner, M./Mühlfeld, K. (2001), "Application Service Providing - Eine Analyse auf Basis des Geschäftstypenansatzes", Arbeitspapiere des Betriebswirtschaftlichen Instituts für Anlagen und Systemtechnologien, Förderkreis für Industriegütermarketing e.V., No. 30, Working Paper, Münster 2001.

Heide, J./John, G. (1990), "Alliances in industrial purchasing: the determinants of joint action in buyer-supplier relationships", in: Journal of Marketing Research, 27 (February), pp. 24-36.

Heide, J. B. (1994), "Interorganizational governance in marketing channels", in: Journal of Marketing, 58 (January), pp. 71-85.

Heide, J. B./John, G. (1988), "The role of dependence balancing in safeguarding transaction-specific assets in conventional channels", in: Journal of Marketing, 52 (January), pp. 20-35.

Heide, J. B./John, G. (1992), "Do norms matter in marketing relationships?" in: Journal of Marketing, 56 (April), pp. 32-44.

Heide, J. B./Miner, A. S. (1992), "The shadow of the future: effects on anticipated interaction and frequency of contact on buyer-seller cooperation", in: Academy of Management Journal, 35 (2), pp. 265-291.

Heidingsfelder, M. M. (1990), "Das Marketing innovativer Informationstechnologien - Eine praxisorientierte Konzeption für die Technologie der Wissensverarbeitung", Saarbrücken 1990.

Heil, O./Robertson, T. S. (1991), "Toward a theory of competitive market signaling: a research agenda", in: Strategic Management Journal, 12 (6), pp. 403-418.

Helper, S. (1991), "Strategy and irreversibility in supplier relations: the case of the U.S. automobile industry", in: Business History Review, 65 (Winter), pp. 781-824.

Hempel, C. (1965), "Aspects of scientific explanation", New York (NY) 1965.

Henisz, W., J. (1998), "The institutional environment for international investment: safeguarding against state sector opportunism and opportunistic use of the state", Ann Harbor (MI) 1998.

Henisz, W., J./Williamson, O. E. (1999), "Comparative economic organization - Within and between countries", in: Business and Politics, 1 (3), pp. 261-277.

Hill, C. L. (1990), "Cooperation, opportunism, and the invisible hand: Implications for transaction cost theory", in: Academy of Management Review, 15 (3), pp. 500-514.

Hitt, M. A. et al. (2001), "Guest editors´ introduction to the special issue strategic entrepreneurship: entrepreneurial strategies for wealth creation", in: Strategic Management Journal, 22 (6/7), pp. 479-491.

Hofer, C. W./Schendel, D. E. (1978), "Strategy formulation: analytical concepts", St. Paul (MN) 1978.

Holm, H. J. (1993), "Complexity in economic theory: an automata theoretical approach", Lund 1993.

Holmström, B. (1979), "Moral hazard and observability", in: Bell Journal of Economics, 10 (Spring), pp. 74-91.

Homans, G. C. (1961), "Social behavior", New York (NY) 1961.

Homburg, C. (1995), "Single Sourcing, Double Sourcing, Multiple Sourcing...?" in: Zeitschrift für Betriebswirtschaft, 65 (8), pp. 813-834.

Homburg, C. (2000), "Entwicklungslinien der deutschsprachigen Marketingforschung", in: *Backhaus, K.* (Ed.), Deutschsprachige Marketingforschung: Bestandsaufnahme und Perspektiven, Stuttgart 2000, pp. 339-360.

Homburg, C./Garbe, B. (1996), "Industrielle Dienstleistungen - Bestandsaufnahme und Entwicklungsrichtungen", in: Zeitschrift für Betriebswirtschaft, 66 (3), pp. 253-282.

Homburg, C./Schneider, J. (2001), "Industriegütermarketing", in: *Tscheulin, D. K./Helmig, B.* (Eds.), Branchenspezifisches Marketing. Grundlagen - Besonderheiten - gemeinsamkeiten, Wiesbaden 2001, pp. 587-613.

Hopf, M. (1983), "Ausgewählte Probleme zur Informationsökonomie", in: Wirtschaftswissenschaftliches Studium, (6), pp. 313-318.

Howard, M. C. (1985), "An overview of some key volumes in a law book collection, or basic sources of information on the legal aspects of marketing", in: Journal of Marketing, 49 (Winter), pp. 162-165.

Hrebiniak, L. G./Joyce, W. F. (2001), "Implementing strategy: an appraisal and agenda for future research", in: *Hitt, M. A./Freeman, R. E./Harrison, J. S.* (Eds.), The Blackwell Handbook of Strategic Management, Oxford 2001, pp. 602-626.

Huber, F. (1999), "Spieltheorie und Marketing", Wiesbaden 1999.

Huff, A. S./Reger, R. K. (1987), "A review of strategic process research", in: Journal of Management, 13 (2), pp. 211-236.

Huff, J. O./Huff, A. S./Thomas, H. (1992), "Strategic renewal and the interaction of cumulative stress and inertia", in: Strategic Management Journal, 13 (Special Issue Summer 1992), pp. 55-75.

Hunt, S. D. (1976), "The nature and scope of marketing", in: Journal of Marketing, 40 (July), pp. 17-28.

Hunt, S. D. (1983), "General theories and the fundamental explanda of marketing", in: Journal of Marketing, 47 (Fall), pp. 9-17.

Hunt, S. D. (2000), "A general theory of competition: resources, competences, productivity, economic growth", Thousand Oaks (CA) 2000.

Hunt, S. D./Lambe, C. J. (2000), "Marketing's contribution to business strategy: market orientation, relationship marketing and resource-advantage theory", in: International Journal of Management Reviews, 2 (1), pp. 17-43.

Hutt, M. D./Speh, T. W. (2004), "Business marketing management", 8th ed., Mason (OH) 2004.

Hutton, J. G. (1997), "A study of brand equity in an organizational-buying context", in: Journal of Product Brand Management, 6 (6), pp. 428-439.

Ihde, G. B. (1988), "Die relative Betriebstiefe als strategischer Erfolgsfaktor", in: Zeitschrift für Betriebswirtschaft, 58 (1), pp. 13-23.

Industrial Marketing Committee Review Board (1954), "Fundamental differences between industrial and consumer marketing", in: Journal of Marketing, 19 (October), pp. 152-158.

Iyer, G./Villas-Boas, M. J. (2003), "A bargaining theory of distribution channels", in: Journal of Marketing Research, 40 (February), pp. 80-100.

Jackson, B. B. (1985), "Winning and keeping industrial customers", Lexington (MA) 1985.

Jackson, D. M./Krampf, R. F./Konopa, L. J. (1982), "Factors that influence the length of industrial channels", in: Industrial Marketing Management, 11, pp. 263-268.

Jacob, F. (1995), "Produktindividualisierung: Ein Ansatz zur innovativen Leistungsgestaltung im Business-to-Business-Bereich", Wiesbaden 1995.

Jacob, H. (1974), "Unsicherheit und Flexibilität: Zur Theorie der Planung bei Unsicherheit", in: Zeitschrift für Betriebswirtschaft, 44 (5), pp. 299-326.

Jap, S. D. (2001), ""Pie sharing" in complex collaboration contexts", in: Journal of Marketing Research, 38 (February), pp. 86-99.

Jarrat, D./Fayed, R. (2001), "The impact of market and organisational challenges on marketing strategy decision-making: a qualitative investigation of the business-to-business sector", in: Journal of Business Research, 51 (1), pp. 61-72.

Jaworski, B. J. (1988), "Toward a theory of marketing control: environmental context, control types, and consequences", in: Journal of Marketing, 52 (July), pp. 23-39.

Jenkins, M./Floyd, S. (2002), "Entrepreneurship", in: *Jenkins, M./Ambrosini, V.* (Eds.), Strategic management: a multi-perspective approach, Basingstoke, New York 2002, pp. 250-263.

Jensen, M. (1983), "Organization theory and methodology", in: Accounting Review, 50 (April), pp. 319-339.

John, G./Weitz, B. A. (1988), "Forward integration into distribution: an empirical test of transaction cost analysis", in: Journal of Law, Economics and Organization, 4, pp. 337-355.

Jopp, K. (1998), "Das virtuelle Kraftwerk", in: VDI nachrichten, 1998 (37), p. 25.

Joshi, A. W./Stump, R. L. (1999), "Transaction cost analysis: integration of recent refinements and an empirical test", in: Journal of Business-to-Business Marketing, 5 (4), pp. 37-71.

Joskow, P. L. (1987), "Contract duration and relationship-specific investments: empirical evidence from coal markets", in: American Economic Review, 77 (1), pp. 168-185.

Joskow, P. L. (1991), "The role of transaction cost economics in antitrust and public utility regulatory policies", in: Journal of Law and Economics, 7 (Special Issue), pp. 53-83.

Jost, P.-J. (2001), "Die Spieltheorie im Unternehmenskontext", in: *Jost, P.-J.* (Ed.), Die Spieltheorie in der Betriebswirtschaftslehre, Stuttgart 2001, pp. 9-41.

Jung, S. (1999), "Das Management von Geschäftsbeziehungen: ein Ansatz auf transaktionskostentheoretischer, sozialpsychologischer und spieltheoretischer Basis", Wiesbaden 1999.

Kaas, K. P. (1992), "Marketing und Neue Institutionenlehre", Arbeitspapiere aus dem Forschungsprojekt Marketing und ökonomische Theorie, No. 1, Working Paper, Frankfurt/Main.

298

Kaas, K. P. (1995a), "Marketing und Neue Institutionenökonomik", in: *Kaas, K. P.* (Ed.), Kontrakte, Geschäftsbeziehungen, Netzwerke - Marketing und Neue Institutionenökonomik, Schmalenbachs Zeitschrift für betriebswirtschaftliche Forschung (Sonderheft No. 35), pp. 1-17.

Kaas, K. P. (1995b), "Marketing zwischen Markt und Hierarchie", in: *Kaas, K. P.* (Ed.), Kontrakte, Geschäftsbeziehungen, Netzwerke - Marketing und Neue Institutionenökonomik,Schmalenbachs Zeitschrift für betriebswirtschaftliche Forschung (Sonderheft No. 35), pp. 19-42.

Kaas, K. P. (2000), "Alternative Konzepte der Theorieverankerung", in: *Backhaus, K.* (Ed.), Deutschsprachige Marketingforschung: Bestandsaufnahme und Perspektiven, Stuttgart 2000, pp. 55-78.

Kaas, K. P./Schade, C. (1993), "Bindungsstärke in Kooperations- und Geschäftsbeziehungen am Beispiel der Dienstleistung Unternehmensberatung", in: *Thelen, E. M./Mairamhof, G. B.* (Eds.), Dienstleistungsmarketing - Eine Bestandsaufnahme; Tagungsband zum 2. Workshop für Dienstleistungsmarketing, Innsbruck Februar 1993, Frankfurt/ Main.

Karakaya, F./Stahl, M. J. (1989), "Barriers to entry and market entry decisions in consumer and industrial goods markets", in: Journal of Marketing, 53 (April), pp. 80-91.

Katz, M. L. (1989), "Vertical contractual relations", in: *Schmalensee, R./Willig, R.* (Eds.), Handbook of Industrial Organization, Vol. 1, Amsterdam 1989, pp. 655-721.

Katz, M. L./Shapiro, C. (1986), "Technology adoption in the presence of network externalities", in: Journal of Political Economy, 94 (4), pp. 822-841.

Kaufmann, L. (2002), "Purchasing and supply management - A conceptual framework", in: *Hahn, D./Kaufmann, L.* (Eds.), Handbuch Industrielles Beschaffungsmanagement, 2nd ed., Wiesbaden 2002, pp. 3-33.

Kay, J./McKiernan, P./Faulkner, D. O. (2003), "The history of strategy and some thoughts about the future", in: *Faulkner, D. O./Campbell, A.* (Eds.), The Oxford Handbook of Strategy, Oxford 2003, pp. 21- 46.

Kemper, A. C. (2000), "Strategische Markenpolitik im Investitionsgüterbereich", Lohmar, Köln 2000.

Kerin, R. A./Varadarajan, P. R./Peterson, R. A. (1992), "First-mover advantage: a synthesis, conceptual framework, and research propositions", in: Journal of Marketing, 56 (October), pp. 33-52.

Kern, T./Wilcocks, L. P. (2000), "Cooperative relationship strategy in global information technology out-sourcing", in: *Faulkner, D. O./de Rond, M.* (Eds.), Cooperative strategy: economic, business, and organizational issues, Oxford 2000, pp. 211-242.

Kim, K. (1999), "On determinants of joint action in industrial distributor-supplier relationships: beyond economic efficiency", in: International Journal of Research in Marketing, 16 (3), pp. 217-236.

Kirsch, W./Kutschker, M. (1978), "Das Marketing von Investitionsgütern - Theoretische und empirische Perspektiven eines Interaktionsansatzes", Wiesbaden 1978.

Kirzner, I. M. (1973), "Competition and entrepreneurship", Chicago 1973.

Kirzner, I. M. (1979), "Perception, opportunity, and profit: studies in the theory of entrepreneurship", Chicago 1979.

Kirzner, I. M. (1997), "Entrepreneurial discovery and the competitive market process: an Austrian approach", in: Journal of Economic Literature, 35 (March), pp. 60-85.

Kirzner, I. M. (1999), "Creativity and/or alertness: a reconsideration of the Schumpeterian entrepreneur", in: Review of Austrian Economics, 11 (1-2), pp. 5-17.

Kleikamp, C. (2002), "Performance Contracting auf Industriegütermärkten: Eine Analyse der Eintrittsentscheidung und des Vermarktungsprozesses", Lohmar, Köln 2002.

Klein, B. (1980), "Transaction cost determinants of "unfair" contractual arrangements", in: American Economic Review - Papers and Proceedings of the 92nd Annual Meeting of the American Economic Association, 70 (2), pp. 356-362.

Klein, B./Crawford, R. A./Alchian, A. A. (1978), "Vertical integration, appropriable rents and the competitive contracting process", in: Journal of Law and Economics, 21 (October), pp. 297-326.

Klein, B./Leffler, K. B. (1981), "The role of market forces in assuring contractual performance", in: Journal of Political Economy, 89 (4), pp. 615-641.

Klein, P. G./Lien, L. B. (2003), "Can the survivor principle survice diversification?" Paper presented at the "Nordic Workshop on Transaction Cost Economics in Business Administration", Bergen, Norway 2003.

Kleinaltenkamp, M. (1987), "Die Dynamisierung strategischer Marketing-Konzepte", in: Schmalenbachs Zeitschrift für betriebswirtschaftliche Forschung, 39, pp. 31-52.

Kleinaltenkamp, M. (1990), "Der Einfluß der Normung und Standardisierung auf die Diffusion technischer Innovationen", Arbeitspapiere des SFB 187 "Neue Informationstechnologien und flexible Arbeitssysteme: Entwicklung und Bewertung von CIM-Strukturen auf der Basis teilautonomer flexibler Fertigungsstrukturen", Working Paper, Bochum 1990.

Kleinaltenkamp, M. (1993), "Standardisierung und Marktprozeß: Entwicklungen und Auswirkungen im CIM-Bereich", Wiesbaden 1993.

Kleinaltenkamp, M. (1994), "Typologien von Business-to-Business-Transaktionen - Kritische Würdigung und Weiterentwicklung", in: Marketing ZFP, 16 (2), pp. 77-88.

Kleinaltenkamp, M. (1995), "Standardisierung und Individualisierung", in: *Tietz, B.* (Ed.), Handwörterbuch des Marketing, 2nd ed., Stuttgart 1995, pp. 2354-2364.

Kleinaltenkamp, M. (1997), "Business-to-Business Marketing", in: Gabler Wirtschafts-Lexikon, Wiesbaden 1997, pp. 753-762.

Kleinaltenkamp, M./Jacob, F. (2002), "German approaches to business-to-business marketing theory - Origins and structure", in: Journal of Business Research, 55 (2), pp. 149-155.

Kleinaltenkamp, M./Kühne, B. (2003), "Asymmetrische Bindungen in Geschäftsbeziehungen des Business-to-Business Bereichs", in: *Rese, M./Söllner, A./Utzig, B. P.* (Eds.), Relationship-Marketing: Standort und Perspektiven, Berlin 2003, pp. 11-44.

Kleinaltenkamp, M./Rudolph, M. (2000), "Mehrstufiges Marketing", in: *Kleinaltenkamp, M./Plinke, W.* (Eds.), Strategisches Business-to-Business Marketing, Berlin 2000, pp. 283-318.

Knight, F. H. (1921 (repr.: 1965)), "Risk, uncertainty and profit", New York (NY) 1965.

Köhl, T. (2000), "Claim-Management im internationalen Anlagengeschäft: Nachforderungspotentiale und deren Realisierung in unterschiedlichen Vertragsverhältnissen", Wiesbaden 2000.

Kosiol, E. (1964), "Betriebswirtschaftslehre und Unternehmensforschung. Eine Untersuchung ihrer Standorte und Beziehungen auf wissenschaftstheoretischer Grundlage", in: Zeitschrift für Betriebswirtschaft, 35, pp. 743-762.

Kotler, P. (1972), "A generic concept of marketing", in: Journal of Marketing, 36 (April), pp. 46-54.

Kotler, P. (1980), "Marketing management", Englewood Cliffs (NJ) 1980.

Kotler, P. (2003), "Marketing Management", 11th ed., Upper Saddle River (NJ) 2003.

Kowalczyk, S. J./Giusti, G. W. (1998), "The H-P way: an application using deliberate and emergent corporate cultures to analyze strategic competitive advantage", in: *Hamel, G. et al.* (Eds.), Strategic flexibility: manging in turbulent times, Chichester 1998, pp. 77-91.

Kreps, D. M./Wilson, R. (1982), "Reputation and imperfect information", in: Journal of Economic Theory, 27 (August), pp. 253-279.

Kuester, S. et al. (2001), "Verteidigungsstrategien gegen neue Wettbewerber - Bestandsaufnahme und empirische Untersuchung", in: Zeitschrift für Betriebswirtschaft, 71 (10), pp. 1191-1215.

Kumar, N./Scheer, L. K./Steenkamp, J.-B. E. M. (1995), "The effects of supplier fairness on vulnerable resellers", in: Journal of Marketing Research, 32 (February), pp. 54-65.

Kunkel, R. (1977), "Vertikales Marketing im Herstellerbereich", München 1977.

LaBahn, D. W. (1999), "Avoiding over-reliance on a single large customer: the impact of technical capability, product development and alternative key customers", in: Journal of Business-to-Business Marketing, Vol. 5 (4), pp. 5-36.

Lachmann, L. M. (1956), "Capital and its structure", London 1956.

Lachmann, L. M. (1977), "Capital, expectations and the market process: essays on the theory of the market economy", Kansas City 1977.

Lachmann, L. M. (1986), "The market as an economic process", Oxford 1986.

Lakatos, I. (1971), "History of science and its rational reconstructions", in: *Buck, R. C./Cohen, R. S.* (Eds.), PSA (Philosophy of Science Association). In memory of Rudolf Carnap, Boston Studies in the Pilosophy of Science, Vol. III, Dordrecht 1971, pp. 91-136.

Lambe, C. J./Wittmann, C. M./Spekman, R. E. (2001), "Social exchange theory and research on business-to-business relational exchange", in: Journal of Business-to-Business Marketing, 8 (3), pp. 1-36.

Lambe, J. C./Spekman, R. E./Hunt, S. D. (2000), "Interimistic relational exchange: conceptualization and propositional development", in: Journal of the Academy of Marketing Science, 28 (2), pp. 212-225.

Lamnek, S. (1995), "Qualitative Sozialforschung. Band 2: Methoden und Techniken", 3rd ed., München 1995.

Langlois, R. N. (1992), "Transaction-cost economics in real time", in: Industrial and Corporate Change, 1 (1), pp. 99-127.

Langlois, R. N./Foss, N. J. (1995), "Firms, markets, and economic change: a dynamic theory of business institutions", London 1995.

Lave, C. A./March, J. G. (1975), "An introduction to models in the social sciences", New York (NY) 1975.

Lawler, E. J. (1992), "Power processes in bargaining", in: Sociological Quarterly, 33 (1), pp. 17-34.

Layer, G. B. (1992), "Dem Systemlieferanten gehört die Zukunft", in: Beschaffung Aktuell, 39 (9), pp. 40-41.

Learned, E. P. et al. (1965), "Business policy: text and cases", Homewood (IL) 1965.

Leffler, K. B./Rucker, R. R. (1991), "Transaction costs and the efficient organzation of production: a study of timber-harvesting contracts", in: Journal of Political Economy, 99 (5), pp. 1060-1087.

Leinfellner, W. (1987/88), "Die Entscheidungstheorie - eine Konfliktlösungstheorie", in: Zeitschrift für Wissenschaftsforschung, 1987/88 (1), pp. 15-30.

Leitherer, E. (1965), "Die typologische Methode in der Betriebswirtschaftlehre - Versuch einer Übersicht", in: Schmalenbachs Zeitschrift für betriebswirtschaftliche Forschung, 17, pp. 650-662.

Leker, J. (2000), "Die Neuausrichtung der Unternehmensstrategie", Tübingen 2000.

Leker, J. (2001), "Reorientation in a competitive environment: an analysis of strategic change", in: Schmalenbach Business Review, 53 (January), pp. 41-55.

Levitt, T. (1980), "Marketing success through differentiation - of anything", in: Harvard Business Review, 58 (January/February), pp. 83-91.

Lewin, K. (1945), "The research center for group dynamics at Massachusetts Institute of Technology", in: Sociometry, 8 (2), pp. 126-136.

Lewis, A. (1941), "The two-part tariff", in: Economica, 8 (31), pp. 249-270.

Lieberman, M. B. (1987), "The learning curve, diffusion, and competitive strategy", in: Strategic Management Journal, 8 (5), pp. 441-452.

Lieberman, M. B./Montgomery, D. B. (1988), "First-mover advantages", in: Strategic Management Journal, 9 (Special Issue Summer 1988), pp. 41-58.

Liebowitz, S. J./Margolis, S. E. (1995), "Path dependence, lock-in, and history", in: Journal of Law, Economics and Organization, 11 (1), pp. 205-226.

Liebowitz, S. J./Margolis, S. E. (1998a), "Network externalities (effects)", in: *Newman, P.* (Ed.), The New Palgrave Dictionary of Economics and Law, London 1998, also available from http://wwwpub.utdallas.edu/~liebowit/netpage.html.

Liebowitz, S. J./Margolis, S. E. (1998b), "Path dependence", in: *Newman, P.* (Ed.), The New Palgrave Dictionary of Economics and the Law, London 1998, also available from http://wwwpub.utdallas.edu/~liebowit/palgrave/palpd.html.

Lilien, G. L. (1979), "ADVISOR ": modeling the marketing mix decision for industrial products", in: Management Science, 25 (2), pp. 191-204.

Littlechild, S. C. (1986), "Three types of market process", in: *Langlois, R. N.* (Ed.), Economics as a process, Cambridge 1986, pp. 27-39.

Lohtia, R./Brooks, C. M./Krapfel, R. E. (1994), "What constitutes a transaction-specific asset? An examination of the dimensions and types", in: Journal of Business Research, 30 (3), pp. 261-270.

Lorange, P. (1980), "Corporate planning: an executive viewpoint", Englewood Cliffs (NJ) 1980.

Lucas, R. E. (1988), "On the mechanics of economic development", in: Journal of Monetary Economics, 22, (1) pp. 3-42.

Luce, R. D./Raiffa, H. (1967), "Games and decisions: introduction and critical survey", New York (NY) 1967.

Luck, D. J. (1969), "Broadening the concept of marketing - too far", in: Journal of Marketing, 33 (July), pp. 53-55.

Lurie, R. S./Kohli, A. K. (2003), "Massenware geschickter verkaufen", in: Harvard Business manager, 2003 (March), pp. 8-9.

Lyon, L., S. (1926), "Salesmen in marketing strategy", New York (NY) 1926.

Macharzina, K. (1999), "Unternehmensführung", 3rd ed., Wiesbaden 1999.

MacMillan, I. C. (1983), "Preemptive strategies", in: Journal of Business Strategy, 4 (Fall), pp. 16-26.

MacMillan, J. (1992), "Games, strategies and managers", New York (NY) 1992.

Macneil, I. R. (1974), "The many futures of contract", in: Southern California Law Review, 47 (4), pp. 691-816.

Macneil, I. R. (1978), "Contracts: adjustment of long-term economic relations under classical, neoclassical, and relational contract law", in: Northwestern University Law Review, 72 (6), pp. 854-905.

Madhok, A. (2002), "Reassessing the fundamentals and beyond: Ronald Coase, the transaction cost and resource-based theories of the firm and the institutional structure of production", in: Strategic Management Journal, 23 (11), pp. 535-550.

Mahoney, J. T. (2001), "A resource-based theory of sustainable rents", in: Journal of Management, 27 (6), pp. 651-660.

Mahoney, J. T./Pandian, J. R. (1992), "The resource-based view within the conversation of strategic management", in: Strategic Management Journal, 13 (5), pp. 363-380.

Makadok, R. (2002), "The theory of value and the value of theory: breaking new ground versus reinventing the wheel", in: Academy of Management Review, 27 (1), pp. 10-16.

Malone, T. W./Yates, J./Benjamin, R. I. (1987), "Electronic markets and electronic hierarchies", in: Communications of the Association for Computing Machinery (ACM), 30 (6), pp. 484-497.

Männel, B. (1996), "Netzwerke in der Zulieferindustrie", Wiesbaden 1996.

March, J. G./Shapira, Z. (1987), "Managerial perspectives on risk and risk taking", in: Management Science, 33 (11), pp. 1404-1418.

Markoff, J. (1998), "Before Windows and internet, there was Ethernet", in: New York Times 18.05.1998, Date of access: November 11th, 1998, available from: http://www.nytimes.com/library/tech/98/05/biztech/articles/18ethernet.html.

Marrian, J. (1968), "Marketing characteristics of industrial goods and buyers", in: *Wilson, A.* (Ed.), The marketing of industrial goods, London 1968, pp. 10-23.

Marshall, A. (1920 (repr.: 1938)), "Principles of economics", 8th ed., London 1938.

Mason, E. S. (1949), "The current state of the monopoly problem in the United States", in: Harvard Law Review, 62, pp. 1265-1285.

Masten, S. E. (1984), "The organization of production: evidence from the aerospace industry", in: Journal of Law and Economics, 27 (October), pp. 403-417.

Masten, S. E. (1995), "Introduction to vol. II", in: *Masten, S. E./Williamson, O. E.* (Eds.), Transaction cost economics, Brookfield (VT) 1995, pp. xi-xxii.

Masten, S. E. (1997), "Empirical research in transaction cost economics:challenges, progress, directions", in: *Groenewegen, J.* (Ed.), Transaction cost economics and beyond, Dordrecht 1997, pp. 43-64.

Masten, S. E./Meehan Jr, J. W./Snyder, E. A. (1991), "The costs of organization", in: Journal of Law, Economics, and Organization, 7 (1), pp. 1-25.

Masten, S. E./Snyder, E. A. (1993), "United States versus United Shoe Machinery Corporation: on the merits", in: Journal of Law and Economics, 36 (1), pp. 33-70.

Mathur, K./Solow, D. (1994), "Management science: the art of decision making", Englewood Cliffs (NJ) 1994.

Mathur, S. S. (1984), "Competitive industrial marketing strategies", in: Long Range Planning, 17 (4), pp. 102-109.

Mathur, S. S./Kenyon, A. (1997), "Creating value: shaping tomorrow's business", Oxford 1997.

McKelvey, B. (1982), "Organizational systematics - taxonomy, evolution, classification", Berkeley (CA) 1982.

Mechanic, D. (1963), "Some considerations in the methodology of organizational studies", in: *Leavitt, H. J.* (Ed.), The social science of organizations, Englewood Cliffs (NJ) 1963, pp. 137-182.

Meffert, H. (1994), "Marketing-Management", Wiesbaden 1994.

Meffert, H. (2000), "Marketing - Grundlagen marktorientierter Unternehmensführung", 9th ed., Wiesbaden 2000.

Menger, C. (1871 (repr.: 1990)), "Grundsätze der Volkswirtschaftslehre", Düsseldorf 1990.

Menger, C. (1883), "Untersuchungen über die Methode der Sozialwissenschaften und der politischen Oekonomie insbesondere", Leipzig 1883.

Metcalfe, J. S. (2000), "Instituted economic processes, increasing returns and endogenous growth", in: *Louçã, F./Perlman, M.* (Eds.), Is economics an evolutionary science? The legacy of *Thorstein Veblen*, Cheltenham 2000, pp. 197-225.

Metcalfe, J. S. (2001), "Institutions and progress", in: Industrial and Corporate Change, 10 (3), pp. 561-586.

Meyer, A. D./Brooks, G. R./Goes, J. B. (1990), "Environmental jolts and industry revolutions", in: Strategic Management Journal, 11 (Special Issue Summer 1990), pp. 93-110.

Meyer, M./Kern, E./Diehl, H.-J. (1998), "Geschäftstypologien im Investitionsgütermarketing", in: *Büschken, J./Meyer, M./Weiber, R.* (Eds.), Entwicklungen des Industriegütermarketing, Wiesbaden 1998, pp. 117-175.

Meyer, R. (2000), "Entscheidungstheorie", 2nd ed., Wiesbaden 2000.

Miles, M. B./Huberman, A. M. (1994), "Qualitative data analysis: an expanded sourcebook", 2nd ed., Thousand Oaks (CA) 1994.

Miles, R. E./Snow, C. C. (1978), "Organization strategy, structure, and process", New York (NY) 1978.

Milgrom, P./Roberts, J. (1982), "Predation, reputation, and entry deterrence", in: Journal of Economic Theory, 27 (August), pp. 280-312.

Milgrom, P./Roberts, J. (1992), "Economics, organization, and management", Englewood Cliffs (NJ) 1992.

Miller, D./Chen, M.-J. (1994), "Sources and consequences of competitive inertia: a study of the U.S. airline industry", in: Administrative Science Quarterly, 39 (1), pp. 1-23.

Miller, D./Friesen, P. H. (1980), "Momentum and revolution in organizational adaptation", in: Academy of Management Journal, 23 (4), pp. 591-614.

Mintzberg, H. T. (1978), "Patterns in strategy formation", in: Management Science, 24 (9), pp. 934-948.

Mintzberg, H. T. (1979), "The structuring of organizations", Englewood Cliffs (NJ) 1979.

Mintzberg, H. T. (1983), "Structure in fives: designing effective organizations", Englewood Cliffs (NJ) 1983.

Mintzberg, H. T. (1987), "The strategy concept I: five P's for strategy", in: California Management Review, 30 (1), pp. 11-24.

Mintzberg, H. T./McHugh, A. (1985), "Strategy formation in adhocracy", in: Administrative Science Quarterly, 30 (2), pp. 160-197.

Mintzberg, H. T./Waters, J. A. (1985), "Of strategies, deliberate and emergent", in: Strategic Management Journal, 6 (3), pp. 257-272.

Miracle, G. E. (1965), "Product characteristics and marketing strategy", in: Journal of Marketing, 29 (1), pp. 18-24.

Mises, L. v. (1940 (repr.:1980)), "Nationalökonomie. Theorie des Handelns und Wirtschaftens", München 1980.

Mises, L. v. (1949 (repr.: 1966)), "Human action: a treatise on economics", 3rd ed., Chicago 1966.

Montaguti, E./Kuester, S./Robertson, T. S. (2002), "Entry strategy for radical product innovations: a conceptual model and propositional inventory", in: International Journal of Research in Marketing, 19 (1), pp. 21-42.

Montgomery, C. A. (1988), "Guest editor's introduction to the special issue on research in the content of strategy", in: Strategic Management Journal, 9 (Special Issue Summer 1988), pp. 3-8.

Moorthy, K. S. (1985), "Using game theory to model competition", in: Journal of Marketing Research, 22 (August), pp. 262-282.

Morgan, B. T. (1984), "Elements of simulation", Boca Raton 1984.

Morgan, R. M./Hunt, S. D. (1994), "The commitment-trust theory of relationship marketing", in: Journal of Marketing, 58 (July), pp. 20-38.

Mudambi, R. (1990), "Entry deterrence: the case of a buyer with market power", in: Review of Industrial Organization, 5 (1), pp. 111-138.

Mudambi, R./McDowell-Mudambi, S. (1995), "From transaction cost economics to relationship marketing: a model of buyer-supplier relations", in: International Business Review, 4 (4), pp. 419-433.

Mudambi, S. (2002), "Branding importance in business-to-business markets: three buyer clusters", in: Industrial Marketing Management, 31, pp. 525-533.

Müller-Hagedorn, L. (1983), "Marketing ohne verhaltenswissenschaftliche Fundierung?" in: Marketing ZFP, 5 (3), pp. 205-211.

Nalebuff, B. J./Brandenburger, A. M. (1996), "Co-opetition", London 1996.

Nash, J. F. (1950), "The bargaining problem", in: Econometrica, 18 (January), pp. 155-162.

Nash, J. F. (1951), "Non-cooperative games", in: Annals of Mathematics, 54 (September), pp. 286-295.

Nelson, P. (1970), "Information and consumer behavior", in: Journal of Political Economy, 78 (2), pp. 311-329.

Nelson, R. R. (1991), "Why do firms differ, and how does it matter?" in: Strategic Management Journal, 12 (Special Issue Winter 1991), pp. 61-74.

Nickerson, J. A. (year not indicated), "Toward a positioning-economizing theory of strategy", Working Paper, St. Louis.

Nickerson, J. A./Hamilton, B. H./Wada, T. (2001), "Market position, resource profile, and governance: linking *Porter* and *Williamson* in the context of international courier and small package services in Japan", in: Strategic Mangement Journal, 22, pp. 251-273.

Nickerson, J. A./Vanden Bergh, R. (1999), "Economizing in a context of strategizing: governance mode choice in Cournot competition", in: Journal of Economic Behavior and Organization, 40 (1), pp. 1-15.

Noordewier, T. G./John, G./Nevin, J. R. (1990), "Performance outcomes of purchasing arrangements in industrial buyer-vendor-relationships", in: Journal of Marketing, 54 (October), pp. 80-93.

Norris, D. G. (1992), "Ingredient branding: a strategy option with multiple benefits", in: Journal of Consumer Research, 9 (3), pp. 19-31.

North, D. C. (1984), "Transaction Costs, institutions, and economic history", in: Journal of Institutional and Theoretical Economics, 140, pp. 7-17.

North, D. C. (1991), "Institutions", in: Journal of Economic Perspectives, 5 (1), pp. 97-112.

Oelsnitz, D. v. d. (1995), "Ingredient Branding", in: Das Wirtschaftsstudium, 24 (10), pp. 791.

Oi, W. Y. (1971), "A disneyland dilemma: two-part tariffs for a mickey mouse monopoly", in: Quarterly Journal of Economics, 85 (1), pp. 77-96.

Oliver, C. (1990), "Determinants of interorganizational relationships: integration and future directions", in: Academy of Management Journal, 15 (2), pp. 241-265.

Parkhe, A. (1993), "Strategic alliance structuring: a game theoretic and transaction cost examination of interfirm cooperation", in: Academy of Management Journal, 36 (August), pp. 794-829.

Pavitt, K. (1984), "Sectoral patterns of technical change: towards a taxonomy and a theory", in: Research Policy, 13 (6), pp. 343-373.

Peffer, J./Salancik, G. R. (1978), "The external control of organizations: a resource dependence perspective", New York (NY) 1978.

Peneder, M. (2001), "Entrepreneurial competition and industrial location", Cheltenham 2001.

Perrow, C. (1967), "A framework for the comparative analysis of organizations", in: American Sociological Review, 32 (2), pp. 194-208.

Perry, M. K. (1989), "Vertical integration: determinants and effects", in: *Schmalensee, R./Willig, R.* (Eds.), Handbook of Industrial Organization, Vol. 1, Amsterdam 1989, pp. 183-255.

Pettigrew, A. M. (1992), "The character and significance of strategy process research", in: Strategic Management Journal, 13 (Special Issue Winter 1992), pp. 5-16.

Pfeiffer, W./Bischof, P. (1974), "Investitionsgüterabsatz", in: *Tietz, B.* (Ed.), Handwörterbuch der Absatzwirtschaft, Stuttgart 1974, pp. 918-938.

Picot, A. (1981), "Transaktionskostentheorie der Organisation", Beiträge zur Unternehmensführung und Organsation, Universität Hannover, Working Paper, Hannover 1981.

Picot, A. (1991), "Ein neuer Ansatz zur Gestaltung der Leistungstiefe", in: Schmalenbachs Zeitschrift für betriebswirtschaftliche Forschung, 43 (4), pp. 336-357.

Picot, A./Dietl, H. (1990), "Transaktionskostentheorie", in: Wirtschaftswissenschaftliches Studium, 19 (4), pp. 178-184.

Picot, A./Dietl, H./Franck, E. (1997), "Organisation - Eine ökonomische Perspektive", Stuttgart 1997.

Pies, I. (1993), "Normative Institutionenökonomik: Zur Rationalisierung des politischen Liberalismus", Tübingen 1993.

Pine, J. B. (1993), "Mass customization: the new frontier in business competition", Boston (MA) 1993.

Plank, R. E./Ferrin, B. G. (2002), "How manufacturers value purchase offerings - an exploratory study", in: Industrial Marketing Management, 31, pp. 457-465.

Plinke, W. (1989), "Die Geschäftsbeziehung als Investition", in: *Specht, G.* (Eds.), Marketing-Schnittstellen, Stuttgart 1989, pp. 305-325.

Plinke, W. (1997), "Grundlagen des Geschäftsbeziehungsmanagements", in: *Plinke, W. /Kleinaltenkamp, M.* (Eds.), Geschäftsbeziehungsmanagement, Berlin 1997, pp. 1-62.

Plinke, W. (1998), "Effizienz und Effektivität im Management von Geschäftsbeziehungen auf industriellen Märkten", in: *Büschken, J./Meyer, M./Weiber, R.* (Eds.), Entwicklungen des Industriegütermarketing, Wiesbaden 1998, pp. 179-199.

Plinke, W. (2000), "Grundlagen des Marktprozesses", in: *Kleinaltenkamp, M./Plinke, W.* (Eds.), Technischer Vertrieb, Berlin 2000, pp. 3-99.

Plinke, W./Söllner, A. (1999), "Preisgestaltung im Produktgeschäft", in: *Kleinaltenkamp, M./Plinke, W.* (Eds.), Markt- und Produktmanagement: Die Instrumente des Technischen Vertriebs, Berlin 1999, pp. 637-693.

Plinke, W./Söllner, A. (2000), "Kundenbindung und Abhängigkeitsbeziehungen", in: *Bruhn, M./Homburg, C.* (Eds.), Handbuch Kundenbindungsmanagement, 3rd ed., Wiesbaden 2000, pp. 55-79.

Plötner, O. (1995), "Das Vertrauen des Kunden", Wiesbaden 1995.

Popper, K. R. (1959), "The logic of scientific discovery", Toronto 1959.

Poppo, L./Zenger, T. (1998), "Testing alternative theories of the firm: transaction cost, knowledge-based, and measurement explanations for make-or-buy decisions in information services", in: Strategic Management Journal, 19, pp. 853-877.

Porter, M. E. (1980), "Competitive strategy: techniques for analyzing industries and competitors", New York (NY) 1980.

Porter, M. E. (1985), "Competitive advantage: creating and sustaining superior performance", New York (NY) 1985.

Porter, M. E. (1991), "Towards a dynamic theory of strategy", in: Strategic Management Journal, 12 (Special Issue Winter 1991), pp. 95-117.

Possmeier, F. (2000), "Preispolitik bei hoher Fixkostenintenität", Lohmar, Köln 2000.

Prabhu, H./Stewart, D. W. (2001), "Signaling strategies in competitive interaction: building reputations and hiding the truth", in: Journal of Marketing Research, 38 (February), pp. 62-72.

Preß, B. (1997), "Kaufverhalten in Geschäftsbeziehungen", in: *Plinke, W./Kleinaltenkamp, M.* (Eds.), Geschäftsbeziehungsmanagement, Berlin 1997, pp. 63-111.

Rabin, M. (1990), "Communication between rational agents", in: Journal of Economic Theory, 51 (June), pp. 144-170.

Raiffa, H. (1997), "Lectures on negotiation analysis", Cambridge (MA) 1997.

Raiffeisen Central-Genossenschaft Nordwest eG (2002), "Über uns - Vertrauen durch Leistung", Raiffeisen Central-Genossenschaft Nordwest eG, Date of access: November 19th, 2002, available from: http://www.rcg.de/.

Rajagopalan, N. et al. (1997), "A multi-theoretic model of strategic decision making processes", in: *Papadakis, V./Barwise, P.* (Eds.), Strategic decisions, Dordrecht 1997, pp. 229-249.

Rajagopalan, N./Spreitzer, G. M. (1996), "Toward a theory of strategic change: a multi-lens perspective and integrative framework", in: Academy of Management Review, 22 (1), pp. 48-79.

Rangan, V. K./Corey, E. R./Cespedes, F. (1993), "Transaction cost theory: inferences from clinical field research on downstream vertical integration", in: Organization Science, 4 (3), pp. 454-477.

Rasmusen, E. (2001), "Games and information: an introduction to game theory", 3[rd.], Malden (MA) 2001.

Rawls, J. (1983), "Political philosophy: political not metaphysical", unpublished manuscript.

Regan, S. (2002), "Game theory and strategy", in: *Jenkins, M./Ambrosini, V.* (Eds.), Strategic management: A multi-perspective approach, Basingstoke, New York 2002, pp. 91-112.

Reid, D. A./Plank, R. E. (2000), "Business marketing comes of age: a comprehensive review of the literature", in: Journal of Business-to-Business Marketing, 7 (2/3), pp. 9-185.

Reinkemeier, C. (1998), "Systembindungseffekte bei der Beschaffung von Informationstechnologien: Der Markt für PPS-Systeme", Wiesbaden 1998.

Reinking, G. (2002), "Continental ändert Zulieferstrategie", in: Financial Times Deuschland 15.04.2002, Date of access: April 15th, 2002, available from: http://www.ftd.de/ub/in/1014399003782.html?nv=se.

Rhoades, E. L. (1927), "Introductory readings in marketing", Chicago 1927.

Rich (1992), "The organizational taxonomy: definition and design", in: Academy of Management Review, 17 (4), pp. 758-781.

Richter, R./Furubotn, E. G. (1999), "Neue Institutionenökonomik: Eine Einführung und kritische Würdigung", 2nd ed., Tübingen 1999.

Rickard, S. (2002), "Industrial organization economics", in: *Jenkins, M./Ambrosini, V.* (Eds.), Strategic management: a multi-perspective approach, Basingstoke, New York 2002, pp. 15-38.

Riebel, P. (1965), "Typen der Markt- und Kundenproduktion in produktions- und absatzwirtschaftlicher Sicht", in: Schmalenbachs Zeitschrift für betriebswirtschaftliche Forschung, 17, pp. 663-685.

Rindfleisch, A./Heide, J. B. (1997), "Transaction cost analysis: past, present, and future applications", in: Journal of Marketing, 61 (October), pp. 30-54.

Riordan, M. H./Williamson, O. E. (1985), "Asset specificity and economic organization", in: International Journal of Industrial Organization, 3 (December), pp. 365-378.

Robin, D. P. (1979), "A useful scope for marketing", in: Journal of the Academy of Marketing Science, 6 (3), pp. 228-238.

Rogers, E. M. (1962 (repr.: 1968)), "Diffusion of innovations", New York (NY) 1968.

Romer, P. (1990), "Endogenous technological change", in: Journal of Political Economy, 98 (5), pp. 71-102.

Romer, P. M. (1986), "Increasing returns and long-run growth", in: Journal of Political Economy, 94 (5), pp. 1002-1037.

Rose, D. (1968), "The service element in added value", in: *Wilson, A.* (Ed.), The marketing of industrial goods, London 1968, pp. 124-133.

Rosen, B. N. (1994), "The standard setter's dilemma", in: Industrial Marketing Management, 23, pp. 181-190.

Ross, S. A. (1973), "The economic theory of agency: the principals problem", in: American Economic Review, 62 (May), pp. 134-139.

Rowe, D./Alexander, I. (1968), "Selling industrial products", London 1968.

Rubin, P. H. (1990), "Managing business transactions", New York (NY) 1990.

Rubinstein, R. Y. (1981), "Simulation and the Monte Carlo method", New York (NY) 1981.

Rudolph, M. (1989), "Mehrstufiges Marketing für Einsatzstoffe: Anwendungsvoraussetzungen und Strategietypen", Frankfurt/Main 1989.

Rühl, A. (1997), "Eine Alternative zum eigenen Lkw-Fuhrpark", in: Beschaffung Aktuell, 1997 (12), pp. 32-33.

Rühli, E./Schmidt, S. L. (2001), "Strategieprozessforschung", in: Zeitschrift für Betriebswirtschaft, 71 (5), pp. 531-550.

Rumelt, R. P. (1984), "Towards a strategic theory of the firm", in: *Lamb, R. B.* (Ed.), Competitive strategic management, Englewood Cliffs (NJ) 1984, pp. 556-570.

Rumelt, R. P./Schendel, D./Teece, D. J. (1991), "Strategic management and economics", in: Strategic Management Journal, 12 (Special Issue Winter 1991), pp. 5-29.

Rutherford, M. (1983), "J. R. Common's institutional economics", in: Journal of Economic Issues, 17 (3), pp. 721-744.

Saloner, G. (1991), "Modeling, game theory, and strategic management", in: Strategic Management Journal, 12 (Special Issue Winter 1991), pp. 119-136.

Sanchez, R. (2000), "Demand uncertainty and asset flexibility: incorporating strategic options in the theory of the firm", in: *Foss, N. J./Mahnke, V.* (Eds.), Competence, governance, and entrepreneurship, Oxford 2000, pp. 319-332.

Schade, C. (1996), "Marketing für Unternehmensberatungen: ein institutionenökonomischer Ansatz", Wiesbaden 1996.

Schade, C./Schott, E. (1993a), "Instrumente des Kontraktgütermarketing", in: Die Betriebswirtschaft, 53 (4), pp. 491-511.

Schade, C./Schott, E. (1993b), "Kontraktgüter im Marketing", in: Marketing ZFP, 15 (1), pp. 15-25.

Scheffler, S. (2001), "Der besessene Kandidat", in: DIE ZEIT 31.10.2001, p. 23.

Scheffler, S. (2002), "Die News-Economy", in: DIE ZEIT 17.01.2002, p. 54.

Schelling, T. C. (1980), "The strategy of conflict", Cambridge (MA) 1980.

Schendel, D. (1992), "Introduction to the summer 1992 special issue on "Strategy process research"", in: Strategic Management Journal, 13 (Special Issue Summer 1992), pp. 1-4.

Schendel, D. E./Hofer, C. W. (1979), "Strategic management: a new view of business policy and planning", in: *Schendel, D. E./Hofer, C. W.* (Eds.), Strategic management: a new view of business policy and planning, Boston (MA) 1979, pp. 1-22.

Schmidt, I./Elßler, S. (1992), "Die Rolle des Markenartikels im marktwirtschaftlichen System", in: *Dichtl, E./Eggers, W.* (Eds.), Marke und Markenartikel als Instrumente des Wettbewerbs, München 1992, pp. 47-69.

Schmidt, R. H./Terberger, E. (1997), "Grundzüge der Investitions- und Finanzierungstheorie", 4th ed., Wiesbaden 1997.

Schmoller, G. (1900 (repr.: 1989)), "Grundriß der Allgemeinen Volkswirtschaftslehre", Düsseldorf 1989.

Schnell, R./Hill, P. B./Esser, E. (1999), "Methoden der empirischen Sozialforschung", 6th ed., München 1999.

Schreyögg, G. (1984), "Unternehmensstrategie", Berlin 1984.

Schumann, J./Meyer, U./Ströbele, W. (1999), "Grundzüge der mikroökonomischen Theorie", 7th ed., Berlin 1999.

Schumpeter, J. A. (1926), "Theorie der wirtschaftlichen Entwicklung", 2nd ed., München 1926.

Schumpeter, J. A. (1928), "Unternehmer", in: *Elster, L./Weber, A./Wieser, F.* (Eds.), Handwörterbuch der Staatswissenschaften, 4th ed., Jena 1928, pp. 476-487.

Schumpeter, J. A. (1934 (repr.: 1961)), "The theory of economic development", New York (NY) 1961.

Schumpeter, J. A. (1942), "Capitalism, socialism and democracy", New York 1942.

Schwartz, G. (1965), "Nature and goals of marketing science", in: *Schwartz, G.* (Ed.), Science in marketing, New York (NY) 1965, pp. 1-29.

Scott, W. R. (1981), "Organisations: rational, natural, and open systems", Englewood Cliffs (NJ) 1981.

Scott, W. R. (1998), "Organizations: rational, natural, and open systems", 4th ed., Upper Saddle River (NJ) 1998.

Selten, R. (1975), "Reexamination of the perfectness concept for equilibrium points in extensive games", in: International Journal of Game Theory, 4 (1), pp. 25-55.

Shackle, G. L. S. (1972), "Economics and epistemics: a critique of economic doctrines", Cambridge 1972.

Shapiro, C./Varian, H. R. (1999), "Information rules", Boston (MA) 1999.

Sheth, J. N./Gardner, D. M./Garrett, D. E. (1988), "Marketing theory: evolution and evaluation", New York (NY) 1988.

Silverman, B. S. (1999), "Technological resources and the direction of corporate diversification: toward an integration of the resource-based view and transaction cost economics", in: Management Science, 45 (8), pp. 1109-1124.

Simon, H. et al. (2000), "Kundenbindung durch Preispolitik", in: *Bruhn, M./Homburg, C.* (Eds.), Handbuch Kundenbindungsmanagement, 3rd ed., Wiesbaden, pp. 319-335.

Simon, H. A. (1945), "Administrative behavior - A study of decision-making processes in administrative organizations", New York (NY) 1945.

Simon, H. A. (1961), "Administrative behavior", 2nd ed., New York (NY) 1961.

Simon, H. A. (1964), "On the concept of organizational goal", in: Administrative Science Quarterly, 9 (June), pp. 1-22.

Simon, H. A. (1969), "The sciences of the artificial", Cambridge (MA) 1961.

Simon, H. A. (1991), "Organizations and markets", in: Journal of Economic Perspectives, 5 (2), pp. 25-44.

Simpson, P. M./Siguaw, J. A./Baker, T. L. (2001), "A model of value creation", in: Industrial Marketing Management, 30, pp. 119-134.

Skarmeas, D. A./Katsikeas, C. S. (2001), "Drivers of superior importer performance in cross-cultural supplier-reseller relationships", in: Industrial Marketing Management, 30, pp. 227-241.

Smit, H. T. J./Ankum, L. A. (1993), "A real options and game-theoretic approach to corporate investment strategy under competition", in: Financial Management, 22 (3), pp. 241-250.

Smith, A. (1789 (repr.: 1976)), "An inquiry into the nature and causes of the wealth of nations", Oxford 1976.

Snow, C. C./Hambrick, D. C. (1980), "Measuring organizational strategies: some theoretical and methodological problems", in: Academy of Management Review, 5 (4), pp. 527-538.

Söllner, A. (1993), "Commitment in Geschäftsbeziehungen - Das Beispiel Lean Production", Wiesbaden 1993.

Söllner, A. (1994), "Commitment in exchange relationships: the role of switching costs in building and sustaining competitive advantages", Paper presented at the "Relationship marketing: theory, methods and applications" Conference, Atlanta, USA 1994.

Spence, M. (1976), "Informational aspects of market structure: an introduction", in: Quarterly Journal of Economics, 90 (4), pp. 591-597.

Spence, M. (1977), "Entry, capacity investment and oligopolistic pricing", in: Bell Journal of Economics, 8 (Autumn), pp. 534-544.

Spence, M./Zeckhauser, R. (1971), "Insurance, information and individual action", in: American Economic Review, 61 (May), pp. 380-387.

Spence, M. A. (1984), "Competition, entry, and antitrust policy", in: *Lamb, R. B.* (Eds.), Competitive strategic management, Englewood Cliffs (NJ) 1984, pp. 446-467.

Spremann, K. (1990), "Asymmetrische Information", in: Zeitschrift für Betriebswirtschaft, 60 (5/6), pp. 561-586.

Städtler, A. (2000), "Leasing in Deutschland: Breitengeschäft wächst weiter - Großmobilien durch Steuerrechtsänderungen gebremst", in: ifo Schnelldienst, 53 (35-36), pp. 27-34.

Stefansson, B. (2000), "Simulating economic agents in Swarm", in: *Luna, F./Stefansson, B.* (Eds.), Economic simulations in Swarm: agent-based modelling and Object Oriented Programming, Dordrecht 2000, pp. 3-61.

Stern, L. W./Reve, T. (1980), "Distribution channels as political economies: a framework for comparative analysis", in: Journal of Marketing, 44 (Summer), pp. 52-64.

Stigler, G. J. (1961), "The Economics of information", in: Journal of Political Economy, 69 (June), pp. 213-225.

Stigler, G. J. (1968 (repr.: 1990)), "The organization of industry", Chicago 1990.

Stigler, J. G./Rothshild, M. (1976), "Equilibrium in competitive insurance markets: an essay on the economics of imperfect enformation", in: Quarterly Journal of Economics, 90 (November), pp. 629-649.

Stiglitz, J. E. (1975), "Theory of screening, education and the distribution of income", in: American Economic Review, 65 (June), pp. 283-300.

Stiglitz, J. E. (1989), "Imperfect information in the product market", in: *Schmalensee, R./ Willig, R.* (Eds.), Handbook of Industrial Organization, Vol. 1, Amsterdam 1989, pp. 769-847.

Stinchcombe, A. L./Heimer, C. A. (1985), "Organization theory and project management: administering uncertainty in Norwegian offshore oil", Oslo 1985.

Stoelhorst, J. W. (1997), "In search of a dynamic theory of the firm", PhD-thesis, University of Twente, Twente 1997.

Stremersch, S./Tellis, G. J. (2002), "Strategic bundling of products and prices: a new synthesis for marketing", in: Journal of Marketing, 66 (January), pp. 55-72.

Stump, R. L./Joshi, A. W. (1998), "To be or not to be [locked in]: an investigation of buyers' commitments of dedicated investments to support new transactions", in: Journal of Business-to-Business Marketing, 5 (3), pp. 33-63.

Sudharshan, D. (1995), "Marketing strategy: relationships, offerings, timing, and resource allocation", Englewood Cliffs (NJ) 1995.

Sundbo, J. (1998 (repr.: 2001)), "The theory of innovation: entrepreneurs, technology and strategy", Cheltenham 2001.

Sutton, J. (1998), "Technology and market structure: theory and history", Cambridge (MA) 1998.

Tang, M.-J. (1988), "An economic perspective on escalating commitment", in: Strategic Management Journal, 9 (Special Issue Summer 1988), pp. 79-92.

Tarlatt, A. (2001), "Implementierung von Strategien im Unternehmen", Wiesbaden 2001.

Teece, D. J. (1988), "Capturing value from technological innovation: integration, strategic partnering, and licensing decisions", in: Interfaces, 18 (May/June), pp. 46-61.

Teece, D. J. (2003), "The strategic management of technology and intellectual property", in: *Faulkner, D. O./Campbell, A.* (Eds.), The Oxford Handbook of Strategy, Oxford 2003, pp. 132-166.

Teece, D. J./Pisano, G./Shuen, A. (1997), "Dynamic capabilities and strategic management", in: Strategic Management Journal, 18 (7), pp. 509-533.

Telser, L. G. (1971), "Competition, collusion, and game theory", London 1971.

Telser, L. G. (1981), "A theory of self-enforcing agreements", in: Journal of Business, 53 (1), pp. 27-44.

Thibaut, J. W./Kelley, H. H. (1959), "The social psychology of groups", New York (NY) 1959.

Thomke, S./von Hippel, E. (2002), "Customers as innovators", in: Harvard Business Review, 80 (April), pp. 74-81.

Thurow, L. C. (1980), "The zero-sum-society. Distribution and the possibilities for economic change", New York (NY) 1980.

Tirole, J. (1986), "Procurement and renegotiation", in: Journal of Political Economy, 94 (2), pp. 235-259.

Tirole, J. (1995), "Industrieökonomik", München 1995.

Tollison, R. D. (1982), "Rent seeking: a survey", in: Kyklos, 35, pp. 575-602.

Townsend, R. M. (1982), "Optimal multiperiod contracts and the gain from enduring relationships under private information", in: Journal of Political Economy, 90 (6), pp. 1166-1186.

Trigeorgis, L. (1995), "Real options: an overview", in: *Trigeorgis, L.* (Ed.), Real options in capital investment: models, strategies, and applications, Westport (CT) 1995, pp. 1- 28.

Troitzsch, K. G. (1990), "Modellbildung und Simulation in den Sozialwissenschaften", Opladen 1990.

Tucker, W. T. (1974), "Future directions in marketing theory", in: Journal of Marketing, 38 (April), pp. 30-35.

Tushman, M. L. (1997), "Winning through", in: Strategy and Leadership, 1997 (July/August), pp. 14-19.

Tushman, M. L./Romanelli, E. (1985), "Organizational evolution: a metamorphosis model of convergence and reorientation", in: Research in Organizational Behavior, 7, pp. 171-222.

Ulrich, D./Barney, J. B. (1984), "Perspectives in organizations: resource dependence, efficiency, and population", in: Academy of Management Review, 9 (3), pp. 471-481.

Utterback, J. M./Abernathy, W. J. (1975), "A dynamic model of process and product innovation", in: OMEGA, 3 (6), pp. 639-656.

Van de Ven, A. H. (1992), "Suggestions for studying strategy process - A research note", in: Strategic Management Journal, 13 (Special Issue Summer and Winter 1992), pp. 169-188.

Vancil, R. F./Lorange, P. (1975), "Strategic planning in diversified companies", in: Harvard Business Review, 53 (January/February), pp. 81-90.

Varadarajan, P. R. (1994), "From the editor", in: Journal of Marketing, 58 (1), pp. i-v.

Varadarajan, P. R. (1999), "Strategy content and process perspectives revisited", in: Journal of the Academy of Marketing Science, 27 (1), pp. 88-100.

Varadarajan, P. R./Clark, T. (1994), "Delineating the scope of corporate, business, and marketing strategy", in: Journal of Business Research, 31 (2/3), pp. 93-105.

Varadarajan, P. R./Jayachandran, S. (1999), "Marketing strategy: an assessment of the state of the field and outlook", in: Journal of the Academy of Marketing Science, 27 (2), pp. 120-143.

Varadarajan, P. R./Jayachandran, S./White, J. C. (2001), "Strategic interdependence in organizations: deconglomeration and marketing strategy", in: Journal of Marketing, 65 (January), pp. 15-28.

Varian, H. R. (1999), "Intermediate micoreconomics", 5th ed., New York (NY) 1999.

Vaughn, K. I. (1994), "Austrian economics in America: the migration of a tradition", Cambridge 1994.

Veblen, T. B. (1899 (repr.: 1998)), "The theory of the leisure class: an economic study of institutions", Amherst (NY) 1998.

Veblen, T. B. (1904 (repr.: 1975)), "The theory of business enterprise", Clifton (NJ) 1975.

Venkataraman, S./Sarasvathy, S. D. (2001), "Strategy and entrepreneurship: outlines of an untold story", in: *Hitt, M. A./Freeman, R. E./Harrison, J. S.* (Eds.), The Blackwell Handbook of Strategic Management, Oxford 2001, pp. 650-668.

Venkatraman, N. (1989), "Strategic orientation of business enterprises: the construct, dimensionality, and measurement", in: Management Science, 35 (8), pp. 942-962.

Voeth, M. (2002), "Nachfragerbündelung", in: Schmalenbachs Zeitschrift für betriebswirtschaftliche Forschung, 54 (März), pp. 113-127.

von Burg, U./Kenney, M. (2000), "Venture capital and the birth of the local area networking industry", in: Research Policy, 29 (9), pp. 1135-1155.

von Neumann, J./Morgenstern, O. (1944), "Theory of games and economic behavior", Princeton (NJ) 1944.

von Weizäcker, C. C. (1980), "Barriers to entry: a theoretical treatment", Berlin 1980.

Walker, G./Weber, D. (1984), "A transaction cost approach to make-or-buy decisions", in: Administrative Science Quarterly, 29 (3), pp. 373-391.

Wambach, A. (2001), "Die Bedeutung des institutionellen Umfelds", in: *Jost, P.-J.* (Eds.), Die Spieltheorie in der Betriebswirtschaftslehre, Stuttgart 2001, pp. 431-445.

Warmbold, J. (1996), "Gabelstapler für Spezialanwendungen", in: Beschaffung Aktuell, 1996 (11), pp. 72-73.

Wathne, K. H./Heide, J. B. (2000), "Opportunism in interfirm relationships: forms, outcomes, and solutions", in: Journal of Marketing, 64 (October), pp. 36-51.

Watzlawick, P./Weakland, J. H./Fisch, R. (1974), "Change: principles of problem formation and problem resolution", New York (NY) 1974.

Weber, M. (1947), "The theory of social and economic organization", New York (NY) 1947.

Webster, F. E. J. (1992), "The changing role of marketing in the corporation", in: Journal of Marketing, 56, pp. 1-17.

Weiber, R. (1997), "Das Management von Geschäftsbeziehungen im Systemgeschäft", in: *Plinke, W./Kleinaltenkamp, M.* (Eds.), Geschäftsbeziehungsmanagement, Berlin 1997, pp. 277-349.

Weiber, R./Adler, J. (1995), "Informationsökonomisch begründete Typologisierung von Kaufprozessen", in: Schmalenbachs Zeitschrift für betriebswirtschaftliche Forschung, 47 (1), pp. 43-65.

Weiber, R./Adler, J. (2002), "Der Wechsel von Geschäftsbeziehungen beim Kauf von Nutzungsgütern: Das Beispiel Telekommunikation", in: *Rese, M./Söllner, A./Utzig, B.* (Eds.), Relationship-Marketing: Standort und Perspektiven, Berlin 2002, pp. 71-103.

Weiber, R./Pohl, A. (1996), "Leapfrogging-Behavior - ein adoptionstheoretischer Erklärungs-ansatz", in: Zeitschrift für Betriebswirtschaft, 66 (10), pp. 1203-1222.

Weigelt, K./Camerer, C. (1988), "Reputation and corporate strategy: a review of recent theory and applications", in: Strategic Management Journal, 9, pp. 443-454.

Werner, R. O. E. (1979), "Legal developments in marketing", in: Journal of Marketing, (Fall), pp. 123-131.

Werner, R. O. E. (1993), "Legal developments in marketing", in: Journal of Marketing, (October), pp. 126-.

Wheelwright, S. C. (1984), "Strategy, management and strategic planning approaches", in: Interfaces, 14 (January/February), pp. 19-33.

Whetten, D. A. (1989), "What constitutes a theoretical contribution", in: Academy of Management Review, 14 (4), pp. 490-495.

Whitney, D. E. (1992), "State of the art in Japanese CAD methodologies for mechanical products: industrial practice and university research", in: Office of Naval Research Asian Office Scientific Information Bulletin, 17 (1), pp. 89-111.

Willée, C. (1991), "Bossard Zug: CAD-fähige Kataloginformation (Fastothek)", in: *Belz, C. et al.* (Eds.), Erfolgreiche Leistungssysteme, Stuttgart 1991, pp. 128-134.

Williamson, O. E. (1971), "The vertical intergration of production: market failure con-siderations", in: American Economic Review, 61 (May), pp. 112-123.

Williamson, O. E. (1975), "Markets and hierarchies: analysis and antitrust implications", New York (NY) 1975.

Williamson, O. E. (1979), "Transaction-cost economics: the governance of contractual relations", in: Journal of Law and Economics, 22 (2), pp. 233-261.

Williamson, O. E. (1983), "Credible commitments: using hostages to support exchange", in: American Economic Review, 73 (September), pp. 519-540.

Williamson, O. E. (1985), "The economic institutions of capitalism: firms, markets, relational contracting", New York (NY) 1985.

Williamson, O. E. (1989), "Transaction cost economics", in: *Schmalensee, R./Willig, R.* (Eds.), Handbook of Industrial Organization, Vol. 1, Amsterdam 1989, pp. 136-182.

Williamson, O. E. (1990), "A comparison of alternative approaches to economic orga-nization", in: Journal of Institutional and Theoretical Economics, 146, pp. 61-71.

Williamson, O. E. (1991a), "Comparative economic organization: the analysis of discrete structural alternatives", in: Administrative Science Quarterly, 36 (June), pp. 269-296.

Williamson, O. E. (1991b), "Economic institutions: spontaneous and intentional governance", in: The Journal of Law, Economics and Organization, 7 (September), pp. 159-187.

Williamson, O. E. (1991c), "Strategizing, economizing, and economic organization", in: Strategic Management Journal, 12 (Special Issue Winter 1991), pp. 75-94.

Williamson, O. E. (1998), "Transaction cost economics: how it works, where it is headed", in: De Economist, 146 (1), pp. 23-58.

Williamson, O. E. (1999a), "Public and private bureaucracies: a transaction cost economics perspective", in: Journal of Law, Economics, and Organization, 15 (1), pp. 306-342.

Williamson, O. E. (1999b), "Strategy research: governance and competence perspectives", in: Strategic Management Journal, 20 (12), pp. 1087-1108.

Williamson, O. E. (2000), "The New Institutional Economics: taking stock, looking ahead", in: Journal of Economic Literature, 38 (September), pp. 595-613.

Witzel, A. (1982), "Verfahren der qualitativen Sozialforschung. Überblick und Alternativen", Frankfurt 1982.

Woodward, J. (1965), "Industrial organisation: theory and practice", New York (NY) 1965.

Yao, D. A. (1988), "Beyond the reach of the invisible hand: impediments to economic activity, market failures, and profitability", in: Strategic Management Journal, 9 (Special Issue Summer 1988), pp. 59-70.

Yates, J. F./Stone, E. R. (1992), "The risk construct", in: *Yates, J. F.* (Eds.), Risk taking behavior, New York (NY) 1992, pp. 1-25.

Yetton, P. W./Johnston, K. D./Craig, J. F. (1994), "Computer-aided architects: A case study of IT and strategic change", in: Sloan Management Review, 35 (Summer), pp. 57-67.

Yin, R. K. (1994), "Case study research", 2nd ed., Thousand Oaks (CA) 1994.

Zajac, E. J./Shortell, S. M. (1989), "Changing generic strategies: likelihood, direction, and performance implications", in: Strategic Management Journal, 10 (5), pp. 413-430.

Zeithaml, V. A. (1988), "Consumer perceptions of price, quality, and value: a means-end model and synthesis of evidence", in: Journal of Marketing, 52 (July), pp. 2-22.

Zerres, M./Zerres, T. (2002), "Der Analysebedarf an der Schnittstelle von Marketing und Recht nimmt zu", in: Absatzwirtschaft, (8), p. 54.

Gabler Edition Wissenschaft

„Business-to-Business-Marketing"
Herausgeber: Prof. Dr. Werner Hans Engelhardt und
Prof. Dr. Michael Kleinaltenkamp (schriftf.)

(Weitere Titel dieser Reihe finden Sie auf der folgenden Seite.)